SEARCH FOR THE LOST
BLACKSHEEP

By Dan Bookout

© Dan Bookout

Published by
Optimum Publishing
Texarkana, Texas

DEDICATION

This book is dedicated to all the families who were left behind:
- ..... to the endeared who endured years of pain and suffering;
- ..... to the living who spent a lifetime wondering about an obscure acronym: POW, MIA or BNR; and
- ..... to the sincere hope that the impact of such an announcement may never be visited upon you, the reader.

Many believe uncertainty is far more devastating to families of those who can't come home. There can be no peace of mind because of the endless association with hope and despair in the same breath. When they live with constant anticipation and frustration, they can have no peace, no satisfaction and no solution.

This is the story of such a family.

Some families would rather receive a KIA report because it includes sure and certain knowledge that allows the full expression of grief. Only with this closure and the final resolution it brings, can healing begin; and, with passage of time, peace can return to the hearts and souls of those left behind.

SEARCH FOR THE LOST BLACKSHEEP
© 1995 AND 2000 DAN BOOKOUT
ISBN #: 1-57397-014-x
PRINTED IN THE UNITED STATES OF AMERICA

No portion of this book may be reproduced in any form, by photostat, microfilm, xerography, or any other means, or incorporated into any information retrieval system, electronic or mechanical, without the written permission of the copyright owner.

This is a true story about real people, but it has been necessary to change the names of some individuals to protect their privacy.
Some literary license has been taken in writing dialogue as it would be impossible to recreate it in its original exact form.

Cover art by Optimum Publishing.
Photographs provided by Vought Aircraft Co. have been credited as such and are used by permission. The remainder of the photographs were either taken by the author or search team members and are used by permission.

PUBLISHED BY
OPTIMUM PUBLISHING
P.O. BOX 7435 ~ TEXARKANA, TX 75505-7435
www.optimumpublishing.com

Two Blacksheep Squadron pilots roll their planes over and pull back the control sticks. As they enter a long dive, their speed accelerates to 300, then quickly passes 400 mph. Crocker sees contrails form behind Bennett's wings.

As they recover from the pull-up, Crocker's vision fades as he courts the edge of a dreaded blackout. Then he looks over at Bennett, and he sees the signal for yet another dive.

They do a wing-over and peel off left into another steep dive. Crocker slides into formation for the attack position. Down they dive... but this time Bennett is slow pulling up. They pass 450 mph, diving straight down, with only the seat belts and shoulder harnesses holding their bodies in place.

Crocker lets out a mental sigh of relief when he finally sees Bennett's Corsair start pulling up. He sees long, graceful contrails form behind Bennett's wing as the hard pull-up narrows his visual field. As the two specks plummet from the sky, the engine hum becomes a shrill scream – a sound that causes the Japanese to call Corsairs "The Whistling Death."

"Bennett's pushing the limit today, but he knows how to handle his Corsair's power. We must have been doing 475 to 500 mph on that dive," Crocker thinks. Crocker knows he must ride the fence between consciousness and blackout because, at 4500 feet, they are too low to relax the pull-up. He groans under the enormous pressure on his body as the nose rises back up to the horizon and safety. He wonders, "That must have been at least 7 Gs."

Bennett's plane suddenly seems to lurch and drop out of formation. As Crocker's plane slows and everything gets back in order, he looks around for his leader.

Nothing.

Crocker shakes his head to clear the cobwebs from his eyes and again scans the skies for Bennett, but to no avail. Crocker has an uneasy thought in the back of his mind. "Did Bennett crash?"

It seems that, in his last fuzzy view of Bennett, the right wing was buckled, then he was gone. "Could that be true?"

Crocker turns back south to survey the jungle. At this low altitude he is even unsure of his own position. From 500 feet he sees no smoke, no fire, no broken treetops, and no sign of an explosion. For several minutes he searches the skies, hoping. Then he searches the jungle below, dreading.

Still no sign of Bennett.

As he heads back to Turtle Bay, Crocker ponders, "If Bennett crashed into that area, he will be very hard to find – he drilled a very small hole in a very large jungle."

CONTENTS

PROLOGUE 1
DEDICATION 2
CONTENTS 4
INTRODUCTION 5
PART ONE: 1941-1949 7
   1   Hometown, U.S.A. – June 3 - December 7, 1941 7
   2   Four Young Men Go to War – 1942-1943 12
   3   Espiritu Santo – The New Hebrides – October 1943 18
   4   Military Search and Rescue Operations – 1943-1949 35
PART TWO: 1987 - 1994 48
   5   The Challenge – September 16, 1987 48
   6   What Do We Do Now? – 1987 - 1988 59
   7   Journey to Espiritu Santo – 1988 80
   8   Search 1 – Espiritu Santo – 1988 98
   9   Road's End – 1988 119
   10   Base Camp Turn-Around – 1988 160
   11   Regroup & Rejuvenate – 1989-1991 173
   12   The Search Continues – 1991 179
   13   A Final Expedition – 1992 192
   14   An Important Discovery – 1994 225
   15   The CILHI Project – 1994 254
   16   The Homecoming – September 1994 294
POSTSCRIPT 308
APPENDIX 316
GLOSSARY OF TERMS 344
ACKNOWLEDGMENTS 349
THE AUTHOR 352

MAPS

Blacksheep Corral (Turtle Bay) 20
Probable Crash Site (Espiritu Santo) 34
Journey to Vanuatu (Pacific Ocean) 84
Vanuatu 88
Espiritu Santo 97

★ ★ ★ ★ ★

INTRODUCTION

America's history is a magnificent and colorful mosaic spanning over 200 years, but the independence we enjoy today is due to the sacrifices of many Americans who gave up their tomorrows. We have established national holidays, national cemeteries and even national shrines in their memory. Perhaps this helps us remember that part of what our country stands for lies in those military cemeteries.

Some still lie, however, in unmarked graves on battlefields where they died. Some still remain on abandoned front lines where our youth devoted their lives and futures to a concept of freedom. These scattered remains of a young generation lie in silent tribute to a nation of freedom for free men and peace for peaceful men. Our devotion to their memory must never die.

When the guns lie silent and rusting in the fields and young warriors are returned to their hearths, we console families who dedicated their sons and daughters to the price of our future and freedom. We then take stock. "Did we get back all we sent out?"

Of those who came home, we count them among the lucky living, maimed, tormented and dead. With these brave men held closely to our country's breast, we proclaim "Peace in Our Time"; we vow "No More War"; we sing "When Johnny Comes Marching Home Again"; and we repent with "The Battle Hymn of the Republic."

But what of those listed as MIA (Missing In Action), POW (Prisoner Of War) or BNR (Body Not Recovered)? From the heat of battle comes joy of America's victories and, just as certainly, woe for American's loses.

America's battles and strife have blessed us because their geographical locations have been elsewhere. The sands of Iwo Jima were not on California's shores. The beaches of Normandy were not on New York's coast. We experienced no Chosin Reservoir, and we claimed no Tet Offensive in our land. Yet, that "elsewhere" has proved a final resting place or unwilling grave for many who could not come back to loved ones after the battles ended.

Free-thinking, peace-loving readers, writers, historians and politicians frequently get no closer to the dirty mess of war than the books they write and read. Their subject is a war that occurred over fifty years ago in a distant land. It was a war lasting five long, bloody years but became an eternity for many valiant volunteers. The characters of their stories often become faceless heroes, forgotten when the story ends.

Many young men volunteered early to fight for our country, instead of waiting to be drafted. They enlisted before the hero stories and movies where glory was born. And, between fights, they gritted blood-stained sand in their food, beds and work places. They sweated from gut-grinding toil as they tried to hold on to island outposts. They unloaded ships and assembled war materials and equipment in sweltering jungle heat. They test-flew untried planes and trained themselves for combat at a frantic, feverish pace in filthy and remote locations. Yet, they did it willingly because they were Americans. And, like the words of the old airmen's song, "Bless'um all, bless'um all, the long and the short and the tall...."

This is the story of 2nd Lt. Wayland Edward Bennett, a daring Marine fighter pilot who gave his life for our freedom. This young man from Texarkana, USA (on the border between Texas and Arkansas), and his family were not and could not be forgotten. This is also the story of four boyhood friends who joined the military, went off to war, and entered into a solemn promise on December 7th, 1941. This is the story of the fulfillment of that *Promise*.

[A] 1941 — HOMETOWN, U.S.A.: (Left to right) D.A. Carson, Wayland Bennett, Robert Sandlin, and Robert Bowden.

PART I
1941 TO 1949

CHAPTER 1

HOMETOWN, USA – JUNE 3, 1941

Wayland Bennett, a tall young man with sandy blond hair, and his twin sister, Wanda, have just finished graduation exercises at Texarkana's Texas High School and are celebrating with friends. He stands stoop-shouldered with a camera around his neck, taking pictures of his pals: D.A. Carson, Robert Bowden, and Robert Sandlin. *(Photo 1-a, page 6)*

They reminisce about hunting in the Red River bottoms and fields north of town. Bowden teases Bennett about his daredevil antics and the way he rode his bicycle faster than anyone else because of his long legs. He remembers how Bennett used to race down to the railroad crossing like he was going to play "chicken" with a train. Seeing the oncoming danger, the engineer would furiously sound his whistle and bell, but Bennett would keep racing headlong toward a certain collision. Then, just as he reached the crossing, Bennett would skid his bicycle to a stop only inches from the train. By then the engineer would be yelling, shaking his finger, and venting some rather colorful epithets.

D.A. Carson adds, "Yes, but it got better when Wayland traded in his bicycle and bought that old Model-A Ford. Can you believe, he only paid $10 for it!" The four lads had attacked the old car with a vengeance and tinkered with it until it became a real hot-rod. In the winter, they raced down the hill on New Boston Road and threw the old car into a violent spin on the slick streets.

The girls talk about dances and skating parties they all attended over the past several years. They enjoyed skating and dancing with Wayland because of his great coordination, good sense of balance, ever-present smile, and ready wit and humor.

Bennett laughs as he plays yet another prank on one of the girls. They all giggle and enjoy his attention. This is really a great day for a graduation, and the last thing they are concerned about is the war in Europe, which seems a lifetime away.

Bennett's parents, who are school teachers, and his older sister Doris welcome the twins to the adult world into which they have graduated. Their two brothers, Richmond Jr. and Wayne, join the festivities when they get home. They all talk about Wayland's plans to attend college in the fall.

Doris, the older sister, has long been referred to as "Big Sis." She is interested in flying and has earned her pilot's license for small private planes. She has no idea she will later lead a hectic life at Braniff Airways, racing across American skies at 175 mph in the giant Douglas DC-3, the most modern, twin-engine airliner of the day.

Richmond Jr. has a head for business and a knack for teaching. He is already in college and plans to get a degree. He will, perhaps, follow in his parent's footsteps as a teacher.

Wayland's twin, Wanda, is a striking blond with the soft, lovely smile common to this happy family. She hopes to become a medical technician, then perhaps a medical doctor, like very few women of the day.

SUMMER AND FALL, 1941

Wayland Bennett enjoys a beautiful summer of swimming, skating and dancing, then enrolls at Texarkana College in the fall. He is unsure of a career direction, but makes excellent grades during his first semester. His study habits are good and he starts concentrating on semester exams by December.

D.A. Carson also enjoys the lazy summer. He and Sandlin make extra money selling fruit jars to local families who store food for winter. Carson has also been working with his father and doing other part-time jobs to save enough money to buy a truck. The CCC (Civilian Construction Corps) camps need men with trucks to transport workers and supplies to work sites. There is plenty of regular work and good pay for those lucky enough to have such a truck, and he can then make enough money to pay for college. Because he needs to work at least a year to pay for the truck, he decides to wait a year instead of enrolling in the fall with Wayland. As his savings grow, so do his work habits and skills. By May or June, he can pay cash for the truck.

But Sunday is a day of rest for all four boys.

SUNDAY, DECEMBER 7th, 1941

This is a typical Sunday morning with Bennett, Carson, Bowden and Sandlin sitting together at Hardy Memorial Methodist Church. Bennett, who turned nineteen on November 21, sits in the middle, as usual, while Carson sits on the end so he can stretch his legs.

Carson is from a working class family on the edge of town. His father has trained him in the family blacksmith trade. He can already weld, rivet, forge and repair almost any working engine. Carson is a large, raw-boned young man who cherishes life and friends. He is strong, but also kind and gentle; however, the time is approaching when he will have to become an altogether different kind of man. He must become a hero in an army of warriors.

Robert Sandlin nudges Carson to be sure he stays awake. Sandlin is a studious young man who hopes to have a career in law enforcement.

His distant dream is to become a lawyer. He is about the same age as Bennett, and they frequently double-date and go to parties together.

On the other side of Bennett is Robert Bowden, the smallest. He is the son of an undertaker, a typical working-class American. He is already proficient as an undertaker and coffin maker due to his father's diligent training. One of his sisters, Helen, dated Wayland in high school; another dated D.A. Carson. Bowden is a comic who will attempt anything when teamed with Bennett.

The pastor, Rev. Mathison, is preaching. He is well liked by the congregation and knows each member by name. He has watched most of the young teens grow up in the church. All seems to be well with the world today in this small southern town.

After lunch the boys go for a ride in Bennett's Model A, then drop into the Paramount Theater for an early movie before going to their separate homes.

As Bennett enjoys the lovely, lazy Sunday afternoon, he hears radio news about a small group of islands called Hawaii. He recalls images from U.S. geography class of little guitars called ukuleles, golden skinned girls in grass skirts, white sandy beaches and pineapples.

On the evening of December 7, 1941, the world drastically changes for these four young men. Grim radio reports from these far-away islands make war an impending reality.

Parents shudder as they recall their own war 25 years earlier. Youngsters, unsure of its implication, vow to do and to be whatever is necessary to reclaim the peace and tranquillity their parents now seem to have lost.

On Bennett's porch that night, the four friends listen to radio reports about Japanese treachery and sneak attacks on Americans in a place called Pearl Harbor. Other young men across America are also listening, and most begin to grow up and make adult decisions. Bennett, Carson, Sandlin and Bowden know they will be involved. As friends, they willingly and sincerely make the usual boyhood vows of bravado, like many American teenagers on that fateful day.

Decades later, three elderly gentlemen still remember that during the evening of December 7, 1941, *A Promise* was made that none of them really expected to be so important in their future. They vowed to each other: **"When I go to some far away place and if, for some reason, I do not come home, don't forget me. Please don't leave me over there."**

This is a day and *A Promise* that none of them can ever forget. It is *A Promise* that will live on against all odds and draw many others into its scope.

These four are not highly educated, politically active or social climbers. Instead, they are just everyday schoolboys from a rural town, like millions of others across the face of a now-changed world. They simply vow to go to war and do their best. But they all also expect to return when it is all over. It is inconceivable that they might not. They think they will just "hop on over to Japan and pop old Bucky Beaver on the head," then come on home. "Nothing to it!" is their shared opinion.

These four young men will represent their loved ones and their country in a manner they can not possibly dream of in their wildest imaginations. They will go to war and each serve honorably. It is not so much what they will accomplish during the war that will touch this nation, but, rather, what they will never forget after it is over. The real challenge and story will be the fulfillment of *A Promise.*

After hearing of the Japanese attack, Bennett tries to recall everything he studied about Japan. He remembers that it is an island nation known as the "Empire of the Rising Sun." It is ruled by an Emperor of god-like proportions to his people. This nation seems to be highly secretive and both isolationist and expansionist at the same time.

After a long talk with his family, Bennett realizes his parents are worried. Long ago they faced another war in which America, the sleeping giant, was awakened to a national emergency. Today, history seems to be repeating itself. A sleeping nation must again arise from the lethargy of a depression and unemployment, and face the imminent dangers of a world at war.

This is not, however, just history repeating itself. This is the present – a shocking reality. President Roosevelt has asked Congress to declare that "Since eight o'clock in the morning on December 7, 1941, a State of War has existed between the Empire of Japan and this nation." The events of this day now absorb Wayland Bennett and his entire generation of Americans.

Bennett tries to respond to this National Emergency on Monday morning by going downtown to the U.S. Navy recruiter in the Post Office building on Texarkana's state line. Recruiters for the various services are doing a booming business, signing up almost anyone who can stagger in.

When it is his turn, Bennett says, "I want to volunteer for duty with the U. S. Navy and fly airplanes."

The recruiter looks over his application and replies, "Your college grades are certainly good enough, but, in order to be accepted for pilot training, you must complete a full year of college. If you'll do that and make good grades, you'll be accepted into the Navy as soon as the spring semester is over."

Wayland really likes the idea of being a pilot. "Big Sis" has taken him for a local flight in the airplane she flies. He enjoyed the ride in the small two-seater, so he agrees to remain in college for another semester. He expects to be accepted into the Naval Aviation Cadet Training Program in April and begin flight training in July or August.

D.A. Carson is also shocked and moved to action. This Day of Infamy forever changes every single detail of the elaborate plan he has laid out for himself. On Monday, he goes to the Navy recruiter's office with Bennett to enlist and says he wants to get into the fight.

The recruiter tells him, "If it's a fight you want, you can have all you want in the U.S. Marine Corps."

D.A. is promptly accepted for training into the most elite Band of

Brothers the world has ever known. They are, by reputation, the world's best team of fighting men with their own special spirit known as Espirit De Corps.

Robert Bowden is only 17 and still in high school. He, like all the others, wants to join the military and do his part for his country. He knows his parents expect him to assume the family casket manufacturing business and become a mortician and funeral director like his father. He has developed a cavalier attitude toward life because he knows where life leads, and he does not look forward to being a mortician for the rest of his life. He enjoys the companionship and camaraderie of his friends, and has no intention of making a career out people's grief and sorrow.

Bowden has learned to be an optimist above all. As the youngest and smallest of the four, the others always try out their new jokes on him. Bowden has had to become tough and wiry from running with D.A. Carson. Running with the prankster, Bennett, has taught him to be quick and wily. Bowden and Sandlin have had to learn to keep up with the two older boys and can outlast either of them.

On Monday evening, Bowden sits in silence, listening to the radio broadcasts about the war in the Pacific. He knows Bennett will be leaving in early summer for naval flight training, and D.A. will be leaving even sooner for Marine training. But for now, Bowden realizes he must stay home and help his father. There is ample reason for concern, as the list of casualties is announced from the attack on Pearl Harbor.

Robert Sandlin, at 18, is already an astute observer of facts. He, like the others, has enjoyed fishing and hunting on Red River. He has also become interested in girls, and one in particular has already caught his fancy. He and Frances have danced, walked, dated and even discussed plans for the future... together. They planned to be married in the summer of 1942, or maybe in January 1943. But now, he wonders if there will even be a next summer or winter. A world at war is a sobering subject for history books at school, but is a frightening reality. No one in this area has been in a war in over 25 years. The enormity of such thought is almost overwhelming. As he listens to the reports of gloom and doom, Sandlin knows he and Frances will have to re-consider their plans because he will eventually be drawn into this war. He is the right age and his country will almost certainly require his services very soon.

CHAPTER 2

FOUR YOUNG MEN GO TO WAR – 1942

As the recruiter suggested, Bennett enlists in the Naval Aviation Cadet program for pilot training in the spring. It was hard to concentrate on his studies while concerned about the war in Europe and the Pacific, but he somehow made it through. Because his grades are so good, he is allowed to leave school in April in response to the national emergency.

He visits the Navy recruiting office, not waiting to be drafted. He volunteers for one of the most dangerous areas of service (the U.S. Marines) and a very high-risk occupation (flying fighter planes). There is no glamorous U.S. Air Force in early 1942, just the U.S. Army Air Corps or the U.S. Navy.

The Navy and Marine Corps are at minimum standard for war. All flying units are, indeed, embryonic, not supersonic jet fleets as depicted in later movies. Cadet Bennett, W. E., is initially assigned to the Naval Air Training Command at Grand Prairie, Texas. He is a quick student who studies hard and learns well.

In June, just before Carson leaves for advanced training, he and Bowden hitchhike to Dallas to "pay old Wayland a little visit." They are greeted at the base's main gate by a rather rude Marine armed guard who snaps, "This is a war-time operation and you will NOT be able to see the Cadet in question, and you will NOT be allowed to come on this base. Ever." So they hitchhike back to Texarkana.

Early in the war, Bowden meets hundreds of the young fighting men returning home. He drives his father's hearse to Union Station Railway Depot where he unloads their bodies from the railway cart; then he delivers the flag-draped caskets to Bowden Funeral Home. These hometown boys have become statistics of the war.

Bowden waits eagerly for his own call to arms, but it does not come. Impatient, he asks a friend who is on the Selection Board when he will be called and finds out, by accident, that he has been classified as "war necessary" – exempted from active duty because of his occupation. He has a fit and demands to be immediately taken off deferred status and placed on the available list. He threatens to quit his job and school so he can enlist.

Bowden is finally allowed to enlist as a U.S. Army medic, which suits him just fine. Of course, he does not yet realize he will serve in several Pacific theater combat zones. He just cannot bear the thought of Carson, Sandlin and Bennett "winning this war without me." He tells a friend, "can you just imagine the trouble those guys will give me if I sit out the war at home?"

After pre-flight training, Cadet Bennett is transferred to the Naval Air Training Commands and assigned to several other bases. He and another fledgling aviator, Harry Johnson from Alabama, become pals. Neither realizes they will later be sent over-seas on the same ship and assigned to the same squadron.

At Corpus Christi, Texas, Bennett is trained to fly, expect the unexpected, and deal with the emergencies that confront aviators. He progresses from the Boeing Stearman Trainer to the famous North American SNJ/AT-6 Advanced Trainer.

He soon falls in love, as only an aviator can, with a bent-winged angel named Corsair – the Vought Sikorski F4U-1. He has never experienced anything like his new sweetheart. Their pulses race to the heartbeat of 2000 horses as they frolic from wave tops to over 20,000 feet. They cavort with clouds and "slide down sunbeams with angels."

[2-a] WHISTLING DEATH: Vought F4U Corsair Bent Wing Angel: 12,582 were built but only a few survive today. Corsairs shot down 2,140 Japanese aircraft during WW2. They flew at over 400 mph, with six .50 caliber machine guns or four 20MM cannons and up to 5000 pounds of ammunition. (Photo courtesy of Vought Aircraft Co.)

Bennett learns how to handle her, then how to soothe and coax her to even greater heights. He soon starts testing his skills with this fast lady, exploring her limits. They soar to exhilarating altitudes and are tantalized by dizzying speeds.

Once they almost go too far in an unknown region, almost passing the point of no return. Knowing his lady friend is capable of over 400 mph, he pushes her beyond to almost 500 mph. She becomes unyielding and hard to manage. After returning to base, he discovers just how close they came to the flight of Daedaleus and Icarius of Greek mythology. She is badly distorted, her skin wrinkled, her wings damaged, and her ribs bent from stress. He has almost pushed her too hard – almost hurt her beyond her ability to forgive him. But somehow she does – this time.

Bennett learned to smoke with his pals as a teenager. Now, with his confidence soaring, he experiments with the nectars of alcohol. Nothing, however, can keep his fancy like his favorite girl.

He is sent to Great Lakes Naval Training Center to train for carrier landings, and is introduced to the USS Wolverine. Thousands of Navy and Marine aviators have courted this old straight-deck carrier. Her makeup has been smudged by many encounters with strutting young sparrows who presumed to be eagles. She humbles more than a few of them too, especially if they ignore her needs. Here, a deft touch and precision speed control means just that. If one comes on to her too fast, she leaves him sweating and groaning in despair when she refuses to accept him on her short, narrow flight deck. If he takes her for granted or thinks she is a sure thing, she rejects his advances and he finds out what the ship's other end looks like. If he makes his pass too fast, too slow, or not straight down the middle, he is refused the landing signal by her big brother, the LSO (Landing Signal Officer).

As training progresses, he is given a choice of services: a commission as a Navy Ensign or USMCR Second Lieutenant. He is afraid if he accepts the Navy offer, he may separated from his new love, the Corsair. The Navy flies off carriers, but not yet with Corsairs. Therefore, if he wants to remain in Corsairs, his best bet is to become a Marine fighter pilot.

Bennett likes the Grumman F6F Hellcat, but after the Corsair, the old Grumman F4F Wildcat is just too tame, too slow, too under-powered and under-gunned in his view. The Wolverine experience convinces him that a Marine island base will be far superior to a cramped life on an aircraft carrier. He is a "hot pilot," like all of his classmates, and feels like he can take on anyone in the Japanese air force and win. That is, of course, the purpose and difference in American fighter pilot training.

In April of 1943 graduation ceremonies at Corpus Christi Naval Air Station, 2nd Lt. Wayland E. Bennett, USMCR, officially enters the service of his country at war. Bennett, Johnson and their classmates go home on a short leave before being shipped to a war zone "somewhere in the South Pacific."

Bennett finds Texarkana a lonesome place when he gets home on leave in the late summer of 1943. Sandlin is a Naval instructor in San Diego. Carson is a Marine Parachute Raider, Bowden an Army medic and Wayland's brother, Wayne, serves on a Navy minesweeper – all somewhere in the South Pacific. His older brother, Richmond Jr., is a Naval Aviator teaching young men to fly. Doris is a Braniff Airways hostess, and Wanda is studying to become a medical technician, but has come home to see him.

New war industries have sprung up in Texarkana. Just about everyone left at home is on an emergency work schedule at the new Red River Army Depot or Lone Star Army Ammunition Plant. The old town is bustling with activity and employment is available to anyone. There are no empty apartments and rationing is in full force.

War has also already taken its toll among old friends at home. Bennett walks over to Hardy Memorial Methodist Church and speaks at length with the pastor he grew up listening to each Sunday. They pray together for the war's successful outcome and a safe return for all Texarkana boys away in the conflict. They also pray for Bennett, who knows he is going where only U.S. Marines can go – a combat area which, for years, has been developed for defense by a very dedicated enemy who is prepared to die before he will surrender or lose a battle.

When leave is over, Wanda drives him to Union Station to catch a train to the San Diego embarkation point. She tells him she is proud of him, and that he looks handsome in his Marine uniform with his ever-present smile. They laugh, talk and cry, and he tells her that she is probably looking at a dead Marine. There will be no fun and games where he is going. He will soon be involved in the serious business of war, where people die.

Wanda waves and cries as the train pulls out of the station. He is more than her brother – he is her twin. They have always been closer to each other than to the other three, and that special feeling for Wayland is more acute today than ever. She will never forget this day and the parting. She will remember this moment, even in the last hour of her life.

SAN DIEGO, CALIFORNIA – SEPTEMBER 1943

Robert Sandlin enlisted in the U.S. Navy in 1942 and was assigned as an ordinary seaman. Because the Navy was looking for bright young men who could think and talk at the same time, he soon became more than just ordinary. They made him an instructor at the San Diego Naval Training Complex, teaching his fellow sailors to win at war, and to bring damaged ships home.

Sandlin married Frances, his girl from back home, and they now live in a small apartment just off base in San Diego. She works in a huge aircraft manufacturing plant, building the Consolidated B-24 Liberator, a giant four-engine bomber. Frances is one of America's finest, a "homefront" hero – "Rosie-the-Riveter."

The crew of one B-24 Frances builds will name it "Beautiful Betsy" when it goes to the South Pacific for bombing and combat duty. After taking off from Darwin in route to Brisbane, this B-24 and its ten-man crew will disappear over the primitive outback in northern Australia's deserted mountains. In spite of ground and air searches, "Beautiful Betsy" and her crew will not be found... for a long, long time.

The Sandlins are part of the hectic life-style of the era – work, work, work – at an emergency pace. They are unaccustomed to entertaining or even seeing anyone from home. One evening they hear an unexpected knock on their door and open it to find an impeccable officer in a Marine pilot's uniform. The gleaming smile can only belong to one person, Wayland Bennett. He has just returned to San Diego from home, where he visited Sandlin's parents and found out where they live. He is awaiting orders to board a ship that will take him to a combat zone.

They laugh and recall times from home. There is the usual exchange of war news and latest information about where everyone is and what he is doing. They talk about Bowden and Carson and wonder when, if ever, they will all be together again. It is a wonderful reunion and Sandlin knows he will never forget this evening.

Sandlin asks about Bennett's flying, and Bennett tells them about his training and new love – the Corsair. This quiet young man doesn't brag in the company of hometown friends, but tells them he knows how to make his airplane go even faster than the advertised 400 mph, and when he is in his plane, "No-one can go faster than Wayland Bennett."

Bennett confides that it is a thrill to leave a contrail across the skies – one way he can show enemy pilots where he is, if they want to try him in combat. He talks about Marine duty, then explains that when a pilot is assigned to a squadron, he is also assigned his own plane, and can paint a name on its side.

Sandlin asks him, "Whose name will you put on your plane?"

Bennett quickly replies, **"Susie-Q."**

Sandlin remembers that is the pet nickname the Bennett children gave their mother years before.

Fifty years later, Sandlin will still remember this evening and how Bennett was like a caged animal – confident in himself, his plane and the Marines, but wanting to get into a fight with the Japanese now, not later. The Sandlins are the last people from home to see Bennett before he leaves for the Pacific Theater, and they will be among the very first to welcome him home.

Bennett, Harry Johnson and several other fighter pilots wait for what seems an eternity for transport to the war zone. Bennett did not train to just sit around the huge naval base waiting for a ship, so he goes over to North Island Naval Air Station and volunteers to fly anything until his orders come through. He serves as copilot on a Douglas four-engine C-54 cargo plane for several flights, and flies a small OS2U Curtiss Swordfish seaplane.

Bennett calls home on September 16, 1943. He can tell them very little about where he is, and nothing about where he expects to go. He cannot tell them he is being sent to a squadron assignment and front-line duty in the South Pacific. Nor that he hopes to fly the most famous WW2 fighter plane – the Vought-Sikorski F4U-1 Corsair. He is thoroughly indoctrinated in warning slogans proclaiming "security first," "phones have ears" and "loose lips sink ships." The significance of that phone call's date won't be known until documents and research recreates events 51 years later.

Bennett, Johnson and other pilots soon board a troop transport ship in San Diego. Their destination is simply "somewhere in the South Pacific theater," and he hopes nothing will interfere with his assignment.

Their transport is a converted Presidential Line passenger ship now named the USS Mount Vernon. After 14 days zigzagging across the ocean, they reach a point halfway around the world. While crossing the equator, they are inducted into the "Royal High Court of the Realm of Neptune" and become members of Navy traditions where rank has no privileges. The pilots are subjected to all the gross indignities reserved for "Pollywogs" by Trusty Navy Shellbacks.

Harry Johnson will always remember that day and the "big old sandy headed guy from Texas who was always smiling." Even though their orders and sailing date were classified on everything else, their subpoenas to the Royal High Court of Neptunius Rex date their equatorial crossing *(Appendix A)*.

Robert Bowden has been an Army medic since April 1943, but no one seems to know where he is. He knows the latest intelligence reports indicate enemy soldiers do not give free passes to men with bright red medic crosses on their helmets. In fact, they seem to use those crosses as targets.

Bowden trained at a furious pace in several different specialties and can do them all well under the most primitive conditions. First and foremost, he a soldier who can fight and hold his own in any conflict. Second, he is a highly trained combat medic who can perform everything from major surgery to setting bones or tending gunshot and shrapnel wounds. Finally, he is a combat-trained dental technician who can, when needed, do some rather amazing dental repairs.

Meanwhile, Pfc. D.A. Carson is a tough and uncompromising fighter assigned to a crack Marine Paratroops Raider Battalion. He has already been to Hawaii, New Caledonia and Guadalcanal – facing the Japanese in combat on its own turf. He knows the enemy is a formidable fighting force, but they are not invincible when met by a well-trained Marine force. The enemy has not been able to vanquish these U.S. Marines, who have learned to survive in the dense jungles during island-hopping campaigns.

CHAPTER 3

ESPIRITU SANTO – THE NEW HEBRIDES
OCTOBER 1943

The USS Mount Vernon silently glides into a secret channel that leads to a gigantic, protected anchorage for hundreds of ships of all kinds. This is the most picturesque setting Bennett and Johnson have ever seen – an island group in the Coral Sea of Melanesia.

Bennett sees dozens of cargo and transport ships, plus hundreds of smaller support ships and boats that seem to be unloading the larger ships. There is a submarine, several PT boats, cruisers, destroyers, LCVPs (Landing Craft Vehicle and Personnel) and LSTs (Landing Ship Tanks and Trucks). Fuel and oil tankers are everywhere. This seemingly endless armada of ships makes it clear that war is not far away.

There is a bustling hub-bub of Navy Sea-Bee Battalions building storage depots on shore. Mud beaches are being turned into crushed coral streets and highways. Quonset hut cities are being constructed, while bomb dumps, ammo storage depots, and huge fuel storage tank complexes are being carved out of jungle and coral cliffs *(Appendix B)*.

Near this beehive a new road leads north to Turtle Bay Fighter Strip Number One. The skies are alive with planes: DC-3/C-47s, PBJ/B-25s, PBYs, C-45/SNBs, TBMs, TBFs and AT-6/SNJs. Old Stearman PT-17s are even here fighting the mosquito population.

As they travel north along the coast, Bennett sees a Norwegian ship anchored about a mile off shore. They pass an entire airport used solely for cargo planes. Another larger airstrip is set up just to handle Bombers. Every lagoon seems to have PBYs and PT boats hidden away. "Boy, if 'Big Sis' could only see this," Bennett thinks.

He sees dark, forbidding jungle on his left, so dense and seemingly impenetrable that it is nothing like the hunting woods back home. Then, off to his right, he sees the dark blue ocean edged by frothy white breakers crashing onto coral reefs. There are also lazy, jade-colored inlets that seem to change to clear, deep blue. Palm and coconut trees lean out over the shallow water, welcoming the incoming tides to white, powdered-sugar beaches. The whirring of jeeps and growl of passing trucks makes all this seem more like a day on a Corpus Christi or San Diego beach instead of a war zone supply depot.

The skies welcome the aviator and invite him to play tag in the grandeur of this tropical island paradise. Further along the road, he sees single-engine fighter planes that are all familiar to him: SBD-2Cs, Douglas Scout Dive Bombers, TBF's, huge Grumman Torpedo Bombers and a Grumman F6F Hellcat. Then he sees his first love, the F4U Corsair.

Rounding a curve, the truck slows in front of pillboxes being built to repel any invading Japanese force. A billowing dust cloud catches up with them and fine, white-coral powder settles onto and into everything. As the procession crawls across the narrow bridge, larger-than-life Marine sentries stand their post, armed with loaded machine-guns. Bennett had experienced a run-in with guards like this back in Pensacola, but he knows these men are all business, and are likely to be much less sociable in this war zone.

[3-a] BOMBER STRIP NUMBER ONE: This airstrip, located on Turtle Bay's southeast corner, provided supplies and parts for many airfields. It was primarily used for bombers and a B-24 is on the runway in this late 1943 photo. There are several fighters parked on the field as standby guards in the event of enemy attack. Trees, revetments and bunkers hide most aircraft. Several PBYs, PT boats, LSTs and cargo ships are in the bay and lagoon.

When the guards recognize the Marine officers, they snap a salute and allow entry into the Marine Air Base's inner sanctum. The view is even more breathtaking when the truck rounds the end of the runway. A TBM lumbers into the air, then two Corsairs flash over the end of the runway.

Quad-mount machine gun tubs at the strip's end track the departing planes for practice. Any Japanese pilot foolish enough to attack this base from the sea must first get past these guns. The Marine gun crews

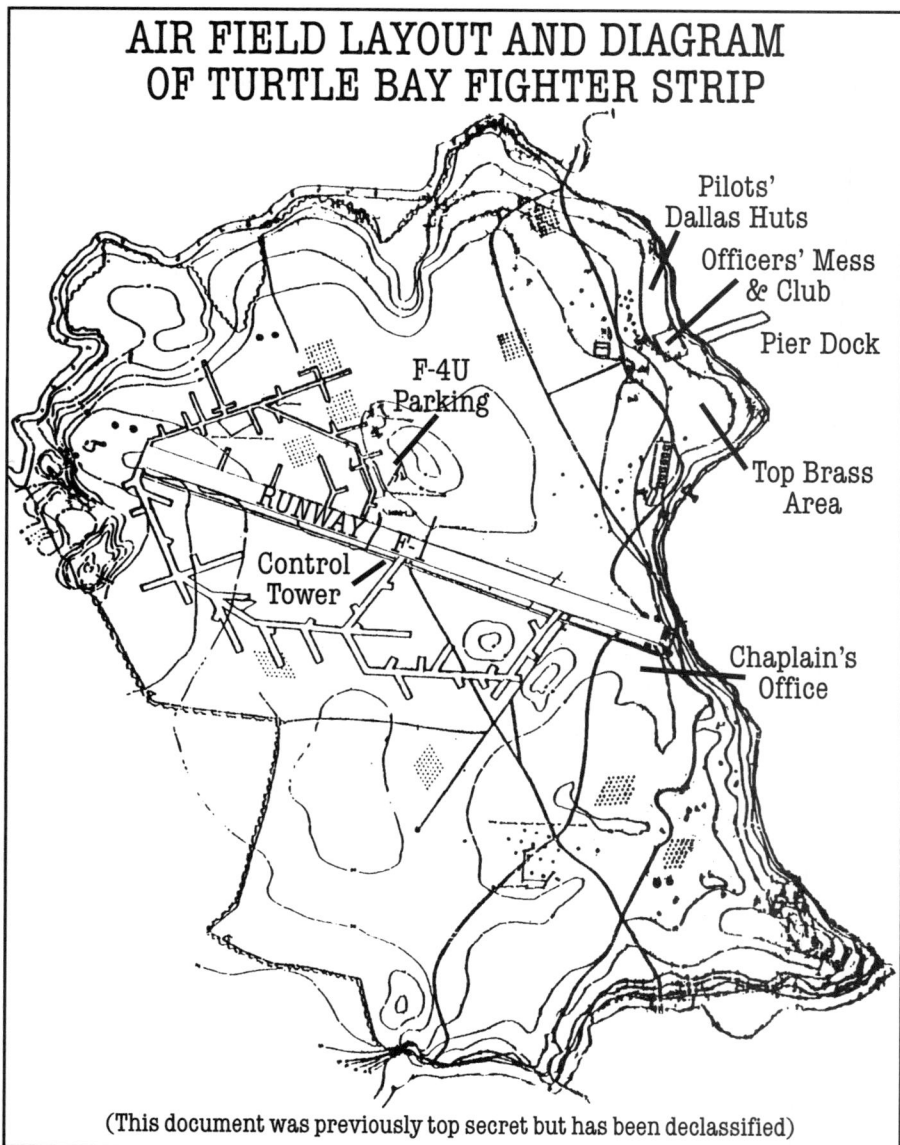

AIR FIELD LAYOUT AND DIAGRAM OF TURTLE BAY FIGHTER STRIP

Pilots' Dallas Huts
Officers' Mess & Club
Pier Dock
F-4U Parking
Top Brass Area
RUNWAY
Control Tower
Chaplain's Office

(This document was previously top secret but has been declassified)

[3-b] BLACKSHEEP CORRAL: *This airfield map shows its facilities including headquarters, dining areas, living quarters, gun emplacements, runway, taxiways, parking and dispersal areas, as well as the location of revetments and hides. It is very clear why information concerning the location of fuel, aircraft, pilots and defensive gun emplacements are such closely guarded secrets. Dedicated professionals such as Marine sentries protect these installations from prying eyes. They do their jobs well enough to really be able to "hand feed the Hounds of the Baskervilles."*

are always on the alert for any plane that does not belong in this area. They guard and protect Turtle Bay Airstrip, where thousands of fellow Marines live and work. They must protect everything in sight because hundreds of airplanes are sitting ducks on the ground. All unauthorized personnel must be kept out, and the Marines do their job very well indeed.

A Dallas hut city appears among palm trees near the runway's end. Hundreds of plywood shells, each housing ten pilots awaiting assignments, stand along white coral streets. Off-duty Marines are cavorting just outside the beach in Turtle Bay's clear, shallow water.

Headquarters are located in a group of Quonset huts surrounded by jeeps, trucks, and a flag pole with U.S. and Marine Corps flags waving in the brisk morning breeze. Here, like every Marine base, are white rocks that look like they were painted only yesterday. Perhaps they were.

Bennett sees new Corsairs being unloaded from an aircraft carrier onto rafts about a mile from shore. After being pulled ashore by small boats, the raft is beached and PSP (Perforated Steel Plating) ramps are laid out. SeaBees use this PSP matting like an erector set to build airstrips with each piece interlocking.

Jeeps, serving as tugs, pull the new fighter planes ashore, then up the hill and into the trees. The planes disappear under a blanket of mechanics who pull off miles of preservative tape. In a few days, all these new cosmoline-covered airplanes will be either at the mercy of young Marine aviators or under the guns of very skilled Japanese pilots. There is no turning back now; home is on the other side of the world.

Bennett and the others stand at attention while a Lieutenant Colonel snaps, "Welcome to Turtle Bay Airfield, gentlemen. You are now part of Fleet Marine Force, Second Marines, Marine Air Group Eleven, Headquarters Squadron."

After instructions are given and orders received, the pilots find their huts, move in and have dinner. The new Marines have homes, food, laundry, a theater, beaches, a Chaplain and a job.

The new men meet other pilots who have just returned from flights and some who are about to leave on combat tours. They learn that many new planes or tired old ones do not return from this field of operations.

"Eat, sleep, and fly, for tomorrow you die." What philosopher could have been so prophetic, so eloquent or so accurate?

Bennett learns about several nearby crash sites. Lt. Snee, BNR, lies in an F4U in the ocean about a mile out from the runway. Another F4U wreck lies in the jungle about a mile south of the field. A mile inland on a hill is an F4U that crashed on approach to landing. The mangled heap of a TBM lies just across the runway. Only days ago, McMahan went down in the mountains about 25 miles northwest.

There was also a mid-air collision of two F4U's about 12 miles north. Sheafer did not make it back. DeCamp survived and was rescued by a "Black Cat," a twin-engine PBY seaplane used for shore patrol and air-sea rescues. But, to be rescued, a pilot must first survive the crash, make his way to the coast and build a fire – a pretty tall order for a crash victim in these jungles.

Bennett wonders as he learns of these crash sites, "How many more will crash, when and where? No," he decides, "the war isn't far away – it's here."

War requires a personal effort just to survive from one day to the next, whether flying combat, maintenance flights, familiarization or training. Trouble anywhere in this tropical paradise means a crash into ocean, jungle or mountains.

New pilots fly a different plane every day – planes that are here to be repaired and made ready for a six-week combat patrol. Some planes have had a hard life of combat flying and received little maintenance attention; these inexperienced young pilots need just as much work. Some replacement pilots in the fighter pool have never even seen a Corsair. Not only do they not know how to start the engine, some don't even know how to get into it!

Bennett blends in well with the other young men at Turtle Bay. His friendly, out-going personality and constant smile soon result in a growing list of friends. He meets the Chief of the airfield controllers, Captain Robert Shaw, and Colonel Smoak, who welcomed them to the island.

Because of the sultry heat, sweat constantly trickles down his spine, mixing with penetrating dust storms whenever airplanes start up – all day, every day. It rains every day and night, always with the same result: wet or dry, it is still dust.

[3-c] SCRAMBLE: *Pilots pour out of the ready room tent and run across dry dust or wet dust (but always some kind of dust) to waiting F4Us. These are shore-based Marine Corsairs with birdcage canopies and with tail hooks removed. When seen from above the dark blue paint blends in with the color of the ocean. When viewed from below the white paint blends in with the sky – You hope! (Photo courtesy of Vought Aircraft Co.)*

The ever-present dust grits in his food, clothes, gun and silver cigarette lighter. At least there are plenty fruits and vegetables on the island, plus rations and cigarettes to trade. Pilots pass their free time swimming, diving, fishing and resting in the cool evening breezes; however all are waiting, wishing and wanting an assignment.

Bennett hopes to soon be assigned to a combat squadron, but will fly as often as possible in the meantime. Relief comes only in the clean, cold air when he is flying in the arms of his sweetheart, the Corsair. The rolls, loops, spins, stalls and dives give this young warrior solace.

Bennett sharpened and honed his flying gear knife to a razor's edge and cut his right hand while putting it back in its scabbard. Although it is sore and possibly infected, he doesn't report it because he doesn't want to miss the next posting of replacement pilots to an active squadron.

Word has filtered back that Major Gregory "Pappy" Boyington, the VMF-214 leader, is returning to Espiritu Santo and needs replacements due to squadron losses. An Executive Officer, new planes and several replacement pilots will be assigned from Turtle Bay. Bennett hopes to become part of Boyington's Squadron and has worked hard to establish a reputation as a team player.

Bennett, Crocker, Johnson and three others are hiding from a torrential downpour in their hut one night in October 1943. An orderly sticks in his head and quickly announces, "You guys are all Blacksheep now."

Early assignment to a squadron means no more delays, waiting or anticipation. This is the news they have all been waiting for. As they go to sleep that night, they search their souls and ask, "Will I be good enough?" And, according to history, they were!

Henry Miller will be the new Executive Officer or second-in-command, but he does not realize what a short time he has to get accustomed to squadron operations. Miller will have to assume command in January when Boyington does not return from a fighter sweep near Rabaul.

The square-jawed Major Boyington once resigned his Marine commission to serve as an AVG (American Volunteer Group) fighter pilot. Some historians claim the AVG were mercenaries who fought prior to the attack on Pearl Harbor. This is not true – they were indeed part of America's quarrel with Japan. They were formed, but not organized as a unit until after December 7, 1941, and their principal combat lasted until May or June 1942.

The AVG pilots flew the famous Kittyhawks (Curtiss P-40) with a distinctive shark's mouth painted on the nose, and were known as the Flying Tigers. This fearless band wanted Japanese pilots to know they were up against the AVG, and they left their marks very well.

Boyington shot down six Japanese planes with the AVG in China and is an "ACE" combat fighter pilot. Now, he is back as leader of Marine Fighting Squadron VMF-214. He also has new kills, as have other Squadron members. Having tasted blood, the Squadron has also shed its own – losses to be replaced by Crocker, Johnson and Bennett.

VMF-214 has no fame or fortune yet, but the pilots are known as the "Blacksheep." Their shield is a black ram sheep with a black diagonal bar to depict their uncertain heritage. The silhouette of an F4U completes the emblem that will soon be known all over the Pacific– particularly to Japanese pilots.

Bonafide rumor (known as "dope") is that the squat, muscular Boyington didn't get along well with General Claire Chennault while with the Flying Tigers in China. Perhaps Boyington was not particularly endowed with the social graces required of an AVG pilot. Well, his job here is not to lead a social tea party. He is already reputed to be a scrapper, both in the air and on the ground. He is called "Pappy" because he is older than any of the Squadron's other pilots. The Major is a skilled and experienced combat veteran who demands and gets his pilots' attention because he works them as a team. He is the kind of leader a young, inexperienced fighter hopes to survive in aerial battles long enough to follow and learn from.

Boyington doesn't always go by the book in combat because he knows what a skilled pilot can do with a Japanese fighter plane. Besides, the enemy doesn't read American rule books. He has made mistakes and survived, then has seen friends make the same mistake the next day and not live to learn that the enemy must not be taken for granted. All squadron leaders are good, but Boyington just has the knack for finding trouble and sensing the time and tactic for a successful strike.

[3-d] HIDE AND SEEK: *This F4U is taxiing out of revetment at a South Pacific jungle airstrip during WW2. Notice that dense jungle foliage has been pushed back by Navy SeaBees who built this airstrip for Marine Corsair squadrons. A dust storm penetrates everything and the pilots pull down goggles before starting engines. Imagine how well the engine's internal operating parts fared in an environment of dirt, dust and mud mixed with oil, gasoline and moving parts; especially when pilots had to fly in combat and almost always over the very deep oceans. (Photo courtesy of Vought Aircraft Co.)*

After flying is finished late on the afternoon of October 21, Bennett stops by a revetment where mechanics are working on the right wing problem he reported earlier today. He asks a mechanic from south Texas, "Would it be possible to get a name painted on my plane?"

The mechanic, who was recently transferred from Corpus Christi, pulls off his fatigue hat and wipes the sweat from his face with it. "Well, Lieutenant, you wouldn't know where I could pick up some cigarettes, would you?"

Bennett laughs. "Come to think of it, I have about five extra packs in my locker that will mildew unless I find something to trade them for."

The mechanic groans at the thought of cigarettes going to waste. "Okay, it'll be ready in the morning."

Bennett smiles and hands the mechanic a scrap of paper on which he has printed: **"S U S I E - Q."**

Bennett remembers he is supposed to finish the paperwork for his new assignment to VMF-214, but it is too late to do that today. He decides, "I'll take care of that after my flight in the morning."

He heads toward laughter and the sound of men at play. Marines refer to this natural crack in the earth at the jungle's edge as simply the "Blue Hole." The 150-foot deep, blue water is fed by clear, fresh and very cool underground springs. A hundred Marine swimmers, who are substituting it for a warm camp shower, now punctuate it.

Gigantic trees over 100-feet tall lean out over this aquatic playground. Some look positively pre-historic with enormous gnarled trunks and huge twisted branches larger than tree trunks back home. Leaves and foliage completely block out sun and sky. This "virgin" stand of trees seems hundreds, or even thousands, of years old with no interruption in growth.

Large vines dangle over the pool, serving as both trapeze and swing. As Bennett swings out over the water, he recalls Sunday afternoon picnics and swimming in spring-fed "Crystal Springs" with his friends.

A peaceful end to a hectic day comes with fading sunlight. This tropical paradise is a Garden of Eden where almost anything grows in abundance. The cold water feels good on his sore, swollen hand.

After a swim, he decides to take in an outdoor movie. This movie setup doesn't compare to Texarkana's Loop Drive-In. This idyllic, natural amphitheater doubles as an open-air church for "Chaplain Pat" on Sunday. The movie is a rerun, so Bennett heads back to his hut after the first reel.

The day's excitement has been one to write home about. He is elated with news he can now share with his family. He tells them of his assignment and writes that Harry Johnson, his old classmate in Cadet flying school, has been assigned to the same squadron. Bennett tells them about meeting several members of the "Blacksheep," and that he has flown in formation with Major "Pappy" Boyington (probably prior to arriving at Turtle Bay since Boyington has not been in the islands since he arrived).

Bennett explains, "A pilot 'belongs' when assigned to a squadron. He can then put a name on his plane's side – a status symbol that proudly displays his new station in life." He continues, "Since I don't have a wife or sweetheart waiting at home, I've decided to honor Mom on my plane. I've already made a deal with one of the mechanics, and when I fly tomorrow, there will be a shiny new *'Susie-Q'* on both sides of my Corsair."

He writes, "Major Boyington seems to have had a hand in the replacement pilot selection, a function normally assigned to the squadron's S-2 officer.

Of course you understand that I can't tell you where I am or this letter will never make it past the censor at HQ." He quickly finishes his letter, then drops it in the outgoing mail slot.

OCTOBER 22, 1943

Peace and quiet reigns supreme at 0400 (4:00 a.m. military time). The sky's velvet blackness displays a dazzling panorama of stars, moon and a few patchy clouds left over from last night's welcome rain. It is getting cold back home on the other side of this planet above the equator, but here it is just opposite. Nightly temperatures are in the seventies in these very humid tropics, and days hover around 100 degrees – unless, of course, it is hotter. Last night was an exception – it was hotter! It is already hot and muggy outside and today promises to be a humdinger.

The mud will be gone by sun-up – replaced by ever-present dust settling onto everything. The 200 planes at Turtle Bay Fighter Strip will all get special attention today. Their engines must be started and tested, and every system given attention to bring it to perfection. They must all be on the line and ready for combat today, because the "Blacksheep" arrive tomorrow and their old planes will be a mess. Bullet holes and cannon fire damage will need repaired, and almost every engine will need major maintenance.

The squadron that replaced 214 is now on the front line, and will stay there for six weeks. If the relief squadron gets a catastrophic surprise by the Japanese and several planes are damaged, then planes from Espiritu Santo must be rushed to them.

Bennett hears jeeps clattering up the hill. The clank and clamor of machinery serves as an alarm clock. Peace is shattered by a bugle sounding "To Reveille," followed by a bell clanging on a hill south of the field. This night is over, and a day that will not easily be forgotten has begun.

The smell of the damp jungle spreads over the base. Airplane engines will soon begin to cough and chug to life. The staccato clatter and rattle of double-row Pratt-Whitney radial engines will settle into a beautiful purr – unique as only an R-2800-8W, 18-cylinder, 2000-horsepower engine can sound.

The war is almost two years old and we're still a long way from Japan, but squadrons like 214 will help to pave the way to victory. Light-hearted and good-natured swearing that accompanies men at war is heard as the Dallas huts begin to stir. Immediately, the sweat begins. "Welcome to the Marines" and "Welcome to the South Pacific" are mixed with a variety of snide imitations of some high-ranking Group Commander.

The cold morning shower is refreshing, as it washes away the night-long sweat. The shave is rough, but the base commander is a stickler for propriety in dress and appearance. Officers and men temporarily assigned to MAG-11 HQ squadron constantly rotate through this command; but, while here, they must adhere to standard rules of military courtesy, conduct, attire and etiquette. After all, Marines must keep up appearances here.

It's different when assigned to front line combat where conduct and courtesies are more relaxed. The best way to succeed here is to not be too different from the standard orders of the day. It could be a long war if assigned to some obscure function in the New Hebrides for some seemingly minor infraction of an insignificant rule.

After the men dress in khaki uniforms, they slowly stroll over to the officers' mess. If they walk too fast or too far, they will be wet with sweat before breakfast is over. Breakfast is hurried because of the heat.

Bennett has time to rush to the flight line to inspect his plane. The mechanic did a "letter-perfect-job." Neatly printed on the side of the fuselage in six-inch letters is the name, *"Susie-Q."* As Bennett hands over the five packs of cigarettes, he wishes he had a picture to send to Wanda and his parents.

"Lieutenant, that paint's still kind'a wet, so don't brush up against it when you get in."

Bennett nods and smiles, "Thanks, Sergeant."

Now, for all the world to see, Wayland Bennett has a plane of his own. Although he won't always fly this plane on missions, it will be known as his. As he hurries to the briefing hut for the day's operations assignments, he looks over his shoulder at the big Corsair and smiles. "The other pilots are going to wonder how I got it painted so fast."

This will certainly be a glorious day to fly. The Corsair, built by Vought-Sikorski, was delivered to the U.S. Navy on April 5, 1943. They are almost exactly the same age; 2nd Lt. Wayland Bennett was delivered to the U.S. Navy nineteen days later on April 24, 1943. They have both logged about 450 hours of flying time. Bennett and his plane are both assigned to VMF-214, and they will both be retired from active duty on the same date. They will remain together for a long time and go home together.

Bennett joins the new squadron members, who are gathering for morning briefing and assignments. He meets the newly arrived Captain Henry Stuckert Miller, who has been in meetings with Colonel Smoak, the base commander. As the new Squadron Exec., Miller will direct today's flights.

The Colonel holds Boyington in a rather acute degree of low esteem, and Miller has been told that it will be his duty to bring some decorum and propriety to the "214 gang." In the Colonel's opinion, "the pilots of 214 are all becoming just like Boyington. They even seem to dress and model themselves after him." It is obvious that he does not like Boyington *at all*.

Miller, a tall Marine from Pennsylvania, is an experienced pilot and a classic Marine who looks like he just stepped out of a recruiting office poster. This well-spoken, by-the-book Marine will keep some of the more valuable squadron records that will be used later by historians. The Blacksheep will soon call him "Notebook Harry" because he always writes everything down in his notebook. He gives the replacements their flight assignments in a cool, efficient manner.

Miller asks Bennett to lead target gunnery practice today, with

Crocker as his wing man. Training records indicate Bennett has, by far, the best gunnery record during training. He eagerly accepts this duty because it means he will be allowed to fire all six Browning .50-caliber machine guns at the same time. Only limited firing was allowed in Corpus Christi because minimum ammunition was available for cadet training.

Bennett is ecstatic when Miller gives him this very difficult assignment; he is on his way to his future and his destiny. There is no time to remember *The Promise*.

Bennett has been assigned Navy 02608, a Corsair with a large "88" buzz number. This plane was photographed last month and the photo published in the Vought-Sikorski company magazine. The birdcage canopy is installed and the tailhook has been removed because the plane is shore-based.

[3-e] **BLACKSHEEP CORSAIR:** *This photo of a Blacksheep (VMF-214) Corsair was taken in September 1943 at Turtle Bay Fighter Strip, Espiritu Santo, by A. G. Simmons. The arrestor hook is removed like many land-based Corsairs and the wings are locked down in an easily reversible field modification. The buzz number on the side of this Corsair looks like an "88." If it really is an "88," then it was named "Susie-Q" by Lt. Bennett about one month later when he paid his mechanic five packs of cigarettes to paint it on 21-22 October 1943. The markings would remain legible for over 50 years. The photo clearly shows the birdcage canopy and removed tail hook, and was important research information for the searches in the jungle. Even small details normally taken for granted could not be overlooked. (Photo by A.G. Simmons – courtesy of Vought Aircraft Co.)*

The plane had extensive maintenance overnight because the right wing did not lock down smoothly yesterday. All Marine shore-based F4U's have their wings locked down; in fact, they rarely fold their wings on the islands. Once the wing lock is tested, Bennett's plane can be returned to combat-ready status. Maintenance reported "88" is ready to test fly. They will take off at 0730 as briefed, so Bennett and Crocker have just enough time to get weather briefings.

Today's routine mission will be an authorized squadron training flight. They will fire guns, test systems, and practice formation attacks and squadron tactics. As always, the last maneuver will be practicing recoveries from steep, high-speed dives – a tactic that Boyington requires every squadron pilot to be familiar with. There will be no time for a solitary Corsair pilot to recover from momentary loss of consciousness during a high-G pull-up while evading Japanese fighter pilots. Pull-up practice is the only way to develop resistance to the deadly blackout phenomenon.

Airplanes crash and pilots are killed almost daily here – many probably due to momentary lapses of consciousness during prolonged pull-up after steep dives at 400 mph when a lapse of a few seconds can be fatal.

The pilots climb into their dusty, gull-wing fighters. Bennett stows the large white, navigation plotter beside his seat and straps himself in. With parachute, Mae-West, helmet, goggles, and assorted flying gear strapped on, he is ready to start the engine. He wonders, "How can anyone swim long enough to get all this gear disconnected in an ocean crash."

After the long checklist is completed, he pulls the goggles down and presses the starter button. Fuel pumps whine as the starter slowly turns the huge 15-foot propeller. He turns on the ignition. The big engine coughs and belches blue smoke from exhaust stacks. As the engine rumbles into action, the oil smoke cloud blows away behind the plane. His eyes sweep the instruments as the engine slowly warms up; all pressures and temperatures are alive and well.

After a moment's warm-up, he signals the Sergeant to remove wheel chocks. The mechanic climbs onto the left wing to act as an extra set of eyes during the long taxi to the strip's end, because forward ground visibility is very limited due to the F4U's long nose. Vision is even more restricted by the dust storm of 20 airplanes getting ready to take off.

Bennett taxis his Corsair down the hill toward the Blue Hole, making snake-like "S" turns while leaning from side to side out of the cockpit. At almost 0730, he signals the control tower that he is ready for takeoff, and looks at Crocker who also signals that he is ready. The mechanics jump off the wings and move away from the two planes.

Crocker, today's wing man, has flown with Bennett before. He was an accomplished college swimmer in Massachusetts, but this rough and tumble outdoor living is new to him. He is an excellent pilot, who is looking forward to becoming a "Blacksheep" combat pilot – and he will.

The propeller blast stirs up a windstorm that keeps the cockpits cool on the ground. Checklists are completed and they are ready for takeoff from Fighter Strip Number One, a dusty jungle strip carved out of coral rock and coconut palm trees.

The control tower, about half way down on the runway's right side, is using light signals to avoid giving the enemy a radio signal to "home into" for an attack. The tower is manned by Captain Robert Shaw, the friendly fellow Bennett met last week at the operations office, and Ed Mazur from Mena, a small Arkansas town about 100 miles north of Texarkana. Although they will never meet, Mazur will play an important role in today's flight – a role he will vividly remember for many years.

The control tower flashes clearance for Bennett and Crocker to move into take-off position. The Corsairs lumber onto the runway and point their noses toward the sea at the strip's far end. Visibility is unrestricted and the 250-foot-wide runway is clear of all other traffic for its full 5000-foot length (almost a mile). As flight leader, Bennett positions himself on the left half of the runway and Crocker moves into take-off position to the right and slightly behind Bennett's right wing.

[3-f] TURTLE BAY FIGHTER STRIP NUMBER ONE:
Notice the wide runway – both Corsairs can take off together in flight position and still have plenty of room left over. Just above the Corsairs are the C-47, Headquarters, Dallas Huts and Turtle Bay lagoons. The Norwegian Freighter is just to the right of the island, along with four downed F4Us in clear, shallow water 60- to 75-foot deep.

At 0729, 22 October 1943, Mazur flashes the green light clearance for take-off. The Corsairs add power and waddle forward, slowly at first, then faster and faster. The big tail rudders deftly swing right, then left, then back right as the pilots point the noses down the runway. Cockpit canopies are slid all the way open, and the pilots are leaning forward to peer around the planes' noses. If the pilot has trouble on take-off and crash-lands in the sea, he will be able to quickly get out of the plane. Goggles are pulled down over their eyes in case an engine cylinder blows on take-off, which would spray hot oil and fire back over the windshield. The mechanics closely watch the take off from the revetments because they worked on Bennett's plane last night.

As the tail comes up, the airplane accelerates faster and arrow-straight down the runway. Then, as the miracle of flight begins, the wheels fold backward and twist into the wings. Doors slam shut, completely covering the landing gear, and flaps retract. The two Corsairs are now committed to flight. Any trouble now would leave them no option but to crash into the sea where Snee and four others wait.

The loaded, quad-mount machine guns track the planes as they flash over the end of the runway. Another hunter, who will soon exact a terrible toll, is stalking this young man who dares invade the kingdom of the skies where only angels tread. As he sees the coral road at the end of the runway, Bennett recalls seeing two Corsairs taking off together like this when he arrived a few days ago.

Crocker tucks it in closer to Bennett as the two planes join up. They climb easily and turn left gracefully as they pass over Turtle Bay's quiet lagoons. Bennett looks down and sees the swimming pier jutting into the shallow waters. As they begin the long climb to altitude, they settle into the planned flight routine. In twelve minutes they climb at 250 mph to 20,000 feet.

While climbing, they constantly maneuver through a series of shallow-banked turns, insuring that no planes are in front of them. Bennett adjusts the elevator trim for a steady airspeed, then shuts his canopy because it will be cold at the top of their climb. He closes the cowl flaps to keep engine temperatures within tolerances. Although left handed, he must fly with his right hand and work the other controls with his left. The cut on his right hand is swollen and sore from infection. He can manage in normal flight with light control forces, but he will have to use both hands for control during high-speed attack maneuvers.

As Bennett signals, Crocker loosens formation and moves right about 200 feet. Bennett noses the fighter over and increases airspeed by 30 mph, then raises the nose back to the horizon. He flicks the controls left and the big plane deftly rolls left; then he brings it level again. Crocker mimics every roll, loop, turn and stall.

Bennett sees two Corsairs in formation below them at 15,000 feet. They may be two new men who just checked out on the F4U. The sight is just too good to pass up because both are flying straight and level. Well, a fighter pilot's game is attack. He motions Crocker and points to the planes far below. Crocker nods and joins up just 20 feet from Bennett who begins an easy right turn. This puts them in attack position and allows them to "slide down the sun beams" onto the two unsuspecting fighters.

If they had been Japanese Zeros, the two "enemy" F4U's would have gone down in flames and glory after Bennett and Crocker make a clean attack from above and behind them. They pull up from the dive, but the other Corsairs never alter their course or acknowledge that Bennett and Crocker are victorious.

Bennett and Crocker zip along, just over the tops of clouds that look like pure white cotton bolls in the fields back home. They perform loops, split-esses and Immelman turns. They experience exhilaration beyond a non-aviator's understanding.

Bennett and Crocker roll their Corsairs over and pull back the control sticks. As they enter a long dive, their speed accelerates to 300 mph, then quickly passes 400 mph. Crocker sees a contrail form behind Bennett's wings.

Bennett is using both hands on the stick. The high-speed control forces are almost more than his right hand can stand as pain throbs to his elbow.

Recovering from the pull-out, Crocker feels his vision fading as he courts the edge of the dreaded blackout. Crocker shakes his head to clear cobwebs from his eyes. When he looks over at Bennett, he sees the signal for yet another dive and thinks, "Bennett's guts must be made out of cast iron to withstand these high speed pull-ups one right after another."

Time passes quickly and they have only enough time for a few more practice maneuvers. They must rendezvous at the target area in seven minutes. Yes, even here the clock is always running. But the truth of the matter is, Bennett's clock is set for a different alarm. He won't get to feel the heavy vibration of his six guns firing all at once... not today... not ever.

As the planes head south, they do a wingover and peel off left into another steep dive. Crocker slides into formation for attack position. Down they dive... but this time Bennett is slow pulling up. They pass 450 mph, diving straight down with their bodies held in place only by the seat belts and shoulder harnesses. As the two specks plummet out of the sky, their engines' hum becomes a shrill scream almost like a whistling sound – the sound that causes the Japanese to refer to Corsairs as "The Whistling Death."

Crocker lets out a mental sigh of relief when he finally sees the other Corsair's nose slowly begin to pull up. He sees long, graceful contrails forming behind Bennett's wing as the hard pull-up narrows his visual field into the early stages of tunnel vision. Crocker knows he is again on the edge of a dangerous blackout.

"Bennett's pushing the limit today, but he knows how to handle his Corsair. We must have been doing 475 to 500 mph on that dive," Crocker thinks.

Crocker knows he will have to ride the fence between consciousness and blackout because at 4500 feet, they are too low to relax the pull-up. The nose is almost back up to the horizon and safety, and he groans under the enormous pressure on his body. He says to himself, "That must have been at least 7 Gs."

The two planes start raising their noses above the horizon and the contrails cease. Bennett's plane suddenly seems to lurch and drop out of formation and Crocker's view. As his plane slows and he gets everything back in order, Crocker looks around for his leader.

Nothing.

Crocker shakes his head to clear the cobwebs from his eyes and again scans the skies for Bennett, but to no avail. He has an uneasy thought in the back of his mind. "Did Bennett crash?"

It seems that, in his last fuzzy view of Bennett, the right wing was buckled; then he was gone.

"Could that be true?"

Crocker turns back south to survey the jungle. He is unsure of his own position at this altitude of 500 feet.

He sees no smoke, no fire, no broken treetops, and no sign of an explosion. For several minutes he searches the skies, hoping. Then he searches the jungle below, dreading.

Still no sign of Bennett.

"Has Bennett become a statistic... in spite of his devotion, dedication and determination?" Crocker wonders.

"Is it possible that his desire to be one of his country's elite fighting men has brought him to earth? Not stricken from the skies by the hand of an enemy, but brought down by fate on a routine squadron training flight? Just after becoming a new member of the Blacksheep Squadron? And only a month shy of his 21st birthday!"

For several minutes Crocker circles the area at low altitude. The adrenaline rush is almost overwhelming. "Is this for real? Is Bennett down?"

As he heads back to Turtle Bay, Crocker ponders, "If Bennett crashed into that area, he will be very hard to find because he has drilled a very small hole in a very large jungle."

[3-g] RECOVERING FROM A STEEP DIVE: *Bennett's plane.*

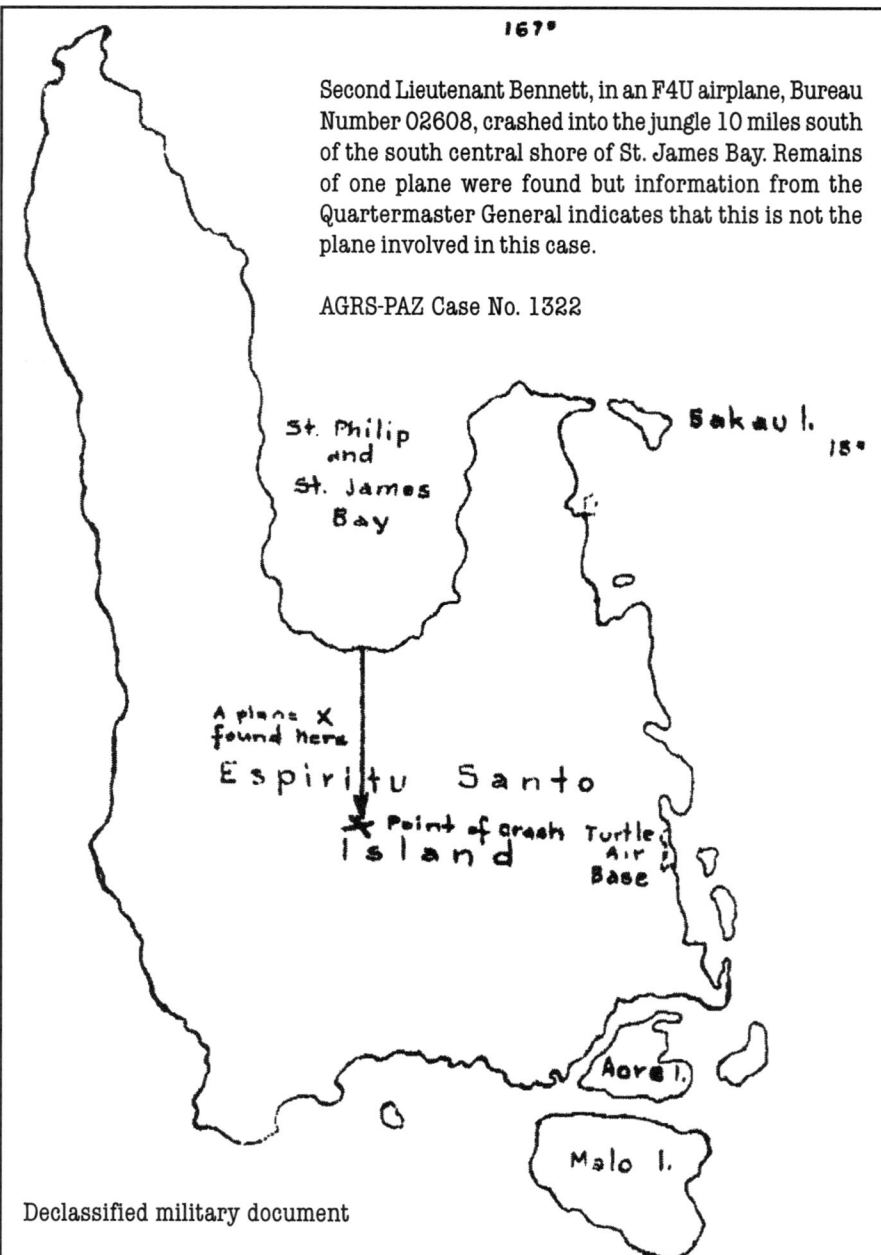

Declassified military document

[4-a] PROBABLE CRASH SITE: *This map indicates the location first reported by Lt. Bill Crocker as the probable site of Lt. Wayland Bennett's crash on October 22, 1943.*

CHAPTER 4

MILITARY SEARCH & RESCUE OPERATIONS
OCTOBER 22, 1943 - 10:00 a.m.

Reluctantly, Crocker turns away from the area. It only takes a few minutes to fly back to Fighter Strip Number One. It is not yet 1000 hours when he lands. He races into the operations tent and reports Bennett's disappearance. Crocker is unsure exactly where he disappeared, but he thinks it was about 15 or 20 miles northwest of the field.

Miller quickly grabs an island map. That would be about 10 miles south of the island's northern edge, in low-lying hills near River Jordan. Some hills are 1500-feet high, but, at least, it is not in the high mountains to the southwest where valleys are very deep and edged by almost vertical cliffs. Miller has seen the area where Bennett may be, and it is not a good spot to go down in a plane, or any other way. It is extremely rough terrain and jungle density is compounded by a lack of trails or roads.

Stunned by the news, other pilots volunteer to fly search missions and a ground search party is immediately sent. Pilot training is also stepped up to an even more feverish pace.

When the search party enters dense jungle, they hire some local natives to guide them into the uncharted and unexplored area. However, the primitive natives do not trust strangers. They are wary and suspicious of Americans, who always seem in a hurry and want to give everyone orders. After the first day, the guides become nervous, and their superstitions take over. They simply and quietly disappear. The searchers try to continue, but there are no trails. They must chop and hack their way through unbelievably dense undergrowth *(Appendix L)*.

Capt. Miller, Harry Johnson, and Crocker continue the air search, criss-crossing the area to no avail. After several days, the ground search is abandoned and the searchers return to base. The supposed crash site is declared unreachable, the location unknown and Bennett's remains unrecoverable at this time. The military explains it with an official acronym: KIA/BNR or MIA.

This all takes place half-a-world away from Bennett's Texarkana home, in the midst of a world at war. The cost, time and manpower necessary to continue the search are simply not available. But Miller, Crocker, Johnson and several other pilots still devote part of each flight to searching for the lost "Blacksheep" pilot.

It is very dangerous to fly the big Corsairs just above the trees at a slow airspeed and perform an effective search at the same time. If anything goes wrong with the plane, the pilot will have no opportunity to bail out and save his own life. He, like Bennett, will certainly be lost to the same wilderness at a time when our nation needs them most... as fighter pilots. Finally, everyone must give up the search.

Miller, another Captain and several pilots who came over with Bennett attend an island memorial service for him in November. The open-air amphitheater is an appropriate setting as "Chaplain Pat" says, "One we have lived and flown with has left us. We will not see him again, but we will not forget him."

He is right. They won't see him again, but they won't forget him either. The Chaplain will later remember the "big old tall lanky boy from Texas, who was always smiling and making everyone else laugh."

Bennett had told another pilot, "Chaplain Pat makes me think of home and my own pastor, Rev. Mathison, who I prayed with for deliverance only seven weeks ago."

These men, who are playing a significant role in events that will change the face of the world, will remember Bennett almost half a century later when a project to find him begins. They will dredge up old memories, both happy and sad. They will search dusty attics and basements to retrieve musty logbooks and documents from those eventful days.

WAYLAND EDWARD BENNETT, MARINE CORPS PILOT, KILLED IN CRASH IN PACIFIC AREA

Mr. and Mrs. R. O. Bennett were notified Thursday of the death of their son, Lieut. Wayland Edward Bennett, in an airplane crash in the South Pacific area.

A telegram signed by Lieut. Gen. T. Holcomb, United States Marine Corps, announced the death of Lieutenant Bennett. He was assigned to the First Marine Air Squadron and piloted one of the famous Corsair fighter planes.

He received his commission in the United States Marine Corps Reserve from the naval air training center, Corpus Christi, Tex, on April 24.

He left several days ago from a west coast port of embarkation, bound for the South Pacific theater of war. The last communication received by his parents from Lieutenant Bennett was sent from the embarkation center.

A graduate of the Texarkana (Texas) high school, Lieutenant Bennett attended Texarkana College and Texarkana Business College. He volunteered for flight training in July 1942. He received basic training at the naval training station, Dallas, Texas.

[4-b] **A HERO DOWN:** *This article, announcing the crash of Lt. Bennett, appeared in the* Texarkana Gazette *in November 1943.*

In late October, Bennett's family receives a telegram from Lt. General T. Holcomb, USMC, informing them of their son's death. The *Texarkana Gazette* then publishes an obituary with a photograph of him in his flying

Search for the Lost Blacksheep

gear and, yes, he is smiling.

Several days after the crash, Miller records the contents of Bennett's belongings and sends them to the Provost Marshall for return to Bennett's family. He files his reports with Marine Air Group 11 Headquarters and notifies the Marine Corps Commandant. Miller states that 2nd Lt. Wayland E. Bennett, O-20609, USMCR, was lost while on an "authorized training flight from Turtle Bay Fighter Strip Number One" *(Appendix E)*.

He then writes an official notification to the next of kin, Mr. Richmond O. Bennett, Sr. Miller reports that the area into which Bennett crashed is "jungle so thick it would have to be seen to be appreciated." He explains, "The trees are over 100-feet tall in the area and have swallowed Bennett and his plane as though it had gone down in the sea." He eloquently describes the base's simple memorial service. His letter is both official and personal, and as the years roll into decades and generations, Miller does not forget. *(Appendix F)*

The Marine Corps lists Bennett and his plane as having been lost on 22 October 1943, and that the plane belonged to VMF-214. Several weeks later it lists a 3 January 1944 loss of another F4U and pilot, Major Gregory "Pappy" Boyington, also of VMF-214 *(Appendix C)*.

[4-c] TRIBUTE TO AN MIA: *These photographs of Lt. Bennett in his flying gear sat on a flag-draped table during the memorial service at Texarkana's Hardy Memorial Methodist Church in November 1943.*

On November 11, 1943, a memorial service for Bennett is held at Texarkana's Hardy Memorial Methodist Church. Bennett's family is all there and, in the absence of his body, a U.S. flag is draped over a serving table and two photographs placed on it. They all hope, however, that they will soon be able to have another, more poignant service.

Bennett's family receives a formal letter dated December 15, 1943 *(Apendix D)*, from group headquarters commander J.A. Smoak, Lt. Col. USMC. This letter officially recognizes the loss of Lt. Bennett on "an authorized training flight" on October 22, 1943.

On March 20, 1944, Mrs. Bennett writes Henry Stuckert Miller with a mother's plaintive cry for her son to be brought home. In it she recalls Bennett's last letter in which he reported having flown formation with Boyington. She also offers a substantial reward for information leading to his recovery *(Appendix G)*.

By the time Miller gets this letter, he has been in combat, promoted to Major and taken over command of VMF-214.

Fifteen to twenty miles northwest of Turtle Bay fighter strip, the jungle floor is quiet, dark and damp. Daily rains soak the island and a triple canopy jungle hides the sun from the mud below. Sheared trees and palms are already repairing themselves in an age-old ritual of survival. Crushed underbrush and vines have sprung back into place and are proliferating. Weeds and grass mingle with new root structure as life begins anew.

Respectful silence is the order of the day, in deference to the newcomer who sleeps here. A tropical breeze searches through the trees. There is an occasional wild animal call and the flutter of wings as birds and bats search for a nesting place.

Scant rays of sunlight allow a hint of the magnificent sunbeams this newcomer slid down to get to this place. On the jungle floor, these sunbeams evoke an angelic setting as a pale halo of light bathes the intruder and his winged chariot as they rest.

The pungent odor of gasoline, hot oil and hydraulic fluids are absorbed by the ancient, soft loam of this resting place. Chunks of man's latest technology are scattered about. The shiny new airplane engine lies buried in fresh mud scars. Only tips of the huge propeller are exposed. Once beautiful, blue gull wings lie twisted and mangled. The tail was ripped away at impact. The fuselage and cockpit rests on its crumpled right side. The broken canopy and shattered windshield lie in a twisted heap. This wreckage bears no resemblance to the once mighty flying machine. The machine guns are silent, and six boxes spilled a neatly-belted 2400 rounds of bullets across the jungle floor.

Through all this devastation, there remains a sign of this once proud bird of prey's nation. The Stars and Bars, identifying it as an American Military plane, show clearly on its upturned left side. They will always face the sky and the God whom its pilot served. In front of the star are 12-inch numbers, "88." Just in front of the cockpit are wrinkled and distorted letters, covered with exhaust smoke and oil. But they brightly proclaim this pile of rubble is named *"Susie-Q."* Farther back in the undergrowth lies the tail section, making this the final resting place for Navy 02608.

Beside his plane, asleep in the arms of his Lord, lies Wayland Bennett. His position makes it appear that he is only taking a short nap. It will be a long rest here, but not permanent. It will take 51 years, but he will be found; and during his wait, he will be remembered by his homeland as always a Marine, always an American, and KIA/BNR.

Immediately following the war, AGRS (American Graves Registration) units quietly recover remains of many Americans who died in battle. They are taken to Hawaii and processed through a very strenuous positive identification protocol. They are then returned to their families, and provided full military honors at funerals befitting warrior heroes.

However, Marine Lt. Wayland E. Bennett is not among those whose remains are returned.

The Bennett family suffers further distress when word arrives that their middle son has been injured in the South China Sea. A Japanese Kamikaze pilot made his bid for glory and dove into the mine sweeper USS Shea, injuring many crewmen including Yeoman First Class Wayne Bennett. After recovering from his injuries, he is given a Purple Heart, but he survives the war.

Bill Crocker becomes a full member of the Blacksheep Squadron two days after Bennett's death, and a combat pilot when the Squadron returns to the Solomons. His six weeks in the Solomons introduces him to a rough and primitive lifestyle, and he adapts well.

[4-d] GLAD TO BE HOME: *This Corsair with birdcage canopy and no tail-hook has considerable battle damage. It is sitting on its tail and the tail-wheel is missing. The left elevator and rudder are shot-up, perhaps by an enemy fighter pilot. At a forward combat base, this much damage could lead to the plane being scrapped and all usable parts placed on other less-damaged planes. (Photo courtesy of Vought Aircraft Co.)*

Boyington's days are now numbered. He is tired, sick and under enormous stress from daily combat. The specter of becoming America's leading Ace allows him little rest. He is unfit for flight, just like the rest of his pilots who are exhausted from flying several strikes each day against the Japanese.

While on a strike in the Northern Solomons, Boyington's plane is damaged, and he is separated from his squadron. While limping back to base in a smoking plane, a light Japanese fighter jumps him. The young Japanese warrior comes out of the clouds and spots the crippled Corsair. He knows he is no match for the enemy Corsair under normal circumstances; but, for his Emperor, he fires anyway.

His aim is accurate as one of his bullets hits the Corsair's fuel tank, just in front of the pilot's windshield. As the F4U bursts into flames, the cockpit is bathed in fire and Boyington must bail out over the ocean. He opens his parachute and lands in the sea, but is promptly captured by a Japanese ship.

[4-e] A YOUNG JAPANESE fighter pilot who knew it was an impossible shot - but for his Emperor he fired anyway. The result was his claim to have shot down Boyington.

Search for the Lost Blacksheep

Although credited with shooting down 28 Japanese planes during his career, Boyington becomes a score for a young Japanese fighter pilot on 3 January 1944.

His Squadron is devastated when he doesn't return. They realize he may never be recovered if he went down in the sea, but hope he will be picked up by an American rescue craft. Boyington is now a war statistic, and nothing will be heard of him until POW's are returned after the war.

America is certain Boyington has been killed, and the Marine Corps awards him the nation's highest honor for heroism in combat, the Congressional Medal of Honor. But Boyington does not die that day. He survives and will be remembered as a war hero.

The Blacksheep return to Turtle Bay for a week of R & R (Rest and Recuperation), and Major Henry S. Miller takes command of VMF-214. He will later be promoted to Colonel.

While in Turtle Bay, they are notified the Squadron is scheduled for reassignment and transfer back to the states. Miller requests that the Blacksheep not be reassigned but be allowed to remain as a squadron. He suggests they pick up pilots and planes to replace their losses and stay in combat. Meanwhile, the Blacksheep are assigned training flights to keep them ready.

One new pilot on the island is Major Royal Monger, a journalist-turned-Marine-fighter-pilot from Chicago. Crocker is assigned as his check pilot; however, since the Corsair only has one seat, the SNJ/T6 training plane is used as a check plane before the Major can be assigned to an F4U.

Because of visual references from the trainer's rear seat, the instructor normally sits there and the new pilot sits up front. However, if these positions are reversed with the student in the rear, his view is very similar to that of a Corsair pilot.

Monger and Crocker fly the trainer over the north edge of Espiritu Santo. Crocker was here before, with Bennett on the day he disappeared. No one is sure why or even how, but the SNJ/T-6 crashes 200 yards off the beach in 240-foot-deep water. Neither Crocker nor Monger survives.

They both make it into WW2 history books, but, like Bennett, as statistics. They have become KIA, MIA and BNR. Some reports indicate Crocker was lost in combat in another island group, but his logbook was returned to his family and cites the above as the facts surrounding his loss. Regardless of what the circumstances were, Bill Crocker was a Blacksheep Squadron combat pilot, and once flew in the company of "Eagles." Perhaps, he still does.

Bennett's friend Johnson continues to fly with the Blacksheep and is credited with combat kills. He survives the war, retires as a Major and returns home to Alabama.

During WW2, VMF-214 records one of the highest kill ratios of any squadron, yet their career spans only 84 days, and consists of only 51 men! In another part of the world, Winston Churchill's comment could perhaps apply to them, "Never have so many, owed so much to so few."

Records confirm that the Blacksheep Squadron shoots down at least 97 enemy planes, with another 35 probables. Fifty more enemy aircraft are damaged and 21 destroyed on the ground. A total of 203 enemy planes are destroyed, probably destroyed or damaged. They also damage and destroy many Japanese ships, barges, vehicles and installations. The history of the Blacksheep Squadron becomes a Marine showcase in books, movies and television. They are all heroes, and in his 1985 book, Frank Walton describes them as *Once They Were Eagles*. They still are.

During the war, the kill versus loss ratio is established, and history records VMF-214's success in that fashion. Some say Bennett was never assigned to 214, while others assert he was just a replacement. The casualty reports list him as a member of VMF-214 when his F4U went down on October 22, 1943 *(Appendix C)*. Perhaps some are afraid historical ratios will be disturbed if Bennett's loss is recorded as a 214 loss, but that is not really an issue.

The facts are simply that 20-old 2nd Lt. Wayland Bennett was selected and assigned to 214 after only two or three weeks because he was an eager and aggressive young pilot. He was special, just like all the Blacksheep, but the story does not end with his loss. It is about his life, friends, hometown and, most of all, about a day when Wayland Bennett finally comes home as a result of the *Search for the Lost Blacksheep*.

THE WAR GOES ON

Robert Bowden is a U.S. Army medic when he comes home on leave. He learns that D.A. Carson is also home from fighting in Guadalcanal. They quickly reunite and mourn the news of Bennett's crash in the uncharted jungles of an unknown island called Espiritu Santo.

After his leave is over, Carson returns to the South Pacific, where he fights through the sands of Iwo Jima as Marines place our flag on Mt. Suribachi. This gentle young man is now a seasoned combat veteran, and will soon become an enraged bull. When pinned down by enemy machine guns and snipers, his choice affects his life and those of his comrades in battle. His actions are well documented in the citation he receives along with his nation's second highest award for heroism and valor – The Navy Cross. His dedication and action surpass the bounds of sanity when, one by one, he sees his squad members gunned down by Iwo Jima's defenders.

Carson makes his move and runs toward an enemy stronghold. With enemy fire in front and friendly fire behind, his survival is a combat miracle. He attacks the enemy pillbox alone. With bare hands, he grabs the hot machine gun barrel from the concrete bunker's slit and jerks it away from the gunner. He methodically does what heroes do and what will later be seen in movies with John Wayne and Audie Murphy. History records a valid assessment of the Marines on Iwo Jima that day: "Uncommon valor was a common virtue."

After such heroism, D.A. Carson walks his last mile on Iwo Jima. Within hours, he will not be so lucky. He crawls up a path into enemy territory, and moves into the sights of an enemy sniper. For the remainder of his life, he will suffer with each step he takes. But he will always remember his pal, Wayland Bennett, and he will never forget... ***The Promise.***

When Robert Bowden arrives in the South Pacific after leave, he suddenly finds himself on Espiritu Santo. Medics in combat zones usually work around the clock, and Bob's lot is no different.

He is exhausted from long hours repairing the damage of war on Guadalcanal's wounded. He also has extra duties as one of only three dental technicians. Each of the thousands of replacements must receive medical and dental exams before assignment to a battle zone. There are no dental technicians in battle zones and medics have a full schedule just keeping the wounded alive under battlefield conditions.

Bowden finally manages a few hours away from the hospital in Luganville and walks up the crushed coral roadway to Turtle Bay Fighter Strip Number One. He has mixed emotions because he is about to venture into a "no man's land" for an Army medic. Trying to get into a Marine Air Base Group Headquarters, alone, with no orders or authorization is real reason for concern.

The U.S. Marines are an independent organization. They even have their own medics – called corpsmen. Renowned as a security force, they are famous for guarding high security bases like Turtle Bay and for always looking for trouble from anyone who wants to pass their checkpoints. They trust no one, and treat everyone like a spy or enemy agent.

"Yes, sir," he thinks to himself, "this ought to be a very interesting day indeed." He is right; in fact, it will be a day that he will never forget, and it will begin a search that will last for over fifty years.

A Navy jeep stops and a sailor on his way to Turtle Bay offers him a ride. During the drive, Bowden wonders how he will pull this trip together. He knows the Marine sentries will first ask for identification and orders. Of course, he has all the necessary I.D., but no orders. He knows the sentries won't be satisfied with just turning him away and denying him entry.

The jeep slows to cross a narrow bridge. and as the following cloud overtakes them, fine white coral dust settles onto everything. The sentry guard shack is at the other end of the bridge, and Bowden sees two rather large guards ignore the sailor and focus their attention on him. As the guards approach the jeep, they carefully point Thompson machine guns directly at him.

The guards know the sailor and ask, "Where'd you pick up the 'mud-puppy,' Joe?"

The sailor laughs and replies, "about ten miles ago."

Bowden knows "mud-puppy" is an uncomplimentary Marine statement directed at all soldiers in general and anyone who is not a Marine. Nothing personal.

One big Marine looks directly at Bowden and insists he produce his I.D. and orders. Bowden hands over the I.D. and tries to explain who he is and why he is there.

Marine sentries are occasionally accused of "not thinking." Some people go so far as to say they only do as they're told, but these two guards are on the offensive as soon as Bowden tries to explain why he has no orders. They explode into action as though they have been waiting just for him all their lives. With both guns now leveled on his chest, one yelps, "Corporal of the Guard!"

The other, with about as much emotion in his eyes as a cobra, barks, "Out'ta the jeep. Hands up, buster!"

As Bowden slowly tries to get out of the jeep, he hears the sailor mutter under his breath, "Oh, Boy!"

The Corporal of the Guard appears, bigger and tougher looking than the first two, and snaps, "Who are you, soldier? What do you want here, soldier? Why, have you come here without orders, soldier?"

Bowden's days as a threat to the security of Turtle Bay have come to a quick and decisive end. He is placed under armed guard and marched up the dusty road.

Bowden thinks his three guards, "act at though they could hand-feed The Hounds of the Baskervilles... they probably do, too."

As he marches past the end of the runway, he looks up to see two quad-mount gun tubs tracking him. He doesn't want to imagine what would happen to him if one of those gunners had to sneeze. Just then the earth shakes with a deafening noise as two F4Us take off. They pass overhead at what seems to be only 25 feet above his head, join into tight formation, then gracefully turn left in their climb. They soon disappear out of sight to the north.

Bowden is very unsure of just what his future holds. In fact, he is very unsure just where he is being led. For a fleeting moment, he imagines a firing squad, because Marines have some really colorful reputations when they are guarding their own, especially one of their own bases.

He realizes, "It is only 0800 in the morning and not really all that hot. Then why am I sweating so profusely?" He thinks of home and his family who are always prepared for a notification of his death in combat. Now, however, he is facing a more difficult question, "How are they ever going to understand how I got shot by Marines at Turtle Bay?"

Bowden sees the bay's emerald green waters and the sugar-like beaches surrounding the small city of Dallas huts. He smells food cooking in the chow hall and hears jeeps darting around the airfield. Over in the revetments, he hears the clanking of machinery and mechanics. He sees blue smoke billow and hears an engine roar as a plane with odd-looking, bent wings prepares for flight. Some planes look like they need major surgery, while others appear ready for the junkyard. A half-century later, Bowden will still vividly recall his every thought on this day at Turtle Bay.

Bowden is taken to a Quonset hut marked only as "HQ-MAG-11." He is introduced to a large, imposing Marine officer who listens impatiently while Bowden nervously tries to explain a rambling story about *A Promise*. After a shaky start, Bowden explains that all he wants to know is where his pal, Bennett, has crashed so he can go get him.

Finally, the Captain seems to have heard enough. Bowden is lectured for several minutes on the facts of life including, "Soldier, the jungle is thick, deep, dark and uncharted. The natives back in the jungle are unpredictable and have cannibalistic backgrounds. We have a world at war on our hands and no time to explore the jungle looking for crashed airplanes. We do know of a few planes and their locations, but we have no ideas about Lt. Bennett's plane. Last week we found a "Wildcat" but cannot recover it. It has a pair of dice painted on the side and "7 Come Eleven," but that is not your friend."

The Captain briefly explains what happened to Bennett and what was done to get to the site. Then, as he stands up, he tells Bowden, "One thing we do need right now is all the medics we can get, and we need to keep them healthy. You can't go into the jungle as if it is just a little walk in the park back home. You cannot search for Lt. Bennett, and, Soldier, you cannot come back to this airstrip!"

So Bowden survives his encounter with Turtle Bay Marines. The Captain is right; Bowden never gets to go back to Turtle Bay. He is soon ordered into combat in the Solomons, Guadalcanal and the Philippines.

1944 - HAWAII

On April 12, 1944, partly due to the circumstances surrounding his loss, Bennett's case is under consideration in Hawaii. As in any conflict when casualties are not found, a permanent status is required. A very rigid protocol must be observed. In a formal and respectful setting, a military board convenes, and the individual remaining cases are administratively considered. Absence of information about crash location causes the board to determine the missing lost through death (KIA) and assigned a status of BNR (Body Not Recoverable).

The Board issues their determination and issues a Certificate of Death based on Crocker's and Miller's reports, and the known facts of his disappearance. This does not close the case, in fact it places it in an always-open status. It is a case that will be reopened by the first shred of information concerning a possible location.

1946

"Pappy" Boyington is released when the war ends, after almost two years in a Japanese POW camp. He is sent to Washington, D. C., to receive The Congressional Medal of Honor.

Bennett had written his parents that he had become part of the Blacksheep Squadron and had flown with Boyington, but some records from the time say "Bennett never met Boyington and cannot possibly have flown formation with him."

If so, Boyington does a very strange thing, from an historical point of view after he is released. Using pen and ink, and with handwriting still so shaky it is barely readable after prison camp horrors, Boyington writes a letter to the family of a mere 2nd Lieutenant whom he supposedly never knew. Boyington expresses his condolences to the family of Wayland Bennett and tells them he enjoyed flying in formation with him!

This is the "Pappy" Boyington who, according to the records, never had Bennett in his Squadron. Since the letter was destroyed in a fire, the family certified they all read the letter *(Appendix I and J)*. We confidently hope that this will someday be confirmed; then, this book's title will be justified.

Bowden returns home after the war is over. He tries mining for gold and other adventures as he starts to put his life on a path to a meaningful future. He finally takes a job with Offenhauser Insurance in Texarkana, where he works with his old pal D.A. Carson. He meets and marries a local girl and raises a family. Bowden progresses to an executive position with the company, and becomes their representative as they sponsor and support hospitals, libraries and museums.

Robert Sandlin finishes the war as an instructor in the Navy College. When the fighting ends, Frances *(Rosie-the-Riveter)* does not need to build any more B-24 bombers.

The Sandlins return to Texarkana where they will raise their children. He begins a career in law enforcement and the development and supervision of the Federal Correctional Center. Sandlin later becomes a judge and serves in that capacity for many years. They are a devout and deeply religious family and teach in their church.

For the next fifty years, Bowden, Carson and Sandlin get together and laugh as they recall their youthful days before the war. But, at night at home, there is always the haunting memory of ***The Promise.***

1947

On August 10, 1947, Mrs. Bennett again appeals to the nation for help, writing this time to General Van Dygriff, Marine Corps Commandant. She asks for any information and volunteers assistance in her son's recovery; but, as one might expect, the complexities of peace are enormous *(Appendix H)*.

The Board's April 1944 opinion is reconsidered after the war, and in Bennett's case without new information to the contrary, the opinion is upheld on 3 August 1949. This is the only way careful and considerate deliberation can be accomplished during war and out of national necessity. No oversight or insult is ever intended toward the deceased or his family. There is no failure to perform any protocol that establishes the BNR classification, and the nation pays tribute to the family on behalf of its loved one's sacrifice.

When a new conflict arises, as it does in 1950, priorities change, not out of disrespect, but out of necessity. Identification of the new casualties from the Korean conflict takes precedence over BNRs from WW2. There can be no searches, only recoveries, and they number in the tens of thousands.

For Bennett's family, the long wait and a lifetime of hope and frustration have just begun. The first notification of MIA or KIA and the BNR explanation start a domino effect of unclosed grief that changes lives in dramatic ways.

What then of the men remembered as the Blacksheep Squadron? Perhaps they are more widely known today than any other WW2 military unit. Some of their deeds place them on an historic parallel with other national heroes, at least in the eyes of a generation of America's television viewers. The reason for their deeds has put them on a pedestal with others such as the "Men of the Alamo." All the legends of the Blacksheep Squadron may not even be true. It is even possible that some of their popularity comes more from journalistic liberties than from actual deeds, but our nation needs heroes such as these to look up to and respect.

After Boyington is released from active duty, he writes a book about the men who would be identified as heroes. The book, which is his account of what happened to these men during the war, is appropriately titled **Baa Baa Blacksheep**. It is a chronicle about VMF-214, not just one man from a squadron. Boyington tells of exploits where blood is spilled and men die daily in the filthy, disgusting business of war. He describes trials and tribulations endured by the fighting men on both sides of the lines of combat and the hardships they all endured. It also tells about his capture and his time and experiences in the Japanese POW camp. It is destined to become a best seller.

Years later, a developing industry picks up the option to rewrite it for television. Their journalistic liberties considerably changed the story's facts, and may be interpreted as a bad representation. However, some feel it brings the history of a long ago war into the present and allows us to appreciate acts of heroism, teamwork and loyalty; conveying such concepts as duty, honor and country.

Even though the TV series is not all factual, it is based on very real acts of daring and heroism. It also displays an age where loyalty, patriotism and national pride have different meanings and really are politically correct.

Boyington admits he was not an exceptional money manager; perhaps this is one reason he permitted too many inaccuracies to creep into his book's adaptation for television. Particularly inaccurate is the impression that Boyington's gang were all refugees from a military court's martial and had no choice but to fly with him in his daring deeds. It must be made clear that the REAL Blacksheep were absolutely NOT under sentence for crimes committed, under house arrest, restriction, awaiting court martial, disciplinary action, or any other discipline as depicted by the TV series. As a form of entertainment, the program became a resounding success. Perhaps it even made American youth want to imitate human heroes instead of robots.

However, the book and series also tell another important story. These deeds were for a common cause, by men who worked, played and died as a team. Perhaps, for that, an element of forgiveness can be extended to those who take literary liberties and make the events of blood and guts more acceptable in our living rooms. It does for some, and perhaps those few are many.

When "Pappy" dies in 1986, he receives another honor reserved for America's heroes. He is buried with full military honors in the Arlington National Cemetery near Washington, D.C., and a Blacksheep team performs the only authorized funeral fly-over remembered by most Marines today.

Some men from the Blacksheep Squadron are still alive today; men who spent their youth in the South Pacific theater. They were at war over azure lagoons. Days were spent in a vast panorama of beauty, etched in fire and gun smoke across picturesque skies of combat. When fighting ended, these magnificent views were punctuated by funeral pyres on the surface of a placid ocean or in the dense jungle undergrowth where death had claimed the victory.

The war has come to an end, but it will never be forgotten. Likewise, many young men will grow old remembering their friends who lie where they fell on the other side of the world. But for three Texarkana men, the memories of one of their friends will be even more poignant because of *A Promise* they entered into on December 7, 1941 – *A Promise* that can never be forgotten.

PART II
1987 - 1994

CHAPTER 5

THE CHALLENGE - 1987 - TEXARKANA, TEXAS

The aging process plagues Robert Bowden. Now in his sixties, his chronic wrist pain has been diagnosed as Carpal Tunnel Syndrome. Surgery is recommended, but Bowden is a very active man who has no desire to gamble soreness against the uncertainty of surgery.

It is time for Texarkana's annual downtown Quadrangle Festival, which is a pet project of Josh Morriss, Jr. and his Offenhauser Insurance Company. Bowden has been Offenhauser's comptroller for forty years, and the festival is his responsibility. Offenhauser donated their old downtown office building to the Texarkana Museum System, and the festival is the annual capital fundraiser for the Museum's operating expenses. Over the years, Bowden has developed a wizard-like skill at organization; he has no time to be sick, laid up or out of action with all the projects he has going on.

Bowden's wife suggests he see a Chiropractor, so he calls one who was formerly an Air Force instructor pilot. The Doctor recently flew his single-engine plane, **The Texarkana Baby,** around the world. After a few visits to the Doctor, Bowden feels better and sees the treatment is effective.

[5-a] The Doctor standing on the wing of "The Texarkana Baby" – the single-engine plane he flew around the world, setting 180 new records.

Although the Doctor is constantly moving from one patient to another, he is friendly and always seems to have a few moments to visit with Bowden, who has always led an active and interesting life. They talk about history, flying and other old interests.

The Doctor knows Bowden is one of Josh Morriss' senior executives who is frequently loaned to community service organizations. The Morriss family's participation in improving the quality of life in Texarkana over the past hundred years and their leadership contributions are legendary.

Bowden, like Morriss, is a quiet and soft-spoken Christian man who knows how to recruit people with the right skills for any project. The Doctor has been recruited for civic duties before, but Bowden is smooth. He has been asking some interesting questions and seems to have something on his mind, but keeps beating around the bush about it. The Doctor wonders, "Bowden may want me to serve on some board or committee, but why doesn't he just come out with it?"

Finally the day comes. While the Doctor treats Bowden, questions creep into the conversation that have no bearing on the treatment. During this office visit, Bowden slowly begins to draw the Doctor into his plan. The conversation seems to lead to an area of interest that Bowden has not been quite ready to bring to the surface. The Doctor remains patient. He knows Bowden will come out with it sooner or later.

Bowden asks about the Doctor's flying experiences, then moves to another question. "Doctor, have you ever heard of a Corsair airplane?"

The Doctor replies that he has.

After a few minutes pause, Bowden tries another question, "Doctor, have you ever heard of The Blacksheep Squadron?"

Again the Doctor replies affirmatively.

"By the way, I've been meaning to ask you, Doctor, have you ever heard of a pilot by the name of Boyington?"

[5-b] A PICTURE WORTH 1000 WORDS:
For those 1000 words, one should read Baa **Baa Blacksheep** *by Pappy Boyington or* ***Once They Were Eagles*** *by Frank Walton.*

The Doctor replies, "Yes, I've heard of him; in fact, he was a friend of mine. I knew him well enough that he presented me some of the World Records I received when I flew **The Texarkana Baby** around the world. I also have several photographs of us together at some major aviation events we both attended."

Search for the Lost Blacksheep

Then the Doctor asks, " Why, Bob, do you know Boyington?"

Bowden replies, " No, I never met him; but, I was wondering, did you ever hear of a place called Espiritu Santo in the New Hebrides?"

The Doctor responds, "Yes, I have. On my way around the world I flew over the area and landed in Guadalcanal. That's where Boyington and his squadron were assigned during WW2, but the name's been changed to The Republic of Vanuatu."

The Doctor then asks Bowden, "Why all the interest in the Blacksheep and Boyington?"

[5-c] **PAPPY'S PLANE:** *The Doctor visits with a member of the Blacksheep Squadron, and is shown the "office" of an AV-8b Harrier – an airplane permanently reserved for Major Gregory "Pappy" Boyington.*

"Well, I'd like to talk to you some day, when you have time, about an old friend of mine from Texarkana who was killed in a crash during the war. He just disappeared one day while on a training flight over the island and never came home. He is listed as MIA."

Now curious, the Doctor asks, "Why did he not come home, Bob?"

Bowden replies, "No one seems to be able to find his plane. He supposedly crashed into the jungle, but they just can't seem to find him."

The Doctor says he would like to hear more about Bowden's friend, and suggests they meet Saturday afternoon at a local coffee shop. After setting the meeting, the Doctor turns and is gone. Other patients have already been kept waiting too long.

So the die is cast and the unsuspecting Doctor is lured into a story of adventure and intrigue that is 45 years old. Bowden is about to pull a string to open a creaky old door that leads to... **The Promise.**

Bowden, Carson and Sandlin have remained close friends while they made careers and raised families. They have often discussed ways and methods to locate their lost friend, but so far, nothing has ever worked. "Maybe, just maybe, now it will be different..." Bowden ponders as he leaves the office.

SATURDAY, SEPTEMBER 17, 1987

There are no phone calls, waiting patients or other interruptions when the two meet in the quiet coffee shop. After a few minutes of idle conversation, Bowden begins. He wants to find out about "current research projects concerning WW2 casualties." He is now direct, to the point and asking some very difficult questions. "Who can do searches for WW2 casualties? How can such things be determined as possible or impossible?"

The Doctor smiles as he remembers his first impression of Bowden. It was obvious, even then, that he wanted to discuss something, and now he comes to the point. "So this is what Bowden wanted to talk about all along, but it seems more than just a passing interest."

The Doctor waits patiently as Bowden continues his rapid-fire inquisition. Then Bowden slowly reaches into his pocket and pulls out an envelope. Inside is an old, worn notebook that has obviously "been around." The 45-year-old journal chronicles what happened to a young Army soldier who tried to get onto a Marine airfield during WW2. It tells about a meeting with a long-forgotten Marine Captain on a now-deserted airstrip, which was once known as Turtle Bay Fighter Strip Number One. It chronicles events, the details of which have long been filed away in musty warehouse archives – events just waiting for someone to initiate an interest in a mystery that is almost forgotten by all but a few who can remember... ***The Promise.***

Bowden gingerly hands the frayed old notebook to the Doctor who slowly reads the contents. Then, after looking at Bowden, he reads them again.

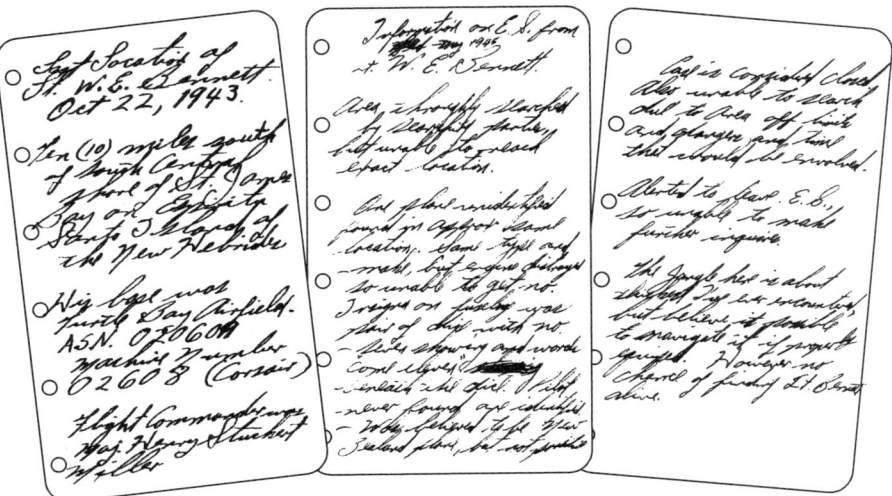

[5-d] PAGES OF HISTORY: These weathered pages from Bowden's notebook reveal a friend who wouldn't give up the search.

The pages are yellowed with age and stained from a thousand readings. The Doctor can barely distinguish the hurriedly written notes that bring back vivid memories. They tell of a young intruder in a place and time where, he was sure at one point, he was about to face a firing squad or be "hand fed to the Hounds of the Baskervilles."

The Doctor reads the following in Bowden's hasty scrawl:

> *Last location of Lt. W. E. Bennett – Oct, 22, 1943*
> *Ten (10) miles south of south central shore of St. James Bay on Espiritu Santo Island of the New Hebrides.*
> *His base was Turtle Bay Airfield ASN 020609 Machine Number 02608 (Corsair)*
> *Flight Commander was Maj. Henry Stuckert Miller*
> *Information on E. S. from Feb.-May 1945 Lt. W. E. Bennett*
> *Area thoroughly searched by several parties but unable to reach exact location.*
> *One plane, unidentified found in approx. same location. Same type and make, but engine destroyed so unable to get number. Insignia on fuselage was pair of dice with number seven showing and words, "come eleven" beneath the dice. Pilot never found or identified. Was believed to be New Zealand plane, but not sure.*
> *Case is closed. Also unable to search due to area off limits and danger and time that would be involved.*
> *Alerted to leave E. S. so unable to make further inquiry.*
> *The jungle here is about thickest I've ever encountered, but believe it possible to navigate it if properly equipped. However no chance of finding Lt. Bennett alive.*

As he finishes reading, the Doctor carefully hands the old notebook back to Bowden and asks, "Just who was Wayland Bennett to you? I sense this means more to you than what is in this book. I'm in no hurry, so tell me what makes this important to you after all these years."

This is what Bowden has been waiting for, and he begins to tell the Doctor the story of the Texarkana Marine who did not come home. Bowden talks about the boyhood friends who vowed with Bennett that a sacrifice would not be made in vain. He tells of the agreement the four boys entered into on December 7, 1941, that they would all return home after the war was over. He tells the Doctor about... **The Promise.**

The Doctor sits through the story without interrupting. He has already sensed what Bowden wants. He suspected it earlier, but is now convinced. When the story is completed, the Doctor leans forward and frowns as he looks directly into Bowden's soul with eyes similar to those Bowden faced once before. A long time ago, a larger-than-life Marine pointed a machine gun at his chest and looked at him with eyes like these: "eyes that had about as much emotion as a cobra." Once again Bowden feels as though he is being examined like a bug under a microscope.

The Doctor carefully frames his next question because he already senses the answer; but, for the record, he asks, "What do you want from me, Mr. Bowden?"

Bowden has waited 45 years for someone to ask him that question. He has told this story many times to many listeners, but no one has ever asked a direct question like this. He knows the Doctor has lived a high-risk life in aviation's fast lane and senses he is becoming impatient. While Bowden was surprised to get this much of his time, he knows it might not be too wise to bore him.

Bowden quickly replies, "I need someone who knows how to do research, someone who can determine the feasibility of searching for and returning Bennett home to Texarkana and his family. I need someone who can determine if a private search can now be made with any hope of success."

Bowden holds his breath, wondering how well he has presented his case. "Have I jumped the gun or moved too fast?"

The Doctor already knows what Bowden wants to hear, but instead he cautions: "The answers you're looking for aren't easy. First, let me point out a few of the problems you'll encounter. You are about to get into a rather mysterious area, Bob, which you know nothing about. And, I might point out, no one else does either, because no one has ever conducted a private search like you propose. You must understand, this is an extremely sensitive subject and also highly restricted. It's a subject that's 100% under military control. Since civilians aren't welcome in these affairs, you're going to meet some very stiff resistance. So, before you give any more thought to 'how nice it would be to just run over to the other side of the world and bring your pal home,' you need to review the other side of the problem. For example, let's go over a little of how hard it will be."

The Doctor explains:

"(1) This is a 45-year-old case of KIA, currently under a BNR classification. It will, by necessity, remain that way until someone reports a sighting or a crash location. Active searches for WW2 casualties ended when the war ended, and none are now underway. Recovery activity in Bennett's case, or any other, will come only after a location report is actually received by the proper authorities – Decedent Affairs and CILHI (Central Identification Laboratory in the Hawaiian Islands).

"However, this case will always be considered government property. The responsibility for all KIA/BNR cases now falls under the supervision of U.S. Military, Decedent Affairs. They are the POC (Point of Contact) for any and all inquiries, and they take their job very seriously. Because these cases are someone's next of kin, it will be an extremely sensitive issue for that family. Government officials are not going to be fond of outsiders who just decide to make inquiries into these issues.

"(2) Generally speaking, no outsider can gain access to an MIA/BNR case if they are not family or next of kin. Family members are usually the only ones who inquire. Information is specifically restricted to one person who had been Designated Next Of Kin (DNOK) by the deceased. An outsider cannot expect a free-flowing wellspring of information because the DNOK is the only person who can gain ready access to details of casualty records and history of the KIA, MIA or BNR.

"(3) Records may be scattered all over government archives, not just 'over in the personnel office' in a nice neat file marked Bennett, Wayland E., 2nd Lt., USMCR. It will be expensive and time consuming to bring all the information together – presuming you can get to it. Then, if you do get to see those records, letters and documents, you may begin to evaluate them in terms of a project. That is slow, time-consuming research that must be meticulously performed.

"(4) You can then discuss the $64 questions such as, 'Where is he?' or, 'Can I go after him?' By the time you get to this point, you'll have already invested a lot of time and money, only to discover you are right where the government was in 1943. The airplane and remains are still KIA/MIA/BNR for a very good and valid reason. It is still a very small airplane, lost in a very large jungle which even the Marines and Army could not find. So, right now, consider doing yourself a very large favor. First, forget it! And next, ask yourself what you think you can afford to do that the government could not afford to do back then? You're not considering just a little walk in the park here, pal. I've been in jungles, and I've flown over a few more. Believe me, this is going to be a very tough project."

Seemingly unimpressed, Bowden asks his first $64 question, "Can it be done?"

The Doctor drops his head, sighs and shakes his head. Bob anticipates a negative response, but the Doctor finally answers quietly, "Yes, I believe it can."

Bowden is surprised to get these answers so quickly, but he's prepared. As an organizer, he asks, "How can we gain access to the information we need?"

The Doctor realizes he is not going to be able to talk Bowden out of the project, so he calmly replies, "In dealing with these problems, someone must absolutely, unequivocally and unquestionably be placed into the information loop by the deceased's family. That person must be designated as the family's representative in these matters for the duration of the search. There can be no changing minds or second thoughts later, and there can be no disagreements between family members. It must be unanimous and permanent. It must also be a legal assignment. Furthermore, an attorney or Notary Public must certify this decision in an official document.

"Once this is done, the new DNOK representative can directly access any information. Any MIA/KIA/BNR case has a stringent set of protocols, and it will be necessary for the DNOK to become part of those protocols. He must never try to go around them, and must become familiar with all procedures. As the family's representative, he can ask questions and may be able to get any existing data from archives and records that were placed in storage and packed away long ago. It will probably take months to track down some records."

Bowden listens intently, weighing every word the Doctor says as he continues. "Perhaps the single most important issue is one with which you have had some experience. You were once a mortician, Bob, and you know government agencies abhor publicity regarding family privacy. Your primary sources of information are going to be those responsible for Decedent Affairs who may not feel at liberty to discuss the case with you or provide requested information. It may, therefore, be necessary to establish secondary contacts, and this will be frustrating.

"It could take months just to gather basic data. You will need to talk to everyone who is still alive who was on the airfield at the time of the crash. You can only hope they will still remember details of that day. Every phone call will be long distance – whether it is to Baltimore, Honolulu, Washington, D.C. or even Espiritu Santo. Initial research will probably cost more than $5000, and it will continue to cost until the day the project is over, or the day you decide to give up."

Bowden does not bat an eye nor waver in his fixed intent as the Doctor continues. "As for the location of Bennett's remains, the area no longer involves a war zone or area of conflict. In fact, the island was abandoned by the Allies after the war and is very sparsely settled today. Indigenous natives inhabit the majority of those islands; so searches can be conducted without restraint, but finding the site may be quite another matter. The site is still where it was, but, unfortunately, you'll need to update the available historical data.

"When research is complete and you start searching, you can proceed to chart the location of each crash site you come to because there will be no convenient chart with all the crash sites printed on it. You will have to hire natives to lead you from one wreck to another, and you must carefully plot the type of each plane and its identification number on your chart. The jungle has natives who live in villages, and each village is connected to the others by trails of sorts. An entirely new generation of natives can still lead you to the old crash sites, but you may have to visit quite a few before you come to Bennett's, and that is a chance you will have to take. When, or if, you locate Bennett's plane, you must turn your chart over to CILHI. They will do the recovery of the remains. And, remember, you may be talking about *several* trips."

Bowden has listened intently to the Doctor's presentation. He is astounded at the easy flow of information and wealth of ready answers. He responds, "I'm certainly glad I talked to you about this. I feel much better knowing that, in your opinion, it is at least possible and not hopeless. By the way, have you ever done anything like this before?"

The Doctor shakes his head and answers, "No one else has either, Bob. Your project will be an absolute first. It's going to cause some eyebrows to be raised in agencies who have this area of responsibility."

Bowden is curious now, and he asks one more question. " If you've never done anything like this before, how do you seem to know all the requirements?"

For the first time the Doctor smiles as he replies, "After our talk in my office, I had an idea of what you had on your mind, so I called some friends in Washington. The first thing they told me was that you are nuts, then they told me in detail how to answer your questions. It's all unofficial and I cannot reveal their names to you. So, to answer your questions, yes, the research can be done, but it will not be easy. The answers to your next two unasked questions are also, yes."

Bowden is almost beside himself with elation and is almost afraid to ask, "What two questions?"

The Doctor replies, "First, you want to know if I will help you with the research. And second, you want to know if I will conduct the search for your friend."

Bowden is stunned; he knew the Doctor was adventurous, but this is more than he could have asked for. The meeting has gone farther and faster than he expected so all he can say is, "What do we do next?"

The Doctor replies, "First, you must get a certified letter of authority signed by each of Bennett's next of kin. That means all brothers, sisters and parents who are still alive. Most important will be the letter from the DNOK. It will then become a matter of time, patience and money. If the family wants my help, I will need to make a lot of telephone calls, and I will need access to a fax machine. I will give you a log of the telephone calls and you can reimburse me."

The Doctor continues non-stop. "Next, once the authorization is signed, the family can make *NO* calls or inquiries on their own. They must make *NO* public announcements about going out to bring Wayland Bennett home. They *MUST* keep this matter out of the newspapers and away from television cameras. If any announcements are to be made, they must come from me. I must have sole authority to speak for the family and in their behalf on this issue.

"If one single question is ever raised about my authority in this research, many potentially valuable information sources will disappear. The family should contact their Senators and Congressmen, asking that I be issued a letter introducing me as their representative. The letter may say that I will be serving as an emissary, acting on behalf of their office in this research and, hopefully, in the search itself. This will create a list of credentials that may later open doors to archives and data banks."

Bowden then asks, "When will we know something of the developments? And when will we have a better understanding of the facts as the agencies knew them in 1943?"

The Doctor answers cautiously, "You must understand, the family will have to first give their authority to someone. Only then can that person make inquiries. If I am chosen to be that person, I'll tell you what I can, whenever I can. But, we must always remember that a single embarrassment or violation of any government protocols could cause the loss of very good friends in areas where we might someday need all the help we can get. To gain this access, I may have to make agreements with those sources that I can't violate. Most of the details I learn will be confidential. So perhaps the best rule will be if I don't give you an answer the first time you ask, don't ask a second time. Is that agreeable to you?"

Bowden replies without hesitation, "Yes."

The Doctor further cautions Bowden. "This must all be agreeable to the family, and they must consent in writing to this agreement before the project can begin."

With much homework to do, Bowden leaves the coffee shop, his head swimming with excitement. He is astounded at his success after so long a wait. He talks to his wife, Jo, when he gets home, and they invite the Sandlins and Carsons over for a visit. Bowden takes the men out into the warm fall evening where they talk quietly on the patio. These once-mighty warriors of a war long ago do something they do every day – they pray to their God for his help because they know they will need it as they try to fulfill... *The Promise*.

Sandlin is enthusiastic about possibilities of a research project and a possible expedition to search for his old pal, Wayland Bennett. He quickly volunteers to be one of the research assistants and help in the communication necessary to supervise such a vast undertaking.

Crocker and Miller once described this search for a needle in a haystack as "a very small hole in a very large jungle." While it seems at times almost insurmountable, the Sandlins are always there, always ready for a late night meeting to discuss newly acquired data. They are both diligent in recording and preserving stories and old details of war experiences. This sizable collection must be organized and fully understood in order to develop a full picture. Of course, everything must be confirmed before it becomes a useable part of the growing list of notes about Wayland Bennett. Reliable information must be developed before the search can begin. This will then become the foundation upon which the complex *Search for the Lost Blacksheep* can begin.

The Sandlins cannot forget Bennett's visit with them in San Diego when he said, "Nobody goes faster than Wayland Bennett, when I'm in my Corsair."

Sandlin, Carson and Bowden also remember that December 1941 evening with the four of them on the front porch and **The Promise**. For these men who survived the war, the greatest test of commitment may not be their service to their country during war and battle, but how, for the next 50 years, they remembered the one of their number who did not return. They were determined **The Promise** to Wayland and to themselves still lived and must be fulfilled.

Later that night, Bowden calls the Doctor at home. He has one final, important question, "Why did you agree to this search for a needle in a haystack?"

The Doctor replies in Latin, *"Semper Fidelis."*

"What does that mean?"

"It means 'always faithful.' It's a Marine pledge to his nation and to each other. You see, Bob, I, too, was once in the Marine Corps, and I remember the value of a man's word. To a Marine, 'Semper Fi' means... **The Promise.**"

☆ ☆ ☆ ☆ ☆

[5-e]
SYMBOLS OF A PROMISE:
*Robert Bowden flew this flag with a yellow ribbon outside his home in Texarkana for years, as he continued his quest for someone to help complete the dream and **THE PROMISE**.*

CHAPTER 6

WHAT DO WE DO NOW? 1987 - 1988

The Doctor has a million thoughts spinning through his mind after the meeting. He spent all last evening on the phone, gathering information which he then sifted through and crystallized into a plan by morning. Finally, at 5:00 a.m., he knew he was ready for the challenge he expected from Bowden so he stretched out on the bed for a catnap.

Bowden seemed genuinely surprised at the preliminary report and the Doctor is glad his assumptions were correct. He knows this new challenge will be far greater than what he accomplished during the last 24 hours. He has planned a trip back to Australia and the South Pacific for some time, and now he has a very special reason for such a trip. It will become far more complex than a comparatively simple flight around the world; and it will be far more challenging than any of the Doctor's previous adventures.

This will be an interesting and strange case because it contains all the right ingredients to make a man like him want to get involved. The Doctor knows, however, that he will be more than just involved. He will represent the men's dedication and the family's dreams in this matter. The boyhood friends and family members are all over 60 years old, so none of them will be able to physically participate on the search teams.

No one can conduct this research or search alone, especially the search in the wilds of an unexplored jungle. The Doctor must draw on his own abilities and those of others. As an independent representative of the family and three remaining friends, he will become a fifth partner in this long ago commitment. He will be the torchbearer for men who made this **Promise** when the Doctor was only two years old.

The Doctor never wanted to be a researcher, but he remembers college lectures when Dr. John Nash repeatedly stressed a basic law of research: "Never discard even the slightest finding when doing research projects. You must save even your mistakes."

As a Senior Intern he found the class particularly interesting because Dr. Nash generated a spark of curiosity that had not previously existed. Although he never intended to conduct research, he had found himself consumed by a search for answers and what they meant to a mystery.

This new project is falling into the same pattern: "How do I start? How should I organize my notes? How do I relate these findings to a final purpose?"

Dr. Nash always insisted on what he called a cardinal rule. "Never try to force a finding to fit your assumption or your hopes for a conclusion. If you do, sooner or later, you will lead yourself into a blind alley with no answers; and your project will become hopelessly bogged down with meaningless trivia. You will become confused, and your goal will become unclear if you try to force trivia into your mysterious jigsaw puzzle."

As the Doctor searches through musty old boxes of class notes taken twenty years ago at Texas Chiropractic College, he smiles as he retrieves notes from Dr. Nash's opening lecture. He was a ruthless taskmaster who, in about three questions, could make you begin to doubt your own best research. No matter how well prepared a student thought he was on a subject, he was never quite ready for Dr. Nash's terrible inquisitions. In his first lecture, Dr. Nash said, "Imagine a spider-web, as viewed under a microscope. It is unfamiliar, with no landmarks or dates. There are no signposts that direct you to turn left or right. Also, there are no arrows that will tell you to go North or South. So, where does it begin? Where does it end? You can never see the entire web, or even the spider, only a dot-sized segment is visible. So which way will you go? And how far will you proceed in this quest?"

The Doctor realizes the ***Search for the Lost Blacksheep*** will begin in much the same way. The early steps will be much like gathering material for a college research paper as he assembles all available information. Some initial data will certainly change as new facts are produced. He thinks, "Ah, Dr. Nash, I could certainly use your help right about now."

The Doctor knows he must take copious notes and throw nothing away. He can trust nothing to his memory – every single detail must be recorded: name of office contacted, date, time, phone number, address, who is interviewed and their position, and even the person's attitude when he hears who is calling and what he wants. All these details may later be crucial because, if a witness dies before the project is completed, it will not be possible to call him back for clarification. Everything must be done right the first time.

Initial research will take patience and a large investment of time and money. It may take years to complete. The Doctor knows the Bennett family and the three friends cannot afford to finance this entire project for the search's duration. Hoping others in the community will financially help with the project, he approaches a few friends, and is stunned by their reactions. While they all wish him well in this adventure, many also want to participate by serving in associated capacities such as support crew and communications, and some just want to do anything they can to help. The concept of a private search for an MIA seems to be of considerable interest to many Americans.

The Doctor realizes it might truly be a teamwork effort if it develops into a community project. He knows from the outset that it cannot be a one-man show or individual effort; but, at the same time, it could be catastrophic if the wrong attitudes are inserted. He is also aware of the necessity for observing the highest standards of ethical conduct throughout. People in official circles will, no doubt, closely scrutinize his adherence to established protocols, and they will retain overall control of any information he is fortunate enough to acquire.

Having been a Marine, the Doctor is well trained in the Marine mentality: "Once a Marine, always a Marine." He will be expected to adhere to the Marine Code of Conduct, even though he is now a civilian. It is a way of life that, once accepted, makes one just a little different from other people. He also remembers another Code of Honor that prevails between men who are officers and gentlemen – a promise to refrain from certain conduct.

In accepting such a code for one's life, changes occur in the person's very character. That oath says in part, "I will not lie, cheat, or steal..." and the oath cannot be altered to suit one's personal needs or be used as an excuse. If one is wrong or makes an error, he must admit it and take his licks. He must never alter the performance of other people's decisions by giving them inaccurate information. That information may require decisions in which men's lives are at stake. The Doctor is sure he will be allowed access to important data on many occasions that will require him to assure a colleague that the "code" is in effect – he must not reveal the sources or the names of those who help in the data acquisition.

He has learned that many customs and politics of Vanuatu will be considerably different from those in America. He and his team will be foreigners there, and must learn the rules and abide by them no matter how different they may seem.

There are no official search parties or active searches for WW2 casualties unless a report is received about the location of the wreck. Most war-dead recoveries were quietly accomplished about five years after the war ended and hostilities ceased. Battlefield burials were exhumed and cemeteries emptied. Most remains were identified and sent home to a hero's welcome. Those who are still missing, such as isolated burial sites and unknown crash locations, have been administratively declared dead and a death certificate issued. Many of those missing cases continue to be listed as BNR (Body Not Recovered).

The Doctor knows what limitations must be placed on any search effort. He will conduct the research and lead the search team, but their goal will not include bringing Wayland Bennett home. The team will only attempt to locate the wreck site, and that is where their job will end. He, as the Search Team Leader, will report directly to CILHI (Central Identification Laboratory Hawaiian Islands) – the Army organization responsible for recovery.

His admiration and respect for CILHI grows as he learns more about them and their duties. Locating the wreck site and identifying the plane's tail number will be the Doctor's only objective. Recovery of human remains contained in or near the wreck is, was, and will continue to be strictly a CILHI matter.

It has already been made clear that the government will not release control or responsibility over a crash site or remains to him or his team. It has been made equally clear that he alone will bear full responsibility for each team member's conduct.

Since this is the first time anyone has attempted a private venture "designed by intent" to find an MIA site, it poses some very scary scenarios to those dignified and studious government professionals. The concept of a "bunch of cowboys prowling around the Pacific snatching gold teeth, guns, and goodies" is almost unbearable to some of them.

Many experts have proposed ways and means to bring MIA's home; but, before this Doctor, no one has ever conceived a plan to include private sector assistance. No one has considered the possibility of civilians developing a solution to a dilemma that is a political hot potato.

Equipment, supplies, personal effects and remains simply must not be disturbed; the site must not be contaminated by turning it into a campsite for curiosity seekers. Stooping to such atrocities will be considered parallel to grave robbing and the desecration of an American war hero's grave.

The Doctor starts gathering information from the family in preparation for contacting government officials. Bennett's twin sister, Wanda, provides copies of letters, photographs, his obituary and the newspaper notice of his death in late 1943. The photograph used in his death notice shows Bennett's big smile and perfectly straight teeth. This will be very helpful later.

The Doctor contacts the Vanuatu Tourism Board and acquires a taped copy of a CBS segment of "60 Minutes," which shows author James A. Michener revisiting the island where ***Tales of the South Pacific*** was born.

To further get a feel for Wayland's life, the Doctor goes to the Bennett family's old home and into Wayland's bedroom. While there, he takes off wall covering and paneling until he finds the wallpaper that covered the walls when Wayland lived there.

They find a copy of the Texas High School graduation program for Wayland and Wanda on June 3, 1941. Bowden brings in an old photo of the four boys at Spring Lake Park, which was made on graduation day. *(Photo 1-a)*

Bowden, Sandlin and Carson share hilarious stories about how Bennett was always a jokester and prankster, and how he had the uncanny ability to "get to you." The Doctor realizes that all their stories are in good taste. He also feels a growing attachment to this young man's memory and realizes why his friends feel obligated to fulfill... ***The Promise.***

[6a] THREE MEN REMEMBER: Three young men who never forgot "The Promise." D.A. Carson, Robert Bowden and Judge Robert Sandlin.

In the course of research, it becomes apparent that this young man had little time to do anything wrong in his life. There are no stories about any wayward days or activities. They seem to have never occurred. He left home when he was only nineteen; and, even then, his activities were restricted and restrained. He lived a completely regimented life in a tightly controlled academic world. His greatest thrills were the high-speed adventures of a Marine Pilot whose daily schedule included flying several types of planes and landing on carriers. It could easily be said that he simply never had the time to get into any trouble.

Some feel that, over the years, negative memories tend to disappear, and those who served in WW2 emerged as stunning young knights of the air. Truly daring young men like Bennett developed personalities that laid a foundation for the rest of their lives. The facts that emerge while researching Bennett's short life apply as well to all the Johnsons, Crockers, Millers and their colleagues. Much is said about the American way of life for which they sacrificed themselves. In reality, however, they were the American way of life, and they will always be our heritage.

Research data is soon steadily coming in on Bennett: name, rank, serial number and date of birth. In addition to copies of several old letters, new ones come from Doris, Wanda and Richmond designating the Doctor as their agent and representative. The family members ask their Congressmen, Senators and the Governors of the states where they live to write letters. These all help identify the Doctor as the family representative and request that any and all help be provided to him in his quest for details.

The Doctor starts absorbing details of Bennett's short life and works along the very narrow boundaries of established protocols. He has no difficulty communicating his needs to officials, and finds it easy to get answers by learning their language and sensing their natural resistance to any inquiry about casualties.

He makes a very special effort not to alienate or offend any conscientious government employee on the other end of the phone. Instead, on many occasions, he lets them carry the conversation. By doing so, they seem more comfortable and at ease by asking him questions about what he needs and when. He is, therefore, able to call on some of the contacts many times over the next several years and develop their friendship. It is obvious they are dedicated and sensitive employees of our government. They will not respond to or appreciate threats and intimidation, but the Doctor has found that a simple explanation of who he is, what he wants and why he wants it opens many doors.

He knows negative tactics will only make his job more difficult in the long run. He does, after all, have some good friends in Washington who will help him, and those old friends do help many times when he needs alternative sources of information.

The Doctor knows he is dealing with many highly placed, ranking officials of the U.S. Government whose lifelong goal is deeply intertwined in research, history, professionalism and MIA protocols. These officials daily deal with distraught loved ones who have waited too long and think they are getting nowhere. They are faced with wrath, rage and retribution from those who are devastated and bitter.

These men and women of Decedent Affairs all practice a strict code of ethics, but still have room in their hearts for sympathy toward the families they represent. Contacting these people exposes a researcher to "a world class team." Sometimes family members get to meet some of them at the "homecoming" of a loved one, the day they have anticipated for decades – a day that could never happen without these behind-the-scenes players. Even though they will shun the title, they truly are the "heroes" of any MIA who comes home.

On that day most families don't even remember to say, "Thank you for all that you've done for us." These dedicated government workers quietly leave the scene of "closure" without receiving any expression of gratitude, and return to their endless task of helping "America's Finest and their Gold Star families."

The Doctor soon learns their secret; it is satisfaction of their own job done well. He knows one is well advised not to go barnstorming around these folk, violating their rules of propriety and protocol. That will always result in hearing a most unpleasant sound, the slamming of doors to further information... but they will even do that in style and with class. The Doctor realizes they already know more than he does, and they have years of experience in waiting. He knows a project such as this will require his best conduct and patience, but will pay off in the long run for the MIA.

The Doctor makes his first call of the day to the U.S. Marine Corps in Washington, D.C., because Bennett was a Marine. He is referred to the Marine Casualty and Memorial Affairs section, then establishes an initial contact with Marine Decedent Affairs. As he establishes a growing list of helpful friends, he learns that many of them really do want to help. Surprised at this turn of events so early in the search, he realizes they will always be reserved and somewhat distant to his questions at first.

The facts that begin to materialize clearly indicate that the Doctor is involved with people who only want to be identified as spokes in a giant wheel of teamwork. So, out of respect to those who have been so helpful, after the searching is done the Doctor seems to lose his notes that have their names, addresses and phone numbers on them. Perhaps he threw them away, and perhaps Dr. Nash will berate him severely for acting no better than a First Year Intern, and conveniently losing some of his valuable research information. (But I doubt it.) Perhaps he, too, has just become another victim of... *The Promise.*

The Corsair's manufacturer, Vought Aircraft, has undergone several major changes in corporate identity since 1943. During most of our search time, they are part of a giant aerospace conglomerate known as Ling-Temco-Vought (LTV). In 1992 they will change back to Vought Aircraft Co. when purchased by Northrop Grumman, then to Vought Aircraft Industries, Inc. in 2000 when purchased by the Carlisle Group. The Doctor calls them to inquire about specific details of the old Corsair. He is connected to a division that maintains historical data on each airplane they ever built, and what a wealth of information they turn out to be!

For example, they know Bennett's plane (Navy 02608) is one of the first batch of production F4Us built. Navy 02608 has a birdcage canopy that has small square windows in it, compared to the later use of a bubble style canopy. The bubble provides better visibility and fewer blind spots from which an enemy aircraft can make an attack. Navy 02608 was equipped with a Pratt-Whitney, 18 cylinder, R2800-8W double-row radial engine. It has a huge fifteen-foot diameter three-bladed propeller.

LTV tells the Doctor exactly where the "soul" of the airplane is located. This is in perhaps the best-protected area – riveted to the pilot's shield (armor plate almost one-half-inch thick). This heavy armor protects the pilot from an attacking enemy fighter pilot's guns. It is what the pilot's seat is attached to; and it is almost indestructible by guns, fire or explosion. The plane's soul is the data plate that identifies the airplane. Stamped into this metal plate are a Navy number, serial number and the date the plane was manufactured. It is an absolute must for a researcher to know precisely what is on the data plate for the plane he is looking for before he begins a search. In many planes the Doctor will visit, the tail will be torn off, the rest of the plane incinerated and the data plate will be the only absolute he can photograph. If the tail still has numbers painted on it, the search team will be fortunate indeed and this will be a second proof for the team.

LTV archivists tell the Doctor that special fabric covers the wings, tail, rudder and elevators; and the first production run of Corsairs have plywood ailerons. They send him a complete set of engineering drawings of the entire airplane. If he finds only one small piece or part of the plane, he can positively identify it as having come from a Corsair with these drawings.

LTV also sends him a copy of an old company magazine that shows a very strange sight – a new, six-month-old Corsair, setting on a jungle airstrip halfway around the world on the island of Espiritu Santo in the New Hebrides. It clearly shows an F4U-1 with a birdcage canopy and no tail hook. This aircraft belongs to VMF-214 (the Blacksheep Squadron), and it appears to have the large buzz number "88" painted on the side of the airplane. *(See photo 3-e)* It appears to be the exact airplane the Doctor is searching for, and it was photographed at about the same time Bennett was in San Diego visiting with the Sandlins and calling his family.

What an odd coincidence that the Doctor is provided with a photograph of the very airplane he is looking for, and ironically, the Doctor never told LTV anything about the number "88." At the time, the Doctor does not know that Bennett was assigned as a replacement to VMF-214.

LTV tells him that no Corsair has ever lost a wing unless it was shot off or otherwise sustained battle damage. LTV suggests that, while Bennett may have pulled the fabric off the wing, he did not pull the wing off the airplane. In their opinion, the main probability of Bennett's crash during his high-speed dive was that he simply blacked out for a moment, but that was just too long at almost 500 mph.

As the phone bill increases, the Doctor develops lists of men who were young in 1943, but are considerably older now. Many had a career in the Marines or other military units. As he tracks them down, one by one, some are amazingly easy to locate while others have died. Some of those he locates and interviews remember even the smallest details from the past with astounding clarity; but some remember nothing of importance to the project. Some have successfully coped with unpleasant memories, but do not want to talk about them. That privilege is respected.

He interviews a remarkable "young" man who remembers Turtle Bay well, and he remembers Bennett. He was then, and is today, known as "Chaplain Pat," and his name is repeatedly given to the Doctor. He remembers the memorial services that he held at Turtle Bay, and all those young "Eagles" who, in their own way, presumed to "Rule the Skies."

All did and all will, but that day unfortunately came far sooner for some than for others. Chaplain Pat refers the Doctor to an old friend who may have been the Captain who Bowden met at Turtle Bay.

The day Bennett crashed in 1943, the Captain was in command of the Control Tower that flashed the take-off signal to Bennett and Crocker. Capt. Robert Shaw was Ed Mazur's boss, and led expeditions into the unexplored jungle in search of many young men and their planes. He had a career in the Marines after the war and retired as a General. He was kind enough to label and diagram the airfield map *(page 20)*.

Later, when the Doctor begins his search on Espiritu Santo, he visits this now-deserted airstrip. He clearly sees where the General indicated airfield positions and many facility locations. Like a time capsule, they are all still in place – including the old control tower. Using the General's letter and charts, the Doctor is able to locate areas where planes received maintenance and where the pilots lived and ate.

The General also remembers the names of many of the young pilots who died with their planes and crash site locations. The General asks the Doctor to visit his old friends and their planes, to stop in the "Punch Bowl" National Cemetery in Hawaii, and to remember him to his old comrades in arms. With a chuckle he says, "Tell 'em, I'll see 'em, soon."

On one trip that the Doctor and his brother make to Hawaii, they keep their word to the General. They follow his orders exactly as he requested. The Doctor and his brother make a two-hour visit to the General's old friends. Of all the people with whom the General served in a lifetime of service to his country, he still, for some reason, remembers Wayland Bennett.

During the research phase, the Doctor realizes he has an opportunity to pay homage to many of his old boyhood heroes. Even when he was a child, these were the men he would try to imitate some day. The men he interviews are captives in an historical time warp – heroes of that day and role models for today.

The General tells the Doctor about his trips into the jungle searching for Bennett, and accurately describes the jungle and its density. The Doctor and his team will soon find that time seems to have stood still and nothing has changed in the past half century. The General remembers the triple canopy that turns the jungle into a sweatbox during a search, and warns that there will be blisters, cuts, bruises and infections. He says a trek of several days will burn off an awful lot of blood, sweat and tears. He also warns the Doctor to be patient with search team members because some people cannot handle the jungle's claustrophobic conditions. While some will remain normal, others will become crybabies, and the worst will resort to foolish acts and attitudes. He also tells the Doctor that if any project ever deserved the support and blessings of Americans, this is the one that he fervently hopes will be successful.

The General refers the Doctor to an old friend who is included in Bennett family letters and Bowden's notebook, Colonel Henry Stuckert Miller. Miller became an attorney in his home state of Pennsylvania after the war and still has a law practice there.

When the Doctor calls Miller, it seems he is always "just on his way somewhere" or "just returning from somewhere else." He willingly shares his time and information with the Doctor, answering questions and revealing personal details of those days that are not found in history books. Although his memory has become clouded by the passage of a half-century, he remembers Bennett and all the others. This is, after all, the often referred to "Notebook Harry" who recorded everything in his little notebook.

Miller explains that Bennett and Crocker had been assigned to fly a section tactics practice session and describes the maneuvers they were to perform prior to rendezvous over the target area for gunnery practice.

He cannot remember exactly where they searched, but he still has copies of all his correspondence concerning Bennett's crash and the details as they were reported to him. He provides copies of his log books concerning the initial search flights, letters of official notification to the Bennett family, personal letters he wrote them, and those they sent him. He also gives the Doctor the names of all the pilots who flew the search for Bennett. Miller remembers being in attendance when Chaplain Pat delivered Bennett's eulogy at the open-air amphitheater that doubled as a church.

He describes, in detail, the difficulty they experienced in low-flying jungle searches as they carefully scanned tree tops for evidence of broken limbs and branches. He remembers that, in a Corsair, the pilot has his hands full in bumpy, low-altitude turbulence. He tells how hot it was in the cockpit and how they had to fly with the canopy slid all the way back to stay cool in the sweltering heat.

The Major explains how the Corsair's gasoline engine is vastly different from today's jet engines. The Corsair's cockpit is full of things to monitor: control stick, throttle, propeller, numerous controls, gauges, mixture, trim tabs (no autopilot), cowl flaps and oil temperature. The pilot also had to watch out for other planes, then start all over again. In the meantime, the pilot tried to scan the jungle floor below.

Miller tells the Doctor that most old gasoline airplanes burned or exploded on impact; and, when they did crash, there was a horrendous fire that consumed everything including the metal structure and engine. When this occurred, the funeral pyre could be seen for a hundred miles as the long, black smoke column marked the final resting place. But, oddly, the Bennett site just vanished as if the plane had gone down in the sea. No fire, smoke or explosion marked *"Susie-Q's"* final resting place.

Miller never got the opportunity to solve this mystery because there wasn't enough time. Boyington returned within a day or two of Bennett's crash, and they all got down to the business of just trying to stay alive. Miller seems to recall that the "88" may also be found on the landing gear doors and cowling sides.

On the outside chance that no one ever thanked Miller and those who tried at great personal risk to find Bennett so long ago, the Doctor expresses gratitude from Bennett's family and friends for that search and for assistance in preparation for the new one.

The Doctor gets other information about the pilots. He tries to contact Lt. Bill Crocker, Bennett's wing man for the last flight. The Doctor hopes he will have just the right details for the research. Sadly, he learns from

Crocker's family that he did not survive the war. However, while interviewing a nephew who inherited Crocker's name and logbook, he learns what the family knows of the details surrounding his crash into the ocean. The nephew is glad to help in any way he can. Although he would like to accompany the search team, his job will not permit him to take off so much time. The Doctor assures him the team will search for him and his family as well as many others.

The Doctor locates Harry Johnson and asks him if he can remember a young Marine named Bennett. It's as if time has stood still for Johnson. He has a good memory and gives details, names, dates and events that are as clear as though they occurred only yesterday. His first recollection of those long ago days is a laugh, then he adds, "I sure do remember Bennett. He was a good pilot, and a big old tall blond-headed kid from Texas who was always smiling and joking."

I suppose one could not say more to Harry Johnson, than "Thanks for the memories."

The Doctor learns the name of the Squadron's former Administrative Officer. Frank Walton was not a pilot, but was assigned squadron administrative duties because he was a big man who could physically control Boyington. It seems that some superior officers were concerned that Boyington would wander too far beyond the policy lines. Walton retired as a Marine Colonel and recorded many historical facts surrounding VMF-214's activities during their tours of combat.

He wrote a definitive book on the activities of those men and the Squadron from WW2 through 1985. **Once They Were Eagles** provides a wealth of information for research as well as a nostalgic visit to the old Turtle Bay. Walton gives the Doctor valuable assistance that leads to talks with other former Blacksheep pilots.

Walton, however, does not remember Bennett. He tells the Doctor that if Bennett crashed just before he was transferred into the Squadron, he was listed as a replacement pilot selected for the assignment. He was probably not carried as an active member, because he died one day before the Squadron returned to Espiritu Santo from their combat tour. Walton was with the Squadron in the Solomon's and never met Bennett. Still, there is the gnawing story of the letter that indicates that Bennett had flown formation with Boyington at some point. *(Appendix I and J)*

The Doctor realizes the lack of documentation should not be allowed to sidetrack the research. He repeatedly comes across the terms "documented" and "undocumented" in archives and records. If an event took place as a part of an official function, it usually generated a report that provides a paper trail right into military archives and history. That is a "documented" fact. However, if an event was of a casual nature, and not a part of an official act or flight, it might not have been mentioned in a report, and thus is an "undocumented" fact because no paper trail was generated. Bennett may well have met Boyington in a casual circumstance, and may well have flown beside him at one time. While his family and friends were sure it happened as he reported in one of his last letters, the Doctor realizes it is, for now, an "undocumented" fact – but, nevertheless, a fact.

The documented report of aircraft loss *(Appendix C)* shows Navy 02608 belonged to VMF-214. It also indicates the squadron to which the pilot was assigned. Both Bennett and Navy 02608 are listed on the loss report as belonging to VMF-214. In the case of Lt. L.W. DeCamp, the aircraft he was flying was Navy 56334 and was attached to VMF-217. Lt. DeCamp was not attached to the same squadron as the aircraft. He was attached to VMF-225, and his loss report was appropriately noted parenthetically. These are documented facts. While it is true that rotational pool pilots, and even squadron pilots, frequently fly different planes, there is no such notation on Bennett's loss report.

It is an unresolved element of the research project; yet, as a matter of curiosity, it seems to be an item that has no paper trail to either confirm or refute the position. Several dozen proposed solutions have been offered relating to MAG-11 custom, squadron policy and historical procedure, but none have a paper trail. All pilots flying under the Blacksheep colors that day went into VMF-214. Miller, Johnson, Crocker, and the others all went to combat in VMF-214.

Another glaring fact is that lying in the jungle even today is an abandoned relic with the name *"Susie-Q"* written on the side of a VMF-214 plane. No other pilot in MAG-11 or VMF-214 ever painted this name on a plane as the name of a mother, daughter, sister or sweetheart! During the war, this was the practice of pilots once they were assigned to a squadron. The only known deviation was in the case of Frank Walton, who was not a pilot, but whose wife's name, Carol, was painted on one of the squadron's Corsairs.

The Doctor receives a copy of the search report for a lost FM-2 – Case #1322 – a fighter plane that had a pair of dice painted on the side with the number "7" showing, followed by the words "come eleven." The search for this report is initiated from notes in Bowden's old war diary. The Doctor makes an inquiry into the recovery procedure concerning this plane, and receives a report that clears up several bits of confusing information. Later research is able to determine the identity of that plane's pilot and the location of his remains. *(Appendix L)*

A search of records allows a separation of the similarities between Case Number 1322 and Crocker's report of the crash of Wayland Bennett. He knows that the only way to completely clear this up is to visit the site and acquire the necessary aircraft identification and type from the wreck. This information must then be plotted on the team chart for proper records. There are no charts available showing aircraft type, tail number, pilot and location of crash site from which the pilot was recovered, so the search team must spend endless hours trekking through the jungle to identify the airplane. What heartbreak this brings when, days later, the team arrives at the site of yet another "wrong" airplane!

The Doctor learns of a book, ***The Final Disposition of WW2 Dead,*** by Edward Steere and Thayer M. Boardman. The very first page of this book contains a letter from the President of the United States that states, "In deep and everlasting appreciation of the heroic efforts of those who, in keeping their country free, made the supreme sacrifice in World War II. The entire nation has been dedicated to disposing of the mortal remains of those honored dead in a manner consistent with the wishes of their next of kin. Signed Harry S. Truman."

This book gives the Doctor an opportunity to peer into areas not normally known by the general public. It gives graphic explanations as to how the government handles searches and recoveries, and how positive identification is accomplished.

The final rule seems to indicate that without a positive identification, there can be no Full Military Honors extended to a casualty at his funeral. This definitive work explains in detail the requirements for a positive identification, and the importance of a complete recovery of undisturbed remains. It also demonstrates the necessity of close inspection of entire undisturbed crash sites, and explains how one souvenir taken by a searcher can be the only remaining way to identify the victim. The Doctor realizes that the entire effort to recover and identify remains can fail if the search team does not observe these protocols.

The Doctor becomes aware of the AGRS (American Graves Registration Service) whose mission was realigned some years ago, and they are today referred to as CIL (Central Identification Laboratory). Several detachments are located around the world where their expertise is required, thus the acronym of CILHI denotes Hawaiian Islands. Other detachment labs are identified such as CILKO (Korea) and CILTI (Thailand). The overall area of the Pacific is assigned to CILHI, which covers not only WW2 casualties but also those from Korea and Vietnam. This lab is responsible for about half of the planet and all of this century's warfare.

After he carefully discusses his project with CILHI and agrees to their guidelines, he calls his research and search team members together to brief them on his findings. He says, "The personnel at CILHI are the epitome of propriety in the performance of their duties. They quietly go about their daily tasks and are, in general, a competent and self-confident organization. In a normal 'day at the office,' they may do mundane things such as aligning a skeleton and teeth for reconstruction and identification purposes.

"However, when a foreign government reports that an old American aircraft wreck site has been located, it becomes a very busy day indeed. An initial report is usually sent to a State Department office or the nearest U.S. Embassy. From there, it is forwarded to the area CIL.

"When the report arrives, a modern computerized science laboratory, equipped with the latest technology, springs into action. Personnel records and squadron history will be accessed in the research department. In moments, a complete list of aircraft and personnel still carried on a missing list will be in the hands of CIL researchers. In a short time, CIL will have narrowed down the list by separating the crashes by type of aircraft. Photographs and blueprints of the airplane will be gathered, along with complete medical and dental records of the plane's crewmen.

"Thus, if the report said a B-24 bomber has been located on a South Pacific island, the CILHI team will have a printout on all missing B-24s for that area and their entire crew files to take with them on the search and recovery mission. A complete historical study is presented of a long-ago day when time stopped for young men aboard an airplane that never reached its destination. In a very short time (only days, really) a complete composite has been formed.

"When a CILHI team leaves their laboratory en route to a crash site, they go well-equipped with the latest technology for locating their position in the jungle. By the time they get into the jungle and identify the airplane, they already know who was on the plane. They take nothing for granted but carefully recover all remains, regardless of the condition, and any associated evidence such as pistols and dog tags that can lead to the confirmation of the casualty's identity.

"They know each crewman's name, rank, serial number, date of birth, how many teeth he had, which ones were filled, and which bones were broken as a child. They will also be equipped with such details as blood type, religion and the date of tetanus shots. CILHI will even know the serial number, make and model of the pistol he was carrying. They will have complete identity of the missing aircraft including serial number, buzz number, engine serial numbers, and a modification and maintenance report on the airplane's history. This list will also include part and serial numbers of all equipment on board.

"Detailed crash area charts will include all documented facts concerning the aircraft's last mission assignment, where it was going, what its target was, what flight path it was assigned, and even the route it was supposed to fly when returning to base.

"The CILHI motto could well be 'The buck stops here.' They have the entire history of the world at their disposal, and they have it close at hand. They also have all the information that has ever been documented about every MIA, and no MIA can come home or be positively identified without them.

"When this data is amassed, CILHI will receive permission to enter the foreign country and orders to depart from the U.S. on their mission. All this is like a concert of players in a giant ballet company that has only one purpose, to return the MIA home to America. Upon arrival in the foreign country, they will be escorted into the region; then, like all good soldiers, they take over manually. This means they walk, wade, climb and hack their way to the site. When they arrive at the crash site they conduct a careful evaluation of the entire area. As in a police crime scene, the crash site and surrounding area are roped off.

"These well-experienced team members have specialties they perform as a well-executed part of this special group. They do to a jungle site what police do to a crime scene. They photograph, identify, brush, sift and collect all evidence and artifacts. They recover everything that is important to the crewmen's identity and spend days marking, making notes and drawing diagrams.

"If one wonders why CILHI exerts so much effort for one B-24 airplane and crew, he must remember that this is a search and recovery of a 50-year-old, four-engine bomber with a ten-man crew on board. This particular plane came down in flames and hit the ground with a terrific explosion of gasoline, oil, and the incidentals of exploding bombs and machine gun ammunition. The fact that this plane hit the ground at approximately 200 mph, and is now scattered over a one-square-mile area, is only a small inconvenience to the experts from CILHI.

"The worst factor they have to deal with may not be that remains have been scattered by the crash and explosions, but scattered and destroyed by wild animals. They persevere, and from daylight until dark for days and weeks if need be, they continue to recover every bone, tooth and old shoe.

"Why do they do this job with such dedication and zeal? Why do they risk their own safety to do such an unpleasant job? Why, then, do they enter a career where most people forget to say 'Thank you'?

"Because they are Americans. They are the U.S. Army, and they also believe their clients (or is it their brothers?) deserve the very best attention they can receive in a final salute and honor."

The Doctor tells the team that in the course of his phone discussions with CILHI, he has discovered the one unpleasant subject that he must make sure he never transgresses. "They have patience with nature, the elements and time, and they can deal with the corrosive damage which accumulates to these casualties. But woe be unto those people whom they classify as souvenir hunters, curiosity seekers, collectors of artifacts, grave robbers and body snatchers. Few are held in lower esteem. One cannot resort to this practice and expect to receive any assistance from CILHI. A responsible search team leader and his dedicated team members must always refrain from this despicable practice."

CILHI has extended their courtesy to the Doctor, even though he admits that he is an amateur. He knows they can have an iron fist if anyone decides to explore the realm of their growl or macho. Flexing one's muscles against the U.S. Army could be an unpleasant experience.

He reminds them, "We need the help of CILHI, but they don't need us. For the quiet 'world class performers' of CIL, patience is a virtue that many searchers may not think they have time to practice. But CIL has the patience and the time to wait until searchers finally just go away.

"Some of their daily duties include such insignificant tasks as scaling ice-covered mountains to reach an isolated crash site. They may jump entire oceans and continents in their daily travels; and, when they get to their 'office,' it may be a crashed airplane on the side of a mountain. If the airplane was loaded with bombs (some of which exploded and others did not) it is only a small bother to them. Of course, when the bombs did explode, they may have caused a small landslide. For CILHI, this is a blessing because only half the mountain now covers the wreck. It is of small consequence to these 'mere soldiers' who just move the mountain side. These are the people who do it with that neat little shovel which all soldiers have strapped to their backpack. Nothing special, just a normal day at the office.

"They also do their work in jungles where small distractions like snakes, spiders and practicing cannibals leave them unimpressed. They can also re-route a flowing river if it gets in their way during the recovery of a crash; in many cases, American casualties are lying on the bottom of some lonely stretch of unnamed river in a foreign country.

"Their work is usually far from civilization, and they may well be surrounded by former enemies of the U.S.; but, for these people called CILHI, there is no cavalry to come to their rescue. They must be totally independent, and they are. They are immune to threats of political influence and/or friends in 'higher' authority. The only threats that seem to concern them are threats from God, and it is obvious they enjoy an excellent working relationship with Him. CILHI never demands, but they deserve the highest degree of respect.

"CILHI has its own sources of information and the assistance of the entire U.S. government. They neither need nor welcome the spectacular or the exposé of a tabloid news media. They have no interest in an 'interpretative reporter' who wants to make a name for himself by writing a sensational article that will leave a blemish on operations he neither understands or appreciates.

"CILHI personnel realize that the worst possible event in someone's life is the loss of a loved one, especially if the loved one cannot be brought home for a decent burial, as is the American custom. They said most amateurs are neither trained nor able to deal with the sensitive and sometimes gruesome questions that can arise: 'How did my brother die? Did he suffer? Was he unconscious when the airplane burned? Was he burned alive?' If one ventures into speculation, it is indeed improper conduct. Some family members or the media may ask these questions. In some cases, they may just want someone to be angry with. CILHI personnel say searchers may find living in a primitive jungle with cannibals easier than trying to deal with the hostile emotions of a distraught family."

The Doctor tells his group he has good reason to believe some of the performance of CILHI borders on the miraculous. "In some of the older cases, there is substantially less than a full set of remains, and CILHI can still make a full and positive identification. CILHI moves in a quiet and studious environment. It may appear that they work miracles and do almost anything but raise the dead, but that is the wrong impression. They do unbelievably difficult recoveries and determine identification through scientific means and technology. This is the job to which they have been assigned and trained, and they are the very best in the world at what they do. Perhaps the only reason they do not raise the dead is because that is not in their mission assignment. Maybe they leave that part of the job to a Higher Command and to a Guy who can do it better. Anyone who goes into the jungle to search for a lost pilot will soon become very familiar with that 'Higher Command Authority' for himself."

The Doctor informs his team, "I have come to hold CILHI in very high regard. The rules under which CIL operates are necessary and they are prohibited from participation in any search except their own."

He then outlines the "CILHI Accords" that will be an integral part of their way of thinking during the Bennett project:

(1) There can be no mass media announcements about what is being done and what is being planned.
(2) There can be no announcement to the world about the "discovery" of aircraft with American bodies inside.
(3) All discoveries of remains must be reported to CILHI, not to the world.
(4) In no case will the search team ever attempt to contact a family represented by the remains found in a crash site that is visited.
(5) The search team must not try to identify the remains, touch them, disturb them or disturb the area of the crash site.
(6) The search team may come and go from the site, but they must take nothing from the site and leave nothing of their visit.
(7) The searchers must never remove anything from a wreck site such as dog tags, bones, teeth, or money and must take no souvenirs such as pistols, knives, rings, bracelets or other personal effects.
(8) The team should leave nothing of their visit, such as trash, paper or film canisters.
(9) The team must take no photographs of remains.
(10) The team must not try to dig or exhume any remains.
(11) The conduct of the team should be as any visit to an American war hero's grave.
(12) The MIA search team leader will assume responsibility for the conduct of the search team."

The Doctor explains, "The rules and responsibilities are very clear, and 'the buck and the blame stops here.' The Bennett search team is a new player, and an amateur who will presume to play with these 'Big Boys.' In other words, if all goes well, they get the credit, but if anything goes sour, they deny any knowledge of the mission."

Sandlin asks, "Who said that before?"

"Must have been on an old TV show about missions which were hard to do," Bowden replies.

They all laugh and the Doctor adds, "Some of you may soon ask, 'What am I doing here?' Perhaps the answer will have to be, 'We were too busy doing something else and may not have been paying enough attention.' This is rapidly becoming a monumental task and an effort of unbelievable difficulty. But at least, it is founded on a decent premise; it is based on a *Promise* which has to be fulfilled."

[6-b] Teamwork: Robert Bowden, The Doctor, The Doctor's Wife, Jo Bowden all working together as a team.

Everyone seems to agree with the last statement and they leave on a positive note, ready for the next step.

The Doctor contacts the Republic of Vanuatu and the U.S. Embassy in the Solomon Islands. The Embassy says they will be glad for the team to search and will assist in any way they can. The Government of Vanuatu is also very helpful; and, on every occasion when a question arises, they do all they can to make answers available to the search team. Their level of cooperation will be fully appreciated.

Vanuatu is a beautiful area, steeped in American history, offering scuba-diving on wrecked ships and wonderful people. The team members look forward to their visit to this island nation in the sun. It will even become a Bali Hai for some of them. After the initial request, the team waits only a few days before permission is received from the Government of Vanuatu to conduct the searches.

The list of people who can be of assistance continues to grow. As the Doctor surveys the growing list of details, he senses it will soon be time to start recruiting volunteers. CILHI has agreed to let the Doctor give speeches about his proposed project, but he must make no assurances or guarantees that the search itself will bring Bennett back to Texarkana.

By now the Doctor realizes that two separate events will happen about the same time: the research phase will reach the point where it will justify the first search mission, and the bank balance will be hovering somewhere near *zero*! The files include more information on Bennett than has been in one place in a long time, and that information is now squarely in his lap. It seems almost every move Bennett made during the last 24 hours of his life is now assembled and ready to use in the search.

As the Doctor completes the research phase, he draws up plans for the proposed area of the first search for Wayland Bennett since 1943. Armed with a rough map of the island and three pages from a yellowed old notebook, he begins. He also wonders if he has lost his mind to think he can ever be successful in this project. He lays out the reference of fifteen to twenty miles northwest of the airfield, then plots ten miles south of the south central shore of St. James and St. Phillips Bay. He sends this all to Col. Miller for confirmation. Miller is unable to recall all the events of so long ago, particularly since he has spent the rest of his life as a very busy attorney, but at least he tries.

From the information available, it appears this search will be in one of the jungle's densest parts. It will no doubt be a brutal experience for the volunteers. Realistically the chances lie somewhere between slim and none. The Doctor believes that any hope for a first year discovery will be very remote. He is unfamiliar with gambling, but after 45 years, the odds against the search must be something like a ga-zillion to one. With time, money, and a vast amount of good luck, it can be done – maybe – just maybe.

Time has come for the Doctor to decide if he is ready to lead the search. Is he strong enough to be the leader, and is he qualified enough? Is he willing to give up who knows how many years to this project? He knows that many years ago, other young men going to war in this part of the world had to face similar questions of themselves. Bennett, Miller, Crocker, Johnson, and millions of others asked the question, and they were. The Doctor must prepare himself physically if he is to be successful in this venture.

The Doctor has had some interesting experiences while working on the Bennett case. On several occasions, while working late at night, he has seemed to sense Bennett's presence. He can almost hear Bennett laughing when he finds himself cornered by his own mistakes. He knows this is not a ghost or apparition; it is more like the good-natured teasing of an old friend who, as Bowden described him, "will always get to you, somehow, when you least expect it." Well, the Doctor decides, since this is not a ghost, it must be a bond of acceptance between two friends, a brotherhood between two pilots. Before the project is over, Bennett and the Doctor will become as close as brothers, and they will have many good laughs, almost always at the Doctor's expense.

The Doctor is aware that everything he has accomplished so far has been done in a well-lighted, air-conditioned office or in his neat, cozy living room at home. The search will be in sharp contrast to those surroundings. They will be a long way from home in a foreign land with people of a different culture and different beliefs. What he is about to embark upon will tax the physical and mental abilities of everyone involved. It will require each member's maximum out-put and perseverance. At the very least, this search is going to be gut-wrenching tough in a primitive jungle. It will be a filthy and exhausting experience until the day Bennett is found.

Suddenly, as he reviews the details, he becomes aware of just how deeply he has been drawn into this irreversible course. He has been selected by the family to be their agent and representative during this project. He is their legal representative and the only one authorized to receive and release information. He is the only person who will be allowed to make announcements. Also, he knows the media will follow this event from beginning to end. It is indeed an honor to represent the family, the friends and Bennett, but this will be an enormous journey into the unknown.

He will not be at liberty to disclose a lot of the information he has and will continue to receive, even to search team members. Much of the extraneous research information is private and personal, and does not need to be associated with the search. He must exercise caution and discretion in these matters.

This is also a first time event with no precedent. There has never before been a private search for an MIA/KIA/BNR. The way it is shaping up, he will not be allowed to fail. The mission must be successful.

The Doctor is a qualified competitor in the quest for Aviation World Records. He has been awarded more records than any man in the history of aviation. Even "Pappy" Boyington has awarded some of those records to him. He does not like to lose, and he does not like second place, so this will not be a vacation for him. It is not a sport or means of relaxation, but a very serious and dangerous obligation.

As he contemplates the search's magnitude, he realizes what the end result will do to him personally: "If I fail to produce Wayland Bennett, no one will ever forget the failure. If I find Wayland Bennett, no one will ever remember my part in this effort."

This is a rather sobering thought for a man who has always protected his reputation by his performance in civic activities. The Doctor knows he will not be able to stop this quest until Bennett is returned to Texarkana. Because of his commitment to an effort he believes in, the Doctor knows there will be no rest for him while the search continues. As he contemplates the search, he realizes how absolutely alone he really is.

He trains physically and mentally as he reads of the jungle's difficulty in previous Army search reports from 1944 and 1947. He has been physically preparing himself with 40-mile bicycle rides for several months.

He has walked, jogged and run through woodlands and river-bottom lands. Even though he begins to feel fit, he remembers the General's advice. He finds himself in better condition than he can remember, except when in the military. But the uncertainty of the jungle is completely different from flying over one in an airplane, as he has done many times.

The Doctor has made friends with many professionals while involved in various civic affairs. Dr. Gene Joyce, a medical doctor who is active in civic affairs, is a Pathologist by specialty. The Doctor spends many hours in consultation with him about what condition to expect of the remains. The variables they discuss concern exposure, impact and fire. But a half-century of exposure leaves many questions and few answers. Dr. Joyce, a quiet and unassuming professional and a deeply committed Christian, is always there when the Doctor needs his advice and support. The Doctor's notes of their first conversations and speculations about what they would find reveal an intense study of cooperation. Those early estimates are almost identical to the remains that are eventually found, in approximately the same condition Dr. Joyce anticipated.

The time the Doctor has dreaded now arrives. He must recruit volunteers for the first year search team.

CHAPTER 7

JOURNEY TO ESPIRITU SANTO – 1988

Now that research is compiled and organized, it is time to begin the actual search. The Doctor has decided he must use volunteers, but knows it will be very difficult to find people who can take an entire month away from work and pay their own trip expenses. It would be nice to find a grant or special fund already in place for an MIA search, but that is not a reality at present.

The Doctor finds discounted advance purchase round-trip airfare from Dallas, Texas, to Sydney, Australia, for about $650 each. The round-trip airfare for the shorter distance from there to Port Vila and on to Espiritu Santo will add another $1000 per person. They also have to scrounge up supplies and gear for the extended jungle stay. With considerations for food supplies and local native help, it will easily come to $3000 per person.

The Doctor calls Mary Jane Dighn, owner of Hotel Santo, for information and advice on native labor and transportation to the jungle drop-off point. Mary Jane assures him she will assist in any way she can. She agrees to introduce him to village chiefs and natives who may hire out for a few days searching for the downed plane. She is acquainted with a few bilingual locals who may be able to serve as interpreters.

The Doctor knows he has stalled long enough and must now find the right team members. He wants young men who are military veterans or at least have extensive Boy Scout training. Both organizations seem to force-feed their members a daily diet of leadership and self-discipline. These candidates will know the basic rudiments of tough physical activity and how to be self-sustaining. Each must be a committed team player who is capable of taking and completing assignments.

There are additional considerations that further narrow the list of prospective searchers, and the Doctor simply cannot allow the search to become a vacation project. It will be a very serious affair, and they will be out of touch with the rest of the world. There will be no room for crybabies because room service will not be available. It will require men of strong mental and physical ability, with an appropriate mix of good attitude and teamwork that will be a welcome factor in the jungle.

The Doctor remembers a military veteran who sat behind him in Dr. Nash's research class twenty years ago. Dr. Tom Chames is a good pilot and also spent time in Vietnam. The Doctor knows he is reliable and will be a superb team player. They have flown all across the U.S. together in the Doctor's plane, and Tom has always been a good traveling partner. They have already shared rain, snow and lightening storms in the sky when flying coast to coast.

Tom Chames is also an excellent doctor who can always find something to laugh at, even if it is himself. He is the kind of natural comic everyone needs to be around on a bad day. When Tom turns on his dry wit and sense of humor, even the clouds go away. He and Bennett would be a good match because he is a lot like Bowden described Bennett. "Besides," the Doctor decides, "maybe Tom can keep Bennett occupied a little, so I can concentrate on putting together this team."

The Doctor climbs in his plane and flies to Marshall, Texas, to talk to Tom. After about an hour of stammering and stuttering about the upcoming trip, the Doctor still has not gotten to the purpose of his visit.

Finally, in desperation, Tom says, "Hey, man, how much longer are you going to beat around the bush with this thing? Are you going to ask me to come along on this trip or not?"

The Doctor is astonished at Tom's response and can only reply, "Well,... Uh, I mean,... Uh, Do you,... Uh,... Do you want to come along, Tom?"

Tom grins and says, "I thought you would never ask. Of course, I'll go. Besides, this guy Bennett seems like my kind of guy."

So, Dr. Tom Chames agrees to be one of the search team members, and he is ready to go now. Since Tom is also a veteran of Dr. Nash's research class, the Doctor quickly puts him to work checking the findings and notes for completeness.

The Doctor continues his search for another member for this first year's search team. He has decided that each team member must pay for the entire trip in advance. Natives in the jungle do not take credit cards or checks, and the doctor does not want to run out of money in the middle of a search. Of course, this is yet another little trick this project has played on him because he never anticipated being responsible for all the money. In telephone meetings with CILHI, they advised him that it is very difficult to make change on a jeep's hood in the jungle. Imagine trying to pay off a chief and twenty natives at the end of the search when everyone is exhausted and no one has any idea where their money is.

Of course, another serious problem would occur if someone loses his tickets or passports, and another discovers he no longer has enough money left for the trip home. That's why the team leader must take responsibility for all of them.

The Doctor learns from Mary Jane that he will have to pay the natives about three dollars a day, and provide them with food while in the bush. She also suggests they bring American food to eat during the search because there will be an alarming lack of it in the bush.

The Doctor contacts a friend who acquires some surplus MREs (Meal Ready to Eat). They contain almost every imaginable type of menu selection, will be quick to prepare, and will meet all the search team's daily caloric requirements. Another advantage of an MRE is that there will be no KP (kitchen police) duties such as washing dishes or scrubbing pots.

The friend who donates the MREs will never know how much money and time his assistance will save them in the jungle in feeding the searchers' ravenous appetites. The Doctor and Tom carefully plan food provisions because they know there will be no corner grocery store to dash over to in the jungle. They plan three MRE's per day for each team member and a few extras to give away – it is a perfect combination.

Before the project is over, the Doctor will make many friends and leave lasting impressions by sharing some of these meals with acquaintances. This leads to endless conversation about how well American military personnel are fed. People want to know if these are normal American military field rations. They are amazed when the Doctor shrugs and replies that these are only a few of the snacks provided American servicemen. He tells them these snacks are only available until it is time to go over to the chow hall, and have a hot meal of steaks, chicken or pork chops. Almost all then want to know if they can enlist in the U.S. military service! The Doctor has a good time talking about the MREs; but, in the back of his mind, he wonders if this is not more of Bennett's humor in trying to get him to become a military recruiter.

A group of Texarkana veterans have stayed attached to each other through their veteran's organizations. They have meetings and work within the community framework to raise funds for several projects. One of their projects is an eyesore piece of property they acquired on the state line and are slowly rehabilitating into a marvelous work of art. This Four States Memorial to military casualties from Texas, Arkansas, Louisiana and Oklahoma is constructed of brick, stone, granite, marble... and a lot of hard work and memories. It includes granite maps of the countries of conflict and marble lists of the names of servicemen who were lost in each area. Mounted on expensive, custom-made flagpoles are the U.S. flag, each of the state flags, and the black MIA/POW flag to help all Americans remember.

The veterans work on this labor of love every Saturday, beginning at dawn. It would cost over one-million-dollars as a contract project, but the veterans have pooled their collective skills and are putting the final touches on this tribute to their comrades and a gift to the people of the four-states area. The Doctor arrives one afternoon about three o'clock with another load of donuts and coffee. He congratulates them on the superb job they have done since last week. As the old soldiers sit and talk, they are eager to know more about his project to the South Pacific and the search for the WW2 casualty from Texarkana. The Doctor explains that he now needs one or two more volunteers to accompany him on the search.

From the crowd of dirty faces and sweating bodies comes a tired voice, "I'll go."

The Doctor thinks someone is just joking and continues to explain that it will cost the volunteer approximately $3000.

Again, from the crowd, comes the simple comment, "I'll go."

The Doctor still fails to take the comment seriously and continues to explain that the trip will last almost a month.

Again a voice comes from the crowd and declares – a little stronger this time, "I'll go."

This is how the Doctor meets Harry Cornelieus, a fine Christian man who will become the search team's elder statesman.

The Doctor is trapped. He has feared all along that someone might volunteer for this very difficult trip, and he would be unable to refuse. Someone who might start out on a cane could return home in a stretcher, or worse. At the very least, he has been afraid of a volunteer who could slow down the progress of their limited search time.

He can almost hear Bennett whispering in his ear again, baiting him, "Ah, come on, let the old guy go. Look at all the fun he'll have if he doesn't forget his nitroglycerin heart pills."

Somewhere along the road of life, the Doctor has been taught that he does not need to fear death and must not make a career of worrying about dying. Something on the order of, "When God wants you, he won't have any trouble finding you, and it will be at a time and a place of His choosing. So until that day, do your very best at what you do and leave the rest to Him."

The Doctor looks into this middle-aged veteran's dirty face. He sees a man who is again ready to put all his tomorrows on the line for someone else. How can anyone say "No" to a man like that? Harry Cornelieus served his time in Vietnam and several other nameless places around the world while he wore the U.S. Marine Globe and Anchor.

Harry, a silver fox with hair almost as white as snow, is over 50 years old. He may not stand as ramrod straight as he once did, but he remains one of "the few, the proud, and *always* a Marine."

He is not volunteering in jest or on a dare. When a man says he cannot go because of the money, Harry says, "I'll go." When a man cannot get off his job for a month, Harry says, "I'll go." And when a man can no longer take such trips because of infirmity or disability, Harry will still say, "I'll go." What Harry means is that he will go for others this time, until they are in shape to volunteer for the next trip. Harry has probably never said a bad thing about anyone in his entire life, and he is one of the shinning stars in the *Search for the Lost Blacksheep*.

With the addition of Harry to the team, the Doctor makes a few last minute arrangements. The team is given a donation of medicines, antibiotics and emergency equipment. They start taking anti-malaria medication in preparation for departure in less than thirty days.

Many of the Doctor's friends are beginning to question the sanity of normal, working class Americans who will risk everything on a search like this for a needle in a haystack. They may even be considering measuring him for a personalized straight jacket for leading a group of civilians on a quest such as this.

When departure day arrives, the pile of gear barely fits into the cars taking them to the airport, or into the airlines weight limitation for the passenger allowance; but they are soon on their way. By midnight, they have traveled from Texas to Chicago, San Francisco and on to Hawaii (about twice the distance across the continental United States).

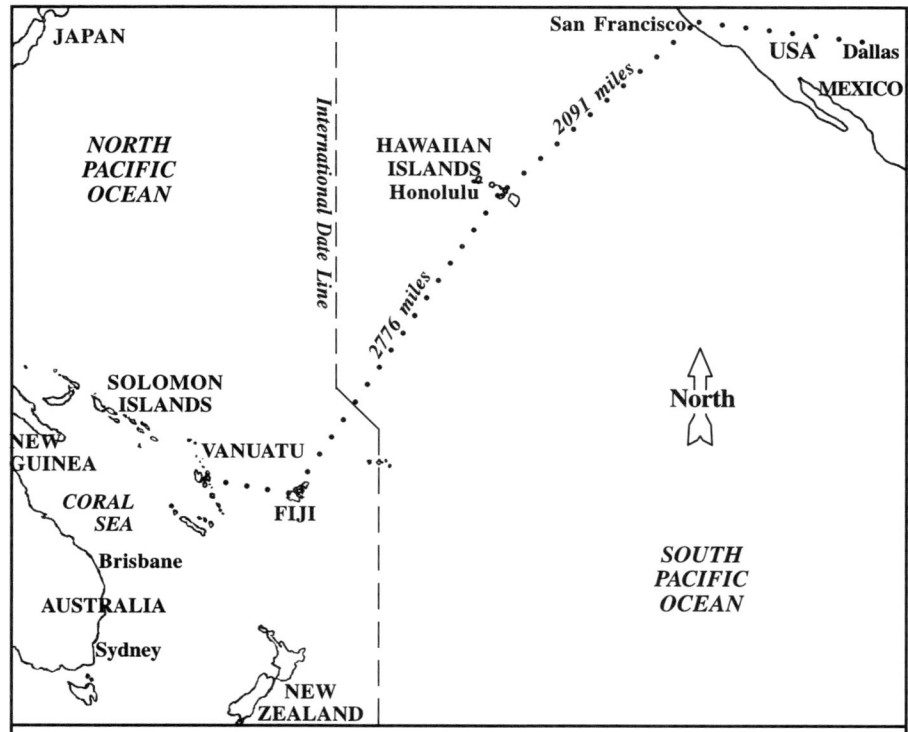

[7-a] JOURNEY TO THE SOUTH PACIFIC PARADISE OF VANUATU: We followed several different routes on our trips to the islands, but the best routing was from Dallas to San Francisco, Hawaii, Fiji, then Vanuatu. The first year we flew from San Francisco to Hawaii, Sydney, then Vanuatu (Port Vila and Espiritu Santo). We also traveled from Honolulu to New Zealand, New Caledonia, then Vanuatu; and from Honolulu to Sydney, Brisbane, New Caledonia, then Vanuatu. One year we flew from San Francisco to New Zealand, then on to Vanuatu. The people are friendly and unhurried in their daily tasks, which may lead to a severe case of culture shock for most high-speed Americans. But you will never forget your stay in the magnificent Republic of Vanuatu.

CILHI & BLUE CHIP FIVE-ZERO

The next day, two rather bleary-eyed victims of jet lag look for a lost command known as CILHI. They finally locate the rather limited spaces occupied by the Laboratories in the old docks and piers section of Honolulu Harbor. It is almost hidden behind mountains of cargo that has just been unloaded from freighters. Cargo ships, waiting to be unloaded, are tied up to the same wharf an old LST used long ago.

The two red-eyed visitors must look like refugees from an all-night Hotel Street binge; but, the Doctor identifies himself, and they are admitted into the administrative offices and introduced to the officer in charge.

For the first time, the Doctor is in the presence of professionals with whom he has only spoken over the phone. Their meeting lasts three hours, and they discuss almost every conceivable detail of the proposed search. The Doctor feels like a new recruit in the presence of people who do this job so well. He tries to make certain the officer understands that he is an absolute amateur and welcomes all the help he can get.

The Doctor is informed that CILHI will receive a new state-of-the-art lab in the very near future, which will be located on the giant Hickam Air Force Base. The Colonel in charge will retire in about seven years, after having served his entire career in this part of the Army. The new lab is a final project he and others have sought for many years. Although he will not be in charge of it for long, he will at least have the opportunity to see his dream take shape.

A sergeant knocks on the door and announces that the Doctor has a phone call, then takes him to a private office where he will not be interrupted. The Doctor wonders who is calling, since no one knows he is here. In fact, even the Doctor is unsure of where he really is, and a sergeant has taken Tom to a coffee shop.

When the Doctor picks up the phone, a vaguely familiar voice tells him about a problem that has surfaced in the Western Pacific region. The voice wants to know more details about it. He is direct and to the point with his request. He wants the Doctor to help him identify certain undesirable individuals in the islands who are busy setting up a disgusting entrepreneurial enterprise.

The voice continues, "A 35-year-old white man known as Fred Folly lives in a rundown shack on the outskirts of Port Vila. He runs a nearly defunct store in town where he sells tours and souvenirs to visitors, and has set up a pseudo-museum to sell island relics and curios. Folly has acquired financial backing from some rather unsavory characters to help him create a business that will invade CILHI's domain.

"He has two accomplices in this project. The first is a 60-year-old freelance photographer known as H.H. Hardington, or Hardy, who photographs aircraft wrecks and crew remains. He is of questionable lineage and has even less morals than he does hair.

"The second is a white woman known as L. L. Laurel, who is about 59 years old, but has lived a colorful life and looks like she's at least 75. She has no pedigree, and is apparently a lady of rather doubtful moral convictions who entertains the two men. Her contribution to the scenario is that of companion and banker for their latest adventure.

"Of course we checked and these are simply aliases in a long string of names they've used all over Australia, New Zealand and the islands.

"What concerns us most is that Folly, Hardy and Laurel have started contacting relatives and loved ones of long-lost Americans. They portray themselves as the only hope for recovery and return of the serviceman's remains. This trio is setting up a black-market dealership for selling remains and personal effects back to these families at unholy prices. If the family does not have the necessary funds; the bones, personal effects, skulls and artifacts are then sold as souvenirs on the black market. This, of course, guarantees the remains will never be returned to the family, and the casualty can never be properly identified.

"Hardy devised this little scheme, and these 'museum pieces and collectors items' are sold to any tourist or foreign visitor who will trade for such under-the-table bargains. Our former enemies in that part of the world pay high prices for American servicemen's remains.

"To the best of our knowledge, Vanuatu's government is unaware of this scheme and has no reason to suspect wrongdoing. However, this terrible trio has asked Vanuatu's government to recognize their 'tourism project' and allow them to advertise as exploring adventures. Of course, with official blessings from the Minister of History and Culture, a cloak of decency would shroud these despicable activities. This is not an uncommon enterprise in other parts of the world, but it is entirely new to the island nation of Vanuatu. The innocence of island natives is intact, and they do not suspect how they are being manipulated and duped.

"Folly is advertising himself as an explorer and aviation crash expert. Hardy photographs remains in graphic clarity, then waxes eloquent about the 'accidental discoveries' that the 'incompetent' U.S. Army cannot locate. The multilingual Laurel contacts the American families, then she and Hardy produce amateur videotapes to sell them. These home movies graphically exhibit the MIA's remains to grief-stricken families, propose their recovery – for a price – then a bargain basement discount sale of the remains is offered. What family can say no?

"Hardy is not overly endowed by ethical restrictions, and one of his specialties is plagiarism. He is extraordinarily good at distorting any criticisms of his activity into an endorsement of his integrity. A once shining light of ethics and integrity no longer brightens his path. He also possesses other skills for vengeance if he fails to get his way."

When the Doctor asks to whom he is speaking, he gets only a cryptic code to use when he verbally reports his findings. The voice says, "It will be best if this conversation is not discussed with anyone. In fact, you will not even need to discuss it with the Colonel. When your search is completed, you will receive a call from 'Blue Chip Five-Zero.'

"If you should choose to write a book after Bennett is found, that will be fine and you are encouraged to do so. After your MIA is returned to his family, you must wait at least one year before you publish a book. We will neither confirm nor deny this conversation, so perhaps you should plan to change a few names."

Suddenly, the Doctor is holding a dead phone. He returns to the Colonel's office, to complete the briefing. It is finally time to leave. The Colonel smiles as he shakes hands and wishes the team well on their search. It will be seven years before the Colonel and Doctor meet again, but that day will be at the happy conclusion of... ***The Promise.***

They pick up Harry, have dinner and catch their plane to Australia. The giant Boeing 747 lumbers into the pitch black skies of Hawaii. Harry falls into a merciful sleep and will not awaken until they land in Sydney. Tom watches a movie as the plane speeds across the North Pacific Ocean at almost 600 mph.

All is serene and comfortable in the cockpit, and the Captain, who has flown millions of transoceanic miles, relaxes after they climb to cruising altitude. The stewardess comes to the cockpit and tells the Captain she has been talking to a Doctor in back who is en route to Vanuatu on a search for an MIA from WW2. The pilot is immediately interested. In his younger days, he knew some of the retired Blacksheep in Hawaii who used to fly with Boyington. The Captain asks the stewardess to see if he may look at the Doctor's notes, if he has them available.

In a few minutes, she is back with two large bound notebooks of notes and research details. Soon the Doctor is escorted to the cockpit where he and the Captain engage in a long, serious conversation.

Four hours later, the Captain finishes the notebooks, then tells the stewardess, "For better flying conditions and safety on tonight's flight, I think it will be necessary to relocate some of the passengers."

The co-pilot and flight engineer look at the Captain; they have no idea what he is talking about. There is absolutely nothing wrong with this airplane, and there is no reason to move anyone for safety reasons.

The Captain tells the stewardess, "Move the Doctor and search team members out of the tourist class seats and relocate them in the first class section for the remainder of the flight. Then serve them the finest steak dinners and a very large bottle of champagne."

The Captain's gesture makes the flight a very memorable experience, and is appreciated by the team. They will soon be wishing for the opportunity to have another one of those hot steak dinners.

The Doctor is learning, however, that this is the way many people will react to the search mission. A deep-rooted sense of loyalty and respect for MIAs is common. It is a feeling that leads ordinary people to make extraordinary efforts to assist the search team.

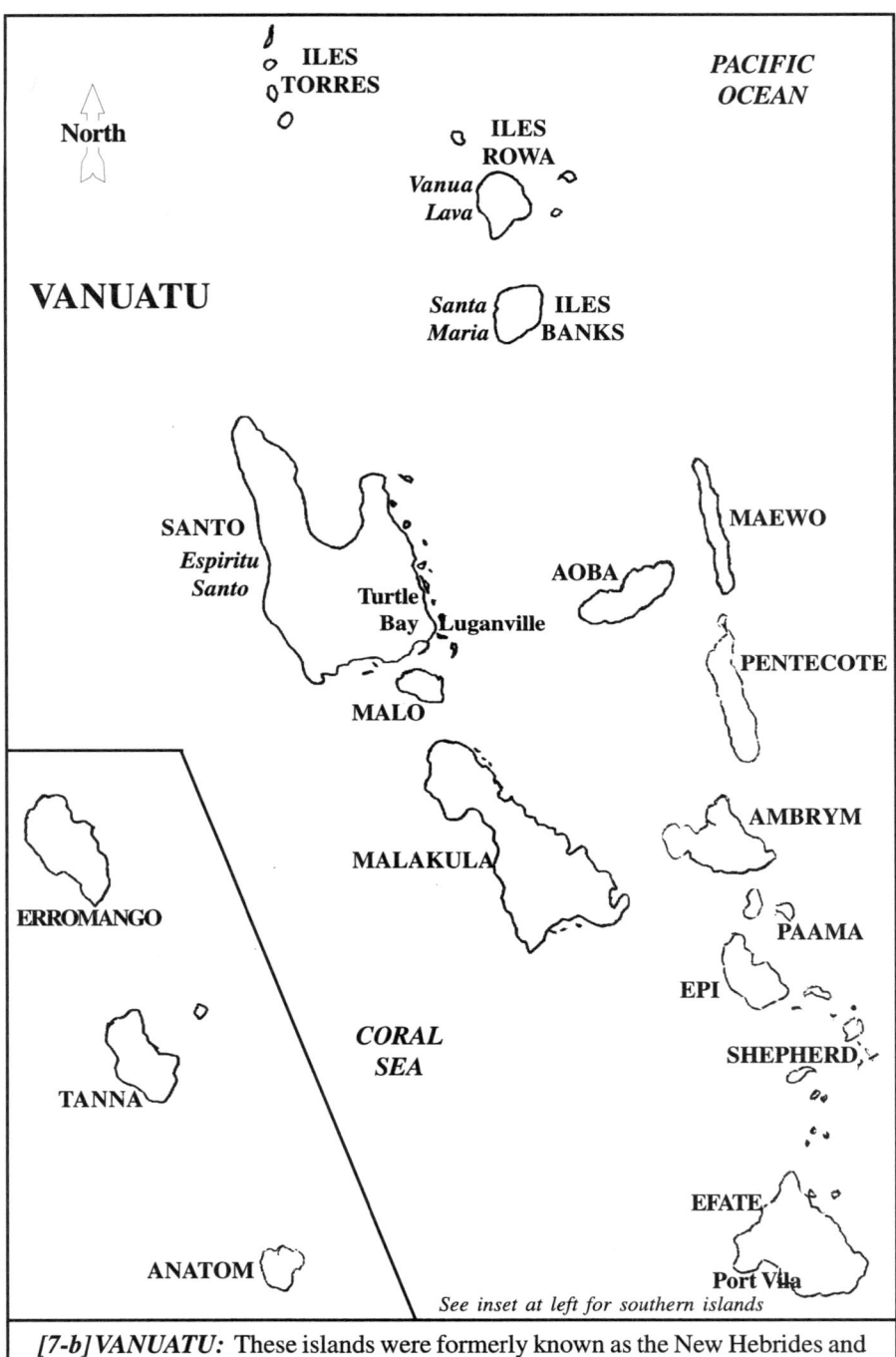

[7-b] VANUATU: These islands were formerly known as the New Hebrides and were an important part of the South Pacific theater during WW2.

BRIEFING – PORT VILA, VANUATU

When the huge airliner touches down at Sydney, the Captain provides a special escort to lead the team directly to a Boeing 727 airliner that has delayed its departure. The 727 crew is awaiting the arrival of some very important passengers; and, as a courtesy to the VIPs, has delayed its takeoff until they arrive. It seems that the Captain of a Boeing 747 airliner, which just landed in Sydney, has brought them in from Hawaii; and he requests they be given first class treatment as a special favor to him.

The search team is loaded into first class on the 727 and it immediately departs for Vanuatu. This common thread of help and assistance will be extended by many to the search team for the duration of the searches until Bennett is found. How humbling to be treated with such honor!

The Doctor had planned to stay in Australia overnight for the team to get a little rest before going on to Vanuatu. However, due to the change of schedule, they arrive in Sydney at least two days earlier than planned, so they proceed to Port Vila. As the 727 lands in Port Vila, the Doctor and team proceed to one of the recommended hotels. They take a long walk on the beach to loosen up some rather abused muscles. Then, after a much-needed hot bath and a short nap, they are ready to meet for several hours with Vanuatu government officials before going on to Espiritu Santo.

The Doctor sends Harry to the government offices to acquire the very latest charts for Santo. While he is gone, the Doctor calls the Ministry of Health to schedule a pre-arranged meeting. They have kindly agreed to provide the team with a special briefing about local precautions, and additional information they need. Soon a local medical doctor arrives at the La Lagon Hotel, and the Doctor learns that, as a courtesy to him, the meeting will be held there rather than government offices.

The search team is briefed for two hours on the various diseases they must avoid. The local doctor asks about what medications the team has with them and agrees with their choice.

He concurs with their anti-malarial medications but cautions them, "Never miss taking the pills! You *must* understand the full implications of a crippling case of malaria if contracted in the bush."

He explains, "The island's snakes and spiders are not venomous. But any bite or puncture wound by a wild animal must be considered poisonous. A mosquito, while not venomous, can certainly be poisonous to the victim. The victim can die just as easily from an infection transmitted by a mosquito bite as he can from a non-venomous snakebite."

"You will also encounter several types of poisonous plants that will cause much grief to the uninitiated."

He agrees with their antibiotic supply and protocols for their use. He stresses the hazards of infections in the bush. He further warns, "You must treat all scratches with strong antibiotic cream. If anyone experiences an injury in the bush that begins to show signs of infection, the search must stop. If the patient does not respond to treatment with antibiotics, he must start out of the jungle immediately. If he becomes unable to walk and has an out-of-control infection, the results can become tragic."

"This makes the danger very plain," the Doctor thinks to himself, but this is one American who already has an intense dislike for all manner of spiders, no matter what their nationality. With a jungle full of wild animals including bats, dogs, snakes and many other biting things, the team is committed to these precautions.

The Doctor remembers telling the team members before they left home, "You will be on the other side of the world from home, and injury or illness would be a terrible way to end a search mission. We are not going for a walk in the park, or walk on the beach. We must stay alert, be constantly aware of our own health at all times in the jungle, and not go in unprepared for our own safety."

The Doctor asks the local physician to look over the equipment he brought for emergencies, and inspect the rest of their gear for compatibility with local conditions.

The local doctor tells them, "The best protection against most of our island disorders is prevention, and the very best method for prevention is a self-contained tent with a built-in mosquito net and dry floor provision – a must for sleeping on the ground. Sleeping bags must have a waterproof cover to keep them dry in rain, on damp ground, and when crossing rivers."

Fortunately, this is exactly the type equipment the team brought from the states, but they are all glad to get the "Good Housekeeping Stamp of Approval" from a local doctor on all their gear.

Before the local doctor leaves, he again cautions the Doctor not to take chances with his team's safety and pay very careful attention to the areas where they sleep. This meeting has been valuable to the whole team; and, in the next seven years, the Doctor will never lose a team searcher to illness.

The next team meeting is with a representative from the Ministry of the Interior who describes the environment in which they are about to take up residence for a few weeks. He tells them, "Our mountains are steep and our valleys are deep; and, when the torrential downpours begin, you must not try to cross the rivers but seek high ground wherever you are. If you can't swim, do yourselves a favor and learn – or stay out of the bush. If you can't swim and persist in crossing flood-swollen rivers, you better make out your will.

"In the bush, a six-inch-deep river that is only ten feet across will become a waist-deep monster a hundred feet across after a heavy tropical rain. These fast-moving rivers have all manner of trees and debris in them which sweep away anything in their path, and it can happen so fast that you will think you're watching a fast forward movie.

"Of course you can also lose all your gear and food, as well as passports and money, in a flash flood river; but it will no longer be of importance to you because you'll be dead by that time. Perhaps, in fifty years or so, someone else can become a hero when he comes to our islands to search for your bodies."

The official appears very calm while making these ominous warnings, but makes his point well to the team. The Doctor gets the picture. "If we can dodge rain drops, maybe, just maybe, we can outrun a raging river." But he decides not to bet all his dry socks on it. Obviously, it will be better to adhere to the safety briefings they have received.

One final note of warning is then passed on to the team. "The natives know all they need to know about rain and all you need to know about weather. When it's raining, or about to rain, the native will want to stay warm and dry in his hut where there is hot food and good company. He will not venture out into the elements. If you try to force him to travel, you will lose your guide and the labor to carry your food and gear. Use a little common sense before trying to take over the jungle as 'Bwana Ben' or 'Jungle Jim.' If you want to become a 'Lord of the Jungle,' listen to your interpreters and they will make you look like a professional."

During the Doctor's research, he came across several letters written by the Bennett family to the Department of Civil Aviation in the islands. While the letters had not been productive when written, they did provide the Doctor with the name of an aviation-oriented office from which to begin local research into crash site locations. This is his next stop.

There the Doctor meets an Englishman who will become a friend and ally during the next several years of searching. Julian Forsyth, Department of Civil Aviation director, is also an airline qualified pilot and aviation expert. Julian is responsible for testing and examination of anyone who wants to fly as a pilot in these islands.

The island's admirable Civil Aviation safety record is, in part, due to his strenuous demands for professional air safety and pilot skill. He is also an historical researcher and shares much of his documented data with the Doctor about the islands and WW2. He is the author of a superbly definitive text on the development of the DeHavilland Gypsy Moth as well as the Tiger Moth biplanes of the 1930's.

One item Julian shares from his files is a declassified document that the Doctor has not seen before. It is an old record of all American aircraft losses from December 1941 until August 1945. The document provides date of loss, type of aircraft, and unit to which the pilot and aircraft were assigned. It also gives personnel information and name, rank and serial number of each crewman in addition to the identification number of the aircraft. *(Excerpt in Appendix C)*

Julian, a world-class gentleman and a legitimate researcher of WW2 archives, volunteers to help the team and becomes a very real asset to the

Doctor. He offers to introduce him to two close friends in the islands who are also researchers and authors, then takes the time to arrange a dinner meeting for them all to get together that evening.

At dinner Julian introduces the team to Dr. Ken Hutton, an island dentist who has been taking care of islanders' dental needs since the 1950s. He is well known throughout the islands as Dr. Ken, and will become a very good search team assistant over the next several years.

[7-c] NEED A TOOTH PULLED? Dr. Ken Hutton, an island dentist, has lived for decades in Vanuatu and personally experienced growth of technology. In early years, his professional equipment included a dental drill powered by the next patient, who would ride a bicycle with a Rube Goldberg attachment of belts and a pulley that turned the slow speed drill – unless the peddler of the cycle pedaled faster or – faster – faster. He was a good friend to the team and a gentleman of infinite wit and humor. I declined his gracious offer to repair a filling – even though he promised I would not have to ride the bicycle.

Dr. Ken tells them, "When I first came to the islands, I had to design and build my office and much of my equipment. In the early days, electrical power was limited and unreliable, causing great difficulty when, on many occasions, power would fail in the middle of a dental procedure.

"Due to the island's isolation, parts to repair electrical generators were not always available and it could occasionally take weeks to acquire them. This meant I would be unable to complete my patient's treatment until power was restored. This prospect for a dental patient was dismal, even if the wait was only a few hours. So," the resourceful dentist continues, "I bolted a bicycle to my porch, removed the rear tire, and replaced it with a belt and pulley that I connected to a drill on my dental chair. I hired natives to pedal this stationary bicycle that turned the drill. When using this device, if a patient cried a muffled, 'Wuffm-Wuffm,' he wanted the native to pedal faster.

Dr. Hutton's ability to design "Rube Goldberg" contraptions such as this is not just a quick fix; many of his devices still work after years of use. When he offers to use the bicycle drill to repair a filling for the Doctor, the Doctor declines as graciously as he knows how.

A very kind gentleman in many ways, Dr. Ken provides lodging for many of the searchers in years to come. He also assists the Doctor by reporting any new information he hears while on visits to his several clinics throughout the islands.

Dr. Ken tells the Doctor about another friend, Reece Discombe. "He is out of the country for a month's vacation, but will be devastated if he does not get to meet you before you leave. Reece has been a New Zealand championship racecar driver, a commercial salvage diver, and an expert at raising ships and their cargo from the surrounding islands. He has been to every wrecked ship in area waters and has engineered the recovery of some very interesting artifacts."

The Doctor remembers that he has been advised during earlier correspondence with the government offices to meet with this highly respected man.

Julian picks up the story. "In the seventeenth century, an English sailing ship came through the islands and named them The New Hebrides. After the ship left, it continued its journey to other islands and was mysteriously lost. Presumably, the ship went down in a storm with the loss of all on board. For centuries the ship's loss was an unexplained mystery to researchers.

"Reece was part of a research team that plotted the estimated course of this ship and superimposed it on the estimated track of the storm. When their research determined where the ship might have encountered the storm, Reece started diving in a systematic search of the ocean floor. Soon they located the wreckage and recovered centuries old artifacts including the anchor and many other treasured heirlooms from the ship – all of which are now on permanent display in the National Heritage Museum in Port Vila.

"The old sailing ship's recovery and the now-solved mystery of its loss have greatly enhanced the islands' history and cultural studies. It has become a valuable reference point in the study of island anthropology, and contributed to knowledge of the native and his social progress over the past several centuries."

The next morning, Dr. Ken and Julian arrive at the hotel to help arrange tickets for the team on the Inter-Island Commuter Airline. Both seem to have rather severe headaches and red eyes. The previous evening, they were kind enough to accept the Doctor's gift of a rather large bottle of champagne that he did not need. Of course, they were certain the team's baggage would not meet required weight and balance computations for the old commuter airplane and were only too glad to help decide which supplies could be eliminated. They were sure the team would not want to ruin the champagne by bouncing it all over the jungle. The Doctor heard from a reliable source that the Champagne came to an untimely end as it was terribly victimized by two white gentlemen who terrorized the bottle until its early demise.

ON TO ESPIRITU SANTO

The Inter-Island Commuter is the only air service between the islands of Vanuatu. This bush plane goes into lonely, nearly abandoned fields and does not have all the social amenities of modern jet travel. They do try, however, to make up for these little deficiencies in many other ways.

The paint job on these old refugees from a salvage yard is a memory, faded into a design that changes with each passing bird. It is an interesting experience to fly on a drafty old plane where air conditioning is a breeze from doors that never quite seem to close. Of course, if one gets cold, he can always lean away from the window, which is no longer there. Just as the passenger climbs on board, he may wonder where the stewardess is... only to discover that the stewardess is a he, and he is the one flying the plane.

Out here one can always recognize the pilot because he is the one who wears clothes. Lest one become unnecessarily concerned that something may fall off in flight, he need never fear because almost everything that can fall off while these planes are in the air, already has.

The Doctor notices that "frequent flyers" with certain religious affiliations are semi-relaxed and can actually slow down the manipulation of their beads until they are visible. However, first time flyers are obviously less at ease, and their beads go so fast that they are only a blur to the naked eye. The Doctor observes many with these beads in their hands as carry-on baggage. In fact, the devout pilot has two... in each hand.

In answer to Harry's question about safety of these old planes, the Doctor replies, tongue in cheek, "Who you gonna' ask, pardner? We're the only ones around here who speak our lingo! Why, of course it will fly; this old plane ain't tired. Folks, this old queen of the skies hasn't flown for twelve years, so you see, it can't be too tired. It's as sound as a dollar. This old girl has flown this route for so long, she probably knows the way from one island to the next better than the pilot does."

About that time the pilot has finished lunch and is ready to brave the elements. The Doctor answers Harry's questioning look with, "Sure, he's okay; he always has lunch in the bar."

These small planes are always fully loaded, if not with passengers, with a mountain of inter-island cargo. The team's first flight carries a lot of both. This first team shares the friendly skies with four big chickens and two small goats. There is even enough room left over for the three medium-sized pigs and a little mountain of fruit and vegetables. The fellow passengers are all natives who, of course, wear little or no clothing. No briefcases out here. Carry on baggage is limited to spears or machetes, although some passengers do prefer bows and arrows.

On the flight, one traveling companion (the one with the bone in his nose) carries at least a dozen huge, live, coconut crabs. These charming traveling companions have their huge pinchers tied up with jungle vines. "N-N-n-n-no-o-o-o problem!" A coconut crab fears nothing on this earth, probably not even God, which may explain why this creature is so ugly.

The Doctor laughingly tells the team, "I happen to believe in both 'The Big Bang Theory' as well as 'Evolution.' The explanation for both is really very simple. Eons ago, at about the time the earth was formed, an angel got into a fight with God; the Angel lost, and that was undoubtedly the 'Big Bang.' Since that time even man has gotten smarter and prettier, and that is evolution.

"The coconut crab was the loser in the 'Big Bang' fight according to my theory. Maybe he too has gotten smarter and prettier since the fight, due to evolution. One can just imagine how ugly he must have been right after the fight, if he still looks this ugly today! Perhaps, even a coconut crab knows better than to cross God now, and each night he probably hopes evolution will help him get prettier. Anything that ugly must be very lonely, and they are, to be sure, unsuitable as pets.

"The only way for most Americans to be safe around this sweetheart of the jungle is for it to be quite dead, and them sitting in a reasonably tall tree. It can inflict a serious injury to the curious or stupid who venture too close to it; for the uneducated, this means roughly fifty yards.

"By divine right, a coconut crab seems most eager to induce agonizing pain to any of the various parts of one's accessible anatomy. At the very least, one may assume this to include, but certainly is not limited to, contusions, lacerations and broken bones. It is said that if certain parts of the human anatomy are so addressed, they frequently have to be amputated. These incidents happen most commonly to people who sleep on the ground in the jungle.

" They perform these attentive little details of personal agony with their immense pinchers. In high-class restaurants around the world, those big things on the ends of a coconut crab's arms are called 'crab claws.' This is so they can charge a higher price when they have sold out of the more common lobster. The reason one eats only the coconut crab's claws is that no one would be able to eat him if he knew how ugly he is."

The Doctor has the whole team laughing by now and finds his ploy to keep their minds off the flight is working. When Tom laughs, it's a mirthful explosion and deep-rooted enjoyment of life itself; in fact, he laughs all over and the more he gets out of control, the more he slobbers. Of course the natives are wondering what these white men are up to.

The Doctor continues, "Another reason the coconut crab is not as popular as the lobster is that the cook can't find a cage strong enough to hold him. He tears up everything he gets close to and is always mad.

"But, the final indignity for the coconut crab is how the cook gets the 'claws.' The cook turns a coconut crab loose on the floor and runs for the door; when the cook arrives there, he turns and makes all manner of faces at the crab. The crab eagerly accepts this challenge, and with his huge 'claws' outstretched, will attack the cook. With the right timing, a good cook can slam the door just at the right time and, presto, 'crab claws.' This is also the difference between a cook and a chef."

The team members, who are hemmed up in the old plane several thousand feet above a two-and-a-half-mile deep ocean, watch with great interest as one of the crabs gets a pincher free and promptly tears off a rather impressive piece of the airplane's metal skin! Right about then, they're not claws any more but, in more common language, "big old pinchers" or something pretty close to it. Harry, Tom and the Doctor watch these crabs with great interest for the rest of the flight.

The Doctor leans over to Tom, and yells loud enough to be heard above the roar of the airplane engines. "Hey Tom, can you imagine this flight with its two dogs, a cat, four goats, and two pigs – not to mention the six other passengers – ricocheting around inside, desperately trying to stay out of the clutches of those coconut crabs if they get loose."

Old Tom relaxes a little, but the natives watch him suspiciously for the rest of the flight. They seem unsure if the American is suffering from a fit or a seizure,... but perhaps all Americans act strangely when they are away from their village too long.

The Doctor steals a glance at their traveling companions. He can imagine them saying, "Those white men must be at least a little strange; after all, look at all the clothes they're wearing. And look, not a single one has a spear or even a machete. And that one doing all the laughing is crying and slobbering on himself at the same time. How disgusting! Wait until I get home and tell the wife about this. Boy, there goes the neighborhood. What are these islands coming to?"

The crabs make the trip to their final destination in style. They make an excellent meal and are considered an island delicacy. However, they do look a lot like the Doctor's worst dream come true: very large and very ugly spiders.

[7-d] BIRD'S EYE VIEW: This high altitude photo shows Espiritu Santo's entire east coast. Bomber One is near the right corner, and Cargo One is just to its left. Half way up the coast is Turtle Bay Fighter Strip One. At least fifty large ships are being unloaded in protected harbors. A noticeable oil slick is from USS Coolidge that hit a mine and sank with a full cargo. The ship is visible 75 feet below the surface.

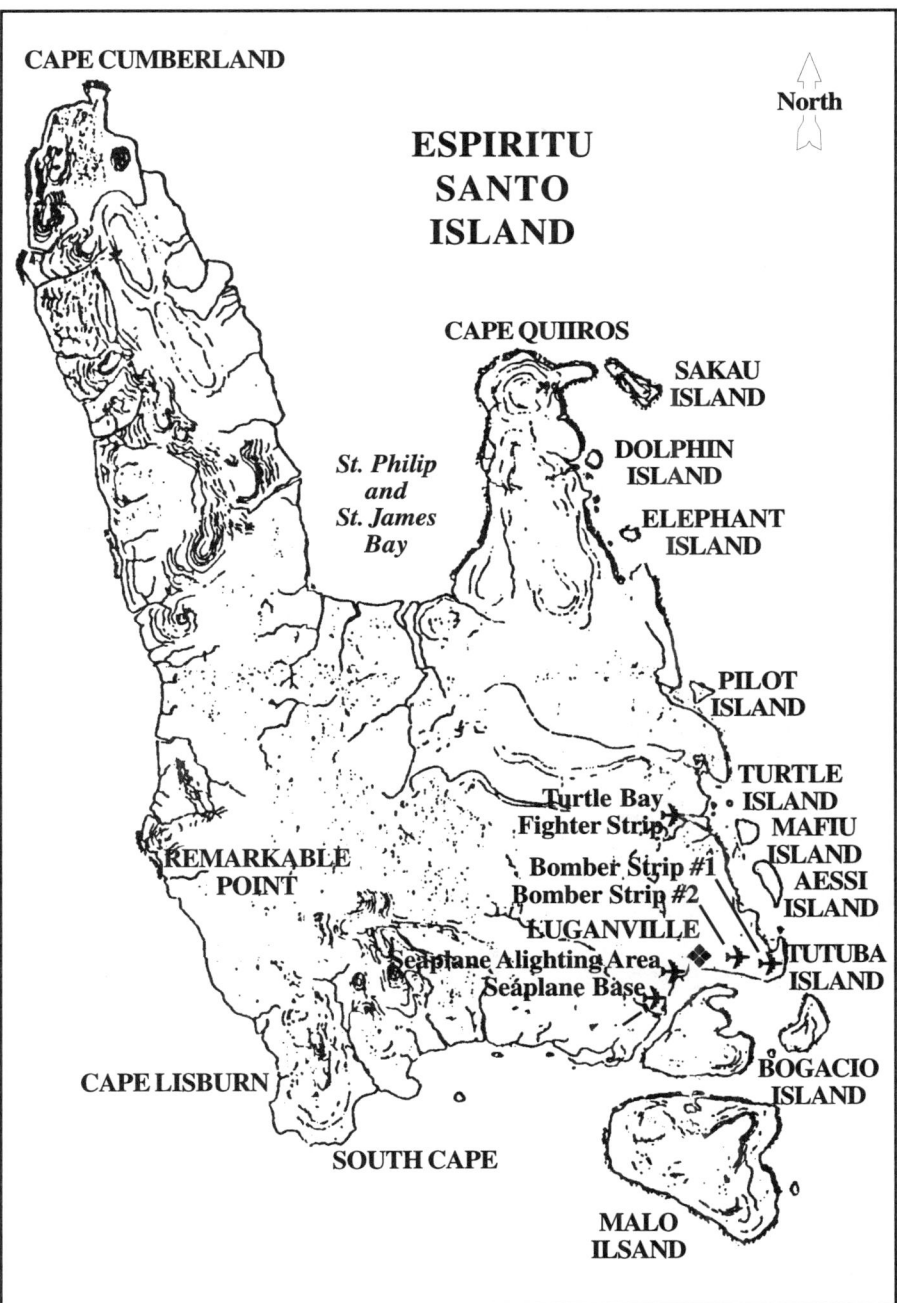

[7-e] ESPIRITU SANTO: The U.S. Military carved a strategic base out of this tropical paradise.

CHAPTER 8

SEARCH 1 – ESPIRITU SANTO – 1988
FIRST STOP – LUGANVILLE

The search team is glad to finally land very near the old Bomber Strip Number One site on Espiritu Santo.

In 1943, this island was an enormous and strategic operations base that supplied most military activity in this South Pacific area. This Island Command was an indispensable supply depot and staging area for aircraft, pilots and their crews. Ships of all sizes delivered men and their equipment along with materials necessary to wage war on an immense scale. When Navy SeaBees built Turtle Bay fighter strip, their orders were to convert this primitive site into a modern airfield within six weeks. But MCB-57 completed their task in approximately twenty days!

[8-a] READY FOR TAKE-OFF: This abandoned airfield was built in 1942 by members of U.S. Navy's MCB-57. It is still smooth and level and I would not hesitate to land my airplane on it now. The SeaBee's work then is still in evidence today, almost a half-century after the Americans built cities of Quonset huts and miles of streets and roadways. The airfields all survived the decades of non-attention. Even the explosive ordinance storage bunkers are still in use today, only now they serve as storage barns and milk sheds. One bunker, built and used as a bomb dump, today serves as a school bus stop.

Today, this abandoned airfield serves the needs of the island's people. The Quonset hut city Bennett saw being built now houses the city of Luganville, a small trading post village that is the last area of civilization before one travels north into the jungle. Less than four square miles resemble a permanent community. It is composed of enough businesses to support the multi-national population that lives and works there. The resident population is composed of a few natives (referred to as "Ni-

Vanuatu") and French, English, Australian, New Zealanders, Vietnamese and Chinese newcomers who have made the islands their home.

The war's influence remains everywhere. A once thriving harbor for hundreds of ships at anchor is now only a peaceful bay. An occasional cargo ship will use the docks to load copra and unload other cargo. Dozens of derelict ships and tons of equipment lie decaying on beaches and in shallow waters.

Espiritu Santo Island paradise is roughly 60 miles long and 40 miles wide. Its topography ranges from white, sea-level beaches to mountains that soar above 7000 feet. While the island contains some 2400 square miles of area, it has less than 40 miles of roadway with only one or two full miles paved.

It rains every single day in this tropical Garden of Eden; sometimes only once a day in the dry season. The rain constantly erodes the roadway, which undergoes at least a daily re-routing due to holes, pits and washouts.

A complete vehicle is rare, and creative genius is common. Rental cars are just a dream, but "limited" transportation is always available from the airport into town. The local taxi that takes the search team into town is the back of an old truck that falls into the "limited" category. It has no doors and fewer windows, and must surely be a refugee from the war. It looks and rides as though it must have already received several awards for service above and beyond the call to duty. Body repairs are the latest technology: a flattened tin can held in place with four screws (no two of the same size). Other repairs defy description, and are held in place with rope, tape, twine and even vines from a tree! None of the four tires and wheels match, and they travel either sideways or another way. Neither of those choices coinciding with the direction in which the truck is pointing.

The sea water atmosphere with its resultant rust and corrosion have taken a terrible toll on some of these artistic creations. Many of the engines seem to run on either wood or coal judging from the multi-colored smoke cloud that is emitted during their asthmatic travels. The ability of a local automobile mechanic and his creative skills give testimony to an old saying, "Never have so few accomplished so much with so little."

When they refer to a new vehicle here, they mean new to this owner. "New" can mean less than twenty years old. "Newer" may mean less than 200,000 miles. "Newest" may mean it runs for the first time in thirty years.

A Quonset hut city appears as the team nears Luganville. The old relic of a truck successfully completes its journey all the way to the Hotel Santo, where it deposits its thankful human cargo at the front door. An unceremonious arrival that is heralded only by the explosive decompression of the right front tire. Following this lead, the radiator produces a huge cloud of steam from which the search team staggeres. As the search team emerges from the clouds, they must look for all the world like arriving saints coming down from glory.

They meet Mary Jane Dighn for the first time under these auspicious circumstances on this momentous occasion. Mary Jane is a beautiful Eurasian lady with golden skin and a pearly white smile. She is fluent in at least four languages that the Doctor cannot even recognize. After meeting her native staff, the Americans have to convince at least three of them that they are indeed not the arrival of saints or even angelic hosts. Mary Jane proudly shows the team her hotel and its open-air restaurant.

She says, "I received your letter which advised us of your arrival. We have made all necessary preparations for your stay." As they pass through the restaurant she comments, "This is where you eat."

With other pressing matters to attend to, Mary Jane politely excuses herself to assign details of the day to her staff.

It seems rather odd to the Doctor that she would tell them where to eat. But, as they survey the deserted dining room, they see a large table of food she has arranged. They promptly sit down and ravenously consume huge quantities of beautifully arranged fruits and vegetables. It is obvious that Mary Jane has gone to a lot of trouble to prepare this food.

In a lowered voice, which befits his station in life as a gentleman and scholar, the Doctor instructs the team, "Make certain we show proper appreciation for this reception by eating as much as we can. In many countries," he whispers authoritatively, "it is considered good manners and a very high compliment to the hostess and her staff."

Tom and Harry are proud to be in the company of a man who is so obviously skilled in the field of international relations. They make certain Mary Jane will be pleased, and only gulps, slurps and burps punctuate the team conversation. For the next twenty minutes the Americans really, really, do impress Mary Jane and her staff in the beautifully appointed Hotel Santo. As a crowd begins to gather, they too are treated to the spectacle of the American MIA search team. The locals have quite possibly never seen such an orgy of appreciation to Mary Jane and her staff of culinary experts.

Finally, the feeding frenzy is over, and team members lean back in their chairs, making appropriate noises. Following the Doctor's leadership, coughs or snorts and the time-honored tradition of stuffed belly rubbing punctuate their compliments.

Mary Jane returns as the search team completes the devastation of these plates of food. She quickly speaks to a curious crowd of onlookers who by now have filled her dining room. The team cannot understand the language, so they just watch with great interest. The Doctor is certain she is introducing them to this gathering crowd.

As she speaks to the crowd, Mary Jane makes appropriate explanations and reports, "These visitors are an American MIA search team. They have only just arrived," she continues, "and are on a humanitarian mission of mercy in search of a lost America brother."

One curious onlooker is a very large native gentleman – the only native wearing sunglasses. The people's questions and answers are conducted in a rapid-fire session using at least several languages including French, Bislama and German.

After about twenty minutes of back-and-forth talk, the Doctor realizes Mary Jane has not asked him to speak. In fact, he has not yet uttered his first word.

Tom slowly leans over to the Doctor and, with a quizzical look on his face whispers, "Hey man, what do you suppose this is all about?"

The Doctor is, of course, a skilled public speaker and globe-trotting world traveler, so he quickly puts Old Tom at ease. Exuding confidence, he whispers his considered opinion as to what is going on. "Well, Tom, you see, it's like this. Mary Jane is probably telling them all about us, and what really nice guys we are. She is no doubt asking them to provide us with all sorts of help. Of course, they can all see how she has demonstrated her desire to help us by setting the pace for cooperation. She probably wants them to see her support for us by throwing this little reception. They are being encouraged to get this message out to all the native tribes that we are her friends and she wants them to treat us likewise.

"Right about now," the Doctor elaborates, "she is asking them to notice what nice table manners we have. She is pointing out we have eaten about 99.4 percent of this wonderful food she worked all morning to prepare."

Old Tom is really impressed with the Doctor's explanation and his obvious grasp of local language and customs, so he eats some more.

Five-and-one-half seconds later, the conversation switches into English, which all team members understand. In their native American tongue, they learn that this little shindig is the annual meeting of the local Kiwanis Club! They also find out this is not a reception laid out for them! And, finally, they learn they are not the guests of honor! The big guy in the sunglasses? He is the guest of honor, and he is the President of the Republic of Vanuatu!

Of course the Kiwanis Club's polite folks probably think the Americans have already been over-exposed to the sun, because their faces are so red, and it must have been a very acute case of exposure too.

In spite of this brilliant display of culture exhibited by the MIA search team leader, Mary Jane doesn't charge them for all the food. On the other hand, and in retrospect, it was quite possibly the most brilliant performance of a traveling floorshow the Kiwanis club ever saw. Yep, Ole Tom and the rest of the search team are really impressed with the Doctor's skill at foreign relations.

Later in the evening, Mary Jane comes to the Doctor's room, where the Doctor is still suffering from an acute case of over-eating humble pie. He apologetically explains what really happened, and how he had translated the conversation as he interpreted it for Tom and Harry. Mary Jane gleefully joins in hysterical laugh that is on the Doctor.

After the laughter is over, they talk of more serious things. As they discuss the search, she explains how she has organized a meeting with some local officials and two local chiefs.

She also tells him about the arrival of a white man who just checked into her hotel and wants to speak with the search team leader. He is from Port Vila where he operates a small museum and curio shop on the beach. He has come to visit with the Doctor about his search for a lost plane. Mary Jane says he is not someone she asked to attend this meeting. She seems embarrassed that he arrived unannounced, and appears uncomfortable because he is not here by invitation.

The Doctor smiles at Mary Jane and says, "Don't worry, I've been expecting him. Is he alone?"

Mary Jane tells the Doctor the man has checked into the hotel alone.

At the meeting, the Doctor is introduced first to Chiefs, then local officials who are notified of the Doctor's plans. Mary Jane quietly translates the conversation into Bislama for the Chiefs and natives.

After an hour's discussion, Mary Jane explains to the Doctor that these Chiefs have consented to let their lands be searched. She says they will also assist the team by providing natives to serve as bearers and guides.

The Doctor explains that he plans to arrive late tomorrow afternoon at the first Chief's village on the island's north shore. It is at "road's end," and the last village accessible by any kind of vehicle.

Mary Jane has also arranged for a truck to take them to his village, and has asked a local trading post to provide food and supplies they must purchase locally for native labor.

The man from Port Vila wears his floppy Australian hat like a badge of honor, and has remained silent during the meeting.

The Doctor is a trained observer, and, in his view, this man has quite obviously not been trained as a gentleman. In fact, the Doctor suspects he may not even be housebroken. He thinks this man's lack of training by his momma is evidenced by the fact that he wears his hat inside the hotel. His wearing a hat in a lady's presence reveals a lack of discipline by his poppa. Even cowboys from Texas have better manners than that.

When everyone else has left the meeting, the man introduces himself to the Doctor as Fred Folly. For some reason, he now nervously holds his hat in his hand. He explains that he has only today heard of the team's arrival in the islands, and wants to get acquainted and see if he can be of assistance in their search effort.

Folly claims to be an explorer of high mountains and deep valleys, and also the island's foremost expert on crashed American airplanes. His modesty, however, permits him to tell only the most amazing stories that somehow relate to his vastly underrated prowess as a pilot. His extensive vocabulary always begins each sentence with the same word, "I." He generously shares a few more stories of his unparalleled skill as an aviator who, by his own estimate, has more flying experience than anyone else in the islands. His description of daring exploits provides an amusing hour of entertainment for the Doctor.

The Doctor no longer has any interest in the man as an aviator because he knows at least 95 percent of what Folly has just described as his own experiences have been outright fabrications. "If he really is a pilot, good enough to have survived so many actual emergencies, he would have to be at least 150 years old. Even the Wright Brothers are not that old," the Doctor thinks to himself.

Folly continues to present his oral resumé and talks about his exploration of the "bush." Folly has already identified himself as a man of questionable integrity and an undeniable pedigree, so the Doctor turns to leave.

Then Folly brags about discovering several American planes with skeletal remains inside, from which he retrieved certain artifacts. He opens an old haversack and empties it with flair onto a restaurant table.

The Doctor instantly recognizes human bones and teeth. This grisly collection of watches, pistols and dog tags is obviously from more than one casualty. He asks Folly, "Are these from American planes and is anyone else aware of this interesting collection."

Folly explains, "I've got a lil' museum fer tourists who sometimes like to take h'm a suv'nir that's a lil' different."

The Doctor inquires, "What's the price of those dog tags and one of those pistols?"

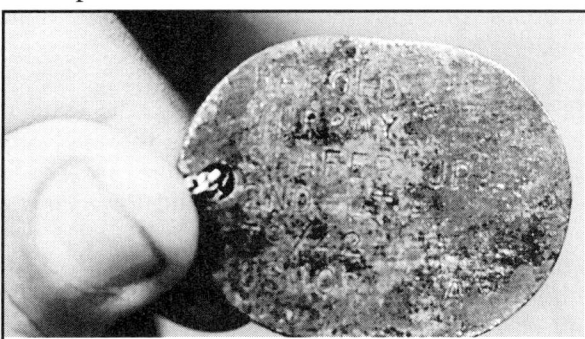

[8-b] ARTIFACTS: This example of a dog tag worn by American pilots now resides in a private museum. Grave robbers, scavengers, souvenir hunters and curiosity seekers collect this type of artifact. It was with the body of an American hero who died at the controls of his fighter plane, along with bones, teeth, personal effects and other assorted treasures for a heartless man's "museum of fine art." He offered them to us for a "reasonable" price, but we were unwilling to participate in his transgression against humanity. It is also the reason we fired him and his cohorts from our search team. We are at least kind enough not to give his real name, address and phone number out of common decency to his family. This is far more courtesy than he showed the family of this American hero.

Search for the Lost Blacksheep

Folly graciously offers to let them go "...for a mere pittance." He indicates that the dog tags are normally worth about $1000 on the black market, and the pistol is worth at least $1500."

Folly explains that he and two partners are in their third year of collecting artifacts. He claims to be showing a profit already and is looking for an additional partner. Since the Doctor's search team will be finding new planes, he is certain his two colleagues would be willing to go along with adding the Doctor as a full partner.

As the Doctor looks through the photograph collection, he realizes this is definitely the threesome he heard about at CILHI. He asks Folly, "Can you lead us back to those planes?"

"Well mate, I just hap'n ta be free an' kin work right now."

The Doctor agrees to hire Folly to take him back to the planes he has already looted. He makes it clear, however, that any work with the team will be under the Doctor's direction and limited to photographing the wrecks. The search team needs each wreck's location, photograph and tail ID number to accurately plot positions on a team chart for future reference and to provide positive identification.

The Doctor asks Folly, "Will it be possible to meet with the other partners in this enterprise? If I'm going to consider being a partner in absentia, I want to know who the partners are, and if we'll all be able to work well together in this business venture."

Folly tells the Doctor, "They're both out'a the country fer now; but, if there's 'nother search later, I'll see if I kin 'range it."

It is decided that Folly will leave early tomorrow morning to photograph wreck sites from which he liberated artifacts.

Folly graciously invites the Doctor to join him in the bar; but alas, the Doctor is tired. He declines Folly's most generous offer, and passes up an opportunity to watch Folly exhibit his unlimited failure and minimal knowledge of social graces.

The next morning, the Doctor assigns Tom and Harry to buy food and rice for their first trek into the bush. By late morning, the team is loaded into another truck, which seems even worse than the one they came into town on yesterday. As they start the long trip north to "road's end," the Doctor surveys the surroundings like Bennett and Bowden did generations ago.

The ride over pitted and muddy roadway is an experience. Native children stare in awe as the truck loaded with white men and supplies navigates around cows and chickens grazing in the roadway. Travel is frequently halted by natives who have never seen so many white men, and the team stops several times to talk with them.

This lovely and serene island seems to be at peace with the entire world. The Doctor wonders where he could ever go for a vacation that will compare to the tranquillity of these pearls of the Pacific.

Everywhere the team looks there is evidence of a war that engulfed this island paradise half a century before. The remaining Quonsets are now homes and trading posts on the town's outskirts. The old fuel storage facilities have been converted into water tanks, irrigation systems and catch basins for rainwater used for washing clothes. Bomb dumps and explosive ordinance depots are scattered about the landscape. Some are now houses, while others are used for farm equipment storage. One dirt-covered explosive storage igloo near the narrow roadway is now a covered bus stop for the few children who attend local schools.

The old headquarters buildings in Luganville are used as municipal offices. On the outskirts of town, other command headquarters buildings are now village meeting halls and small local government offices. Local missionaries have converted some of the better buildings and larger Quonsets into small churches and convents.

Bridges that were hastily thrown over creeks and rivers have received little, if any, attention in the last fifty years. Many have been in constant use, most without guardrails, and none have two-way traffic. As the truck passes over some rickety old bridges, clear waters reveal many colorful tropical fish below them. Other river bottoms are still littered with equipment discarded by allied forces. Men who once filled these oceans and skies as combatants used these rivers and beaches for rest and recuperation. The river's clear waters and reflected hues from moss-covered relics make an interesting study of a discarded time.

[8-c] HIGHWAY ONE: This maintenance-free road has an indigenous coral base. You can see ruts made by trucks that haul supplies to northern villages. We took this route to the vicinity of Bennett's crash area. It was the beginning of the long journey home for Lt. Bennett. One must travel through dense jungle when leaving this highway.

As they proceed northward, it becomes obvious that few, if any, vehicles travel along these now deserted roadways. The Doctor sees the eastern shoreline where small craft and PT boats were once parked, always alert for another sneak attack. In every quiet lagoon, PBY Catalinas from Black Cat squadrons of flying boats were kept ready for immediate take-off – always prepared for attack against any enemy, whether it be a marauding Japanese ship, or the open ocean ready to swallow a downed American pilot and his crew.

The jungle is held back by sections of PSP matting that once covered airfields. It has been converted into gates and corral fences surrounding small farmhouses and barns to keep out ever-present goats and pigs.

The truck soon passes Matevulu College, a grade school and middle school for Luganville children. No children from mountain villages attend this school and some villagers rarely, if ever, come this close to civilization.

THE TURTLE BAY EXPERIENCE

The truck slows to a crawl as they start across a narrow bridge. A following cloud of dust overtakes them; and, as they emerge, the Doctor feels he has entered a new dimension of reality. He senses the memory of larger-than-life Marine guards who await their arrival at the other end of this bridge. As the truck strains past remnants of an old guard shack, the Doctor imagines Bennett and Bowden standing here.

From this exact spot, young Marines once challenged all visitors to this base. The Doctor expects to hear an order to "Halt!", followed by a terse, "Out'ta the truck, Buster!" Next a yelped, "Corporal of the Guard," followed by a walk with fearless men who could face an attacking armada of the Imperial Japanese Fleet – guards from another time who personally hold back enemies with one hand while they "hand feed the Hounds of the Baskervilles" with the other.

The Doctor is tired, and jet lag has not been diluted with rest. He shakes his head to clear away these images from the past. For some strange reason the truck suddenly stops with an overheated engine. The driver informs the team they must wait here two hours while the overheated truck rests.

The Doctor wearily climbs out of the old truck and tells Tom and Harry he is going to walk around and stretch his legs. They head for the nearest tree to grab a catnap.

In preparation for this trip, he read Boyington's and Walton's books and interviewed several "Blacksheep." All those stories of MAG-11 and the VMF squadrons' adventures began here.

The Doctor has an overwhelming urge to walk through an opening in underbrush ahead, and soon finds himself at the entrance to a deserted and abandoned airfield once known as Turtle Bay Fighter Strip Number One. This is the beginning of a long afternoon that will leave him with a strange sense of deja vu that he has never before experienced.

As he slowly walks up the old roadway, the Doctor seems to sense someone watching his every move. So far, the someone he cannot see has not challenged him but actually seems to sanction his presence. Perhaps he is being observed and tolerated as a visitor. Although he is not a superstitious man, he feels the hair rise on his neck.

The Doctor has a strange sensation as though some unseen escort is giving him a guided tour into the past. Even before the tour begins, there emerges a feeling of kinship with a guide dressed as a young Marine.

Somehow the Doctor feels rather than hears unspoken instructions, "If you'll not stare directly at anything, you'll be allowed to look beyond your dimension into a higher level of understanding."

Then a new sensation seems to rise from an area of rusting steel just off the roadway. Walking by, he recognizes it as a long ago defensive position described by the General. It is the quad-mount machine gun installation that tracked every passing plane. Strangely, it seems new and recently oiled.

The Doctor senses the presence of men still guarding these skies against all attackers. For practice, they track departing planes and arriving intruders into this domain.

The Doctor is startled and ducks as a flight of large birds takes off from where Corsairs once made formation departures. These birds are like the ghosts of F4U's as they pass only twenty feet above his head. They climb, then make a graceful turn to the left over the lagoon and disappear to the north as they soar up to meet angels.

[8-d] TURTLE BAY R & R: A place where pilots swim, relax and fish during their periods of rest and recuperation after a six-week combat tour. The white, untarnished beaches and the shallow turquoise waters are clear and calm. Located just outside the Dallas Hut living quarters, the men of Turtle Bay saw this every morning, and, for some, on the last morning of their lives.

Down to the right, at water's edge, the Doctor seems to see new fighter planes being unloaded from the rafts that bring them ashore. Without looking, he senses an aircraft carrier anchored only a mile off shore. Jeeps pull the planes up the hill, then park them in shadows under trees. With practice, the vision becomes clearer. Waiting Marines quickly peel off protective tape and cosmoline preservative.

The Doctor sees the swimming pier and beach, then a ghostly aroma of food drifts from the officers' dining hall. Crushed coral streets meander beneath coconut palms, overrun by grass and underbrush. The Dallas huts are gone, but the Doctor feels their presence and sees where they were placed. Pilots rest and relax between flights under the palms.

The guide seems to be saying, "Over here is the outdoor movie

Search for the Lost Blacksheep

theater that doubles as a church." The Doctor senses a saddened Chaplain who seems to be saying something the Doctor cannot quite hear.

The guide admonishes, "Don't look. Just listen and feel."

Obeying the suggestion the Doctor hears, "...someone is gone from us, with whom we have trained and flown. We will not see him again, but we will not forget him..."

As they move on, the next stop is Mag 11 Headquarters. The building and flagpole are gone, but the white painted rocks are still in place – as though they were painted only yesterday.

From inside MAG HQ, he hears a jumble of voices, and the loudest seems to be saying, "Ah-Ten-Hut!"

Then another voice, "Gentlemen, welcome to the South Pacific."

Not wanting to eavesdrop or intrude, the guide moves on.

As they cross a trail now used only by cattle, the Doctor realizes the General indicated this wide-open area was used for cargo arrival. It is where C-47's unload high priority parts which are needed immediately. One of the Corsairs in the distance is waiting for the new carburetor, and another needs the new propeller.

The ready room for briefing new replacements is just next door. The Doctor hears a muffled briefing from inside the tent, "...I would like for you to take charge of this very difficult part of our training."

And over there is the area where Capt. Robert Shaw supervised aerological operations as his men made their own weather forecasts.

Down this hill, planes are scattered and hidden in "hides" under the largest trees. Right over there is the maintenance area where planes are parked in revetments. Some are undergoing repairs for injuries received at the hands of young pilots who last week didn't even know how to start the engines.

There seems to be an aura around some new planes that look odd because they appear to have bent wings. Many are receiving various types of attention. Some have engine cowlings removed, and what appears to be major surgery is underway. The guide steps aside as a new fighter plane taxis into a revetment and is surrounded by a swirling cloud of dust that settles on everything. As the engine coughs its last breath, the Doctor hears a rattle and clatter as the huge propeller comes to a stop.

As another Corsair prepares to leave, the Doctor hears a battery hum, boost pumps whir, then a starter's whine as it cranks a huge engine. The engine coughs, and a belch of black smoke is followed by a swirl of blue smoke as the engine accelerates into life. As the engine stutters its distinctive sound, a young mechanic leaps onto the wing, and the big fighter slowly begins its long taxi to the runway's end.

Following his guide, the Doctor walks down a ramp area, and they pass two young men. They are wearing leather jackets and yellow Mae-Wests, and carry parachutes on their shoulders. One is old at 25 with a crew cut and sharp piercing eyes, looking as though he just stepped out of a Marine recruiting poster. He seems to be a Captain while his young friend wears shinny new gold bars of a 2nd Lt. on his collar. The youngest has a soft southern drawl that sounds like East Texas, and he is smiling like he belongs in a toothpaste advertisement.

They almost seem to acknowledge this visitor as they pass, but they do not speak. The Doctor thinks perhaps they did not see him, but his guide says, "They know you're here."

The pilots are deeply engrossed in conversation because they are preparing to fly a gunnery practice mission, and nothing else is important to them right now.

In the distance, the Doctor sees a Corsair receiving a mechanic's close attention. The Sergeant is painting something just under the windshield. Although the painting is not quite finished and it is too far away for the Doctor to see clearly, he makes out a few letters. It seems to be "S-U-S-I-E" something. He is unsure.

The Doctor does not believe these are ghosts, yet he is being granted a rare opportunity to visit a reality of memory. The memory of these men will remain here for as long as men study history and write books. They are not illusions, but the memories of young men during an uncertain time of terrifying war, and an airfield that was their last contact with a place of peace. Tomorrow, perhaps, they will take these planes into a combat zone to the north. Regardless of what fate befalls them there, they will return to the serenity of Turtle Bay to rest and relax.

The guide moves over to a Corsair with its tail jacked up. The men working on this plane back away as all six machine guns open fire in a staccato roar. The smell of gunpowder and burning cordite fills the still air. The sweating pilot leans forward in the cockpit and peers through the gun sight. He seems satisfied as he gives a thumbs-up signal to the mechanics. These greasy, shirtless, sweating armorers repair the guns and reload the wings with heavy boxes containing 400 rounds each. The machine guns are receiving final adjustments for a point of convergence where all six .50 caliber guns will focus their fire on the same point ahead. Next week, they will focus on a young Japanese pilot in the skies over Rabaul in the Solomons; and, as these guns return him to his Emperor, he will be welcomed home as a hero.

The Doctor detects a strangely familiar smell back under the trees where a mechanic is repairing the tail of a Corsair that strayed under the guns of a "Tojo Tommy" last week. The repair dope and fabric have a distinctively pungent odor, which many pilots today no longer recognize because this form of repair is as obsolete as the Corsair the young mechanic now works on.

As the guide leads the Doctor out onto a broad expanse of runway, they pause and look left and right before crossing. The crushed coral surface is over 250-feet wide and 5000-feet long. Long ago it was rolled and packed, then oiled and packed again. It has survived the elements and onslaught of the encroaching jungles. It can still be used as an airfield today. As they walk, the Doctor sees a control tower halfway down the runway on the south side, while an old boxing ring and baseball fields are in a clearing on the left.

Warplanes of other ghost squadrons that no longer exist are south of the airfield. The dive-bomber and torpedo bomber methods of attack are no longer used in combat. Young pilots are no longer taught the antiquated strategies of the past, and they no longer practice such methods of delivery. But they will always live here as they did a half century ago.

Parked everywhere under palm trees in the tropical breeze are new TBFs and SBDs, and each squadron has an SNJ/T6 training plane. The SNJs are constantly in use preparing new replacement pilots for the latest combat maneuvers. Each successful combat strike develops new tactics that must be taught to Turtle Bay replacements by flying an SNJ in simulated attacks. All the men here are ready for assignments to engage the enemy at war. Very few seem to be over the age of twenty.

Fuel storage tanks are carefully camouflaged under the trees on the hill. Today they still sit next to the tennis courts of Matevulu College Junior High School where they are camouflaged by a brilliant display of jungle flowers and used as a modern septic sewer system.

The Doctor realizes that, even though he is escorted by the memory of people who lived here, he is still an intruder. He feels the runway gunners' eyes on him as he trespasses into their realm.

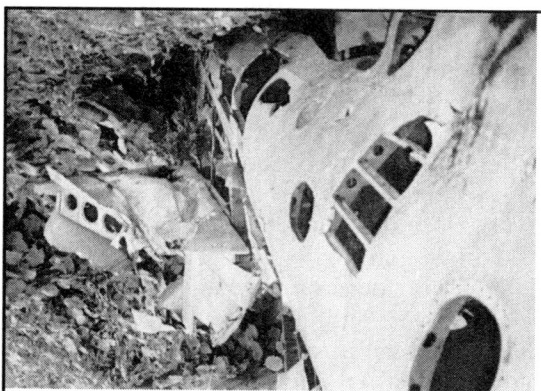

[8-e] AVENGER: The TBM/TBF Avenger is like the torpedo bombers that were stationed in the island campaigns of the South Pacific. When damaged to a certain degree, they were pushed to one side of the airfield and stripped of usable parts. As the war moved toward Japan, these relics were left in the maintenance area of the islands and were quickly claimed by jungle. They now lie as sentinels, awaiting the return of young shirtless, sweating mechanics and sergeants, corporals, and privates who loaded guns and bombs for the next mission.

The guide shows the Doctor a beautiful new TBF Avenger in pristine condition under the trees. Somehow the Doctor understands that this very airplane will always remain at Turtle Bay. In his research, he found reports of an old derelict TBF that was once abandoned and pushed into a ditch where it remains today. It almost seems that, in this plateau of understanding, everything is ageless. For the men and aircraft he has seen during this eerie walk, even time is meaningless.

The Doctor feels a sensation of being allowed to see things as they once were and will always be. He knows these men are not ghosts because even today some are not dead, and the airplanes are not his imagination or just relics. The protective revetments and bunkers shield the planes from attackers who will never come.

As the Doctor walks through the old maintenance area, he carefully avoids eye contact with anything or anyone. He smiles as he realizes what it is to sense, feel and hear on a different frequency than ever before. This is like an old radio station that he listens to for a while; then, as he changes stations, the music is still there, but he cannot hear what he is not tuned into. Never before has the Doctor been allowed to listen to this station because, always before, it was unknown; but now he knows the frequency, and he knows he will be allowed to tune in again, someday.

He clearly hears a clank of tools and mechanics at work in the maintenance area, and the clang of cowlings being removed, then replaced around Pratt-Whitney engines. The engines are being pampered and soothed by young experts who know how to make them purr like kittens. A special relationship exists between a mechanic and his plane. It is on a higher realm to which a pilot is rarely, if ever, admitted. The laughter and language in a maintenance area are unique.

Engineers and pilots are not needed, and their opinions are seldom accurate. The engineer had his chance at perfection when he designed and built the airplane. The pilot is the one who always uses and abuses the plane, then brings it home in need of a mechanic's attention. As certainly as a mechanic cannot understand the fighter pilot's world of combat when he is alone or under attack over enemy territory or over a deep ocean, the pilot will never be able to really communicate with an engine on the same level as a mechanic. It is almost as though two separate ethereal levels exist, if assigned to one level it is best to not intrude on the other.

The Doctor is a chosen guest today, here by approval of these men from the past. He senses he is not here by accident and is not just being tolerated. He is no longer viewed as an intruder, but is accepted as a guest under escort. Even before he can ask a question in his mind, the answer is clearly provided. For some reason, which he does not yet understand, he has been brought here to experience this realm. He knows that everything he has been brought here today to experience happened. He has already learned that he may return and will be welcome. During this walk, he has learned so much already, yet there seems to be infinitely more to know.

The guide stops near the base of the control tower where Ed Mazur is on duty. Thousands of others are at work on the field, and hundreds of airplanes are parked everywhere. Take-offs and landings begin early in the morning and last until late afternoon.

Here the slogans and posters of another time take on a special meaning: "Fly then Fix," "Haste makes Waste," "Loose Lips Sink Ships." The Doctor spends time in reflection and recalls other people, places and things from his research: Boyington's Gang, the Blacksheep, Walton's book, Miller's letters, Crocker's flights, Johnson, McMahan, Snee, Shafer and DeCamp.

The guide knows this visitor is a skeptic, but he has still been allowed to peer through a tear in the portals of time. The visitor has been prepared for this trip through research, yet neither science nor religion can define today's events. Still, this visitor is unafraid, and questions neither his mortality nor his spirituality as he absorbs these senses. The guide allows the visitor to experience a meeting with knowledge of the past not found in textbooks. The Doctor is exposed to actual people and actual events. He strolls through an element of time that continues for the men of Turtle Bay as though no time has passed since these events occurred.

From his vantage point near the runway's edge and close to the control tower, the Doctor sees a long line of S-turning planes as they slowly taxi to the end of the runway. As the planes point their long noses toward the sea, pilots wearing cloth helmets and flying goggles pulled down over their eyes peer at the control tower around their planes' big engines. A light signal from Mazur, and the engine's gallop changes into a throaty roar – the challenge of a tiger on a leash. There is no time for timidity or swagger. Now is the time for young Eagles to take charge and be in command of a machine that will hurtle through the skies at over 400 mph.

Mechanics watch reverently from revetments as they wipe oil and grease from their bodies and tools. This is their pilot, their guns and their plane. Last week, when some of these pilots came to the island, they did not even know how to start the engine. Some had never flown a Corsair. The mechanics patiently showed them which side of the plane to climb up to get into the cockpit, and carefully explained how to start and care for the Corsair's giant power plant.

That is all over now, and this young pilot is about to fly a new plane. He is their charge, and they have more than just a passing interest in him. The young pilot is not yet aware he belongs to these mechanics and they own him. He is the new kid on the block and is driving their plane, not his.

But they also know he is a fighter pilot who must seek out the enemy and fight him alone; and, for him to be successful, he must be allowed to boast and brag a little with the other pilots. Yes, they know he will strut and swagger tonight, and he will stand a little taller in the new shoes of his self-confidence. He will begin to believe in himself and his ability to fly this brute of an airplane.

Very soon now he will be ready for transfer into a combat squadron, but eventually, he too, will return to Turtle Bay. It will be these mechanics he will come to first when he returns. It will be a mechanic who will hear his confession as they lean on the tail after his flight. The young pilot will share his fears about the roughness of the engine and his concerns about the grabbing brake. It will be a dirty face who is always bumming a cigarette that the pilot will come to with his mortal problems. And the kindly old Sergeant will absolve him of today's sins of riding the brakes during landing and over-speeding the engine during takeoff. The mechanic will bestow his forgiveness and give the blessing of yet another flight tomorrow.

At the rising of the sun, he will be permitted to fly again with his sweetheart, and they will chase angels and slide down sunbeams once more. Last week when this airplane came ashore on a raft, it was covered with preservatives and tape. When that was all finally removed, the engine was started for the first time since the ferry flight from the factory.

Only five weeks ago, when this plane arrived at the West Coast Naval Air Station, it was taxied straight to the docks. An hour later it was loaded onto the carrier, and the big ship slipped out of the harbor when the night was dark. Now that it has been cleaned and prepared for flight testing, it will be a replacement for one of the Blacksheep Squadron's losses.

Those Blacksheep pilots seem to go through airplanes and engines like no other squadron. Major Boyington never lets up on new pilots, and he is always after them to shoot better than the enemy, and repeatedly attack fast. He force feeds them on training for new attack formations, then weans them on combat, always at full throttle. Air superiority means to attack faster, higher and more often, and Boyington leads them in their attacks as a team.

They scorch gun barrels and over-boost engines. They fly three and four missions each day and collapse into sweaty bunks at night. The mechanics at the forward base cannot possibly keep up with the abuse to these planes when they fly that much, because combat operations take a terrible toll on planes and pilots. On the other hand, however, their Squadron is just about the hottest thing to ever hit the South Pacific. They may run the guts out of these engines and go through gun barrels like candles in a blackout, but they do more damage to the enemy and his planes than anyone ever thought possible.

This new kid who is test-flying the plane is an eager beaver, who can only think about going north with Boyington. He has a shinny new commission and shiny new gold bars; neither are as old as the new plane he is flying today. At least he is a decent sort from back in East Texas somewhere. He finally got the word he was being assigned to Boyington and VMF-214, and now the mechanics can't seem to get him out of their hair. He volunteers for every flight and is training all day, every day. He acts as though he has a divine appointment to keep and only very little time to get there.

Last night he was after the mechanics to paint a name on the nose of his plane. The paint is still wet this morning and it won't last six weeks; but, if they both get back this way in six weeks, he will probably want a bunch of Japanese flags painted on anyway.

"I'll re-paint the name and do the Japanese flags for free," thinks the mechanic. But for now the kid has parted with five fresh packs of Chesterfields, and fresh smokes are like pure gold around here. Although the young pilot is friendly and always smiling or laughing, the mechanics watch him like a hawk. He is so young he shaves only because the Corps requires him to. He has not been around airplanes long enough to have a gruffness in his voice which comes with having to yell over the engine noise. But that will come with time, if he has enough time left.

The love-hate relationship between pilots and mechanics goes far beyond military rank relationship, and mechanics love a pilot who takes care of his plane. If he does not take care of it, they will growl, murmur and swear at him when he cannot hear. As the throaty roar of the engine fills Turtle Bay valley, the mechanics all turn toward the runway as if a ritual worship is taking place. They watch as the youngster in the new plane puts the spurs to his mount. They coach and cajole him and condemn him at the same time. The kid is a good Corsair driver, but still they watch him as they would a cobra and trust him even less.

One screams, "Stop fishtailing my airplane, kid, you're all over the runway!"

Then from another, "Stop riding those brakes, pal, or you'll have a brake fire and a flat tire to land on."

A third barks, "Back off that power, Junior, and don't over-boost my engine."

And finally, "Watch out for the cross-wind, Bub. I don't have any spare wings or propellers if you ground-loop."

The mechanics all grow quiet as the tail of the airplane comes up and they sense he is committed to flight. If anything goes wrong now, he will join the others who lie in the ocean about a mile off shore – those who were forced to ditch in the water, but, for some reason, could not get out in time and are still with their planes.

As the Doctor watches, he can sense the mechanics' attention as the Corsair lifts a little and the miracle of flight begins. The main landing gear folds backward and disappears as if by magic with a twist into the wing, while the tail wheel folds into the tail. When the doors slam shut over the landing gear assembly, only a smooth lower surface remains where wheels and struts had been. The mechanics turn away from the runway and clean their tools again; the ritual is over for now.

The kid will be back in a couple of hours or so and he will have no complaints because the airplane is in perfect condition. However, if he goes too fast today, he is going to smear those new letters that were painted on the side of his plane last night and this morning. But trying to tell these kids to slow down in a Corsair is like trying to go slow on a Saturday night date. "It ain't never gonna' happen," the mechanics think to themselves.

The guide stops near a tent marked "Operations" and turns to look at the Doctor. A young pilot races into the tent where he makes a frantic report that stuns the other young men. It sounds as though he is saying, "We were pulling up at 5000 feet and his right wing just seemed to buckle, then he was gone."

The Doctor says nothing, but he understands this is the way a morning began long ago.

[8-f] THE BLUE HOLE still exists like it did during WW2. It is a deep, clear pool of fresh spring water about a half mile from Turtle Bay fighter strip. Ancient trees still spread their gnarled branches and are festooned with long vines serving as swings and trapezes for those wanting to rest and relax at the end of a busy day.

The guide leads the Doctor down a dark and lonely trail that was once hammered by a thousand feet as pilots and mechanics walked to and from the Blue Hole. This natural crack in the earth is the same today as it has been for generations. Filled with fresh cold water, it forms a natural playland that almost seems out of place here. The trees are festooned with vines, ropes and cables that young men improvised as trapeze and swings. They have ample vines to swing from, so there is no waiting for a turn at play.

The Doctor imagines some of the men looking toward him as one of the men waves, but no one says anything. They know he is a pilot, and they know why he has come to the island; but, for now, he is not one of them. Not yet.

Suddenly, the guide heads off the trail, and the Doctor struggles to keep up as they move through an almost impenetrable mass of underbrush. "Where are we going now?" he wonders.

Then they seem to be standing beside a demolished Corsair. It is a new plane and the paint still shines, but the engine has been torn off and wings ripped away. The tail is a mangled pile of useless scrap that sheared off during final impact. This new Corsair was attempting to land at the field when a young Eagle misjudged his altitude and airspeed.

Too slow and too low, when just above the trees in a Corsair can be a "snake eyes" roll of the dice. The young pilot lost when he frantically force-fed the huge engine more power than he could control and the plane snapped into a pure "torque roll." It rolled onto its back and passed beyond human control. When it settled into trees, it started to cartwheel and exploded into a gigantic ball of flame. Black smoke billowing toward heaven lit another Gold Star in the Halls of Glory as another fallen "Eagle" returned home.

"It happened only yesterday," the guide seems to say. "The pilot was the swimmer who waved at you. This was his first flight in a Corsair, and his monument no longer bears any resemblance to the sleek Corsairs on the airfield."

Strangely, the Doctor senses that it is almost time to go. Somehow, he knows this visit is coming to an end, and he must move on up the coastal road. It is almost time to begin the search.

The Doctor senses a message from his guide. "This wreck will remain here for generations, and we will not remove it. Someday men will gaze upon this monument and question its purpose. Some will wonder of its contribution to mankind. Only a few will remember the purpose of our sacrifice, and some may question what we stood for. Perhaps, men such as you will try to explain. You have chosen to begin this quest, and you must do it alone. We cannot show you where to look for the answers you seek. The man you seek has met his test and now you must meet yours. You will receive no glory for trying, but we will always remember that you tried. You have accepted the challenge of your search, and the responsibility of the search is your test. When you are in doubt we will always be here. Always. You know where we are and you know how to communicate."

The Doctor asks, "Can I communicate tomorrow? Can others do as I have done today?"

The guide seems to say, "Many can, some will, but very few really want to."

As the guide's image starts to fade, he says, "Don't worry about today having damaged your soul or spirit. We're but a small part of immortality, and we wish you well. Your visit with us today has done you no harm, so farewell my friend and do not give up. Remember, 'Semper Fi.'"

"Yes," the Doctor says, not really to anyone but himself, "Semper Fi... the Promise."

The Doctor shakes his head as if to clear away the remains of a dream, then proceeds with the work he is here to do. He records the

Corsair's number and the TBF's data plate information. He is alone and the guide has left. As he returns to the airfield, there are no planes, no tower, no tents – only a silent ghost town of memory. The history lesson, and the walk through what appeared to be a time warp, has ended.

[8-g] REFLECTION: I was deep in thought with the setting sun as I stood at the end of old Turtle Bay Fighter Strip Number One. I was not alone with my thoughts. I sensed the presence of men who served here over a half century ago – sweaty, shirtless young men who stopped in their toil to remove their hats as they bowed their heads and bid farewell to an old comrade. These young men seemed to occupy a different plane of existence than I – perhaps a time warp. Though no words were spoken between us, their existence somehow seemed real. They gathered around as I began to write a prayer...

As I stand by the sea, and look out at the sun,
I remember the youth, and these men of the gun.

They took a full measure, of life and its fate,
And when that time came, they flew on to a date.

They courted the angels, in a time of despair,
As they chased the sunbeams, on the wings of Corsair.

God, don't be offended, by their clamor and roar,
Just give them a pass, to fly and to soar.

Irreverent at times, impossible at best,
These men of the Blacksheep, have all passed the test.

The Doctor

...and as I finished, I sensed their approval. As I turned to leave, I wished them the best from Chaplain Pat and whispered, "The General said to tell you, he'll, see you soon." I was tired and exhausted, and I may not have gotten it all right. But as I walked away, I got the distinct impression that they had their right arms raised and in the old Marine salute, "Rrouff – Rrouff – Rrouff."

The Doctor reluctantly walks back to the truck knowing he has been among Marine friends. This has been an experience he did not think possible. It has not been frightening, but, instead, invigorating. As he reaches the far end of the runway, he turns back to where a short while ago were hundreds of men and scores of airplanes. Slowly and deliberately he brings up his right hand and holds it in a salute to the men of Turtle Bay. The Doctor knows they are watching, and he senses their approval.

As he walks over a small hill and down to the truck, Tom and Harry come running over and Harry bombards him with, "Where have you been? We've been looking everywhere for you!"

Tom senses something has happened and asks, "Are you okay? You look as though you've seen a ghost!"

Finally realizing there is something different, Harry asks, "Is anything wrong?"

The Doctor smiles, "I only went for a short walk around the airstrip, and yes, I'm fine now. In fact, I seem to have finally overcome the jet lag and my fatigue is gone. I certainly feel stronger and more relaxed than I did when we stopped. And no, Tom, I have not seen a ghost. You know I don't believe in such things."

Tom and Harry both want to explore the airfield and see what the Doctor has seen. But the Doctor speaks quietly and in a lowered voice, "Fellows, at some point in time, you may see what I've seen today, perhaps the next time you pass this way. I hope so. But for now we need to get this search team on the road."

As far as the Doctor knows, Tom and Harry never did get the tour of Turtle Bay.

CHAPTER 9

ROAD'S END – 1988

The Doctor rides in silence for what seems like hours. Traveling in the back of a truck, which has had no shock absorbers since the invention of dirt, is torturous to certain parts of one's anatomy. It does no good to switch positions because that part of your body is also sore. The blessing is you only crash onto those body parts half the time, the other half you're flying around frantically grabbing at anything to prevent being launched into outer space.

As they ride in the silence of their thoughts and the panic of their transorbital insertion, they pass villagers coming down from the "dark bush." The Doctor says, "These natives are referred to as 'bushies' because they live far back in the mountains and rarely, if ever, come into areas of civilization."

Tom and Harry notice that a few have bows and arrows, many have spears, and all have machetes. Most of the men have various size bones in their nose.

Suddenly, Tom spins around and remarks, "I'm certain the native we just passed has a human leg bone in his hand."

Harry, serenely asks Tom, "Which one?" *(meaning "which leg bone?")*

Tom frantically points, "That great big guy we just passed, the one with the long spear." He screeches, "Stop the truck, let's go back and see if he's a cannibal. I'm sure that was a human bone."

Harry speaks with a slow drawl and tries to calm Tom. "Look, Tom, I can have them stop this truck, and you can go back and ask the guy if it's a human bone he's carrying. However, I might point out, if your scholarly observations are correct and it *is* a human leg bone, he must be mighty proud of it if he's wagged it all the way down here from the mountains. He might even be a collector of leg bones."

Tom replies, "Yeah, yeah, stop the truck, I'll go back and see."

Then Harry, in his unflappable wisdom, finally gets through to Tom as he calmly says, "By the way, Tom, if he's proud of it and if he's a collector of such things, he might just want to add yours to his collection. And, pardner, you're gonna' be standing there all alone, arguing with a machete."

The light just starts to dawn for Tom as he asks, "Where are you going to be, Harry?"

Search for the Lost Blacksheep

Without a moment's pause Harry answers, "When your feet hit the road, this truck's leaving, and I'm gonna' be long gone by the time you get to that native."

Tom's interest in human anatomy seems to decline and they don't stop. The Doctor is relieved.

The truck ricochets from one hole in the road all the way to another as it hurtles down the pitted roadway. The Doctor is certain that most, if not all, his internal organs have been dislodged. He sincerely hopes they will grow back to where they were originally attached; but he is sure some will never again function as intended.

The truck slows, then stops, as they pass another group of natives who look only slightly less ferocious than the first. The native driver has just recognized an old relative.

Soon natives, who to the Doctor look less friendly than the one with the leg bone, surround the truck. Some have large tusks from wild pigs that roam the islands in packs – pigs that are about as tame as an Arkansas Razorback in the last quarter of a championship football game with Texas Longhorns. The natives wear them as symbols of their achievements and ability, presumably as warriors. If the tusks are any example of the animal's size and ferocity, they must be just about the same size as a Texas Longhorn.

Tom, who has a very ornate section of dental bridgework, whispers to Harry, "Do you think they collect teeth from the foes they vanquish in combat. I'm permanently attached to my teeth and would certainly hate to lose them."

Harry again puts Old Tom right at ease with his opinion. "Most of the folk in the world with cannibalistic backgrounds do not collect teeth; they just take the whole head."

(For the record: the search team never encountered either a headhunter or a cannibal while in the jungles of Vanuatu. At least no one told them they did!)

The Doctor laughs to himself, "Harry really, really knows how to get Old Tom's attention; sometimes he gets his goat, though."

Most of the natives are wearing their formal attire, which is very close to nothing, when they go to town for a little visit. For eons they have been bare-chested and bare-breasted, which is as normal for them as clothing is for Americans. The men may wear a breech cloth arrangement held in place by a G-string, if they have one. If not, they simply wrap a banana leaf around whatever part of their anatomy they do not wish to bump into a tree with, or feed to a renegade coconut crab, who was born mad and goes on a rampage while the gentleman is asleep on the ground. The jungle has an abundant supply of banana leaves to use for all kinds of purposes.

The ladies' attire is somewhat less complicated and may consist of a G-string if she belongs to a more affluent warrior. If not, a vine may be wrapped around her waist with various ornaments attached in the front, various lengths of grass in the rear. There are not very many ornament shops in the jungle and grass doesn't grow well there, either.

"I wonder if this is an original 'grass skirt,' which grew longer and fuller in 1940s movies?" the Doctor thinks to himself.

The deeper they go into the dark bush, the more primitive tribesmen become. They are now in the "dark bush" where nothing seems to have changed for a thousand generations, give or take one or two. The machete seems to be natives' only apparent modern element of attire. Big natives carry big machetes; little natives carry only slightly smaller machetes, but they all have machetes!

Time, as Americans understand it, does not exist in the jungle and nobody has a watch. There is also no television, telephone, sidewalk, radio or 911 to dial for help.

Houses were left behind in Luganville. Out in the bush, there are only native huts made of woven bamboo and covered with coconut palm thatched roofs. Some have bamboo doors, but all have dirt floors.

The truck stops again and the team talks to some natives from a village which sounds like "Sara." They are blessed with a resident missionary, thank the Lord, from the Churches of Christ.

As they talk with one villager through a translator, they convey their reason for searching the jungle for a crashed airplane. He says there are many crashed airplanes in the "dark bush," and two are only a couple of hours away. He pauses and looks all three Americans over from head to toe.

Tom turns and looks at the Doctor, then silently mouths the question, "Why is he looking at me that way?"

Then the native continues with something that sounds like, "Well, maybe three or four hours for a white man."

The Doctor removes his hat and looks almost straight up to the vicinity where he thinks God might be and says, "Oh boy, I can tell it's gonna' be one of those days."

Upon hearing the Doctor's comment, old Tom starts slobbering again, and even Harry finds a little more than a smile in that one. The Doctor knows they must always go into the jungle with a sense of humor, and laugh when they get scared, because laughter is a common language. But, when Old Tom slobbers, the natives must think he is ferocious because they always begin to back away from him. The Doctor keeps Old Tom slobbering every chance he gets.

The native volunteers to take the team to the airplanes tomorrow or the next day or the next, but the search team has a pre-arranged meeting with a chief in another village. They decline his invitation, thinking they will get to it later. As it turns out, the Doctor will later regret that decision. He should have gone with him then; but, of course, everyone makes a little mistake now and again, and that one was all his.

[9-a] HERE WE ARE a long way from anywhere and very near nowhere. Also very near Lt. Bennett.

Back in the truck, the driver seems to have a new destination that he is absolutely bent on reaching, and very soon. He must think he is driving either a rocket to the moon or a bat out of somewhere else. One loses track of time and speed when racing through the jungles, but the Doctor wonders what the hurry is as the truck cruises at about 50 mph.

"Nice drive," Tom says nervously.

"Great driver," Harry adds. "I wonder how long he's been driving?"

When the truck reaches the top of a small hill, the driver slows down about one-half mph. As they go over the rise and the roadway drops out of sight, the team has the distinct impression of having become airborne, or at the very least, being in a roller-coaster.

The Doctor can see about 35 miles up the northwest arm of the island and all the northeast arm. He can see for miles across the big bay of St. James and St. Phillip, and about a million square miles of ocean – all of which seems to be somewhere in the vicinity of straight down.

He can only take in this vast panorama with his peripheral vision. His straight-ahead vision is locked on an almost vertical cliff from which the extremely narrow roadway has been hacked out, and the roadway seems to be only three, maybe as much as four, inches wider than the truck. The cliff rises vertically to the left of the roadway and at the very top, if one has time to look, he may see the "100-foot-tall trees" that Miller wrote about.

The Doctor misses some of this panorama because he is preoccupied with the left side of the truck and a shower of sparks, smoke and flying rocks. The driver acts like he is perfectly in control and not in the least concerned that his passengers may faint.

To the right, the part of the roadway that the right side tires are supposed to roll on is conspicuously absent. The space beneath the tires seems to drop hundreds of feet "sta-rate down," as Old Tom will later describe it. The view ends abruptly in a green sea of dense jungle far below.

If the brakes fail on this vehicle, we are going to "drill a very small hole in this very large jungle, too," the Doctor says.

At the end of this perilous roadway there is a turn to the right, and the driver does not seem to have noticed it... yet! A *very* sharp turn to the right, and the driver has not begun to slow down... yet! This is at least a ninety-degree turn to the right, the last half of which is accomplished in a broad slide that ends in a cloud of dust of simply unbelievable proportions.

When the truck stops, team members are frozen in their seats as though welded there. They are each holding on to the metal dash and doors with such force that fingerprints will remain permanently imbedded there. The truck floor will almost certainly have to be replaced because of heavy pressure from team members' feet as they subconsciously searched for a brake. As for the seat cushions they were sitting on... what seat cushions?

When the dust cloud subsides, the team staggers or bails out of what must be the scene of a terrible accident. As they check their anatomy for completeness, they notice the driver is missing. They frantically look under the truck and back up the roadway for his mangled and lifeless body. They find nothing. He seems to have been thrown from the truck with such force they will have to search for him in the bush.

Finally, Harry says calmly, "Are we looking for the driver?"

Old Tom is almost in a panic already and jumps right into this one with a voice driven only by adrenaline, and making sounds very similar to Barney Fife. "Are we looking for the driver? What do... Who do you think we are looking for, Harry, God?"

Very calmly, Harry jerks his right thumb over his shoulder to where the dust-covered truck is sitting squarely in the middle of a village. "Something" is standing there, surrounded by squatting villagers.

"Are they praying?" the Doctor wonders.

The "something" seems to be gesturing as any self-respecting, modern day fighter pilot would, using both hands to describe single-handed accomplishment of some aerial feat of daring. This can't be, but there stands a real live ghost!

Well, it turns out not to be a ghost or a ghostly fighter pilot after all, but a man, who looks like he might be Moses delivering "The Ten Commandments" from Mt. Sinai to the natives. But he is not that either. He has all the appearance of an albino – including a white, bushy hairdo and white skin, and he seems to be dressed in white.

"Wait a minute," the Doctor thinks, as he looks more closely. "There can't be any albinos in the tropics."

As the Doctor finally comprehends what he is seeing and before he says a word, he realizes he is looking directly into the open mouth of another albino.

Old Tom realizes, a full second after the Doctor, that the albino is the missing truck driver – covered from head to toe with a liberal coating of powdered white coral dust that the truck created when it skidded sideways into the exact center of the driver's home village.

Harry, in yet another of his many classic understatements, says, "The driver."

Old Tom does a lot of slobbering; in fact, the whole team does. They can't figure out if it's them or the driver who looks so funny. Maybe it's just relief that follows panic. Things get funny when they realize no one is hurt. Thanks to the daredevil driver, the team has finally arrived at road's end, with a grand finale... and "on a wing and a prayer."

As they look around and get their bearings, they notice the natives are not laughing; nor do they seem very friendly.

Tom groans, " Oh, I hope we didn't get here just in time for supper, and I sure hope these guys are friendlier than they look." Then, with a crocodile smile for the natives to see, Old Tom growls at the Doctor in little more than a whisper, "Hey, man, I thought all those books we read said these guys are pygmies? Well, I can tell you, they are getting bigger all the time. Look at them, even the runts are bigger than I am."

Tom is obviously suffering from some deep-seated, emotional, stress-related trauma. It may be originating from somewhere deep within his panic-driven worst nightmare. Probably from very near where the Doctor's spiders live.

Tom says, "I've heard several stories that these very natives, or their very recent ancestors, practiced the fine art of cannibalism until only a few years ago."

The Doctor quietly interjects, "praise God!"

Tom continues as if he hadn't heard the Doctor, "The custom is supposedly still practiced in some remote villages of the dark bush."

Harry adds, "I always heard that cannibals didn't eat until just after sundown, and sundown's still about an hour away."

Tom groans, "Thanks Harry, I really needed you to share that little pearl of wisdom with me right about now. It might interest you to know, I've always wanted to ask someone that question, but I just couldn't find anyone who might know."

The team soon learns that the natives are as concerned about the white men as the white men are about the natives. As they stand in the middle of the jungle in what seems to be a Mexican standoff, the Doctor remembers to thank God for this day. It has been a beautiful day, and he fervently prays it will stay that way. But, as he takes the time to put a postscript on the short prayer, he says, "Just in case everything gets worse from here on out, I sure am glad I have a God to come home to." Then he makes a mental note to be sure that all future team members know how to pray.

A tall slender Chief comes out of a hut and seems to be sizing up the team. He speaks rapidly in a language the Doctor can't even begin to understand and the interpreter seems to have vanished.

"How convenient," the Doctor thinks.

The native Chief gestures wildly and emphasizes every statement with a very long spear.

Tom is back to normal by now and whispers to Harry, " Why does he keep licking his lips while he puts the mean eyes on me?"

As always, Harry is calm and replies in a whisper, "I think he blames you for the dust in his soup and salad."

The Doctor decides it's time for a few gifts, so he carefully digs into his pack for a bag of peppermint candies to share with the children. He finally gets one young boy to come closer to see the candy. The Doctor unwraps a candy and puts it in his mouth to demonstrate what it is. The native children are shy and innocent and have no idea what candy is. So, as the child comes closer, the Doctor puts another one in his mouth. Finally, the five-year-old grabs one the Doctor is holding out and races away to join his companions behind a nearby tree. Soon another child timidly comes forward and holds out his hand; but, as the Doctor hands it to him, he just looks at it. So the Doctor unwraps another and pops it in his mouth. After a few more native children get treats, the Doctor has a mouthful of candy.

Tom purposely asks the Doctor all manner of questions during this exercise. However, the Doctor can only gurgle to answer because, if he takes the candy out of his mouth, the children will do likewise. Tom sure enjoys getting the Doctor in such a predicament.

After he gets home, Tom will do an elaborate pantomime of that day's events, much to the enjoyment of his children and their friends. In fact, he will tell that story a lot; but, invariably, he always begins to slobber as he tells it.

Harry enjoys the children and has a large assortment of "slap bracelets" for them. The natives have never seen such bright florescent colors, and soon every child in the village is wearing one. Then, as if on cue, every lady of the village, young and old, comes over to Harry wanting a bracelet for their ankles. They love the bright colors and are soon parading around the village wearing their new ankle attire – some with one on each ankle.

The Doctor remembers a box of cheap LED crystal watches he has in his pack. He offers one to the Chief, who promptly puts it in his mouth. He is obviously not too impressed with the taste, so the Doctor shows him how to put it on his wrist. The Chief, with the watch strapped to his arm, watches the Doctor warily with a cold glare of indifference. Soon all the village's men are wearing watches, and none of them know what a watch is or how to tell time. The natives excitedly jabber their approval each time the numbers change on the watch faces.

Harry says, "I haven't seen this much excitement since the day Dad brought home our first TV set."

The team will later learn that some natives sit alone on a log and stare at the watch for hours. Some are kept as treasures long after the batteries run down and the watches cease to function. A native has no concept of time. If he needs to go somewhere, he just goes and will get there sooner or later.

The Chief seems to loosen up a bit, and the interpreter soon reappears. As the Doctor speaks, the Chief actually smiles once during the conversation.

"He seems friendly enough for the moment and not too hungry," Tom observes.

The Doctor explains the purpose of their visit and search. He asks if the Chief will help them search the jungle in his territory, and if he will allow them to hire his people to carry gear and act as guides to crashed airplane sites.

The Chief seems genuinely interested in their search for crashed airplanes. He agrees to let them search and says he will hire out his men. He adds that the Doctor may have any of his tree fruit as well as fish in his rivers. His men will guide the team to wrecks and help build campsites. Their labor will cost three dollars per day for each man. This is a reasonable arrangement, and a deal is struck by a shake of hands. The Chief does not understand the handshake.

Tom says," Maybe you can make a better impression on him if you bow or kiss his feet."

The Doctor assures the Chief that, on completion of the search, any unused food or camp gear will be given to him as a gift. This part of the deal makes the Chief happier than a kissed foot, and he beams his pleasure.

The Chief then looks directly at Old Tom and smiles at him.

Old Tom smiles back and mumbles through clenched teeth, "Hey man, I wish he wouldn't do that!"

The Doctor offers to give Tom the floor so he can admonish the Chief to "stop looking at him that way," but Tom declines his recognition.

When the interpreter goes back into a hut with some friends, natives surround the team. They are curious about Tom's clothes, which include a bright red shirt and blue neckerchief.

The Doctor knows the Chief cannot understand a word he is saying, but Tom is not too sure about this. The Doctor decides the time is right to get Tom's goat once and for all.

Speaking in a normal tone of voice, he addresses the Chief as though they are old friends carrying on a usual conversation. "Now, Chief, I know you fellows are cannibals and frequently eat each other."

A glance at Tom shows his mouth agape in surprise, so the Doctor continues. "In the event any of your people get the idea they would like to try some white meat, allow me to offer a suggestion."

Another glance at Tom and it is clear the speech is having the desired effect, so the Doctor continues again. "I will make you a present of Tom, and we can offer him up as a human sacrifice; but, he is so ugly you may not want to eat him."

Tom is stunned because the Doctor has pointed to him during this conversation and he is certain the Chief can understand.

Harry is standing behind Tom and gnawing his knuckles to keep from laughing. He can see that Tom is very near the panic stage by now, as the Doctor continues. "You might want to keep him as a pet while you fatten him up a little. But I must tell you, Chief, he does have a terrible mood when he wakes up in the morning. And be sure to make him sleep outside because he has really bad breath. And another thing, Chief, you probably need to know he is only partially trained so it might be best if you keep him in a cage or even chain him to a tree."

The Chief looks at Tom and back to the Doctor. He nods his head and then smiles at Tom again. Tom is very near apoplexy by now, and Harry and the Doctor cannot hold back their glee any longer.

As their laughter echoes through the jungle, Tom vows to the Doctor and Harry, "You guys may as well get ready for it, because someday and some way I will get even for this."

Even today, when the Doctor and Harry are around Tom, they are on the alert for his revenge. Old Tom will have his revenge someday, and it will probably be spectacular.

CHIEF ROBERT'S HOUSE

Since it will be dark soon, the Chief gives rapid-fire orders to natives gathered nearby. He announces that the team will be lodged for the night in a house near the River Jordan, about four miles away.

The Chief says he will send his men to this house early in the morning, and their search team can begin the first day from there. "Houshimiblong-big fella-Jif-rober-long-reva." This seems to be the address that loosely translated means P.O. Box: "The House which belongs to the Big Chief Robert near the River." Zip Code: "It will be made available for the team to sleep in tonight."

Everyone knows where the hut is, or so it seems. Evidently, this delightful little grass shack is in a picturesque setting on the banks of the River Jordan. The villagers all understand the team will be spending the night there, and when, "Sunhimi comlong revabinbi wego longtop." This apparently translates into a period of time that means "When the Sun comes up along the River Jordan, which it will do by and by, the team will make their first journey into the mountains."

The team gathers the remnants of the candy and gifts, and once again mounts the truck for a short drive to the river. They warily watch as their driver again mounts his aging steed. Then they leave the Chief and his village in a cloud of blue smoke and white dust.

They travel down what appears to be nothing more than parallel ruts in thick jungle that blocks out the fading sun. This long dark tunnel finally comes to an unceremonious end near a river, and they find themselves in a very small clearing with a darkening sky giving clear signals that their first night in this jungle is about to begin.

The Doctor reminds them of an old Bible teaching about, "When we all get to River Jordan, we will cross over into Glory." Then he adds, "Well, here we are at River Jordan, but if someone 'up there' is about to take a load across the river, I really hope we can wait a little longer."

The truck is soon unloaded and the driver prepares to return to Luganville. The team is glad not to be making a night trip back with this driver. They are left with one native to assist them.

They survey their new surroundings, particularly the grass and bamboo shack that looks forlorn and forbidding. A stale, musty smell of burned copra is almost overwhelming as they peer inside it's black interior. Dampness of old smoke and old mud brings back clear memories of a Port Vila Health Officer's lecture and vivid images of so-called "non-venomous snakes and spiders."

This shack seems to be held together by spider webs, a fact that does not go entirely unnoticed by the Doctor. The vast collection of webs in various geometric designs convinces him that a very large community of giant spiders is about to be disturbed inside this dank entomologist's paradise.

The Doctor is talking to himself when Harry asks, "What are you murmuring about, Doc?"

The Doctor replies, "I really *do not* like spiders, Harry."

[9-b] FIVE STAR INN: On the first night of the first trip we stayed in "housblongrobert." Dear Mom, having a great time. Made some new friends today. No, Mom, I don't think he is a cannibal. He has given us a nice house to stay in. Running water – about a mile away. Nice view – about ten feet. Great nature trails – when we hack them. Lovely smells – burned coconut. Charming neighbors – about one ga-zillion spiders. Snakes? Naww – haven't seen a one, today. Write soon Mom. Address? – Hhmm, I'll have to get back to you on that Mom.

Chief Robert's hut is about 15-feet wide by 20-feet long and is constructed of bamboo poles tied together with vines. Woven split bamboo siding covers its windowless walls. The coconut tree thatch roof is patched in many places with large banana leaves. Its floor is composed of designer dirt, except where roof leaks provide a modern mud motif. Architecturally sound, it seems to be a simply amazing feat of engineering. Native huts all appear to be assembled in such a way as to prevent invasion of both light and circulation. Inside, the residue of a thousand fires built on its dirt floor correlates with a noticeable lack of a chimney. Sanitary amenities are lacking but are amended by many nearby trees. This chateau shows signs of having been built in about 1492!

The Doctor's decision is swift and certain: he will sleep in a sleeping bag under a tent tonight. As he turns to walk out of the hut, he redesigns the four-foot high, narrow doorway with his head. When the kaleidoscope of stars subsides, he starts to build a fire about twenty feet away from the hut. During this exhibition of his superior Boy Scout skills, Tom and Harry stow their gear inside the hut in case of a sudden rain.

The remaining native is obviously impressed as he squats on his haunches about twenty feet away and watches the Doctor with impassive interest. When the very small fire dies out, his attention seems drawn to a vigorous wrestling match between the Doctor and a reluctant tent. He is perhaps moved as he bears witness to the Doctor's survival in this battle-to-the-death with a tent that appears to be quite dead.

The victorious team leader again directs his attention to ashes and burned matches but little in the way of a meaningful fire. (Even Smoky the Bear would be proud of this display of pyrotechnics.)

Finally, the fire is beginning to vigorously burn paper, leaves and a twig or two. Seizing this opportunity, the native, camouflaged in smoke, saunters over and picks up the single piece of wood that seems to be burning. Mumbling, he wanders into the hut with the burning branch that the Doctor is sure he will use to burn it down.

Knowing this will kill all the spiders, the Doctor smiles in complete agreement. Maybe the native is curious and wants to see just how big the occupants really are, so the Doctor ignores him. Soon the native is back. This time he drags the now harmless tent carcass into the hut's darkness; "probably to bury it," the Doctor mutters.

Five minutes later, the Doctor stares in amazement as the entire hut fills with billowing smoke.

Harry advances a theory that the native may be offering up the tent as a burnt offering sacrifice.

Old Tom finds that possibility rather amusing, but the Doctor does not since he had no other protection against elements.

With smoke pouring out of the single doorway and seeping through the walls and thatched roof, the hut must be blazing furiously. From inside the hut, the native appears bathed in putrid smoke and looks like a heavenly visitor as dense smoke even seems to rise from his bushy hair.

The native then takes the Doctor's sleeping bag inside. Consumed with the thought of no tent or sleeping bag, the Doctor investigates. This time he stoops to enter and, through clouds of smoke, he sees that the native seems quite at home and very content, sitting on a log holding his hands over an open fire.

Harry says, "Oh, I see we are having hands for dinner."

The native grins, and in the darkness of the smoke filled hut, there appear two large white eyes perched above a toothy grin.

Now ready for conversation, the native mumbles to himself, "Yumi cuk bimbi Kae kae." He places pots of water near the fire and becomes a picture of domestic tranquillity. He alternately mumbles for a while then repeats his earlier phrase, "Yumi cuk bimbi Kae kae."

Harry begins to laugh and Old Tom starts slobbering again.

The entire scenario finally gives way to a hilarious insight into native life in Vanuatu's jungles. By his actions, he invites them to move into the hut and out of the rain that will start in a few minutes. "Gentlemen, a nice warm fire in this hut will provide all of the heat and light we will need."

He fails to mention that a choice of flavors is available in the smoke they will breathe all night. This diet is particularly abhorrent to spiders and snakes. When exposed to this form of environmental pollution, they surrender the hut and run for the nearest jungle.

It seems to concern the native that anyone in his right mind would sleep outdoors with wild animals and other creatures. It might be of immense interest to him to know that many "civilized" white men do such strange things. But with a perfectly good hut and almost all the comforts of home readily available, he may have some difficulty understanding these white men who seem to lack enough sense to come in out of the rain.

As soon as they get moved inside, it promptly begins to rain. Big time rain!

For the rest of his time with the team, this young native is referred to as "George," and they often hear him struggle with the word "George." Before the search is over, he will become known and referred to as "George," even by other natives.

In the smoke-filled hut, the team attempts to communicate with George and surprise themselves more than him. George uses words in his pidgin language along with hand signals and facial expressions. He continues to repeat the same phrase, "Yumi cuk binbi Kae kae."

Tom, Harry and the Doctor struggle with this mysterious chant until they finally get its meaning. They begin to realize their first lesson of the evening in humility.

The Doctor laughs as he tries to interpret for Harry and Tom, and it comes out this way. "You gentlemen have come half way around the world, to conquer this jungle. Perhaps the best way to impress us with your skills as campers is to do your cooking inside, out of the evening rain. By doing so you will warm this lovely bungalow, and all of the charming little spiders, snakes, bugs and assorted creatures will leave. You will stay warm and dry, and we can talk about how best to prepare a flying fox or a bat for the hot evening meal. I do eat food like you do. Also, such an intelligent decision will discourage the inevitable gathering of mosquitoes around warm-blooded animals such as we are. They like to eat about this time of day, you know."

"Pretty smart for a guy who doesn't even wear clothes," Tom says. Tom is a man of unique character with a very dry sense of humor that often keeps Harry and the Doctor in convulsions.

[9-c] SUPPER FARE: Natives think bats and rice on a banana leaf are a magnificent meal after a long day in the jungle. You can see one hanging on a limb held by an adventurous Tom.

Soon George has dinner prepared, and the team is amazed at the aroma that fills this jungle hut. It almost reminds them of mother's home cooking back in America. They laugh at themselves as they eat fillet of cold beans over hot rice, and what a feast it is! The food is dipped onto a fresh banana leaf by the native cook's dirty fingers. The hot rice quickly warms the cold canned beans, and steaming coffee from a canteen cup is superb. In his haste to drink hot coffee, Tom burns his lip on the metal cup and he is thrilled. The MREs will keep until later.

Harry tries to get George to say, "Coffee is served, gentlemen. Hand picked by Juan Valdez."

The team is ready for a bath and bed, but their pantomime becomes more like a comic opera. The dust-covered actors try to convince George of their dire need for a bath. George appears unfazed by their efforts.

Unable to communicate with him, they become lost in their attempts. Suddenly, Old Tom is on the floor in a fit of laughter while Harry is holding onto a wall doing the same.

The Doctor becomes frustrated in his efforts to establish contact with George and finally gives up. In desperation he leans over to Harry and begins speaking some sort of pig Latin derivative. His words of wisdom sound like something out of an old Red Ryder and Little Beaver comic book.

Gleefully Tom relates the Doctor's words to Harry, "Hey, Harry, You tell'um native we wantum bath. He tell'um us way to running waters. We wash'um good and smell'um better."

Between fits of laughter and streams of tears, the Doctor and Tom decide that with 22 years of higher education, five degrees, 4 years of Chiropractic College, and 2 years of internship, they are absolutely helpless. Their skills in the language arts are seriously lacking, and they are now certain this little guy is in serious doubt as to their sanity.

So, in this den of spiders and bathed in smoke, they climb into sleeping bags; and, like Bennett and all the others in the jungle, lay down to sleep in the arms of their Lord. They realize they are not alone, but who could know what is in store for them next.

They are awake by 5 a.m., feeling well rested and rapidly recovering from jet lag. George is preparing breakfast of hot coffee and huge thick crackers. These waterproof crackers, referred to by the natives as "bis-kit," are similar in hardness and taste to a dog biscuit. The team is certain they will not enjoy this breakfast. They are also certain that no cook on earth could have intentionally abused human food in this fashion.

As he turns the bis-ket over in his hands, Tom says, "It may be a combination of rock and bone."

Harry adds, "and it may be a leg bone, Tom."

Quietly observing their dining skills, George slips into the teacher role again. Perhaps his thoughts are, "I am becoming very concerned about you civilized white men. A person with even minimal IQ should know one of these large "bis-kets" is a complete meal. They are, of course, prepared thick and baked hard to protect them against night dampness. They are best eaten after dipping in hot coffee or powdered milk, much like you Americans dunk your donuts. Once softened they are quite tasty when taken with a sprinkle of sugar or salt. They are particularly good with hot soup or beans. And so, gentlemen, as we say in French, 'Bon Appetite.'"

Following George's example, they dip bis-kets into their coffee to soften them. The blob that emerges is large, hot and also soft enough to eat. Harry, the Doctor and Tom agree they are going to have to watch this little guy very closely.

MT. WIMBO

At about 7:30 a.m., the Chief, true to his word, sends the men to guide the team. As the natives stand, talking in their language, the search team just looks at each other and shakes their heads. They are unable to understand the language at all!

Finally, George comes to their rescue and says something like, "Dokta spoz yumi broer blong yu wego longreva. Binbi cumlong weembo. Man hemiblong jifrober hemikum. Wekaekae weslep. Wego longtop plenhemi faldown bird blonghemi kilum ded. Armblong hemibrok spozwego."

Putting their heads together, the team is certain this means, "Well, Doctor, you gentlemen seem to be through with your morning tea. Do you suppose you and me could just stroll along this here river for a ways? Assuming that will meet with your approval, by and by, we will come to a small mountain, which we refer to as Mt. Wimbo. We will be met by my step-cousin third removed and a few of his colleagues."

[9-d] NATIVE TRAVEL GUIDES: The native labor we hired when we searched for Bennett's crash site. Immediately behind them is the entrance to the dark bush, where they live in huts made of woven bamboo and thatched roofs. They lead a primitive life without education or the modern conveniences we call civilized. The natives we met were all friendly and gentle folk who were as amazed at us as we were with them. They speak neither English, French nor German, but have their own dialect known only as "language." It can be translated into a style of pidgin language, then French and English – a very complex but necessary mechanism for communication. None can read, write, spell or count.

They interpret his further communication to mean, "He is, of course, married and one of his five wives is the daughter of the village Chief who is really a very nice guy who is semi-retired. He is about seven feet tall and carries a three-foot-long machete in one hand and a six-foot-long spear in the other. We refer to him as Chief Robert, but since you are our friends you may call him Sir. As you are aware, these most elegant accommodations you enjoyed last evening represent one of his many property assets. They were provided to you as a courtesy of this very fine gentleman. When we arrive there, we will make evening camp, and entertain you with war stories.

"On the following day, one of our friends will lead you on a little mountain climbing to the top of Mt. Wimbo. Upon reaching the top of this small hillock, you will presumably find an aircraft that crashed long ago. I am of the firm opinion that this plane is of WW2 vintage that you so ardently seek. It has fallen among trees in the forest and has one wing broken off. If it were a bird, of course, it would be quiet dead. And now if you gentlemen will be so kind as to pick up your pitifully small packs, my friends will all think you are ready to go. These nice fellows with me will bring along all of rest of the assorted junk that you have seen fit to bring with you. Shall we now proceed?"

The team finds a good sense of humor indispensable. Well rested and freshly fed, they are ready to tackle the first day of a long trek. They travel along a narrow jungle trail where one or two swamps and a couple of mud seas break the monotony of the deep bush. By the time they arrive at the River Jordan, each trekkie has a walking stick.

When used by a skillful swordsman, these sticks can fend off spiders, snakes and rogue elephants. An unskilled user will tend to fall on them and inflict various injuries, which may be bragged about later as "battle scars." And thus, appropriately equipped, the search team courageously demonstrates their leadership by leading the way across the shallow and seemingly tame river waters. As they step into ice cold waters, which must have spent last night as an ice cube in the mountains, they are chilled to the bone. But the search team continues to exhibit their resolve as cold water gets deeper and deeper. Soon Tom, who is in front, reaches a point about one-third of the way across where water is about four-feet deep and the bottom is covered with round and very slick river rocks.

[9-e] LOW WATER: River Jordon is only a small creek by Texas standards, but don't bet your life on it when the rain begins.

While using his walking stick to maintain his balance, Tom just disappears! As he goes under he lets out a yelp, which the Doctor interprets to mean something like, "Shark!" However, it is nothing to be overly concerned about. Tom has simply reached the permanent riverbed that is about 20-feet deep and very clear. Harry is certain Tom is playing submarine because of all the bubbles, some of which seem to contain unintelligible words. The Doctor can see Tom standing on the bottom with bulging eyes, holding his stick up so that it protrudes exactly one foot out of the water.

Later Tom excitedly explains that he was standing on the river bottom holding his stick up so we could find him. After Tom surfaces, Harry retells this story with great delight.

Safely on the other side, the three adventurers collapse on the bank to catch their breath. As they lie there, panting, they behold an almost bizarre vision. The sight of ten heavily loaded natives, apparently walking on the surface of the same river the team just walked across the bottom of, attracts more than a little of their attention. When the completely dry natives arrive, they see open-mouthed amazement on the American's faces.

The search team seems impressed by natives skilled at walking on water while carrying heavy loads. George, the native with the two-word vocabulary, which the three white men can understand, tries to explain. "Yumiwok longhea!"

Why of course! Tom could easily understand this, and Harry agreed, so they translate for the Doctor. "Gentlemen, be not dismayed and despair not. As you may have noticed our island paradise is composed of hard granite-like stone that is almost impervious to river erosion."

To emphasize Tom's dialogue, George is tapping the granite river bottom with his walking stick. It seems to be only two inches deep at that point.

Tom continues to interpret for George, "But, alas, we also have sand stone which is quite susceptible to erosion and the river's persistence. Therefore, an astute traveler must always note the presence of two large piles of rocks on either side of a river. We are by your standards illiterate and backward because we cannot read, write, spell or even count. However, you may assume piles of rocks to be an unwritten sign that announces a shallow river crossing. As you have just noticed, water upstream from these rock piles is only ankle deep. On the downstream side, as you have just experienced, a dummy may expect to find the sandstone bottom washed away. This hole is commonly about fifteen-feet deep, and they are frequently littered with bones of those who would presume to lead us through our own jungles. And now that we all understand just who is leading whom, shall we proceed?"

The Doctor scratches his scraggly beard and mumbles to himself, "Tom and Harry are so perceptive to native sensitivity. Don't you just love folks like that?"

The temperature soon increases to what is only slightly less than incredible; a little later it cools down to a bearable 110 degrees – in the shade. As the team walks for miles over rocks, more rivers, and about half the island's topography, they are thinking about taking their first break. By now, of course, the Doctor has become skilled at simply trying to stay alive while Tom and Harry are just trying to keep their leader in sight.

As if also able to read their minds, George announces, "Spell." This word seems to mean, "Let's rest a spell."

George probably interprets the responding grunts and groans as meaning, "Thank you, Jesus."

George graciously waits for them to catch up, and the three weary travelers collapse into personal states of semi-coherent consciousness. They are in the middle of a small coconut grove, so the natives climb the trees and cut down fresh coconuts. They deftly open them with two licks from a very sharp machete. With the top thus removed, the cool, fresh coconut drink is truly "a pause that refreshes."

The team soon finishes off about a dozen of these sugar free drinks as they watch the natives practicing what seems to be some ancient tribal ritual. The natives neatly slice a spoon shaped sliver from the side of green coconuts; then strike the skull-sized (and shaped) coconuts in half with a single well-placed blow from their machetes. Using their spoon, they eat whatever is inside. George saunters over to the visitors and demonstrates how to eat the inside of a (gulp!) coconut. Really very tasty and filling, it also replaces lunch. With mangoes and papayas for desert, a few of life's vital signs seem to return to the exhausted team. After this welcome pause, the Doctor wanders over to the river to brush his teeth. When he returns, everyone is waiting and he tosses his toothbrush and toothpaste into the medical pack.

The Doctor also puts away his eyeglasses for protection. They are already useless and covered with mud, sweat and tears; but this would be a terrible time to break them. The Doctor is unable to read anything smaller than a gigantic billboard without glasses, but at least he can manage to talk without them.

After a dozen river crossings and several hours of sweating, it becomes painfully apparent that something is going to have to be done about a rather severe case of "raw" that the Doctor has developed in the cleft of his entire posterior.

The Doctor has been warned about dangerous infection of open sores in the jungle. It feels as though this problem area is glowing in the dark, and the Doctor is certain he will be unable to bear this personal torture for much longer. It feels as though it will most certainly require immediate treatment. If untreated, the entire area may have to be amputated in another ten minutes or so.

As he calls for a "spell," the Doctor blindly gropes around in his pack for the white tube of antibiotic, a powerful creme guaranteed effective if used liberally and promptly. An appropriate application may even preclude the use of a sling, so the Doctor's haste is certainly justified. Finally, he locates the elusive tube and rescues it from the clutches of the medical pack.

The natives sit transfixed as they watch the white Doctor lower his pants and underwear. The Doctor squeezes a liberal portion into his right hand. Then, from a perfectly natural position of balancing on both knees and left elbow he applies the treatment with gusto. As the paste goes onto the severely reddened target area, the Doctor lets out a huge sigh of relief, "Aaaaaahhhhhhaaa!"

After they get home, Tom will tell this part of the story much better than the Doctor does, and while telling it, he will howl with laughter as he animatedly and graphically describes the drama to anyone who will listen. But, alas, only this edited version will make it past censors.

To hear Tom tell the story, "the Doctor suddenly begins to moan, 'Oh, No!' As he sits straight up from this glamorous position, his eyes are pools of disbelief. With his mouth open in dismay, he feels as though a variety of his body parts are ablaze. His body is tensed in reaction to pain as his feet fly straight out. The Doctor already knows the agony of this defeat is from a handful of Pepsodent® toothpaste, not antibiotic creme."

At this point in the story, tears begin to stream down Tom's face and he screeches, "Now the Doctor makes a grab for his pants in an attempt to pull them up."

With great elaboration, he describes the Doctor's 100-yard dash to a nearby river. Then Tom gets down on his hands and feet to demonstrate how the Doctor looks when he abandons the idea of pulling his pants up as he trips over them in his dash for the river. Tom gleefully imitates the yelp of a kicked dog and attempts to show how the Doctor looks as he frantically tries to run on his hands and feet. Tom's description of the Doctor's very red posterior, sticking straight up in the air, covered with gleaming white toothpaste, frequently needs a translator.

Tom says, "The spectacle looks like a coconut crab on a chain gang." However, by this point in the story, Tom notes, "My peals of laughter are only matched by the Doctor's hoots of agony."

Of course, by this time in Tom's dissertation, the listener will no longer be able to understand him, as he will degenerate into yet another orgy of slobbering and laughter.

After returning to the states, when the Doctor calls Tom on the phone, he always begins the conversation with a question, "Hey, Tom, have you got any Pepsodent®?" Tom always knows who's calling and howls with laughter.

A year or two later the Doctor conducts an experiment in a conference hall filled with hundreds of other doctors. Wanting to demonstrate his suspicions of Tom's mental instability, the Doctor waits until a deep discussion of mental health and emotional disorders is well underway. Innocently, of course, the Doctor leans over and quietly says to Tom, "I have to go out and brush my teeth, could I borrow some of your toothpaste?"

Tom's face muscles clench tight as he murmurs through gritted teeth, "All I have is Pepsodent®, watch where you put it."

Ready for this, the Doctor replies, "No problem, Tom, my room has a fire extinguisher in it."

As anticipated, Tom degenerates into depths of madness. His howls of laughter completely overwhelm him. Unable to maintain his professional decorum, he has to leave the conference hall. As he does so, about 800 sets of glaring eyeballs follow his departure.

But of that day in the jungle, Tom will swear he saw smoke and fire arising from the shallow river.

The Doctor claims, "It was only a few bubbles."

As Tom's self control becomes history again, he cries, "Yeah, but you looked as though you were biting bubbles."

Tom is usually primed for laughter by this point as he describes the natives' reactions. He puts on a solemn face and vows they were totally mystified by the reactions of the white man who came to the jungle so he could sit in a river.

Later, in a Dallas restaurant, Tom tells this story to some colleagues.

The nice folks in the next booth share the Doctor's thoughts about Tom, "I can tell – they think old Tom is going mad!"

They press on after the fire is out and finally reach Mt. Wimbo. They easily decide to make camp by the river at the base of a nearly vertical cliff of moss and trees, because that is exactly where the exhausted team collapses.

There are fish at least 18 inches long in the river. George walks up while the team is admiring them. He points to the fish, rubbing his belly as he says, "Honkry?" The three white men are so tired they can only nod. George snaps an order to the other natives.

One native chops down a small bamboo stalk with his machete, strips its branches, then sharpens one end into an evil looking spear point. He holds it in the open flame until it is tempered into a viscous looking weapon that won't be affected by dirt, rocks, scales or bone. He also chops a short length of vine that he takes with him as he meanders down to the river. He only weighs about 110 pounds, but within a few minutes he triumphantly marches back into camp with at least sixty pounds of fish on the vine – one for each native and team member.

[9-f] GROUP THERAPY: Today's native meal is "rice and something." Yesterday it was "rice and something else." Tomorrow it will be the delightful "rice and what's left." Served "piping hot on individual banana leaf." Fresh, of course, and eaten with the finest "polished fingers." The drink of the day is "fresh coconut milk," served *"en husk." Or one may choose to drink the ever-tasty, muddy-water milk shake served "on tap." Attire is formal... hats optional.*

The fish are wrapped whole in banana leaves gathered by other natives. A small stick holds the assembly together. The leaf-wrapped fish is then laid in an open fire and cooked for about twenty minutes. The old standard rice is prepared in boiling water pots. The baking fish has an absolutely unbelievable aroma. When unwrapped, the fish and rice make a superb meal with no fat, salt or other additives. The rice is simply piled on a banana leaf and provides sufficient calories after a long day's march, and the baked fish is so tender it falls apart when eaten... fish eyes optional. This search team may never again eat fish as tasty as those served on a banana leaf in the jungle that night.

The first village Chief has cordially sent Chief Robert a message that Americans are in his neighborhood. Soon after camp is set up, they receive a royal guest as Big Chief Robert comes to their campsite. He really is over six-feet tall and so is his spear. The search team learns he is a very friendly gentleman who responds very nicely to "Sir."

Natives build a standard bonfire and talk for hours in the several dialects of their language. Since Chief Robert and George are related, they talk vigorously about these white men's super skills. The Chief casts a knowing glance and patronizing nod toward them as George describes their jungle skills at jumping over small rocks and leaping over little logs – at least this is how the team chooses to interpret the dialogue.

About 8 p.m., bird-sized mosquitoes attack in force and wreak havoc on the team. They notice natives moving from one position to another, trying to always sit in billowing smoke, and they realize this is a natural way to ward off such insects. As they dive for the mosquito net, they discover to their chagrin they only have one. It's not large enough for everyone, so they decide to share it as best they can. They lay their sleeping bags out like spokes on a wagon wheel with the mosquito net in the center, then crawl into the bags with only their heads under the net, and are safe from marauding mosquitoes. However, they soon learn that 13 heads under one mosquito net provides an interesting night of togetherness.

Imagine being this close to a band of natives who don't bathe! The assorted body odors are only slightly better than a bad dream. They also don't brush with Pepsodent®... anywhere. This bad breath bunch leaves the Doctor back pedaling into the farthest recesses of his sleeping bag. With a sigh of resignation, the team consigns itself to a night of snoring, snorts and other odiferous noises – most of which are directly attributable to Tom, an accusation he vigorously denies.

A final insult to this collage of misery is natives who talk in their sleep in a language on the order of a growl. This nocturnal serenade continues **all night long.**

Even Harry is mumbling the next morning as he relates how the native sleeping next to him seemed to be having dreams of a more amorous nature. After fending off this fellow's subliminal dream schemes for hours, Harry was forced to sleep with one eye open until dawn.

Tom screeches in delight and his laughter echoes through the forest as Harry tells this story.

The team is up at 5 a.m. After a night of rain, morning dawns humid and muggy. Today they will attempt to scale Mt. Wimbo's heights. Chief Robert has told the natives there are two airplanes on top instead of just one. The team is anxious to begin the climb, which, according to the team chart is a small mountain only 1500-feet high. It is shaped like a mesa and should be relatively flat on top. However, after last night's rain, its almost vertical walls will be covered with wet, slippery moss.

While the team is preparing for the climb, an English-speaking missionary comes by their camp en route to one of his native churches. He tells the story of an airplane that is about four miles away on a large mountainside. He has never been to the wreck, but his traveling companion was there several years ago. He says it's easily accessible, but no one ever visits the wreck because it's so far away from roads.

After yesterday's march, they're all suffering from sore muscles, various scratches, cuts and bruises. The Doctor is afraid this climb may be difficult for them all, but especially worried that it may too much for Harry who has been eyeing Mt. Wimbo's vertical climb. Now there is a graceful alternative.

The missionary pastor graciously offers his assistant's services as a guide, and helps them chart the mountain where the plane is located. It doesn't seem like a hard journey, so the Doctor asks if either Harry or Tom will care to visit that site.

Harry accepts this challenge and the project becomes his, while Tom and the Doctor will go to the top of Wimbo to investigate the planes there. He packs for a three-day journey and is soon ready to depart. The team agrees to regroup at this campsite in three days. If Harry should get into trouble due to an injury or is delayed for any reason, he will send back a note. Soon the missionary, his companion, Harry and one native disappear into the jungle.

[9-g] DR. TOM CHAMES, shown at the base of our "small hillock," was an excellent team member and reliable man to have as a climbing partner. We had a few laughs about our "trials" while climbing up to the top of this small mountain. When it's raining and the moss is slick, you learn to communicate with your inner self. When I see him at meetings, there's never a dull moment watching the eyes of our friends as we tell "The Tales of Mount Wimbo." And sometimes, at dinner, when I mention that I need to brush my teeth, I worry about Ol' Tom. I think some others are worried about him, too – his wife for one.

Tom and the Doctor believe they can get to the wrecks and chart them along with positive identification before noon. They are equally certain they will be back in camp before mid-afternoon. According to their plans, it does not matter what the planes' identification reveals; they will take nothing and leave nothing, in accordance with the CILHI Accords. They will only photograph the planes' identification and the presence of remains for CILHI, then leave everything as they found it until CILHI can make a recovery.

The Doctor and Tom again review the briefing rules, then pack a tent, food and medical supplies for a quick trip. They leave the rest of the supplies and gear at base camp.

As they begin their climb, the mood is one of sober concentration. They are not real mountain climbers, so they choose a route that will not be vertical – an easier zigzag path across the mountain's face. They begin the journey along a muddy pathway that soon becomes a TRIAL instead of a trail. It becomes a longer than normal climb as they switch back and forth across the mountain's face. Thus a 1500-foot hill becomes a considerably longer climb of almost two miles. At times it is possible to look 50-feet down and see where they were hours before.

At first, their trail is covered with only rotting leaves and plant vegetation. But as they climb higher, they reach mud and moss fields... and mudslides. The vertical run-off from last night's rain has loosened soil in many places, resulting in a smelly mixture of mud combined with slimy moss. Everything on the trail, including the climbers, is soon covered with this slime. Even the face of the cliff and protruding roots and trees are slick and covered with ooze.

It is now a nightmare of risk and hazard for these amateur climbers who don't know enough to turn back. It was a mistake to begin this climb in the first place, but judgment has taken a back seat in their search for Wayland Bennett. However, this lack of judgment can and will become one of the more serious risks for any search team. An amateur cannot comprehend the meaning of necessary escape routes, nor understand the difference between turning back for safety as compared to giving up and failure. Both reasons may have frustrations, but one will allow a return engagement at a later date. This team is not so well endowed with judgment and continues to persist in their climb.

[9-h] PICTURE PUZZLE: Sorry, we're all out of sidewalks and telephones. We are searching for Navy 02608. Can you see it? Perhaps now you can appreciate why Crocker couldn't see it either... or why Miller never saw it and could not show us on our chart where he thought Bennett was. Look again – are you sure you can't see a crashed Corsair?

After several hours, they are perhaps half way to the cliff's top. From this lofty vantage point, they can see all the way to the tip of the northwest arm of the island, about thirty miles away. But, even worse, they can see the entire valley and river directly below them.

The team has already climbed too far and is now perhaps 800-feet high, clinging to the moss-covered side of an almost vertical cliff. Okay, so it is only 80 degrees. They have no escape route and cannot turn back. In the event of a slip, the outcome will be certain for they have pushed themselves beyond reasonable limits. To compound this situation, as they round a bend in the narrow trail, it simply vanishes! Last night's rains caused a landslide for a space of at least 40 feet. The trail is completely erased, and a ragged slash of fresh mud, rocks and roots is all that remains. This mess is loose and unstable, and it is finally obvious that the trail is not suitable for travel even by Tarzan and Jungle Jim.

Tom says, "Hey, buddy, this looks serious."

As the Doctor surveys their plight, he can only agree. Here they are on a trail slick with mud, rotting underbrush, and moss, which has been steadily dwindling in size and is now only six inches wide. In fact it is so narrow, they have no room to move about and explore other possibilities. They can only face the cliff and move sideways like a crab along the trail. It is at least an 800-foot fall to rocks and river below.

The climb has led to other discoveries that produce a mumbled response from the Doctor, "Yes, but the trail isn't my only problem.

The chaffing and rawness from yesterday is back and has started to plead for some rather immediate consideration. Explaining his plight to Tom, the team leader asks, "Have you got any ideas?"

The Doctor honestly never intended that to be funny; on the contrary, it was far from amusing. But Tom starts laughing so hard that he is oblivious to the Doctor's next suggestion. It's probably just as well.

When Tom settles down, the Doctor asks, "Are we ready to proceed?"

Tom manages to reply, "Yep."

This situation needs a decision, so the Doctor chooses to try out the only words he has learned from their native guide. With authority he orders, "Wego longtop."

Upon receiving this order, a native turns left and starts climbing straight up the cliff, like a squirrel back home in Texas. They hope to climb up above the slide, cross over it, then descend back to the trail.

Demonstrating determination compounded by lack of alternatives, the Doctor tries to whistle the tune of Rogers' and Hammerstein's "Oh What a Beautiful Morning." Fortunately, he finds that no matter how hard he tries to whistle, the only audible response sounds like "Whew."

Tom is murmuring. Tom does that a lot and the Doctor asks, "What did you say, Tom?"

Tom's reply is a rather weak and breathless question, "I said, can we do this?"

The Doctor cheerfully responds through clenched teeth, "Sure, Tom, it's a piece of cake, and it's no step for a stepper like you."

It seems to work and they survive, but it would have been so much easier with a 50-foot length of rope or a helicopter. Up the cliff, across the slide, and down to the trail is a lot easier said than done. After returning to the narrow trail, they hug the cliff and work forward about four inches at a time. The trail is narrower than before, in fact, it seems only as wide as their feet with no room to spare. They are holding onto roots and grabbing at cracks in the stone cliff. Their hands and fingers are bruised and sore, and their knees are cut and bleeding... not to mention trembling from exhaustion.

The Doctor is in a spread eagle position, pressing his body into the cliff when he hears Tom mumbling something unintelligible again. He slowly turns his head left, and looks at Tom with the only eye not actually embedded in the cliff.

From Tom's muddy, moss covered face comes no sound, but his mouth is moving vigorously. At first the Doctor thinks he's chewing on a piece of jerky, but that doesn't seem possible. The Doctor decides to move forward another three feet, then turns to look at Tom again. His mouth is still moving, but he's still not making any sound.

"Is Tom talking to himself or to me?" the Doctor wonders.

Seizing the opportunity afforded by a giant sapling, at least two inches in diameter, the Doctor hangs on like a Koala bear. He turns around to address Tom, whose mouth is still moving but without sound. Tom's face is contorted in pain, and he's a mess of mud, slime and moss. Tom looks rather dismal today, the Doctor thinks, but he knows they must both look about the same.

The Doctor is panting and out of breath as he asks, "Hey, Tom, are you okay, pal?"

Tom slowly replies, "Yes, I am fine."

"What are you eating, Tom?"

Tom reluctantly growls back, "Nothing."

"Oh well, I keep seeing your mouth moving, but I can't seem to hear the usual noise, and I thought you might be eating jerky or something."

Then, Tom takes the Doctor completely by surprise when he says, "I'm not eating, I'm praying."

"Uh, oh!" the Doctor groans. "Here I am just barely... *pant*... hanging onto this root... *pant*... trying not to fall completely... *pant*... off the face of the earth... *pant*... and Old Tom is about to say... *pant*... something funny that may cause me to... *pant*... lose my grip on this mouth full of mud... *pant*... *pant*... I really don't need this right now."

The Doctor bravely attempts to secure his grip. He can't stand the anticipation so he says, "Hey, Tom, what are you praying about?"

Tom grimly replies, "I'm making a deal with God that if he will just help me down off this mountain, I ain't never gonna' let you get me into another mess like this."

Desperately the Doctor hangs on, as he whispers to Tom, "Say, old man, while you have him on the line, you better ask him for some soap and water to help you come clean, 'cause, pal, you're a mess!"

By now Tom really does look like a creature from the Black Lagoon – of course the Doctor can't see himself to realize what a pair they make. But neither of them can afford to laugh because they might lose their grip and fall.

They are completely exhausted as they wearily make their way around an uprooted tree trunk. Suddenly the trail becomes as wide as a freeway. Well, maybe it is only two-feet wide... but it certainly seems like a freeway. More importantly, it's dry with no mud or moss. They crawl over a small ridge and are miraculously on top of the cliff.

With breathless prayers of, "Hallelujah, thank you Jesus, and amen," they try to catch their breath as they lie panting in the mud. They rest in silence for a long while, considering the miracle that has led them safely to Mt. Wimbo's top.

Finally, when they can spare the breath to speak again, the Doctor asks, "What took you so long, Tom?"

Thinking the question is over, Tom croaks, "Hey, man, you were in front and were slowing me down."

Still panting, the Doctor continues his question, "No, Tom, why did it take you so long to ask for the help? Right after you started praying, the trail got wide and dry, and we easily made it to the top."

With a voice as cracked with emotion as his hands and knees, Tom growls, "You know, if you had helped pray a little, this climb might not have been so rough."

As the Doctor attempts to laugh, Tom croaks, "Why are you laughing? That was serious trouble back there, man."

The Doctor smiles and offers Tom a canteen of water, "No, Tom, you get all the credit for this one."

Tom is perplexed as he growls, "Whaddaya mean?"

The Doctor replies, "You see, Tom, I've been worried about this climb all day. So, I started praying when we left camp because I knew we were going to need all the help we could get."

Tom still does not understand and asks, "So?"

The Doctor's answer is slow and deliberate and finally registers with Tom, "The climb didn't get easy until you prayed and made your deal with God. Thanks, pal."

Neither climber speaks for awhile, and just because their eyes are closed does not mean they're asleep. As the Doctor contemplates future searches, he makes a mental note to advise future team members of a few facts of life out here. He will have to add this to their field notes when he gets back to base camp.

On many occasions, the Doctor is deeply concerned about what lies ahead of them. At such times, he will only pray once a day, but that prayer will last all day long. Because he is responsible for the whole team's safety, he can never completely relax. On several occasions, such as this one, it will take other team members' help, as well as their prayers, just to make it through the day. "Yeah, it's tough," he reflects, "but it's worth it!"

After this sobering meditation, the Doctor and Tom rest for about thirty minutes before moving into their search area. They drink a little water, then stiffly shuffle along the trail. It seems like every single muscle in their entire body is sore and complaining. Their hands and fingers are a wreck, and their knees will require some attention when they get back to base camp.

[9-i] NOT DEJA VU: This is a long way from anywhere and very near nowhere. It can be very demoralizing when you have been walking for several days and your guide points out that you are only going to go just beyond that last hill. It can be even more discouraging when you get there and realize it is not even the type plane you are looking for. But it is important to record the plane type and number on charts and search notes for the benefit of others who may be searching for this particular MIA.

Harry, Tom and the Doctor have already visited several airplanes on island coastal areas. The Doctor even experienced an enlightened afternoon around Turtle Bay with "Old Friends." But they will soon be at a wreck that has only been seen by a handful of natives since it crashed.

While they make their way through the forest, a native guide makes a pathway with his machete. As he hacks through underbrush, the Doctor contemplates all the past year's preparations for this visit.

Research and preparations are over; speeches to awestricken crowds are also over. The first physically hard march and mountain climb are finished, and they are now involved in a serious and meticulous phase of data acquisition.

Each remote wreck must be properly identified, and photographs must prove the type of aircraft as well as its identification numbers. The presence or even suggestion of human remains and personal effects must be photographed for CILHI. Today's visit will almost certainly lead to a site where an American hero has died in his country's service. These deaths are not a result of combat with enemy pilots or even strikes made against enemy bases. Unfortunately they were only training flights against an enemy as old as flying itself.

An old aviator's warning reminds new pilots early in their careers. "Flying, in and of itself, is not inherently dangerous. But the sky, like the sea, is terribly unforgiving of mistakes." The men who make their sacrifice on the island of Espiritu Santo are none-the-less heroes. No matter what the cause of the crash, good men have made sacrifices for good reasons – all with a common cause – for their country.

Many of the crashes here were due to the dreaded blackout phenomenon. Young pilots wearing no G-suits repeatedly practiced recovery from high-speed dives. Some accidents were due to mechanical problems with new airplanes, or any airplane for that matter. Inexperience caused some accidents, while others were due to over-exuberance.

And, in a day before radar was used for traffic separation, the skies were full of young men with 400-mph hot rods – two airplanes coming directly at each other had a rate of closure of almost 800 mph. To lose sight of an airplane for only a second or two could be fatal. And what of a sky full of airplanes doing the same thing? Sooner or later the inevitable happens, and two planes make contact, at almost the speed of sound!

Imagine a new pilot searching the sky for another plane; picture him peering over his left shoulder, then forward and ahead of his plane. Follow his gaze as he looks over his right shoulder, then above and below. Give him a moment to focus on his engine instruments. Then he refocuses outside, where he resumes his visual search pattern. How long did it take? Fifteen seconds? Ten seconds? Five?

Imagine a pilot looks straight ahead and sees nothing. Give him fifteen seconds to search the skies then look straight ahead again. No plane existed there seconds ago. Unfortunately, during a fifteen-second scan, the pilot is shot down or becomes the victim of a mid-air collision.

This is the bottom line for a pilot, and there are no second chances. There are seldom any survivors because, after an 800-mph impact, the fall begins. At the end of a long fall is another impact with the ground or ocean that occurs at a speed in excess of 150 mph. Usually the site erupts into a ball of fire, and the ensuing inferno consumes almost everything. The site marker in 99% of these crashes is a funeral pyre from which pilot escape is highly unlikely because he is by now either dead or unconscious.

Inevitably, some will ask, "But why didn't he eject like they do in movies?"

This very good question deserves an equally good answer. There were no ejection seats at that time of aviation history.

If someone is fortunate enough to survive the first collision with another plane, he must remain conscious, reach over and unlock the canopy, then slide it all the way back to open position. He must then simply unstrap and disconnect himself from an airplane that is totally out of control as it falls, turning and twisting in its final death throes.

During this time, the pilot has no time to panic because each move must be calculated and measured in a pre-arranged ballet of survival. If a wing has been lost for any reason, the rate of roll may approach 1,000 degrees per second. The pilot will not be able to move, much less escape from his plane. If any time or altitude remains, he can fight enormous forces of gravity and the propeller blast slipstream, but he may be able to overcome even this obstacle.

On a very good day (and this is probably not one of those days) he can climb out of his cockpit and fall away from the plane just long enough to clear any falling debris that accompanies such an event. Then he must manually pull the ripcord or parachute opening device. If the parachute opens in time, it may be possible for the miraculously uninjured pilot to find a clear, level area to land. If not, he must come down hard in 100-foot-tall trees of a hostile jungle.

If still uninjured by this final insult, he might figure out how to get out of the parachute harness while in trees. If he can manage this, he may be able to drop only 40 or 50 feet to the ground without too severe an injury. Then he can simply walk out of the jungle to the distant shore. Of course it will be fortunate if he is only 10 miles inland. All he has to do is take a little walk through a jungle that even Marines cannot penetrate.

Upon arriving at the nearest shoreline, he can build a fire that will be reported to a Black Cat squadron. An Air Sea Rescue Catalina will land in the ocean and send a raft to pick him up. With a lot of luck, he can be back at his base within a few minutes.

Perhaps an expert Las Vegas gambler can give some idea of the odds of this pilot's survival so far. However, if the pilot should run afoul of lady luck in any scenes depicted in the above scenario, it may be a very long time before he can come home. It does not take a rocket scientist to solve this equation. With so many "ifs," "maybes," and probability factors at work, even an amateur can see an absolutely enormous set of odds *against* survival.

This is the story of the last few seconds of life on this earth for many young men who flew airplanes in WW2. Most are unconscious when they contact the ground. Many are killed during the collision with the other plane. Some are still in a blackout when their end comes. The Doctor knows of only one who survived, and the search team is able to visit the plane from that one-in-a-million chance for survival.

The Doctor thinks "How great it will be if this first plane is *Susie-Q*." But he knows that is highly unlikely. Not even a gambler will take those odds.

Suddenly, the natives gather around something in the waist-high saw grass. They excitedly chatter, and George says, "Kae kae."

The Doctor thinks, "Surely they don't want to stop and eat here." Then he sees that the object of their interest is only a snake, not venomous, but certainly one with an enormous potential to inflict many serious puncture wounds. His teeth are like needles and they curve back into his mouth. His victim would be unable to pull away, and considerable soft tissue injury could result in serious infection. It is apparently a Boa relative that eats infrequently and, judging from his smile, this one seems to have just finished a rather substantial meal. His hugely distended belly indicates something on the order of a chicken or perhaps a small pig. The snake is less than ten-feet long and, having dined recently, is lethargic and unexcited. The natives are trying to decide how best to keep him captive until they return to base camp. It is apparent that they intend to dine on snake and rice tonight. They finally decide not to kill it and seem to lose interest in this prospective meal. Without refrigeration, the natives know exactly how long a fresh kill will remain edible before it begins to spoil. To kill him now will not meet those requirements.

The natives stop after walking another hour through dense underbrush. George begins to point and chatter about something just ahead. It is obvious no one frequents this lonely, deserted hilltop that surveys the vast Pacific Ocean. There is only jungle and mountains for miles in every direction. But here, in this peaceful setting of huge and ancient trees, timeless ages are kind to visitors and intruders. In this thick undergrowth on top of Mt. Wimbo, a small gully has become home for such an intruder.

George is chattering again, "Plenstap hemided manblong hemigo longreva binbi kumcanal."

By now we understand this means, "The airplane that crashed here is dead, and the man who belongs to this airplane has gone. He went along a river, and at some time thereafter he came to a village by a canal."

The Doctor knows that "canal" is the term for a village that long ago was by a large canal. Today that village has grown into a larger village. It is apparent the natives know the fate of this pilot and the story of his survival, because he was rescued and returned to the military base in Luganville.

George has just announced their arrival at a plane crash site. The area is densely forested, and no sun lights the quiet jungle floor. Undergrowth blocks any view of the plane. Tom immediately starts taking photographs of the site from the gully's edge.

The Doctor uses his walking stick to point out which bushes must be cut down to provide a view that outlines the wreck's position and condition. He carefully walks around the site's perimeter. He sees shattered remains of a once proud tribute to technology and man's best efforts in aviation.

[9-j] OH, SAY CAN YOU SEE? The American Star and Bars were clearly legible on this Corsair. The cowling flaps and trim tabs are undamaged and still operable. Clearing back the jungle allowed drawing and photos to be made of the aircraft parts and their location. These photos were given to CILHI.

    This is a Navy plane painted dark blue on top with a cloud-white bottom. The star and bars on the fuselage are easy to recognize and photograph when the natives clear away some brush. The vertical stabilizer is missing and horizontal stabilizers are a shambles. The gully is only 30-feet wide where the plane seems to have penetrated tree cover and came to rest here long ago.

    The right wing is a crumpled mass of junk with three machine guns installed. The left outer wing structure is almost complete, although it is without any evidence of fabric cover. Three boxes of .50 caliber ammunition are neatly preserved in the left wing, and the belted ammunition leads to three machine guns which lie rusting in mud on the gully floor.

    The armor plate to which the pilot's seat is bolted is intact and undamaged. On closer inspection, he sees that the aft fuselage is intact, including the tail wheel but no tail hook. A small access panel sprung open near the cockpit during impact. Inside are well-preserved radio black boxes. They appear to have many operable components and only need cleaning and bench testing.

    The rear part of the engine is clearly visible along with the accessory section at the engine case's rear. Much of the component assembly is easily identifiable, but it is obvious to the Doctor that this Navy fighter plane crashed, then burned.

    The Doctor surrenders his spot to Tom for photographs and carefully approaches the cockpit. The seat adjustment slide tubes are undamaged but have rusted in a pile. The cockpit no longer exists because of the intensity of a post crash fire, which consumed everything that would burn. This explains why no fabric remains on wings or shredded tail. Seat remnants are twisted and bent but the contour shape is still visible.

[9-k] FINALLY FOUND: This Corsair was identified and plotted, along with each aircraft site we visited, on the chart we gave CILHI. As we paid our respects to these men, we remembered General Shaw to them. This was one of the planes he searched for after it disappeared.

Suddenly, this search is completed. The data plate is still attached to the armor plate. It is scorched and covered with moss and rust but is the only identification still attached to the basic airframe's hull. The true identity of this wreck is Navy 55334, F4U-1. Lying next to the seat is a panel that is the left outer skin of the cockpit. The canopy slide rail is still attached but covered with mud and moss. This is an important area of the plane and may provide valuable details regarding its identity.

The Doctor carefully wipes away some moss and finds white paint. As he gently removes layers of moss, 12 inch buzz numbers appear. This plane is number "33" and definitely not Lt. Bennett's. He asks Tom to photograph the number 33 and the data plate.

The Doctor calls the natives away from the wreck. He has finished his site inspection. When Tom gets back to the gully's edge, they mark this position, identification number and buzz number on their chart.

Tom asks, "What do we have here?"

The Doctor explains, "The identification and buzz numbers indicate this was a Corsair. According to the Loss Report, Lt. L.W. DeCamp was flying it when it crashed. The natives said the pilot survived the crash and returned to his base.

"While the plane is chewed and mangled, some of its damage doesn't appear to have been caused by impact with trees. Some appears to be deep slashing wounds. The tail and right wing have not received usual and customary damage. When wings are torn off, trees frequently rip them off. A tail is commonly the area of least damage, yet this one is chewed and mangled like the right wing.

[9-1] TIME CAPSULE: Lying in a lonely gully, the wreckage of Lt. DeCamp's Corsair is also a time capsule. Heavily damaged in the crash, the left wing is intact. When this wing was separated by impact, it was spared the indignity of being consumed by the fire that followed. It remains an excellent study of the 1940s aluminum structures. Perhaps in another 50 years someone  *will study these airplanes that were manually riveted by humans and built in a "jig," one at a time. Of the 12,532 built, very few remain, and even fewer fly. But for anyone who has ever seen the "bent winged angel," perform, they will always remember the unique sound of the airplane the Japanese referred to as "The Whistling Death."*

"There is no major damage to the pilot seat, which is odd. Normally a 150 pound pilot is wearing as much as 30 pounds of equipment, and this 180 pounds may be amplified as much as 20 times or more during a crash. If the pilot is strapped in his seat, both he and the seat will be hurled forward in a killing impact. Since the impact weight is at least 3600 pounds, the seat rails will bend and break. The seat and its occupant will be thrown into the instrument panel, then through the windshield and canopy. Death is mercifully instant, if the pilot is not already dead or unconscious.

"This plane was not under any semblance of control at impact because of the damage to the right wing and tail; however, the natives' story indicates this pilot survived. His presence in the plane at time of impact is not substantiated by the condition of the seat and vertical-adjust slide tubes. In fact, it seems the pilot may not have been in this airplane at all!

"Their story about the pilot's survival may be true because I haven't seen any evidence of a parachute near the seat. He may have survived because he used his parachute. If so, then why did he leave his plane in the first place? Why did he not try to land in a flat open area near the river where he could save himself and his plane? That seems a much safer solution than jumping out in flight, hoping for a good chute opening and a landing that leaves one unscathed.

"A parachute evacuation will only be chosen by a pilot who has experienced an event of catastrophic proportions, which leaves him no other choices? No pilot will choose to execute a high-risk bailout over hostile jungle unless painted into a corner. And what caused the unique slashing damage to the wing and tail of number 33?"

Tom is reading the loss report and whistles, "Did you know the Marines lost two F4Us from Turtle Bay on the same day, and this is one of them?"

The Doctor looks back at the ruined plane's tail. "Of course, that's it, DeCamp was hit by another plane! That's what chewed his tail and wing. He couldn't control his plane, so he bailed out. This plane was empty when it crashed and was completely out of control as it came into the trees."

Tom looks at the Doctor and asks, "Okay, if that's true, then where is the other plane that was listed as missing?"

[9-m] MID-AIR COLLISION:
Marine Aviator Lt. DeCamp experienced a mid-air collision with another fighter plane from Turtle Bay in this F4U Corsair. This plane did not survive, but the pilot parachuted to safety. A report of a later aircraft loss reports a Lt. DeCamp was killed. We hope not.

Tom is on the right trail; the other plane may have been the reason this one came down. It may also have received serious damage, and it may be close by; or it may have limped for miles before it crashed.

George has been a good teacher, and the Doctor is getting the hang of some of his language skill. He decides to try an idea on George that may be productive.

He begins slowly, "George, frenblomi, spozplen hemided gotwan broerblohim spozhimi diecloseup longtop Wimbo?" Roughly translated, "George, you are a friend who belongs to me. Do you suppose this plane which is dead has got a brother? And maybe this brother is also dead, and very close by on top of this mountain?"

George nods and points as he says the magic words of, "Closeup longtop weembo." This means, "Yes, on top of this mountain and very close."

The Doctor looks at Tom, then to George and says, "Wego," which means, "We go there now."

George rattles orders to the other natives who gather the gear and begin to hack away at underbrush. After five minutes of work, George says, "Westap, plenbroer blohimided himigat wanman himided."

By now Tom is getting the hang of the language too, and repeats, "We stop here. The plane we have just seen which is dead has a brother, and it is dead also. It has one man inside and he is dead too."

The Doctor is confused, they are standing in deep jungle under trees, when he asks, "Plenhimi staplongwher?" Meaning, "The other plane which stopped on Wimbo is where?"

George looks at the Doctor as though he is a child who must be shown how to do every little thing. "Stap longhere," George says impatiently, and then to prove his point, he makes a chopping motion with his machete at a bush.

The bush is different because it has a metallic clang to it. They are standing within three feet of an airplane, but due to underbrush density, neither the Doctor nor Tom has recognized it. This second airplane is less than 200 feet from number 33!

[9-n] CAMOFLAGE: This F4U-1 Corsair crashed into a jungle so thick we could not recognize it as a plane from only three feet away. Removing jungle underbrush covering these wrecks is very similar to yard work you try to escape at home. You hire someone else to do it – unless there is no one around when you need them – then you get out your trusty machete and go to work. These wrecks are well preserved by moss that covers them within weeks and underbrush that hides them from the eyes of all who would intrude on their misery.

Tom begins the camera work as the Doctor points out brush to be removed. This airplane is different in several ways from the others they have seen. It is also a Corsair; and, as brush is removed, it appears almost intact. Upon inspection, the horizontal stabilizers are largely undamaged, and the elevators are almost air-worthy. Vines that grew through the wreck are all that impair the vertical stabilizer and attached rudder. As natives move vines, the rudder swings freely in almost undamaged condition. But stranger still, even the fabric on the rudder and elevators remains intact.

The butyrate and nitrate-base dope that is used to paint plane fabric is explosively combustible. Any contact with fire, no matter how small, and the fabric disappears in a blazing inferno. The fabric's condition clearly indicates the rear part of this airplane has not been exposed to a post impact fire. The vertical stabilizer is the first area of investigation since it is still attached to the airframe. Using a handkerchief, the Doctor begins to peel away a 50-year collection of slimy green moss, then carefully wipes the area with a soft cloth.

[9-o] SHAFER'S TIME CAPSULE: This F4U-1 Corsair still has fabric on the tail and the "mil-spec" is still clearly printed. The airplane has some interesting features as a "time capsule." Even though the plane has been here for over a half century, many parts are useable – a common condition for these old planes. This victim of a mid-air collision apparently came down under control. A post-impact fire consumed the fuel in the nose tank and destroyed the cockpit, but the wings and tail are still attached. A souvenir hunter stripped it of its machine guns and many of the historically important features that could have been studied by historians, scientists and archaeologists. All the bones, teeth and personal effects also adorn the walls of a self-proclaimed "explorer" who has a museum where he sells "artifacts" at "reasonable prices."

    The protective cover of trees and underbrush has allowed moss to flourish, sealing and preserving this wreck in a natural cocoon time capsule. The navy blue paint on the tail is untarnished by heat or fire, and the darker blue lettered identification number seems to have been applied only yesterday. "Navy 56263" is so clearly perfect and legible it seems a shame to leave it unexposed for the first time in a half century.

    The doped fabric is still tightly drawn over structural framework. Printed on the fabric are the letters "MIL-SPEC." With vines and underbrush removed, the controls slowly move in the breeze with an eerie cry for lubrication. On the fuselage's moss-covered left side is a large star, still brilliantly white. The wooden radio antenna mast stands erect from the top of the fuselage. The plane is pointed northeast and both wings are in their proper position.

    Behind the plane is a forest of huge trees. So how did this plane get here without tearing the wings and tail off? There seems to be no crash path or scatter pattern to this wreckage and that is also odd. The windshield and rear view mirrors are in excellent condition after so long without attention.

    Peering into the fuselage's tail cone reveals a mute testimony to "Rosie the Riveter" of WW2 home front fame. Military men flew these planes into combat, but the ladies of America build them. Wives and daughters worked in aircraft factories while mothers and sisters put the assembly together; they should see this example. Even an assembly line quality control inspector would be satisfied. His stamp of approval is still clearly legible on the parts he inspected.

[9-p] ROSIE-THE-RIVETER'S LEGACY: A Corsair that belonged to VMF-217. After 50 years lying in mud on the mountains, this airplane had "Hot" ammunition, and the powder was still dry. There is still fabric on the tail's control surfaces and the controls all work. After a half-century's abuse, "Rosie-the-Riveter's" plane and her quality of work remain an historical challenge to so-called modern technology.

    The interior of the fuselage is perfectly preserved. It is painted with bright lime green, zinc chromate primer, which has prevented corrosion and deterioration. The primer is not cracked and has not started to peel away.

    The walking beam elevator controls are undamaged by the crash and indicate a slow-speed impact. They still function on command, as do the elevators and rudder. The rivets did not loosen or shear on impact. The lap joints and butt joints did not buckle or fail in this crash, and the work would still pass inspection today.

    The fuselage's right side is caved in, but the once beautiful airplane's symmetry remains. There is enough structure left to use as a reconstruction project pattern. In fact, there are enough parts on this island to build at least one airplane and most parts for many more. Perhaps the island's legitimate historians will soon decide to save war artifacts before they are lost forever to ravages of time and elements.

    The Doctor moves along the trailing edge of the left wing where he can see segmented flaps. They are fully extended in preparation for a landing. None of the controls were torn off by the crash and even the ailerons are still attached. The left wing tip has retained its graceful curve and even the handhold is not deformed. The handhold is a small slot on a wing's outboard end that is just large enough for a mechanic to place his hand into. The pilot prepares for flight by spreading his folded wings, and mechanics pull them down into locked position before takeoff.

    The fabric has been burned from this wing by a fire following impact. Wing ribs and spars suffered very little damage during the crash. The trusses and braces are in the same position they were rigged for long ago. Even the leading edge of the wing retains its aerodynamic shape.

A large angular-shaped access door is closed; but it snaps open, ready for inspection and service, when the Doctor presses the release buttons. He slowly lifts the door; and, as it opens for the first time in 50 years, it creaks and groans to reveal a diary of effort by dirty and sweating armorers. Corporal Jones wrote his name on the inside of this door in 1943! With greasy hands and bare arms, they prepared this plane for flight. Three well-preserved boxes of ammunition lie protected from the elements.

[9-q] HOT STUFF: When the left wing access hatch popped open, we found boxes neatly packed with 2400 rounds of .50 caliber machine gun ammunition. The belted ammunition was fed into the machine guns' breach and they were ready to fire. These old guns only needed a good cleaning, then they would be ready to fire. We realized this should be considered "live" ammunition and extremely unstable. This is definitely not something you would want as a souvenir. It was designed for a death knell for a Japanese combatant over 40 years ago and is just as deadly, if not more so, today.

The Doctor visualizes a crew chief making final adjustments to the point of convergence of six guns. Each box is full and contains neatly belted bullets ready to fire at an enemy ahead. Some bullet tips are painted different colors to define their purpose. Armor piercing bullets will penetrate fuel tanks and aircraft engines. Tracers have a phosphorous spot on the rear that glows when fired. Evenly spaced in the belt, the tracers allow a pilot to watch his stream of fire into a target. The remaining bullets are incendiary for starting fires when the plane strafes an enemy airfield. When the gun bay door opens, three belts of ammunition disappear into a feeder assembly, which directs ammunition belts into machine gun breeches. This combination of six heavy machine guns allows a Corsair to take down any aircraft in the sky.

These three machine guns are still aligned and focus on some unseen enemy plane. Although these guns lie silent and rusting, they are still very dangerous. The ammunition is very well preserved and may still be hot. Since it has been undisturbed and remained dry, the old ordinance is very dangerous and looks ready to fire.

The Doctor gingerly removes one bullet from the belt, sticks it into the end of the gun barrel and gently twists it off. The small cylindrical powder granules inside are clean and look new as he pours them onto the wing.

Tom lights a long twig with a match and sticks the flame into the small powder pile. With a blinding flash and cloud of acrid gun smoke, all questions are answered as suspicions become fact. The entire 2400 rounds are still capable of doing a job they were built for 50 years ago. This ammunition may even have been made during the war at Lone Star Army Ammunition Plant in Texarkana.

> *Author's note:* A warning is appropriate at this point. Anyone who visits an old aircraft wreck will wonder if the ordinance is hot and dangerous. This description is provided in the hope that any visitor will understand it still is. All old ammunition should be considered unstable and unpredictable. Of course, this example could easily have been omitted from this book, but then a visitor to a wreck might want to try an experiment of his own. This example is provided as a warning to anyone who would tamper with bombs, rockets or any guns in an old wreck. Hopefully they will accept this description and refrain from conducting excursions into their natural curiosity. A safe example of their condition is herein provided, and it is sincerely hoped for one's own safety, there will be no need for an amateur to explore the condition of any explosive ordinance.

The Doctor closes the access doors in the wing panel and snaps the latches back into place, but one latch crumbles under pressure. The wing is a graceful sweep upward where it joins the side of the fuselage. The gull wing construction of the plane clearly denotes a Corsair. The air scoop in the wing root is not damaged from striking trees on the way down. Inside the air scoop, a cooling radiator looks new because it has been protected from the elements. Doors under the wing still cover landing gear. Inside is a white-painted landing gear strut with an undamaged wheel and brake assembly, and this tire and tube may still contain air serviced by a Turtle Bay mechanic during WW2.

The left side of the forward fuselage received major distortion during the crash, and the entire section burned. Cowling still shrouds the engine and cowl flaps are closed. This power plant and its accessory section must hold a complete history lesson on how airplanes were built and serviced in the 1940s. Fuel lines and oil hoses snake into every part of the engine and surround the starter and generator. The undisturbed ignition system is now obsolete.

The plane seems to have arrived here under a pilot's control, in a nose-down attitude with level wings. The engine is buried at a 45-degree angle in the jungle's soft dirt floor. Two huge propeller blades rise from leaves and undergrowth on each side. One protruding blade has been torn off and seems about ten inches shorter than the other.

The nose's right side shows more evidence of intense fire. The metal skin has melted away and the right wing's fabric is also gone. That wing is severely burned and several components have simply melted away. Its ammo boxes and machine guns lie rusting in mud and rotting jungle. The Doctor visualizes a fire that must have been located behind the fuselage's firewall because it ate away the nose section as it consumed both fuel and oil tanks.

The canopy and windshield sustained no impact damage but lie on the fuselage's left side. The cockpit's right side is burned away, along with the seat and instrument panel. There are no bones in the cockpit like George had expected. Earth has been freshly dug away and there is no brush or foliage near this cockpit. The Doctor and Tom are not the first to discover this site. Someone else has recently been here, and his search was confined to the cockpit area.

The Doctor asks Tom for the identity of the second plane and pilot lost on the same day as number 33 in the gully. Tom soon produces the plane's number and the pilot's name, rank and service. This is the other missing plane!

For over a half-century this plane and its dead pilot waited for someone to come. And when that someone came, he was a grave robber, a thief who ransacked the pilot's skeletal remains and removed all his personal effects. This is not the work of natives; they could have done as they pleased for 50 years. This happened recently. In fact, the Doctor saw this pilot's name printed on a dog tag that Fred Folly offered for sale. The pistol, bones and teeth of this American hero are now being offered for sale to the highest bidder in a two-bit souvenir shop!

This search of Mt. Wimbo is over, but neither plane belonged to Bennett. However, it has allowed the team to imagine what may have happened here. When this mid-air collision occurred, DeCamp was able to get out of his mortally wounded aircraft, which had been slashed and mangled by the second aircraft's propeller. As he descended to safety in his parachute, his aircraft crashed out of control into jungle where it exploded and burned. He was later rescued and returned to Luganville.

The second plane appears to have received no structural damage, but the propeller blades that pull it through the air must have sustained fatal damage that forced it to land. But the plane appears to have been fully controllable and responsive to the pilot's commands.

That assumption leaves several unanswered questions. Why did it come down so near the one it struck? Why did the pilot not choose an easy forced landing on level river delta at the mountain's base? Could this young Marine have decided to risk an inevitable crash very near his companion's plane? Did he intentionally land here with the purpose of helping the other pilot who bailed out of his stricken plane?

This second plane was apparently brought into this area at a very slow speed and stalled just above the trees. It nosed over only 45 degrees and fell though tree tops onto the ground below. It obviously did not come in at high speed because that would have scattered airplane parts along a crash path. It did not shed wings or cartwheel through trees into total destruction.

The Doctor wonders, "Perhaps this is the resting place of an American hero who willingly gave his life to try to save a fellow Marine!"

Any pilot knows that survival from a forced landing begins with a level landing area and ends by coming in at the slowest possible speed. This was a slow speed landing, but it in the worst possible location.

The Doctor shares his opinion with Tom. "This pilot was in control of his plane during the crash. However, due to an unexpected injury or unconsciousness at impact, he was unable to simply get out and walk away. Perhaps he suffered a broken back. If the remains were available for study, a broken vertebra might allow recognition of this hero and his sacrifice.

"But the desecration of this American war hero's resting place has caused irreparable damage to the final chapter of his life and his death. The damage caused by someone stealing his skeletal remains forever casts a spell of doubt over why this pilot did not get out of his plane. It may even prevent recognition for his courage and final heroic act."

This scenario will forever remain with Tom and the Doctor as one possibility of how it happened.

As Tom and the Doctor leave this site, they have all required data and photographs for their CILHI report. They will also report about activities of a certain Mr. Folly and his two pals, Laurel and Hardy.

Within an hour, they are back at the cliff's edge, preparing to climb down. The hot sun has dried the jungle and the cliff face is now more accommodating. Two hours later they arrive at base camp to rest and recuperate while they wait for Harry.

CHAPTER 10

BASE CAMP TURN-AROUND

At 4 p.m. on the fourth day, base camp is quiet when suddenly a new sound penetrates the jungle. Harry is back, and he has learned a new call from natives who accompanied him on his search. It sounds like a cross between a yodeling love call from Arkansas hills and the "Ssoouuii" of a championship hog-calling contest.

[10-a] BACK TO BASECAMP: Harry Cornelius and the native search team at Base Camp.

Tom and the Doctor are glad to have Harry back. He had a successful journey and carefully transfers his notes to their team chart. He took site photographs and identified the aircraft as a B-25 bomber, but dressed out in U.S. Marine war paint.

That means it is a PBJ, and the location matches a report of where one crashed in 1944. Plantation owner W.T. Robertson and Major Palmer both filed reports about this plane and it's crew.

The Doctor first learned about PBJs and their use while conducting research before the first trip. During WW2, the PBJ was commonly used to escort smaller planes and served as mother ship or nursemaid for fighters over long water stretches. The PBJ crew included a navigator for long inter-island flights, such as a 700-mile flight from New Hebrides to the Solomons.

Harry made an effective visit and there is no doubt about this plane's identity. He recorded the identification numbers and reports evidence of human remains and personal effects. The team's research notes contain

160   *Search for the Lost Blacksheep*

the name, rank, and service number of each crewman aboard this PBJ.

Harry describes his visit to the wrecked PBJ to Tom and the Doctor. "It was cold and lonely, with low hanging clouds and a drizzling rain shrouding the crash site. The wreckage is covered with moss and underbrush and very well preserved."

The Doctor explains, "That is partly because it has always been wet in those mountains since its crash. Without a complete oxidation cycle of wet followed by drying, only minimum rusting and corrosion can occur. Airplane wings and tails seem to survive best when they have been broken away before a post impact fire."

"Well, this airplane hasn't changed since the day it arrived," Harry adds. "Even fabric on control surfaces remains intact."

Harry confirms the original report. "It flew directly into a cliff's rock face where it exploded and burned. The wreckage is well preserved and confined to a very small area. One wing is almost complete and easily identified. The rear fuselage, which is always the last part to arrive at a crash scene, is not severely damaged and contains a tail-gunner's seat and guns."

The Doctor adds, "Early reports of its loss indicate that it left the base during rainy weather and immediately flew into clouds. As the bomber circled to gain altitude, the pilot set the course indicator to a heading that would lead him to his next destination. It did just that.

"The PBJ was still in clouds where it struck the vertical cliff face about 300 feet from Mt. Tabwemesana's top. It has not been disturbed since its arrival there, probably because it's so difficult to reach.

"Approximately a month after its crash, Major Palmer reached the wreckage after an arduous climb. It takes about a week to get there from Roads End. But Harry started from here, well inside the mountains and the jungle, so he got to the site and returned in only less than four days."

[10-b] AN AMERICAN CASUALTY: Another twin-engine B-25/PBJ that cartwheeled through trees and exploded. This wreck gave America six "Gold Star Families" – the regrettable cost of freedom all Americans enjoy today.

The team is elated with their searches so far and has recorded the location of over a dozen planes. The report of the "7-come-eleven" airplane is not yet on their chart. They know it is neither a Corsair nor Bennett's, but it is in the area and needs to be accurately plotted, so they break camp early the next morning for a two-day trek to the Wildcat site.

Search for the Lost Blacksheep

By now, they have their routine down to a science and know it is far easier to let Harry take the lead on a long march. It will be a long walk, but they are on the way out of the jungle. An easy march like this does not take all the wind out of their sails, and in three or four days they will be back in Luganville. The team is in excellent physical condition by now, and even the jungle and its people no longer seem quite so mysterious.

The Doctor learned a lesson from an old Marine General, "Let the men do their best; sometimes they will surprise you."

While in the jungle, the Doctor lets Harry set the pace of their march. Harry is an invaluable team asset who, by example, shows everyone else how to walk, march and trek for days at a time. He starts a little earlier and takes a few more rest stops; but, with Harry in the lead, they cover more distance. If anyone plans to keep up with Harry all day, he better bring along a good pair of track shoes.

One day in the jungle, Tom and the Doctor sit on a log panting and trying to catch their breath after hours of following Harry. The Doctor looks over at a rather dilapidated Tom and says, "This must be one of those days, Tom."

With a quizzical look on his sunburned face, Tom asks, "What days?"

The Doctor finally recalls a nursery rhyme he has been trying to remember all day; it's something about a race between a rabbit and a turtle. As he finishes the story, the Doctor pants, "Tom, I think I've just been mauled by a giant turtle."

The two grown men expend much of their remaining energy in fits of laughter and rolling on the ground as they picture Harry as a really fast turtle. They have a good time for a few precious minutes until they look up into Harry's face looming over them. He says, "Well, if you gentlemen are ready, perhaps we can continue?"

The Doctor groans, looks over at Tom and says, "Uh-oh!"

In an equally exhausted voice, Tom replies, "Yeah, that's what I thought you said."

Mid-afternoon they set up camp in the coconut and mango grove where they stopped on the trip in. The natives busy themselves making a meat stew that fills the jungle with an aroma that begs to be tasted. The team is so hungry, even boiled rice smells good.

Tom has been on an MRE, rice and canned food diet for what seems like a very long time. Finally, when his taste buds can stand the temptation no longer, he says, "Man, I've got to have some of that. It smells like barbecue on my patio back home."

He walks over to the natives' fire where a pot is boiling and the stew smells delicious. As he stands there talking with George, he watches as they dip a small snake, two lizards and a rat out of the stew.

Tom suddenly scurries back to the safety of an MRE dinner. Later he explains, "Man, the contents of those MRE dinners are far more predictable. There's no telling what else was in that native stew!"

It was just too much for a man of such delicate culinary sensitivities as Tom or the Doctor!

HEADING BACK OUT OF THE JUNGLE

The next morning the team departs the area by 8 a.m. and proceeds across almost level trails that lead to the island's north shore. When they arrive at the site of "7-Come-Eleven," they stay only long enough to get its position transferred to their chart. This plane has also been recently pilfered; it is obvious that Fred Folly's grave robbing business is booming. Parts of the remaining airframe have been chopped apart with an ax, and the machine guns and other artifacts have been removed.

The next day is a long, hot march back to the original village and "Housblong Bigjif Rober." The jungle is insufferably hot and a breeze non-existent. The temperature is 105 degrees, so they must drink plenty of water along the way to ward off the effects of dehydration. Harry's stamina is amazing and always appreciated, except in a hot jungle when others are exhausted from the physical demands of the past two weeks. But the "Silver Fox" is one of the very nicest people one can ever hope to have on a search team, and has a very dry sense of humor.

Harry, a strong advocate of the POW/MIA movement, spends much of his personal time at home involved in the activities of Vietnam Veterans and Veterans of Foreign Wars. He always seems to be available as a volunteer for any work assignment.

He has been working on Tom for at least a week to make a donation to Texarkana's Veteran Memorial project. Probably out of sheer desperation, Tom has finally agreed to make a substantial contribution.

"Uh, oh, here comes Harry, it must be my turn," the Doctor mutters.

Harry catches up to the Doctor just as they start across River Jordan again. Harry begins with the fact that the memorial in Texarkana is almost complete. He quickly moves on to the issue of flags and custom flagpoles that will look so great in front of the monument.

For some reason, it is important to Harry for the Doctor to understand at this very moment, in the history of the universe, how nice those flagpoles are going to look. It is imperative that those very poles and no substitute of lesser quality be used, even though it might be cheaper. The monument needs those poles very badly, and they are needed now!

"How great, how badly, and how nice," are the Doctor's exact choice of words as he encourages his feet to just make it to the river's other side.

They are about waist deep in water, a cold current is tugging at their balance and the coconut-sized river rocks are just about the world's slickest. The Doctor wishes he had been born with suction cups on his feet like the natives seem to have.

Harry notices the Doctor is not answering; and, thinking his leader has not heard his "sales pitch," begins all over again.

After several slips and falls in cold river water, the Doctor is absolutely breathless. He crawls from the river on the far side and collapses in the mud. He closes his eyes, seeking only one or two second's pause, hoping he will be able to catch his breath soon. His body is screaming for rest, and his brain is fuzzy from a lack of oxygen. Soon, his brain detects an almost human chattering. Then it becomes louder.

As the Doctor opens his weary, blood-shot eyes, he sees Harry about ten inches away from his face. A terrible thought crosses the Doctor's weakened brain, "If I don't make some show of life pretty soon, he's gonna' give me mouth-to-mouth resuscitation."

Harry is yammering on about flagpoles, totally oblivious to the Doctor's stupor. Receiving no intelligible response he asks, "Can you hear what I'm saying?"

The Doctor groans, "Yes, Harry, I hear you quite nicely, thank you."

Harry immediately makes his move, he has the Doctor right where he wants him, flat on his back and unable to move. "Now, Doc, let me tell you about these flagpoles."

The Doctor is in a highly weakened condition and may soon become a raving lunatic if he does not get some peace and quiet. But he makes one last grasp at sanity as he heroically grabs Harry by the front of his shirt. The breathless Doctor can only whisper in a strange croaking sound, "Harry, please, I beg you to do one thing for me before I die, and I will so appreciate it if you will do it right now."

Harry is as chipper as he has ever been as he responds, "Sure, Doc, what's that?"

The Doctor continues, "Well, Harry, I was wondering if you will sell me one of those flagpoles? Right now! Right here! I'm not sure I can make it through this trip if I can't have one of those flagpoles. I will pay you any price as soon as we get back to civilization, or I'll write you a check when we get back to town, but I have just got to have one of those poles."

It must have been just the right thing to say, because Harry doesn't bring up the subject of the flagpoles again.

Years later, in front of the new monument, the Doctor will smile as he remembers a day in jungle mud and the persistence of a guy named Harry who made a lot of it possible and made a dream come true. "You know, old Harry was right all along; that new monument would never look quite as nice as it does now with anything less than those special poles. It's a great monument and tribute to all the men who made sacrifices during conflict."

ANOTHER TREK INTO THE JUNGLE

When the team returns to Luganville, they receive a message from a local native who has been to a plane in the bush. The Doctor visits the small woodworking shop where the native is an apprentice. As he interviews the man's supervisor, the native is brought into the discussion. The supervisor, who is a lay preacher at a local church, asks the native to describe the plane's location and how long it will take to make the trip. He then offers the use of his truck and the native as a guide. The truck seems to be held together by its paint job, but his gracious offer is accepted.

[10-c] WHAT IS IT? Harry back at Hotel Santo with a gift from our native search team members.

The team carefully avoids going into the restaurant when they arrive at Hotel Santo. Mary Jane can't afford many surprises like they demonstrated last time. Because Harry has a cut above his ankle that looks infected, the Doctor asks him to stay behind and write out reports of aircraft visited so far.

They pack for a fast in-and-out five-day trip and quickly load the truck. The Doctor anticipates it will take only four hours to drive over a new route to the jungle because they are going into a completely different area, in lower mountains on the island's south side.

The Doctor is driving and carefully negotiates holes, ditches and very narrow bridges. This roadway is sharply lined by cliffs with sheer drop-offs and is quite a challenge. He must struggle with the old truck and constantly change gears. None of the controls are where they were when it was built.

They pass several incoming natives who are loaded down with produce from their mountainside gardens. Many have never seen an American, a white man, or a truck like this. Come to think of it, the Doctor has never seen a truck like this either. Perhaps that is why the natives stare in open-mouth disbelief as the truck wobbles down the narrow trail. The Doctor dodges a cow grazing in the road.

The native in the back intently watches every move as the Doctor navigates around potholes, but he remains silent. He seems quite taken with the Doctor's driving skill and nerve. He came with the truck and Tom thinks he is the truck's regular driver. Old Tom is as nervous as a cat, but he too remains silent.

The Doctor parks the truck at the end of the road and they load their packs for a fast march to the crash site. The native carries part of the team's load as they go deeper into the hills on foot.

Two days later they arrive at the crash site of another F4U in the mountains, and its position and identification are plotted on their chart. This plane made a late pull-up from a high-speed dive, and scattered junk over 300 yards of jungle. The pilot did not survive, but his body was recovered two weeks after the crash. Tom and the Doctor spend only two hours photographing and recording information at the site.

Corsair crash photos clockwise from top left.

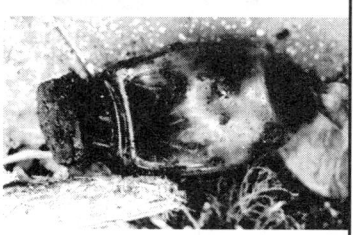

[10-d] CATCH ME IF YOU CAN: The Corsair was a terrible foe for the Japanese. Its speed and engine power made it hard to catch. It also had devastating firepower, and the distinct advantage of some of the world's best-trained fighter pilots. But even this combination could not overcome collision with the huge and ancient trees in primitive South Pacific jungles. The wrecks and trees stand in mute testimony to sacrifices of nations at war. If undisturbed these wrecks will provide interesting study subjects someday when we graduate from war into humanity. I would love to be present when students, 200 years from now, try to figure out what a propeller was for.

[10-e] UNVEILING THE SOUL: This is the rear wall, or bulkhead, of a Corsair cockpit. The armor plate survived forces that completely destroyed the airplane. Even fire failed to distort the thick steel protective armor plate. The "soul" of this plane was clearly visible, even after 50 years. Also visible were the vertical slide tubes that help keep the pilots seat in place. They were broken because crash forces exceeded design limits. The pilot died when he was thrown into the instrument panel then out of his plane as it disintegrated in the crash.

[10-f] MALARIA VIAL: Robert Bowden was part of the "Malaria Police." MAG 11 Commander Lt. Col. Smoak enforced Malaria controls on his pilots. They were required to always keep their atropine with them. They could continue to ward off malaria attacks as long as they continued to take their medicine. This young aviator was in compliance and the vial was found in his plane – 50 years later. The atropine was melted by the post-impact fire but still sealed.

They are very tired but begin their return trip. They cross a final river onto flat, open terrain about three miles from the truck, then throw down their gear and collapse. They have learned a little of the native's dialect and have taught him a little English, but conversation is limited at best.

The sky soon darkens, and Tom groans at the thought of another night in the bush. He says, "Boy, howdy! I sure wish we didn't have to go those last three miles to the truck. Why didn't we park it here?"

The native picks up on about every fourth word Tom says but the only part he seems to understand is, "We go truck." Wanting to be helpful, he volunteers, "Me go truck."

The Doctor thinks, "Of course, what a superb idea. After all, since you are the regular driver, it will be much easier for us. You go after the truck and drive it over here while we rest and wait for you. Then we won't have to walk that last three-miles in the dark or spend the night out here again."

As the Doctor hands over the keys, the little native takes off at a gallop in the truck's direction. Tom and the Doctor fall into a deep sleep, and the native is back in an hour or so, shaking them into consciousness. He has the truck parked only five feet away with the engine running. It looks like a chauffeur-driven limousine to them.

They gratefully throw their gear in the truck and climb in. As it starts moving, both Americans fall asleep. The Doctor remembers starting up the trail but that is all; Tom remembers nothing else. It is a deep and fitful sleep with dreams of sharp turns, quick stops and grinding gears... and a nightmare of racing along black jungle trails and over a roadway edged by a cliff that leads straight to eternity.

About 1 a.m. the truck arrives at Hotel Santo's front door. The two men stagger to their rooms and sleep until noon the next day. When they visit the truck owner that afternoon, he asks how their trip fared and what they discovered during their search. After discussing the trip at length, the Doctor just casually expresses his appreciation for the truck and driver.

They notice an odd expression on the owner's face.

The Doctor continues, "I really don't like those fast in-and-out trips. They're physically exhausting and a terrible way to conduct a search, but they do save a lot of valuable time. By the way, we really appreciate your driver being so helpful. Once we got into the truck coming back, I fell asleep and didn't wake up until we reached the hotel."

Tom nods his agreement. "Yes, we both just passed out until we got in at about one this morning, thanks to your driver."

The truck owner has a look of utter shock on his face and shakes his head in dismay. "You mean you guys came back last night?"

After they both nod agreement, he continues, "Look guys, no one travels on those mountain roads at night. They have blind curves and cliffs that are extremely dangerous even in daylight, and that truck doesn't even have headlights! And it has very little in the way of a brake system. But the part of your story that interests me most is... what driver are you referring to? I don't have a driver. I loaned you the native as a guide."

Perplexed, the Doctor looks over at Tom and asks, "Did you drive back, Tom?"

Tom shakes his head and replies, "No, the native was driving when I fell asleep; you were already asleep."

The Doctor looks at the truck owner and says, "Well I guess he drove us back; if he damaged anything I'll be glad to pay for its repair."

The truck owner is shaking his head now as he says, "Now wait a minute, let me get this straight. You're telling me that you came back last night along mountain roads, in this old truck that has no brakes and non-existent lights."

The Doctor replies, "Yes. That's right. Why?"

The truck owner slowly and carefully explains, "That native has only been out of the dark bush for one week. Before you arrived here, I had to teach him to wear clothes. He's never been to school, and can't read or write. Your guardian angels must be to working overtime because this is truly a miracle."

Tom's face is pale and his mouth is open in surprise as he asks, "What day is this?"

The truck owner says, "Saturday."

That night, for the first time in their lives, both Tom and the Doctor sit on the back row of a native Seventh Day Adventist village church. They can't understand a single word the preacher says during his sermon, but it doesn't matter because Tom and the Doctor have already gotten the message.

A NIGHTTIME TRIP INTO THE JUNGLE

During their absence, Harry has been busy. He has asked everyone in town about crashed airplanes and, surprisingly, has picked up some interesting leads that need to be investigated. But Tom and Harry must now get home. Another search will have to be organized for next year. Their trip back to America will have a two-day layover in Australia for rest, then a three-day trip home.

The Doctor wants to check out Harry's leads before he leaves, so he sends Tom and Harry on to Australia while he completes the search activity for this year.

Harry has heard of natives at Matevulu College, near the old Turtle Bay airstrip, who might help. The Doctor rides out to the school on a truck delivering food supplies. When he arrives, a school principal leads him to a rear school ground where three natives are building a fence.

The most promising site is in the mountainous foothills about three days march into the jungle, but he does not have three days. He offers to hire them for the weekend if they will lead him to this crash site, and the principal agrees to give them time off to act as guides.

The Doctor pulls four strong, battery-operated flashlights out of his pack and explains that this trip must be made at night, using the lights. The natives are very skeptical about going into the jungle at night, and it is clear they have never done anything like this before. However, they are soon in the back of another truck, taking a long ride into unfamiliar bush on another road that leads nowhere.

None of these natives speak English, but fortunately the Doctor can carry on basic communication with them by now. The sun goes down just as they arrive at road's end, and the jungle is soon as black as the inside of an old shoe. The four men carefully pick their way down a trail that leads in the direction of the crash area. They walk for hours, and stumble across wild cattle in one jungle area. The natives are terrified of cattle in the darkness.

They are halfway across Apouna River when two natives whip out machetes and begin flailing away at the water. As they climb out on the other side, the Doctor notices they have several long, black eels in their hands. In the pitch-black night, while crossing the river, they noticed a group of eels swimming in the cold water. A fire is promptly made and the natives enjoy eels baked in a banana leaf and served on a bed of hot rice. The Doctor sits in the shadows and watches as he eats an MRE. The natives probably think this white man is retarded for refusing to eat such a delicacy.

After their meal, they resume their midnight trek with flashlights through dense jungle. It is an exhausting trip and they are deep in low, interior foothills by morning.

They reach the crash site at 7:30 a.m., and the Doctor immediately recognizes the burned-out hulk of an SBD Douglas Dive-Bomber. This is a frustrating disappointment, but it is one more plane that can be placed on the team chart and turned over to CILHI in Hawaii.

Within two hours, the Doctor is ready to make the return trip. The natives have never seen a white man walk like this before. The walk into this site took almost 12 hours, now this white man wants to return. Natives are unaccustomed to haste, and they do not take 24-hour walks either.

In the course of the search for Bennett, almost thirty sites will be visited and plotted. And every one of them is the wrong airplane... except the last one. Any searches must be conducted in this manner in order to acquire reliable data. The most disappointing and frustrating trips will be when, after several days marching, a searcher reaches a wreck from a different direction; and, on examination, finds he has already been there – last year or the year before.

As the Doctor records this crashed Dauntless, he knows it is this year's last site. He must now rejoin the rest of his team in Australia, then return home. The monsoon season will soon render these jungles impassable. Rivers will rise to dangerous levels, and even natives will not cross them for several months. And, as the search ends, the Doctor notes that he has spent 24 of the 28 days on this island in the bush.

BACK TO CIVILIZATION

The team chart has many notes on its edges, and tail number and type of aircraft are labeled on several locations. Loss Reports have been marked with yellow highlights that denote occupants and unit to which those planes once belonged. The Doctor makes no notes as to the presence of remains in planes in case he accidentally loses them later. Many notes are in a shorthand code that only the Doctor can decipher; and, years later, he will be glad he used those codes.

The Doctor has been gone 36 hours when he arrives back in Luganville. The principal of the school where these three natives work will later write a letter to the Doctor and explain how this in-and-out night trip with short supplies and only three natives is something that even natives have never done before. In fact, they have never even heard of such a trip before.

The Doctor becomes a new legend that natives talk about around their campfires. They tell the story over and over about their trip with "White man, Doktablong himiwak longreva waklongbush sunhimided, manhimigat nostap, manhimigat noslep, manhimigat nofrad." This roughly translates into, "The white man who is the Doctor walks along the river, and he walks along the trails of the jungle bush at night after the sun has gone down. This man does not stop to rest and he does not stop to sleep. This white man is not afraid."

The Doctor and the principal become friends, and he writes the Doctor and tells of these stories *(See Appendix Q)*. The truth is really very simple: the Doctor is so tired most of the time on searches he does not have time to be afraid of anything; it just never crosses his mind.

At Hotel Santo, the Doctor bids farewell to Mary Jane and her staff. He arranges for a $500 reward for any Chief who reports the undisturbed location of Bennett's remains. The report must only be given to Mary Jane and not shared with Fred Folly. If Bennett's plane is found and Folly manages to get there before CILHI, it will be a nightmare come true. A plan must be devised to keep him away from the Bennett site. When Bennett is found, no one on the islands must know of its location until CILHI has removed all remains. But how? For now it seems an impossible task; maybe, when the Doctor gets a little rest, he can work on this problem.

On his way back to Port Vila, the Doctor pays little attention to his fellow passengers, coconut crabs or animals. He has a month-old beard and has lost 20 pounds. He looks tired and haggard as he steps off the plane and is met by Forsyth and Hutton. After three hours of discussions about the search and its results, the Doctor asks for a little time to clean up and take a short nap. The short nap turns into an 18-hour marathon of pleasant dreams mixed with nightmares about coconut crabs.

Finally, when he is presentable, he contacts Forsyth and Hutton, and they spend all afternoon drinking coffee at La Lagon Outdoor Restaurant. Discombe is not expected back from New Zealand for at least ten days, which means the Doctor will not be able to meet him this trip.

The Doctor explains his meeting with Folly. Both Hutton and Forsyth are aware of Folly's activities, but are in no position to interfere. And, as far as they know, neither is the Doctor since he is just a foreign visitor.

The Doctor calls Folly and asks him to come to the restaurant. Folly, who is not a very bright man, thinks he is being invited to the island's finest hotel for dinner. His financial instability does not allow him to dine there unless someone else is picking up the tab.

When Folly arrives, the Doctor orders coffee to be served outside on the verandah. Folly seems hurt, but the Doctor is not on call today. Sweets must be a luxury that Folly cannot afford, because he puts six spoons of sugar in his coffee.

The Doctor explains the feelings of all Americans and the problem a family endures when a loved one is designated MIA. He tells Folly why he must decline his generous offer of souvenirs. Then he asks Folly for any photographs of aircraft he has visited and a bill for his services, which he pays.

The Doctor then adds, "It will not be possible for me to make an investment in your business venture now. Nor will I be able to use you in future searches. However, if you have information to sell, I will be willing to pay for facts that lead to a complete recovery of Bennett, his airplane and all his personal effects. This can only be in the form of a reward for an undisturbed crash site."

Folly asks, "Am I fired?"

The Doctor explains, "Due to your involvement in questionable activities, it will be better for the search team's reputation if we do not have a permanent relationship."

Folly replies, "I'm fired."

The meeting is over, and the Doctor rejoins Hutton and Forsyth. He explains how his meeting with Folly ended.

Hutton and Forsyth tell him they will talk with Discombe upon his return, and start asking about old crash sites. They will all regularly communicate through letters, telephone and fax machines (which are new to the islands).

As the Doctor prepares to board his plane to Australia, he sees Folly with a white man and woman in the parking lot. Folly is gesturing wildly toward the Doctor, but his voice is drowned out by an airliner's starting whine. The Doctor knows he will probably see both of Folly's companions in the future under uniquely different circumstances. But, for now, they are left to their deviate plans and lifestyle as the Doctor leaves for Australia.

The Doctor catches up with the rest of his team in Sydney, and gets a good night's sleep in a luxuriously soft bed. After almost a month in a South Pacific jungle, the ten-hour flight to Hawaii is almost over before it began. The Doctor turns a written report and copies of their team chart over to a Sergeant from CILHI in Hawaii.

Some volunteers pay dearly in the search for Wayland Bennett, but no one pays as high a price as Harry. When their airliner lands in Dallas,

Harry contacts his Dad in Texarkana. He tells him when they will arrive on their commuter flight, and Harry's Dad drives out to the airport to meet him and bring him home.

You can well imagine a father and his son who are best pals and haven't seen each other for a month. As they drive home, they excitedly discuss Harry's month in the jungle, search events and airplanes he visited. When they cross a busy intersection, a motorist drives through a stop sign and there is an accident. Harry's father is killed instantly. Everyone grieves with Harry over this tragic loss of his father, but they all know how proud Harry's father was on that last day.

Harry is a real hero in the search for Wayland Bennett, and he contributed more than anyone else. No one on the team will ever be able to forget his father's death or forget the part Harry Cornelieus played in fulfilling... **The Promise.**

After the funeral, the Doctor receives a call from someone named "Blue Chip Five-Zero."

After the Doctor files his report, a voice asks him to please convey his condolences and regrets to Harry's family for their loss from "a friend."

The Doctor passes the message to Harry, who has no idea who this "friend" is.

CHAPTER 11

REGROUP AND REJUVENATE – 1989

As soon as the Doctor catches his breath from their first long search mission, he starts planning for a second search to begin in August 1989. The first step is reviewing all notes and the team chart from the first trip.

While reviewing field notes, he finds a reference to a "prayer meeting on Mt. Wimbo." "That's right," he remembers, "I've got to include that in preparatory instructions for the second search team." He knows it should follow an explanation about what happened on Mt. Wimbo and decides it should be something like this: "During a search, you'll learn to pray, and you'll probably learn to do it well – long before we find our MIA or get to the first mountaintop. You will, I believe, become very accomplished pray-ers before the first week is over! Some individuals may even become eloquent at it.

"Besides, it's very lonely in the jungle, and we'll rarely search as an entire group due to time constraints and financial limitations. When we divide into smaller, fast-moving one or two man teams with only one or two natives, you're going to need someone to talk to. You'll be very much alone, your friends will be far away, and you'll have to be totally self-reliant.

"Some of you may even try to delude others into believing you've begun to talk to yourself; but, my friend, you and I will know different. Only, by then, you won't be ashamed to admit it to either your friends or to yourself.

"The trials and tribulations of doing something so completely beyond the pale of normal, for most people, will indeed test one's mettle. Uncertainty may test your resolve in different ways. It will assuredly test your self-confidence. It will almost certainly explore the limits of your confidence in whatever power you turn to when you're in a jam.

"There are always some who feel untouchable because they have experience in the military or other walks of life. This sometimes tends to make them a little over-confident in certain areas. As members of our search team, you're all personally experienced and skilled in several areas, but any of those are just part of a much larger and completely self-sustaining team.

"As for this team leader, no matter what my previous achievements may have been as a part of a larger organization or team, I still sometimes find myself in trouble far beyond my abilities to succeed alone. And, on most of those occasions, it's not even remotely my exceptional skill or leadership which causes this team to come through unscathed.

"On some occasions, such as we experienced Mt. Wimbo, success is due to someone on the team who makes a spiritual acknowledgment. Some experiences may lead people to make a deal or a promise. Perhaps it's those deals, promises and prayers that will ultimately lead to success in our search for Wayland Bennett.

"Even though a team leader may fervently try, no one person can ever be entirely capable of pulling off a search like this alone. Our team needs a lot of assistance from all members, as well as from God himself.

"During our first trip I realized this more than ever before. On many occasions, I was very concerned about what was ahead of us. During those times, I only prayed once a day, but that prayer lasted all day long. The leader is responsible for the safety of the entire team and can never completely relax. But it takes other team members' help, as well as their prayers, just to make it through the day."

"Yeah, it's tough," he reflects, "but it's worth it!

A DILEMMA

Soon after returning home, the Doctor sustains a serious injury due to a fall from a 15-foot ladder. It will require several surgeries and many months of intensive rehabilitation. It is immediately obvious that he will be unable to lead a search in 1989. Harry is still recovering from his accident and will not be able to lead the team, and Tom has just opened a new clinic and cannot be out of his office for a full month.

The question arises, "Who will go on the search in 1989?"

The Doctor finally recruits two young men, Pat and Paul, who agree to make a search for Bennett. They grew up together and were members of the same Boy Scout troop where they achieved the highest rank of Eagle Scout. Both are capable, but neither knows anything about airplanes. They will be entering college in the fall and are eager to have one last adventure before they settle down to four years of academia. Almost like brothers, they will make a good team. Yet, from his hospital bed, the Doctor feels uncertain about sending these two into the bush alone.

He has maintained contact with Julian Forsyth and Ken Hutton since the first search. They introduced Reece Discombe into the team's inner circle, and he is indeed a gentleman as well as a scholar. Reece is one of the most knowledgeable men in the islands concerning the nation's economic growth and social development. He has more than recommendations from Forsyth and Hutton; he has bona fide credentials.

Reece was originally from New Zealand and served in many South Pacific islands, including the New Hebrides, during WW2. He liked the islands so well that, after the war ended, he decided to return and make his home there. When they arrived, Reece and his new bride, Jean, were the only white people living there. They raised four daughters there and all are citizens of the New Republic of Vanuatu.

Reece and Jean have lived a colorful life in the islands; and he became a hard-hat salvage diver after the war. In his work, he was frequently away from home for months at a time. He became acquainted with America by diving on wrecks of sunken American war ships. The salvaged materials and supplies left him with an impression of America as a most wonderful place. Due to his experiences, he has had several articles published about WW2 history and South Pacific development.

Reece writes the Doctor about his eyewitness account of activities with the old AGRS unit when it came to Espiritu Santo in 1947. "I was in Santo in connection with my salvage diving business. One day, while at St. James and St. Phillips Bay, I saw an American Navy LST-711 beached on shore. I'm sure that ship kept detailed logbooks of where it went and what it recovered. Perhaps those records will help in your search."

The Doctor knows that LST-711 was chartered by the U.S. Army, 604th Quartermasters Corps, American Graves Registration Company. Its voyages helped AGRS disinter buried remains of WW2 battlefield dead. Since CILHI is AGRS's successor, they will have a list of all crash sites visited and bodies recovered on that ship's two island voyages.

Reece's letter continues, "This big ship had beached itself like a whale and its two huge front doors were swung wide open. I went up to the ship to see if I could get a haircut from their barber, and they were very cordial. One officer told me they were in the islands to retrieve bodies of American war casualties from battlefields and aircraft crash sites. They let me take a tour of the ship and we passed through a large storage area in which many flag-draped aluminum coffins were stacked.

"Four soldiers with inverted rifles stood at attention in the room's four corners as an honor guard for American bodies that had already been recovered. Many bombs had also been recovered which would later be dropped overboard at sea. The officer said these bodies would be taken to Hawaii for identification, then sent home to their families.

"The search and recovery team's motorized equipment included two LCVPs landing craft and six DUKW amphibious vehicles. Since some Americans had died in bays and lagoons where their planes crashed or on ships that sank, recovery team personnel included divers to make recoveries from those submerged aircraft and ships. The recovery teams were very well equipped and searched the jungle every day, but the war had been over for almost two years, and the jungle had reclaimed and hidden many of the crash sites."

In his letter, Reece volunteers to assist the Doctor in searches and in outfitting future teams.

This offer is an answer to the Doctor's prayers. With Reece's knowledge and information, it is obvious all that remains is for the Doctor to notify Vanuatu when the team will arrive. Reece can serve as team leader for the two young men who have volunteered.

Reece and Jean Discombe become priceless friends who assist the search in many ways. Their assistance and support will help lead to ten or twelve crash sites in the bush of which he hears stories. Each plane will be located very close to where he indicates on the chart. The recovery of Wayland Bennett in an undisturbed condition will also be a direct result of their assistance. They will, of course, deny this, but they will always be considered important spokes in a large wheel of people who cared and helped.

Reece and the Doctor spend many hours on long-distance telephone calls, and later in person, discussing the unique American custom of returning its war dead home to native soil. The American government is one of the few who practice this custom to such a high level of science and dedication. But even more interesting to Reece is the idea of a private search, independent of government authority, and without government assistance. He is intrigued by the friendship that is a driving force behind this "first ever" private search effort. No such team has ever visited the islands before in search of one specific airman lost during WW2.

Reece does not just live in the islands, he loves Vanuatu and its people. As a citizen, he carefully explains their customs and rules that should be followed when dealing with native tribesmen. He helps the team locate friendly Chiefs and natives who will be helpful and ethical in conducting searches.

Reece will also serve as a communications link for more than seven years of constant research and several search missions. He answers a barrage of inevitable questions that arise each time a new detail is established.

Since Reece has explored all the islands, he warns the team of the various perils they could encounter, such as some dangerous mountain plants. He also explains the dangers of malaria, infection, and various spiders and snakes found in the bush. He gives them stern advice to prepare against that day when someone becomes incapacitated several days into the bush and insists they always remember the shortest exit route in case of an emergency. Only one question will matter at that time he warns, "How long is it going to take to crawl out?"

Due to Reece's cautions, the Doctor decides all teams will carry a little more reserve medicine and food.

The Doctor realizes that Reece and Jean Discombe, Julian Forsyth and Dr. Ken Hutton are all honest, sincere and caring individuals who represent their new country well as Ambassadors of Goodwill. Their help contributes to each team's fondest memories about one of the most beautiful places on earth.

The Doctor knows Pat and Paul will be well-advised by these dear friends while in the islands. He trusts these four valuable team members to look out for the two young men as they do their part to help fulfill...
The Promise.

In the summer of 1989, Pat and Paul leave Texarkana to search the jungles. The two young men have youthful enthusiasm in their favor and little else. They are going to keep searches alive in the jungles and make natives aware of the Doctor's intent to continue searching until Bennett is located.

THE SECOND YEAR'S SEARCH

Pat and Paul arrive in Port Vila where they meet Reece and Jean Discombe, who will assist them while they are in Vanuatu. The two searchers are unaware of the problem with Folly and his pals, Laurel and Hardy. The Doctor has not briefed them in this arena of subterfuge, so they can concentrate all their efforts on the search.

The two young men proceed to Espiritu Santo, then to the island's deserted north shore. They make camp on a beach and begin to explore jungles south of River Jordan. They find one plane that they identify as a Dauntless SBD; and, for two weeks, they explore several areas where they have been assigned to search for the lost Corsair. They visit several villages and meet several Chiefs, but are unable to reach *"Susie-Q."*

One interesting fact seems to constantly surface as they work with natives who tell them, "White man longVila himiluk longreva longtop himigat oneplen nemblo him 88 faldon himided man himisay native frenblohim nowuk Americans. Manblo America himigat novatu blohim frennohep Americans."

And so an alarming story begins to surface. "A white man from Port Vila is looking for an airplane that he says belongs to him. The plane name is number "88," and the man is searching high and low from rivers to mountaintops. The airplane has fallen down in the jungles and is dead. The white man from Vila has told all natives they are his friends, and his friends must not work for the Americans. He has told the natives and Chiefs that the white men from America have no money."

On one trip into the bush, Pat and Paul are led in a huge circle for a week, then the natives tell the two Americans, "Someone has stolen the airplane. It is no longer here."

That night while the Americans sleep, the natives abandon them in the jungle! Fortunately, the veteran Boy Scouts find a river that they follow to the island's north shore. Once there, they get a ride back into town and make their telephone report to the Doctor, who instructs them to continue their search using other natives.

THE TEAM RETURNS HOME

By the time Pat and Paul return home, they have successfully covered much of their assigned jungle search area. Although they were unable to locate the Bennett site, they bring back considerable information about a new native attitude they encountered in one village.

It becomes apparent to the Doctor that Folly, Laurel and Hardy have become more than a little interested in the Bennett case, and are prepared to go to rather extraordinary lengths to beat the American MIA search team in a race to the unknown crash site.

Fred Folly and his companions have decided that discovery of Bennett's airplane can lead them to a fortune. However, they know they must first get to the crash site and loot it before anyone else can notify authorities. So, the project is no longer simple research and leisurely searches; it becomes a race to the finish and one of the teams lives half a world away from this jungle-shrouded racetrack.

But equally helpful forces are at work on behalf of the search team and its goals. Hutton, Forsyth and Discombe have also become aware of efforts by others on the island to interfere with American searches, so they increase their efforts to acquire information, which they fax to the Doctor on a weekly basis. Reece employs his own natives and Dr. Hutton's friends to travel from Vila to Espiritu Santo to collect information. Once they learn anything new, they return directly to Reece and share it with no one else on the island.

Although this may now seem like a hopeless race to some, the Doctor stays in close contact with Reece Discombe. He also keeps CILHI, as well as the mysterious "Blue Chip Five-Zero," informed of each development.

By early summer 1991, all the latest information is assembled, and the Doctor is ready to recruit a new team to go back into the bush.

CHAPTER 12

THE SEARCH CONTINUES – 1991

The Doctor has been unable to personally conduct searches for two years due to recovery and rehabilitation necessary after his accident; but, by summer of 1991, his mobility and health are nearly normal. He still walks with a limp and has only partial use of his left arm, but is determined to lead this year's search. He has maintained a positive attitude, and his physical condition is about as good as it is going to get.

He is looking forward to meeting the Discombes for the first time. They have kept up steady communication by phone and fax, but it will be a delight to meet them in person. Their friendship has brought a new outlook to the searches and creates a lasting friendship in the islands.

When the Doctor reaches the Discombe's home in Port Vila, Jean bets him he will never find Bennett. The Doctor accepts this challenge because he has never considered the possibility of failure. After all, he reasons, the island is only so big, and Bennett's wreck will have to eventually surface. Neither Jean nor the team leader will later recall if the challenge is based on finding Bennett during that year's search or at all. But, several years later, both Jean and the Doctor claim to be winners of a steak dinner. The final outcome has a special meaning for all the search team.

In the Doctor's continuing discussions with Reece about the islands and wrecks there, Reece points out the location of several PBY Catalinas. He says, "These long-range patrol aircraft were used extensively during WW2, and many were assigned to this area. As conflict advanced toward the Japanese homeland, the New Hebrides mission assignment was no longer required. Espiritu Santo was left far in the rear and the entire military operation, including vast supply and maintenance operations, was relocated north to the Solomons."

Reese further explains, "When the fast moving war machine advanced northward across the Pacific, supply priorities underwent a dramatic change. All unserviceable equipment was dropped from an asset list, became a liability and was redesignated as a spare parts unit. War-weary vehicles and damaged airplanes required more time and manpower to repair than acquiring replacements.

"As military units from Turtle Bay hastily relocated combat operations to other islands, a lot of materials and supplies were simply abandoned. This included several non-operational PBY's that were simply towed into a deep ship channel and anchored. Scuttle valves were left open, accidentally of course, and the problem of an abandoned derelict was solved in a few minutes. At least six PBY's lie in less than 150-feet deep clear water, while some planes are only 70-feet deep; all less than one-half mile from shore.

"The Turtle Bay harbor floor is littered with wrecks of harbor tugs, PT boats and service equipment of every imaginable type. It was much easier to dispose of equipment this way, rather than pack and forward it to a new advanced supply base. Evidence of many of these disposal sites still exists on hundreds of islands throughout the North and South Pacific. Mountains of supplies and aircraft were abandoned on island groups such as the Carolines, Marianias, Philippines, Aleutians, Solomons, as well as Espiritu Santo in the New Hebrides.

[12-a] SUCCESSFUL CRASH LANDING: This C-45/SNB crash-landed in 1943. The only injuries were a bloody nose and broken finger. Even the tail wheel doors remain in place and open, which indicates that the wheels were lowered for landing, resulting in a ground loop as it slid off the runway. It is still in good condition, even after years of exposure to highly corrosive salt-water spray that it receives daily, and it is a perfect example of why airplanes are built of aluminum.

"By the end of hostilities, there were many aircraft on Espiritu Santo that were no longer needed for combat – some new and still in crates. By many accounts, over 450 aircraft were left on one island at the end of the war. They are truly Ghost Squadrons of the sky and the list includes:

   175 - B-24, four-engine bombers
   129 - B-25, two-engine bombers
    73 - F4U, one-engine fighters
    29 - TBF, one-engine torpedo planes
    64 - SBD, one-engine dive-bombers
    18 - C-47, two-engine cargo planes
     9 - C-45, two-engine transport planes

"On Espiritu Santo, Million Dollar Point is of interest to any student of history and WW2. Destroyers and freighters lie on the bottom in less than 150 feet of clear, protected harbor waters. I have done a lot of diving in that harbor and it is truly amazing."

Reece continues, "The President Coolidge, a 600-foot-long Presidential Liner that was pressed into service during the war as a troop transport, missed a protected harbor channel and entered a minefield. A large hole was blown open in the bottom of her bow when the front of the ship struck a mine placed in this harbor's mouth as a protective defense against Japanese submarines. The Captain attempted to back the Coolidge out of the minefield and into a channel, but backed it into another mine in the process. With two holes in the ship, it started to list to one side and settle in the water.

"The Captain knew his ship was mortally wounded and attempted to beach her near the lighthouse. If he could run her aground, she would sink no lower, and her cargo could be salvaged. He called for full speed from the engines, but his ship had already taken on so much water she could not accelerate. This huge transport's bow crashed into a coral ledge at a very slow speed and ground to a stop. The front of the ship slid up onto a ledge while the stern was still in deep water. As her stern settled lower, she slid off the ledge and sank in shallow water.

"The ship and cargo were lost only 200 feet off shore at Million Dollar Point. The giant hulk rests on its side with her bow only 70 feet below the surface. Due to the seabed's slope, the stern descends to a depth of slightly more than 200 feet.

"Our island's resident diving expert lives just across the street from Hotel Santo. He acts as curator of the Coolidge wreck and leads diving tours into it every day. No souvenirs can be removed, but it is loaded with adventure. The Republic of Vanuatu is fortunate to have such a man of integrity who maintains Coolidge's history as an intact tourist attraction. Conservation of these historical resources attracts divers from all over the world to Santo.

[12-b] DIVING AND EXPLORING FUN AWAIT THE ADVENTURESOME IN VANUATU: *The bays, coves and lagoons are full of relics and evidence of WW2 activity. Most artifacts are in remarkably good condition. Diving tours of destroyers, tugs and a variety of ships (including the USS Coolidge, which lies in shallow water) enhance the wrecks of aircraft such as the AT-6, TBF, F4U, SBD2, PBJ, C-45, and PBYs. Million Dollar Point is where tons of supplies were dumped when the Americans left the islands.*

"There are several Corsairs and TBF's just off the shore at Turtle Bay in 60 feet of water. But the most impressive site can be dived with either scuba or snorkel at Million Dollar Point where the allies dumped cartons, boxes and crates of unneeded supplies. Mountains of supplies litter the beach and shallow bottom. Amateur snorkelers can explore shallow bottoms scattered with engines, cranes, silverware, vehicles, tools of every imaginable description and everything from old coke bottles to metal food serving trays."

Reece concludes, "Many other Pacific islands are also dumping grounds for vast supplies provided to American men at war. Shiploads of new, crated airplanes were left on beaches of lonely deserted atolls. In Guam and Palau, rumors abound of long narrow pits or trenches filled with metal crates containing new fighter planes. Some sites are reported to include all supporting parts and tools necessary to maintain them as combat squadrons. Many were shipped in metal and wooden crates approximately 15-feet wide and 15-feet tall and some were even 40-feet long. They were buried in trenches and covered over, having never been unpacked. What a treasure trove these will become when they are finally unearthed."

Prior to the search for Wayland Bennett, there was no ongoing search for WW2 aircraft lost in the islands. In fact, many WW2 records and archives are sketchy and do not provide certain information about location, identity, aircraft type or whether remains exist in the wrecks. In some cases, AGRS or CILHI has already removed the remains.

Island crash sites were not being plotted and reported to either U.S. officials or Vanuatu's government. The native islanders have no interest in these matters now; but, perhaps in the future, they will eventually report and record all sites. Such efforts in international relations could enhance the cultural and educational development of these islands, and their cooperation would be greatly appreciated by those involved in a humanitarian effort to return war dead to the country for which their sacrifice was willingly made.

The Doctor has recruited his brother, Roger, for this year's search. Roger is a Vietnam veteran who was once a member of the Navy SeaBees assigned to Chu Lai. He says little about his time there and would rather enjoy the present, wasting no time reliving an unpleasant part of the past. One of the squadrons that uses an airstrip SeaBees built in Vietnam is an old friend – the Blacksheep Squadron, again at a field created for their use by the Navy.

Roger is a gentle giant with a heart of gold. His sense of humor helps keep the entire team in good spirits and well entertained when the going gets tough. Roger will not hunt for sport because he cannot bear the thought of killing any animal and always has a collection of stray dogs and cats that become pretty good pals. He is committed to a non-violent lifestyle unless someone hurts an animal or kicks his dog. If and when this occurs, that person better just run like a devil is after him because, most likely, no amount of explanation will get him off the hook.

[12-c] SO-O-O-O GOOD: After what feels like months in the jungle and 36-hour-long days of walking and stumbling along primitive mountain ledges, this could be referred to as the "pause that refreshes." It gives a whole new meaning to the term "cool, refreshing and on tap." This creature of the dark bush is only Roger; and the coconut fresh from the tree is truly one of Mother Nature's masterpieces. It is always cool and tasty. I believe Vanuatu has the world's finest coconut milk, but you need a native to get into one. He can open it in about four seconds; but it will take you about half-a-day.

A new recruit for this year is Ben, a stranger who professes an undying loyalty to the memory of fallen comrades of any war. He is unknown to any of the team, but seems easy-going and claims a military background. After they get to the bush, the Doctor discovers that Ben is a fake and phony with no military background, but by then it's too late and the search must go on.

Ben constantly tries to impress anyone who will listen, even the natives. He brags about his heroic exploits in various military units as if he is an unsung hero. This is the first alarm that goes off. Ben has never flown an airplane; but, like Folly, thinks he is a bonafide aviation expert.

At first he is at least funny; however, when the going gets tough, he is no longer entertaining. Ben becomes more of a burden than asset in the jungles because he is afraid of everything: jungle, night and natives. Everyone soon sees him as a sissy and crybaby.

In the jungle, Ben works hours on his tent and sleeping quarters, then summarily declares it to be his space and off-limits to everyone else. He isolates himself in the silence of his own fantasy world.

Roger and the Doctor get up first and prepare hot water and coffee for everyone. Other team members and even the natives always pitch in to help as they arise. Once coffee and breakfast are ready, Ben emerges from his tent with his hair looking like a firecracker has combed it. He announces his awakening by using the same script day after day, "Aaahhhh, I love the smell of napalm and gun smoke in the morning!"

As anyone knows who has ever smelled napalm and gun smoke early in the morning, he probably slept with the taste of fear in his mouth, too. Ben probably just likes to watch "Apocalypse Now" reruns. Hearing that line each morning gets to be old and a pain in the ear, but Ben must have spent a lot of time practicing those words, so Roger and the Doctor say nothing but just look at each other and grin.

[12-d] A DAWN WAKE-UP CUP: Early morning was our only time for relaxation. We were guests of the village Chief and were treated to this Royal Suite for our accommodations. We declined drinks of Kava and dining with him because we were unsure of what he meant when he invited us to "stay for dinner." We were afraid recent advertising posters claiming "no more cannibals" may not be widely read here; so we just sat around eating rice and something from a stew pot that was served on a banana leaf. As we ate with our fingers, we thought that, in the future, we should perhaps "polish up on our social graces." The bananas were breakfast and the plastic bag of water was our shower.

Roger and the Doctor choose old, wide-brimmed, soft hats and mundane long-sleeved khaki shirts and pants or old T-shirts and shorts. But Ben is decked out in his stylish safari hat, autographed tee shirt, and a silk scarf around his neck. He is wearing his designer "Daisy Duke" short khaki pants and knee-high socks. Yep, old Ben is a sight to see in the jungle, at least the natives are impressed.

The Doctor and Roger wear lightweight, high-top tennis shoes, which they also recommended to Ben before they left the states. However, Ben did not heed their warnings and is determined to wear a pair of very heavy and almost knee-high combat boots he picked up at an Army surplus store. Ben also insists on wearing a backpack stuffed with about fifteen pounds of sweets. The team never understands the significance of his pack, which Ben jealously protects, but he refuses to share its contents with anyone.

After walking about four hours the first morning, they arrive at a dry riverbed covered with round river rocks. Ben constantly falls and slips and his legs are tired from the combat boots and pack.

The going is very hot and pretty rough in the riverbed. Suddenly, a combination of fatigue and exhaustion take over, and Ben cannot seem to get his second wind. He slips and falls into a small mud puddle in a riverbed, landing on his back like a stranded turtle. He appears to be stuck between two giant rocks that are at least four inches high. His heavy boots and near-exhausted state leave him without sufficient strength to kick himself out of this predicament. He cannot seem to wriggle free or even roll over.

The other team members start laughing at the sight of Ben flailing around in the mud, trying to get out. He is covered by black mud that seems to match his new mood. Of course, an appropriate number of color photographs must be taken to record his skill as a jungle man before anyone helps him out of the mud. His designer costume is shamefully tarnished and matched only by his choice of wild epithets vented on trees, rocks, rivers, mud, everyone present, and even some who are not. This sight and the resultant living color photos are absolutely hilarious.

Soon after this episode, he is given the nickname "Bwana Ben."

The natives rarely laugh in white men's presence. In fact, they didn't even laugh when the Doctor applied Pepsodent® by mistake. But on the day "Bwana Ben" gets stuck in the mud, even the natives are amused. Yep, old Ben actually becomes a legend around native campfires. Well, he always did want to be a superstar.

Ben is often a source of entertainment, and some of it is legitimate. But he also has a dark side that will later become a problem.

Upon advice from CILHI, the Doctor keeps all research documents confidential and team notes are not accessible to all team members. When absolutely necessary, a team member may be allowed access to certain items, but many notes are in the Doctor's own form of shorthand. Ben seems to take exception to this.

It is dark and quiet one day as the team cautiously picks its way through thorns and other dangers that may lurk around the next bush. Even the natives are concerned because they are far away from usual trails in thick underbrush. Everyone is walking with his head down and sweating with the enormous effort of making a very small trail through dark, quiet jungle. As they chop their way through a particularly thick area of bush, a horrendous growl and furious barking of an enormous dog greet the team.

This is the worst place to be attacked by anything, and the natives send packs and gear flying in every direction. This huge, fanged monster must be protecting a lair and babies, and the sound seems to come from the very bushes the team is hacking into.

Everyone is terrified, including the natives. In panic, the natives draw their machetes for battle against the huge attacker. The white guys are easy to spot; they are busy climbing up the largest available tree.

The Doctor is a little slow on the uptake and can only find a tree about three inches in diameter. As he scurries to the uppermost branches, he is only about four feet off the ground, and precariously swaying back and forth like a possum in a pear tree. Surely the large attacker will just gnaw off whatever part he can reach, because the Doctor can get no higher.

Roger, ever the animal lover, is patting his knee and whistling, "Here, boy, good dog."

"I wonder if that dog can understand English," thinks the Doctor. "If not, he might just eat Roger." The Doctor vividly recalls the first page of Bowden's notes where he describes the "Hounds of the Baskervilles."

The Doctor tries to climb higher as the dog resumes its furious barking again. He looks around for the monster that seems to be just beneath his tree. All he can see is Ben, sitting on a log and suffering from severe fits of laughter as he busily takes color photos for posterity and history. Ben has somehow acquired the ability to bark like a very large dog.

The natives are astounded that a white man can put such realism into an imitation of a very mad dog. Ben becomes somewhat of a legend on the island because of his animalistic tendencies. In every village the team enters, Ben is called upon to perform his act for chiefs and natives. Ben enjoys the attention, and this time it is well deserved.

After a week of hard jungle march away from any roadway and a day-and-a-half's climb, they are on top of a mountain that is in the area where Bennett is presumed to have gone down. The agenda is serious, and the Doctor is consumed with details of the search and his intense desire to find Bennett on this trip.

While searching in the jungle, the Doctor briefs the natives each morning after breakfast. This helps establish a bridge of understanding to span age, time, language, customs, understanding, education and culture. This morning his audience includes 20 native searchers who have been hired to "beat the bush." Of course none of the natives speak English or understand what he is saying, but they pay courteous attention to the Doctor's rapid-fire instructions. He assigns one white man to accompany each group of natives and the area for each party to search. The briefing includes the procedures to follow when an airplane is located and what to do in the event of an injury.

Among the photographs Vought Aircraft provided the Doctor is an F4U-1 Corsair, taken on the island of Espiritu Santo in September 1943. It appears to show the buzz number "88" – the airplane Bennett crashed in less than one month later. It clearly shows the airplane with a birdcage canopy and no tail hook. There is also an excellent 8" x 10" color photograph of a Corsair in flight. The Doctor carries these photographs with him on the trips to Vanuatu.

The Doctor covers details that may help them identify an airplane: the large white American Star and "88" on the plane's side, and six machine guns in the wings. All these details are amplified by passing around the color photograph of a Corsair supplied by Vought. As the Doctor passes the photograph around for the natives to see, he says, "This is what we are searching for, gentlemen!"

The natives have never seen a photograph before, have no idea what an airplane is, and are quite amazed to see just what they are looking for. The Doctor can readily see that he has really impressed these natives with his educational briefing, and their excited chattering seems to indicate that they are paying close attention.

As the Doctor stands, he declares an end to the briefing and a beginning to the search by saying, "Wego."

In their language this means something really profound like, " Okay, folks, it's time to go to work and punch the old time clock, so let's hit it."

Pleased with himself, the Doctor thinks, "Boy, I really scored this time, because all the natives are wearing serious looks on their faces. I really got their attention today."

The natives all jabber excitedly and shake their heads as they leave for their assigned search areas.

The next four mornings, the Doctor repeats his daily briefing before their search. "Wow!" he thinks, "What a leader I must be to get so much territory covered in three or four days."

On the fifth morning, as the team is about to depart a campsite, one native with a serious look on his face shakes his head from side to side. As he tries to communicate his question, he finally brings the Doctor to his knees in despair.

The Doctor finally realizes that, in all the grandeur a search team leader may enjoy, he must always reserve a small private niche into which he can crawl and hide. Especially when he realizes what a super job he has done in failing to make the natives understand. It should be a place where he can eat lots of humble pie and not be disturbed.

This native has finally made the Doctor realize they cannot understand how they will ever be able to find something so small as the airplane in the jungle! Each day the Doctor has displayed the photograph of the airplane and told them, "This is what we are looking for." The Doctor is stunned when he finally realizes the natives are looking for an airplane the size of the one in the photograph!

In the haste of each briefing and his assumption that the natives understood, the Doctor has led them to believe the impossible. Since the Doctor is a white man and obviously in charge, natives believe every word he says and have been trying to please him as best they can.

In an attempt to correct his mistake the Doctor takes a machete and draws a scale outline on the ground so the natives can see what size the plane really is. Communication has finally taken place, and the natives smile and nod their heads. They begin to jabber and point to a nearby valley and a distant mountaintop.

The Doctor decides the moral of this story is keep a good sense of humor and never take natives for granted. He had become so intent in the search for an airplane that he failed to remember the vast culture gap.

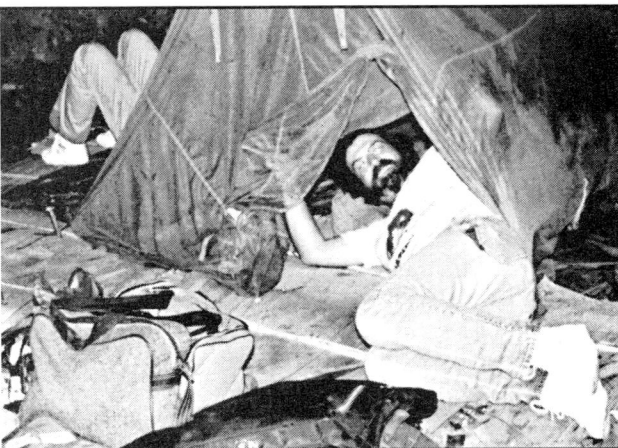

[12-e] "HOME, HOME ON THE RANGE": These "Cowboys" have had it for the day. This is what happens when the search team's fearless leader forgets all but one mosquito net. You learn to share it with others who have the breath of foul beasts and talk in their sleep.

As a result of this miscommunication, the past several days have been wasted and the team is, once again, heading back to town in an old truck.

A new group of natives has joined the truck driver for the long ride into town. As the truck labors up a small hill, the road is passing through dense brush that overhangs the road, which was probably built by the "Flintstones." As the truck grinds almost to a stop, a furious dog suddenly attacks it again. These natives have not been exposed to this noise, and they jump out of the truck and scatter in every direction, yelping and hollering with machetes flashing in their panic. The natives think a huge, drooling monster is attacking them.

As the team rolls in laughter, they notice that even the driver has jumped ship and is running as fast as he can away from the vicinity of the truck and dog. The search team jumps out of the truck and makes motions as if confronting this fanged monster and beating it away. Soon the yelping of a dog running away in defeat is heard.

To the natives, this clearly indicates that the white men have victoriously saved the day. The natives cautiously return, while the white guys stand protective guard. The driver remounts his truck and, as the team jumps on board, the truck leaves the scene in a cloud of smoke and dust. As he drives away at high speed, the driver continues to throw hurried looks over his shoulder to see if those ferocious dogs are gaining on him.

It was perhaps the fastest ride to town anyone ever experienced. To the best of the team's knowledge, the natives never learned that the attack was from Ben. But they must certainly think the Americans are brave when under attack, because they got out of the truck and chased away the attacker. One can imagine, however, what would have happened if some mangy old mongrel had wandered out of those woods about then; the team would have passed the natives as they ran up the road.

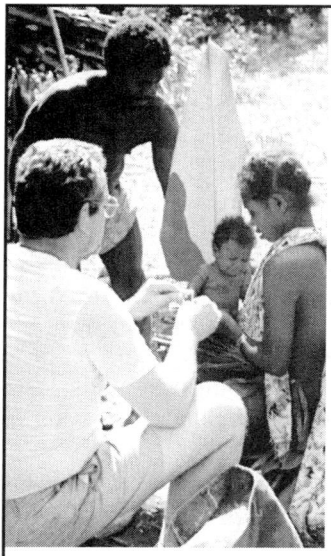

[12-f] THE JUNGLE TELEGRAPH: Word spread quickly, *"whitemanlongmerikahimicomhimlongdoktablonghim."* This seems to be rather loosely translated into something like, "White men from America are coming, one is a Doctor." They will come from miles away, weeks for us.

Each day, before the search began, we had "office hours," and treated dozens of patients from infant to senile. Some ailments only God could diagnose, because I certainly had never seen anything like them. Most had never seen a white man before, much less a doctor.

It was sometimes difficult to determine what scared the children more, the white man or the Doctor. The parents, like parents the world over, admonished them with words that meant something like, "SS-ssshhh, stop that crying! Do you want the white man/doctor to see you cry? Shame on you!"

[12-g] JUNGLE CLINIC: No doctor can say "no" to someone in pain. We never asked for payment, but it seems a universal law that, "Payment is expected at time of treatment unless prior arrangements have been made. Insurance accepted." Natives paid with food they brought as gifts for treatment. I'm not too sure what it was, but it sure was tasty.

This patient said something bit him and it sounded like he said, "spider or snake."

"Uuhh-huuh! Yeah! That's what I thought you said; and all this time, I thought you guys didn't have things that bite in the night, like spiders and snakes."

    This year's search is long and hard and, although it does not produce any new aircraft, it confirms a large area where there are no planes. It is a successful search in many ways because the team makes new friends and sees Mary Jane again, this time under slightly different circumstances than on our first trip.

    The team members will return home with priceless tales to keep friends laughing for hours. They understand now why the Doctor warned them, when they signed up, that they must always remain searchers who can laugh at themselves and the hardships they encounter. They must be able to take hardships with a grain of salt or the trip can become a frustrating and very unpleasant adventure.

The Doctor knows he must not take himself too seriously either. He must keep a good sense of humor above all else. The good times and experiences always lend balance to hard times that eventually come. He knows he must be patient with both natives and team members and not take out his frustrations on anyone. He tries not to become angered at disappointments, because he will get pretty beaten up by the search and journey.

He realizes he is the only one who knows the entire story, and this will have to satisfy the others. By keeping the team's attitude right, adversity presents no problem, otherwise, it may lead to dissension and unrest in the weakest team members. He tries to condition the team to realize that any airplane they find is a success. By doing this, they learn not to be too frustrated if their search fails to produce Bennett as soon as they would like.

The Doctor is trying to show them how to turn lemons into lemonade and turn disappointments into compliments for everyone. He knows it is important to preserve the friendships with which they started so that everyone can participate in making a good report to help their friends at CILHI. This creates a better relationship among the team rather than vilification against one another.

The Doctor tries to contact Peter, the missionary in Sara, but to no avail. Peter is frequently in the bush and on trips to other islands, but the Doctor wants to talk with him about those planes he spoke of three years ago. Perhaps next year the Doctor and search team can find him. Peter is also taking English lessons, so, they may even be able to converse in their own language next year.

Before leaving Vanuatu, the team has dinner with Hutton, Forsyth and the Discombes; and they all start planning for next year's search. The Doctor is pleased that Folly is not in the restaurant, and has not approached him this year.

During dinner, the Doctor is introduced to a white lady who lives in the islands; her name is Laurel. Although he has not met her before, he already knows who she is. He remembers seeing her briefly from a distance as he boarded his plane to leave the islands in 1988. She and a white man were talking to Folly, who was gesturing wildly and pointing to the Doctor at the Vila airport.

She is introduced as a co-producer of island films, working in concert with a man who currently has pressing business in America. However, the Doctor remembers his briefing about their business activities, and he can imagine the grief Hardy must be visiting on one of America's Gold Star families.

Laurel offers her services as an interpreter on any of the next search missions in the bush. She also makes other offers of her services, but the Doctor turns these down as well. Out of respect for the others at dinner, the Doctor remains courteous to Laurel, and assures her that he will contact her if he needs an interpreter next year.

While declining her favors, a warning signal comes on in the back of his brain – something about a woman scorned. Since the Doctor is not always accused of having a brilliant bedside manner, saying "no" to this pig was easy, but he will also become a target of her retribution. At least, he does not have to worry about taking some sort of "swine fever" back to America.

Laurel was once a beautiful woman, well educated in Europe. Sadly, she abused both her mind and body; and, unfortunately, she never broke either the habit of alcoholism or on-demand promiscuity. The number of these transgressions is beyond her ability to remember or count today, and her age is rapidly catching up with her. She will not be able to acknowledge this element of her mortality either, and that will truly be to her everlasting shame.

After dinner, the Doctor notices Ben and Laurel seem to be having a long, animated discussion about something. The team soon heads back to the hotel; but, when they arrive, the Doctor notices that Ben is missing. One dinner guest says he last saw Ben in the restaurant bar. Another says Ben decided to stay and talk further with Laurel, so the matter is dismissed.

Ben misses breakfast with the team the next morning, but is back by mid-morning. He makes no mention of his meeting with Laurel or what they discussed. It is probably just as well; Roger and the Doctor have heard enough war stories from Ben. Actually, Ben turned out to be a pretty good searcher after they got him used to the ways of the jungle.

Nothing seems out of the ordinary, and the Doctor suspects nothing to be out of place, but Reece and Jean have been watching Ben very closely. They don't trust him, and it is clear to them that something is not quite right about him. Dr. Hutton and Roger share an opinion that Ben could have no good reason for a relationship with Laurel. She is almost twenty years his senior and not nearly as attractive as the raven-haired beauty who waits for him at home.

CHAPTER 13

A FINAL EXPEDITION – 1992
PREPARING FOR THIS YEAR'S SEARCH

After they return, the Doctor begins to put together a team for 1992. An Australian TV news service contacts him for information about the search. They want to film at least part of it as a documentary for Australian viewers. After preliminary discussions, the news service realizes their schedule will not be compatible with the planned search month.

Then, in late 1991, the Doctor receives a call from an independent film producer named Hardy, who claims to makes documentaries about South Pacific islands. Mr. Hardy, it seems, has heard about the searches from some of his island friends.

"Imagine that!" the Doctor thinks to himself.

Hardy says, "I'm interested in opening a dialog of preliminary discussion about filming your next search."

The Doctor muses, "So finally the rat is going to show his face."

He schedules an appointment for January 1992 to meet with Hardy so he can make his position and intent known.

When Hardy arrives in Texarkana for their first meeting, one of his first questions is, "Will it be possible to meet the other team members?" He adds that he has heard of a team member named Ben.

"Now, isn't that a surprise?" the Doctor asks himself.

Hardy seems, for some reason, to be in a hurry to meet Ben as soon as possible.

"Naw," the Doctor answers himself, "it's not really a surprise."

The Doctor has his own surprise ready for Hardy in the form of Bowden, Carson and Sandlin. He asked them, as project founders, to attend this meeting with Hardy, and they all arrive about the same time Hardy starts asking about Ben.

Hardy is a man of little stature and even less hair – a "prissy" type to whom the Doctor takes an immediate dislike. He remembers, "Hardy was the third person at the Vila airport with Laurel and Folly in 1988."

Hardy thinks the Doctor does not remember him from then, but that assumption is his first mistake. There will be others he will perform with even less grace.

The Doctor knows this meeting will steadily define Hardy's true lack of character and a purpose that has no honor or integrity.

Hardy immediately tries to start impressing the three older gentlemen and makes the unforgivable mistake of revealing his real intentions. He says, "I want to record everything about the amazing discovery of Wayland Bennett on film. I'll direct the film, edit it, then sell it to various news agencies with whom I have contract in several countries."

The four men inform Hardy that Wayland Bennett's family has not given permission for such an event, and the Doctor asserts, "I will not endorse or participate in such a project without the family's full approval."

At Hardy's insistence, the Doctor and Bowden leave the room to call one of the family members. "Blue Chip Five-Zero" has already briefed him on how to handle this situation. The Doctor and Bowden confer privately before returning to the meeting.

The Doctor tells Hardy, "The family is firm in their convictions. They will require that any documentary must be tastefully done and with no mention of Lt. Bennett by name. He can be referred to as what he is and nothing more: an MIA who has not been forgotten."

The Doctor explains that he and Bennett's three childhood friends are authorized by the family to decide about any such project. "They have requested that we insure that no filming be allowed unless it is done with the highest moral and ethical standards with no unsavory production.

"Since you are not an American, you would have to give the family complete editing privileges of your final product. They also require that there be no criticism of the U.S. Government or any of its agencies.

"There are also some other restrictions if you decide to produce a documentary under these conditions and we agree to let you do so. It must be limited to the search for Bennett, and under my absolute authority. There will be NO filming of Bennett's remains and any documentary inserts must also be limited to Bennett. You will not be allowed to 'dub' film clips of any other American casualties into the Bennett documentary. You cannot take any still photographs of other American casualty remains. Those are the conditions."

This is not what Hardy has come all the way to America to hear, and he is incensed; but the Doctor still doesn't give him a chance to reply.

"In all matters of the search, my agreements with other agencies such as the CILHI Accords will take precedence," the Doctor adds.

Bowden sees Hardy's frustration and picks up the conversation. "We want it to be perfectly clear that the Doctor will be in charge of everything, including ancillary shots that may not be included in your final product without his specific approval. The Bennett family's loss has been a private grief that has spanned a half-century. They make their wishes very clear, and they will not tolerate exploitation of their grief or their loved one's memory. The sacrifice willingly made by Bennett and any other American must not be tarnished in any form whatsoever!"

Hardy realizes he is up against a brick wall and powerless to change anyone over to his way of thinking. "The Doctor is intractable; and the other three won't waver either. I'm surprised these people have made such strong demands."

Finally, when he realizes he can't get anywhere by arguing, Hardy makes an offer. "I'll agree to provide ten-thousand-dollars to be applied to transportation and search team costs."

The Doctor looks at him with those snake-like eyes that Hardy will later say make him so self-conscious, and says, "What about the conditions we have set forth?"

Hardy then sees he is beaten and agrees to unconditionally abide by the terms and conditions the family set forth.

When the Doctor leaves the room to get some papers, Hardy uses the opportunity to question the three men about their choice of the Doctor as team leader. Try as he might, he cannot get the Doctor replaced.

Hardy ponders, "The Doctor poses a real threat to my success in this venture. He is hard to get along with and steadfast in his demand to adhere to those so-called 'CILHI Accords,' whatever they are."

While in Texarkana, Hardy finally meets Ben and they spend a couple of long nights in a local bar, where they seem to have an agenda of their own.

Bowden, Carson, Sandlin and the Doctor are unaware of and not invited to any of these meetings.

The team continues to make preparations for this year's search and does not hear from Hardy again until mid-June, when he calls the Doctor and asks if their plans are still the same.

Hardy then offers the Doctor a private deal: "Just allow me and my crew to follow along in the jungle and film as I see fit. I won't mention Bennett in the film. I'll just observe the team and film them at work."

The Doctor ponders, "Even a blind man can see through this scheme."

The Doctor flatly refuses the offer since it has been proposed to him instead of the Bennett family. It is also different from the offer that was approved by Bennett's family and friends.

Finally, in desperation, Hardy agrees to go by the original plan and sends money for team transportation.

The Doctor is aware of what has been going on in Vanuatu and knows what Laurel, Hardy and their friend, Folly, have in mind. It is also apparent that Ben will somehow be involved in their plans. CILHI has been kept informed of Hardy's proposals, and so has "Blue Chip Five Zero," who is deeply concerned about their activities.

Even after the Doctor challenges Ben's reasons for making this year's trip, he is still adamant that he wants to "finish what I started." Somewhat reluctantly, the Doctor agrees to let him go, but decides to keep an eye on him.

Pam, a young pilot who wants to go on the search, approaches the team in early June. She is told about the film crew and advised that this search will not be a walk in the park, but she is an outdoors person and seems to know what she is doing. She agrees to abide by the rules and work as a team member, so she is accepted. Little does the Doctor realize how close she and Ben will become during the search trip.

BACK TO VANUAUTU

After they arrive in the islands, the team has two days to purchase any necessary final supplies.

The Doctor and Roger meet with Reece and Ken Hutton, who have heard several rumors about the film director and his friends, Laurel and Folly, during the past year. They bring the Doctor up to date on what has happened and make him aware of the rumors.

Reece has a friend in the islands who is a widely known and well-respected missionary. After learning that the search team will be going into a new region, the missionary contacted Reece. He advised him of certain idiosyncrasies to be expected of a Chief from that area.

Reece tells the Doctor, "This Chief is about thirty years old and already has five wives. He fancies himself quite a man with the ladies, according to the missionary."

The Doctor replies, "Perhaps anyone with five wives in the same house, or on the same planet for that matter, can fancy whatever he pleases."

They both laugh, and Reece continues, "The young Chief has been alerted to the impending arrival of the Americans, and his first question was, 'Are there any American women in the search team?' The missionary didn't know if any women would actually be coming into the bush, but he and the Chief had a long and revealing discussion. The missionary contacted me so I could warn you of the Chief's attitude."

Reece then takes the Doctor and Roger to meet with the missionary at his office.

After introductions are over, the missionary gets right to the point. He is concerned for any women who may accompany the search team. He relays the content of his talk with this Chief and his conditions for cooperation with the search team.

The missionary adds, "This is not an uncommon demand to be made of unattached women in any group. It is best if the woman be identified and introduced as 'belonging' to one of the search team's men. She must not go into the jungle unattached; she must belong to one of the men. And she must be introduced as the, 'White woman blong white man'."

The Doctor makes it very clear that he will not be subjected to this demand, and assures the missionary, "I will not allow the Chief to make his demand on our young lady."

As they return to the hotel, Reece asks the Doctor, "Do you plan to tell Pam about this meeting since some of the Chief's conditions for cooperation will involve her when you reach his village?"

The Doctor replies, "I don't think I'll tell Pam right now. We'll just have to take a chance that the Chief is bluffing about all this. If he is really serious about Pam, I'll just escort her back to Luganville.

But Reece and Roger cannot let this opportunity for a joke on Pam die on the vine. When they get back to the hotel, the Doctor goes over to a pharmacy to get a supply of antibiotic creme. Unknown to him, Roger and Reece head straight to Pam's room to tell her the story. With full-blown amplification and appropriate distortion, they tell Pam about what the missionary said.

Pam is absolutely stunned at the implications of the proposition the Chief will make to her.

With no idea of the turmoil Pam will go through before morning, Reece and Roger drag the story on in great detail, and end with, "...if you agree, everything will be okay. The Chief knows where Bennett's plane is located; and, if you refuse, the trip will end in failure."

Once they finish the story, they adjourn to a restaurant where the rest of the team is eating. In their haste, they forget to tell her that the Doctor has already decided that compliance with the Chief's demands is not an option.

The next day the Doctor briefs Pam. "While we are in the jungle, you should act like you belong to me. You should stand behind me when we meet the Chief and do what I say. Native wives are always subservient to the men."

Pam has been up all night worrying, and the Doctor is concerned that something is terribly wrong. After a few questions, he finds, to his horror, that Reece and Roger never told her the end of the story.

She finally tells him, "I didn't sleep at all last night. I kept trying to figure out how I can comply with the Chief's demands. I didn't want to but I was afraid that if I refused it would hurt the team. If fact, I was afraid it would keep us from searching the area and cause the entire trip to end in failure."

The Doctor thinks, "Boy, that must have been a very long night for her, but she has spunk and no one can ever deny that she is concerned about the search's outcome."

He explains to Pam, "As an escorted woman who belongs to a man, you will not be a target of opportunity, and the subject of your availability to the Chief should not come up. It is possibly a custom in some of the more remote villages, including this Chief's. But you will not have to face this problem in the jungle with nowhere to run or hide. We are a team and we all look out for each other. Nothing like that is going to happen to you."

Pam is clearly relieved and ready to go on into the jungle.

The Doctor makes a mental note to have a little chat with Reece and Roger about their idea of "teasing" Pam.

Meanwhile, Ben has found an old friend in Vila, Laurel, and they are keeping to themselves. This is his second trip and everyone has grown more relaxed with him, but he does seem somewhat distant this time. He seems quiet and contemplative and seldom attends functions with the entire team.

The Doctor assumes Ben is resting and keeping himself occupied while waiting for all the meetings to end, but the Doctor will soon have another meal of humble pie. And his assumptions about Ben's activities will come back to haunt him.

With the crisis over about the Chief and Pam, the team flies to Espiritu Santo and back to Mary Jane's hotel.

When they arrive, natives are celebrating their Day of Independence so they can't go into the bush for two days. This gives the team a chance to relax and recover from jet lag after their long trip.

Ben is off on some private adventure, while the Doctor is hiring villagers and talking to Chiefs from the regions of this year's search.

Finally, everything settles down so they can depart for road's end. This is all familiar territory, and the villagers are old friends. The Doctor and Roger have plenty of toys for the children, and Pam makes an excellent nurse assistant for the Doctor while he treats natives. She has a quick wit and natural smile, and the natives like her immediately.

At the last minute, Pam sprains her ankle, and it appears she will be unable to go into the jungle at all. Pam is crushed at the thought of not being able to go along on the search mission, and the entire team feels bad about her ankle. Pam is afraid of being left behind, and the Doctor knows he cannot leave her in a strange village. Emotionally, she is in no condition to stay anywhere other than with this team.

The Doctor talks to the village Chief, and soon a native brings Pam one of the very few horses on the entire island to save the day. She will be able to ride the horse for the first day of travel to the base camp at the village of Jenetavara. She can then rest in the village for a day or two while her ankle heals enough for use. She can then join the team at a more distant camp.

Jenetavara is deep inside the jungle and sits on top of a steep mesa over 150-feet above the river. It is a breathtaking view, and the village Chief is the team's old friend Robert. He is very friendly and has no ulterior motives in his friendship with the Americans. He agrees to have his people help Pam and make her feel at ease as a village guest.

Pam is delighted to see that this is a no-risk situation, and accepts the hospitality of the Chief and his family.

The next morning at dawn, the team bids Pam farewell and begins a long, arduous climb to the next campsite. The search area will be high in the hills and a long distance from Pam. But she will be able to see the mountaintop where the team will camp in the cloud-shrouded distance.

During the trip into the bush, Ben stays close to Hardy, the film crew director. They always bring up the rear of the line and have deep conversations about some mysterious topic. These discussions always come to an end when the Doctor or Roger walk nearby.

Roger and the Doctor have an idea that something is brewing, but they can't waste time on suspicions about these two.

They spend four days scouring mountainsides and talking to many different villagers. Several leads have been developed, and plans are well underway to eliminate mountainsides in the search area. The team is closing in on the elusive Bennett site by process of elimination. When their systematic search turns up nothing, it defines the area where he is not located. Thus the area of highest probability grows smaller daily.

If Bennett is not found in the valley where the team is now searching, they will move the base camp into a final region on the charts. It has been a well-kept secret by the jungle, but Bennett's discovery appears to be only a matter of days away now. If all of their information has been correct up to this point, Bennett will come home this year.

THE DOCUMENTARY & DECEPTION

During the search, the team communication liaison, Phyllis, stays at Hotel Santo to conduct interviews. She records all new information from missionaries, natives and Chiefs.

A missionary from a church and school in Santo comes to the hotel each day to swim in Mary Jane's private, freshwater pool in an attempt to rehabilitate an old injury. This morning, he and Phyllis spent a lot of time talking about the search team, and he asked how things were going.

He told her an interesting story that causes her great concern. It seems he met a search team member named Ben, and is concerned about Ben's motivation and honesty. He admits that he does not like Ben, and feels like Ben has a problem with his heart and soul.

The missionary tells her that he told Ben and a film director about the location of an unvisited WW2 plane that still has remains of an American pilot and crew inside. And the site is in the area of the search for Bennett's plane. He said he even explained the location and drew a map of the site because he knew Ben was a part of the visiting MIA team.

Evidently, this meeting with Ben took place on the day before the search team left Santo! As the team liaison, she sat in on all briefings and planning sessions; and she knows, for a fact, that Ben did not give this information to the Doctor before they left.

She ponders, "Why would Ben withhold this information when the purpose of this trip is to find Bennett? Something is very seriously wrong!"

Phyllis is pondering all this while having dinner in the hotel restaurant, then she sees a familiar face. It is Folly, and he has come to Santo to meet with a Frenchman sitting at the next table. The Frenchman knows Folly, and tells him the results of a trip he just returned from. It seems he went into the bush to hunt wild pigs in an area Folly referred him to. He tells Folly that he came upon a crashed airplane, which contains the remains of two Americans. He then sells Folly the crew's personal effects that he stole from that crash site.

Phyllis wonders, "Did that man accidentally find that plane, or did Folly send him to hunt for it... instead of hunting wild pigs?"

When Folly finishes with the Frenchman, he comes to Phyllis' table and starts asking questions about the team and their location. He asks, "Has there been any trouble on the search yet?"

She replies, "I haven't heard of any. Have you?"

Folly smiles as he replies, "I think there's about t' be, and I'm on my way to visit their jungle camp."

Folly adds that he has business with the film crew director and is supposed to take artifacts and remains back to one of the first year's planes that will be used in Hardy's documentary. He plans to leave at dawn for road's end and, with luck, will reach the team in two days.

Phyllis has been involved with the team since the beginning and is very aware of their plans. She knows that nothing like this is supposed to happen.

The team has been in the bush for over a week. Phyllis asks herself, "How does Folly know where they are and what they're doing? What is his plan for trouble? What kind of trouble? And what about the remains and relics being photographed? Filming those disturbed artifacts could really cause trouble!"

She knows this is all in clear violation of the CILHI Accords. She has been married to the Doctor for over thirty years and is certain he will never deviate from the agreements he made with the Army in Hawaii.

Phyllis had already decided that she should try to get a message into the bush to the Doctor. Now that she has overheard the conversation between Folly and the Frenchman, and talked with Folly, she knows she has to warn him.

She tells Folly, "I haven't seen or heard from my husband in several days, and I really want to get a letter in to him to let him know how much I miss him. Would you mind delivering a personal message to the camp, since you are going that way? I would be happy to pay you to deliver my little 'love letter' to my husband."

Phyllis returns to her room and hastily writes the details of her meeting with the local missionary and includes everything she overheard between Folly and the Frenchman. Finally, she includes the cryptic comments of trouble that Folly mentioned, and explains that Folly has a bag of artifacts and remains that he evidently removed from a wreck on top of Mt. Wimbo. She securely seals the envelope and returns to the restaurant to give it to Folly.

At dawn, Folly leaves the hotel with her letter in his pack. Two days later the Doctor is near Jenetavara when the natives tell him, "White man himicum." ("A white man is coming into this part of the jungle.")

The Doctor waits on the trail; and, sure enough, Folly strolls into the clearing about an hour later.

The Doctor has no need for conversation with Folly, who unstraps his pack and hands an unopened letter to the team leader. "A letter from yer missus, 'luv letter,' she said."

Without a word, the Doctor reads the letter and is stunned by its contents. The information about Folly is no surprise because the Doctor has anticipated it for some time, but the part about Ben is the worst type of treachery because he is an American and a search team member.

It doesn't take a rocket scientist to recognize what Ben and Hardy have been planning all along, and the time has come to see if Ben is really this treacherous. The next move must be his own; then there will be no further doubt of Ben's real intentions.

The Doctor and Folly return to the base camp and call the team together for a meeting.

The Doctor explains, "A native on the trail today gave me new information about a plane that lies within our search area. It is on the area's south side and we need a fast-moving team to proceed there immediately. I'll take one man and make a fast, forced march, then rejoin the team at "Brokestone" in a week. Ben would you like to accompany me?"

Strangely, Ben chooses to forego the opportunity to visit this new site with bodies inside.

This is exactly what the Doctor expects Ben to do; in order to be a movie star, he must stay with Hardy. Folly has brought all the props for this film, and their setting will be on top of Mt. Wimbo.

Since Ben has declined the trip, he is given instructions to continue searching down the north face of the mountainside they have been searching. If nothing is found, he is to move the team into the final search area and look for Bennett's plane in the northern region.

The Doctor then says he will take Roger with him. They will take only a small pack of food and leave the balance of their gear with Ben and the natives, who will bring all of it to Brokestone when they come out in five days. The new site the Doctor will be visiting is not explained to Ben or the remainder of the team.

The Doctor adds, "Ben, if your team finds Bennett, notify Phyllis at Hotel Santo. If we find Bennett, we'll send word to you in the bush."

Roger already realizes the plan has changed dramatically; things are happening too fast. He knows something is wrong, but says nothing.

With the instructions given, the Doctor and Roger leave Ben with his assignment. On the trail, the Doctor explains the information contained in the letter.

He admits his concerns to Roger. "If Ben continues to search on this mountainside, he will be through in four days. If he moves into the final area of search, he will be south of Sara. At least two planes are there, in an area tightly controlled by an old Chief who has not allowed outsiders into his area for over forty years. I haven't mentioned these two unconfirmed reports to any team members.

"The situation has reached a point where our next move is a gamble. I may regret my decision, but I think my bet is covered. I think we can leave the area and safely check on the plane to the south because Ben is too preoccupied with the film crew to move into the last search area. If I'm wrong, the Bennett site may be lost to us forever; but if I'm right, we can report two more sets of remains before Folly can get to them."

[13-a] A WALK IN THE PARK? So you want to just "run over to an island" half way around the world; then "take a little walk in the park" so you can "bring your MIA home." Believe me, it's worth every drop of blood, sweat and tears you shed, every ounce of fat you burn, many miles you walk along dark bush freeways, and every dollar you spend doing it. Look at the thick jungle and imagine a wild dog attack that sent us all scurrying up giant, two-inch diameter trees to escape. Then imagine Roger slapping his leg and calling "Here boy, nice doggie." Or even the phrase from a popular country western song "Bad dog – no biscuit."

As they walk along the trail, the Doctor is deep in his own thoughts. He knows the consequences to the Bennett family if he is wrong. He also thinks of the possibilities if he can report the airplane to the south, and two American families will be very happy if he is correct.

He ponders, "Okay, Wayland, which way do I go with this deal? Is this a roll of the dice? Am I expecting too much from lady luck?"

The Doctor knows Wayland took chances because he raced trains and spun his old jalopy in the street. He pushed his angel to the point of wrinkled wings in Corpus Christi, and he pushed himself and Crocker into tunnel vision on the last day.

The Doctor takes a big breath and smiles. "Yep, I think old Wayland would take the chance, and he would roll the dice just like this."

The search is closing in on Bennett, and one plane to the south has already been found and looted. The Doctor is now certain that Hardy and Ben have cooked up a plan to go to Mt. Wimbo where they will make Ben a star... and nothing will deter Ben from this plan. The sad part for Ben is that he is committed to a shameful course of action that he will regret until the day he dies.

Two days later, the Doctor and Roger arrive in Luganville and are briefed by Phyllis about the events mentioned in her letter.

The Doctor and Roger proceed directly to the missionary's home and ask for confirmation of all details of the plane he told Phyllis about, and any other information that he may have to offer.

The missionary gives them the entire story, which leaves no doubt as to the agenda Ben and Hardy have been working on. It also seems obvious that the plane the Frenchman looted may be the same one the missionary told Phyllis about.

The missionary is kind enough to take the Doctor to a cattle yard where the Frenchman is working. They quickly find out that the Frenchman shares Folly's total dislike for missionaries, preachers, foreigners and Americans; in fact, every time he says "Americans," it almost sounds like a curse. But there is one thing he does like – money. And enough money loosens his tongue a lot.

Once they interpret his uneducated, broken English, it comes out something like: "Folly bought all that there stuff 'ceptin one little ole gun. He and his pal, Hardy, are tellin' all them natives not ta werk for ya 'merikins. They sed yar team ain't got no money ta pay thar bills and ya ain't honest 'cause yar 'merikins. Hardy and one of yar guys named Ben are gonna take yar girl with 'em ta film the findin' of a plane on Mt. Wimbo as though it's a first find.

"Then Hardy and yar Ben's gonna' come back here, then I'm suppose ta take em off ta where I found that stuff Folly bought the other day. They're a gonna take all them bones and stuff from that one and move em all down ta his place in Vila. Folly and his friends sell them bones and personal stuff ta them dead men's fam'lies. If the fam'ly can't afford ta pay their price, they sell it all ta some tourists who'll pay fer it.

"They are tellin' all the natives ta not work fer ya and not ta tell ya anythin' 'bout crashed planes. Folly's done talk'd ta' three Chiefs who've agreed not ta help ya find any more o' them planes."

Wow, what a turn of events! The Doctor, Roger and even the missionary are surprised to learn that Folly, Laurel and Hardy have conceived such a devious plan. The Frenchman refuses to take the team to the crashed airplane site, but does let slip that he took a native with him when he went there. The missionary knows the native and agrees to take them to his house to talk with him.

Fortunately, the Doctor has been prepared for most of this plan. Now he has confirmation that a race is on for the location of any undisturbed wreck. If found by the wrong team, the site will be plundered and stripped of remains and possessions. Folly, Laurel and Hardy's business venture is in full swing, and they have involved natives.

The Doctor and Roger are disappointed to learn that Ben is right smack in the middle of this plan, but there are still a few surprises yet to surface. They still do not think Ben is aware that his new friends are selling the remains of American servicemen. Unfortunately, they are also wrong on this assumption.

Because the film crew did not to go with the Doctor, they missed an opportunity to film an exclusive discovery. Or Ben could have become the hero of the search and made an even more exclusive discovery if he had followed the Doctor's instructions. Instead, he switched to his new agenda and lost an opportunity to find Bennett and much more.

Even though some problems were anticipated, it is still disturbing to realize that the team has been betrayed from within its own ranks. It will be very important to keep all future information under a close security blanket. The Doctor knew he was an easy target for any team member with a wrong attitude or intention. As leader, he has been busy with search details and concerned with his team's well being. Meanwhile, Ben has been plotting to establish himself as the leader.

Ben is willingly being manipulated by Hardy. In his desire to become a superstar, he has become a pawn of Laurel's and Hardy's revenge. His price is cheap and he is easily lured into a quest for fame and fortune. To become the film director's star, all he has to sacrifice is his honor. Search details are endless and the opportunity has always been there for someone of Ben's character, and he is beginning to show his hand.

The Doctor now realizes Ben has asked a lot of questions lately about Turtle Bay and island history. He has also been asking more questions about Bennett's family lately and has too much interest in the crews of the Mt. Wimbo planes. Since Ben did not visit Mt. Wimbo, the Doctor wonders, "Why he is interested in it now?"

The Doctor is beginning to have a good idea what is going to happen. In fact, right about now Ben is following the film crew up Mt. Wimbo. The film they shoot there will forever show Ben's shameful desecration of fellow Americans' graves. "Yep, old Ben is certainly some kind of superstar and his film debut will show what he truly is," the Doctor says to himself.

THE DAUNTLESS

Roger and the Doctor are now physically exhausted. They have been on daily searches in the bush for ten days and then a forced march directly to Luganville. They are drained after interviews with the Frenchman and missionary. They are not ready for another trip into the bush, but time is running out. They must visit the plane the Frenchman looted before it is ruined forever. This is their only hope to record its occupants before Folly and his friends desecrate this plane.

The missionary takes Roger and the Doctor to see a native, whose name is Larry. They are not surprised when Larry says the Frenchman clearly did not trust or like him. When they reached the area, the Frenchman made Larry wait for him below a waterfall near the crash site. Larry says he could hear the Frenchman moving wreckage to get to money, dog tags, bracelets, watches and rings to sell to Folly. He thinks the Frenchman also took the dead crewmen's wallets.

The missionary finally convinces Larry that the Doctor and Roger are conducting a humanitarian search that observes the customs of their land, and that they have no intention of reselling any artifacts or bones.

With the missionary's help, the Doctor and Roger hire Larry to guide them to the site. They agree to meet the next morning at 7:30. The Doctor will bring food and supplies for the rough journey over some of the island's most rugged terrain.

This site is just inside the search area's southern boundary, and the Doctor is sure it is not *Susie-Q*. Although the wreck may not be Bennett's, one thing is certain: if they fail to visit this site, both occupants' identification will be forever lost. They cannot fail to at least look at the site and record the plane's identification numbers.

Larry is reluctant to make the trip the next morning because of impending rain. He does not want to be blamed if they fail to reach the plane due to weather. They must cross a river that will become impassable if hard rains occur. If a native takes an assignment, he feels honor-bound to insure the trip meets the white man's expectation; Larry is no exception to that rule. He would rather not go and be assured of his status in the community, than to go and fail.

The Doctor finally convinces Larry that his reputation and performance will not be criticized if the team fails to reach the plane due to rain. He will not be blamed for any failure and will be praised if the trip is successful.

At 8:30 a.m., the three men set off down a dim, narrow trail. After 30 minutes' march, the Doctor suddenly becomes aware of Larry's intelligence. One minute they are in rolling terrain and in the next moment they are looking straight down into a chasm that is at least 400 feet deep.

"Another vertical cliff! Boy, it's going to be another one of those days," the Doctor thinks.

Far below is a small, meandering stream, but they must first go straight down the cliff like a cat. There is a big difference between climbing and descending an almost vertical wall. Climbing up is hard, but climbing down is an almost totally blind maneuver. A trail of sorts simply disappears over the cliff's edge, complicated by ever-present mud and moss.

The Doctor and Roger cannot even see where to put their feet as the three slowly and carefully inch down the steep wall. No one can be in a hurry here. They gingerly work their way diagonally across the cliff's face several times, gradually moving downward. A light rain begins after almost three hours, and soon runs down the cliff's sides in rivulets. Below, they see the stream only 100 feet away, and notice its surface is still and calm.

An hour later, they arrive at the bottom of the gorge where the Doctor and Roger think about a rest stop. But Larry is making some noise about, "Big fella wata himicum nostap." This means, "The big water will be coming soon and we cannot stop now. We must move onto higher ground."

By now the placid creek is receiving a heavy downpour's runoff. The Doctor carefully looks for a pile of rocks on each side of the river to denote a shallow water river crossing. He does not want to duplicate an earlier mistake by ignoring those signs.

[13-b] CROSSING THE JORDAN:
Roger and the Doctor cross the River Jordan. The fast-moving water is only ten inches deep here, but it drops to 20 feet just ahead and currents make it very hard to cross. The native guides know the river crossings so we don't just disappear. These jungle rivers become uncrossable after even a few hours of rain. The natives know better than to cross them during the monsoon season's daily rain because they can be very dangerous for both visitor and native. At least seven American airplanes, including Bennett's, are within five miles of this crossing.

The ten-foot-wide, lazy stream has rapidly widened to fifty feet. The normally ankle-deep water is already over two-feet deep, and seems to be visibly rising. Larry also seems to be telling them that the water will soon be ten-feet deep and very fast moving.

The Doctor has been advised that natives know all they need to know about weather, and all the team needs to know about crossing rivers. He was also cautioned that a calm river surface is easier to cross. Movement on the water's surface indicates a fast-moving current below; and, the deeper the water, the more dangerous the crossing.

The message is clear: they must cross immediately if they are going to cross it at all.

The three hold onto each other and start across the swift, rising stream that has risen to three-feet deep. Larry's estimate was fairly accurate. Only a few minutes later, the rising water is frothy and ill-tempered and has changed from a calm stream into a treacherous-looking monster.

This is not the time or the place to fall as Tom did several years ago. If anyone loses his balance here, he will be swallowed by the dangerous river and rapidly swept downstream at the river's mercy. An out-of-control river can also contain other bizarre, unanticipated hazards.

With the crossing complete, they climb out on the other side. As they look back, they see limbs and trees with entire root systems coming down the river crosswise. If they had encountered these charming obstacles while crossing the river a few moments before, they might have had a very serious problem with an even more dismal outcome.

The three men quickly start climbing the almost vertical opposite wall. Thick moss and a dense collection of rotting leaves cover the steep rock face. The three must search for each individual niche for their hands and feet. Rain is pouring down in sheets and complicates the climb because they must look up into it as they climb.

The river canyon below is rapidly filling with water from the boiling, muddy river. It is now roaring like a passing freight train, and rapidly carries its cargo of trees and stumps below the climber's feet. Chickens and a cow, along with hundreds of coconuts, have become the river's victims – all swept by in a foaming, raging mass en route to a final resting place somewhere in the sea.

Such little encounters just help pass the time of day for a search team when in rough mountainous terrain. If the jungle is deep with steep terrain, the team must anticipate fast-moving water as a natural phenomenon. The Doctor and search team members have all learned a little about results of inclement weather and its aftermath.

The Doctor has learned that a native is always the very best guide, and knows how to co-exist with nature. The wise team will do what a native does in a rainstorm, which is usually nothing. Jungle life is slow and methodical, and no one seems to be in a hurry. Natives will usually not travel when it rains, but stay in their huts with family and friends. When on the trail, natives will occasionally simply crouch under a tree and make an umbrella or head cover from large banana tree leaves. If they have more time, they will make small, one-man shelters from those leaves in about five minutes flat.

Larry learned long ago to take no risks with uncertainties of weather and wind in the jungle because that is not usually conducive to longevity or old age. Natives do not like to travel in late afternoon because they do not want to take the chance of getting caught in the jungle after dark. They know that any injury in the jungle at night might make them unable to defend and protect themselves from marauding wild animals, which always seem able to find an injured person in the bush.

The Doctor learned on a previous night march that encounters with wild cattle and pigs at night can be frightening. One cannot see well enough to escape in the dark, but an animal can see well enough to attack. A wild cow or bullock protecting a calf can be a formidable opponent at night for an unsuspecting "rhinestone cowboy."

During a short lull in the rain, the three men successfully make it to the canyon rim. They are so relieved to be out of this canyon of terror, they just sit down in the mud. They watch the rain and raging river sweep by below as they catch their breath. As much as they will try to make light of the river crossing later, this has been another close call.

Roger looks over at his brother and says, "You know, big brother, no one is ever going to believe things like this happened over here."

The Doctor shakes his head grimly and replies, "You're exactly right, but most of all, I sure hope Mom doesn't believe it. Because I'm still your big brother, and she still holds me responsible for your safety when we're together. And frankly, I would prefer to take on this river in a rowboat than to have to explain to her why or how I let you get into a mess like this."

The Doctor can tell by the far-away look in Roger's eyes that he is recalling some other adventures they've experienced while growing up. The Doctor ponders, "Mom really does still expect me to take care of him, and I still try, Mom."

As he stands stiffly, he puts his arm around Roger and says, "Ready, Rog?"

Roger groans a mocking, "No," and stands to his full height of over six feet as they both limp away behind the small native.

[13-c] **AMERICAN JUNGLE MAN:** *This is what we looked like after several days in the jungle, and we probably smelled worse. One often-repeated phrase of either praise or complaint was "are we having fun yet?" It is agony just getting one foot to fit in front of the other when going up and down these small hillocks. During these little walks no one ever "sits down to rest" – they just fall down and wrestle with the agony of muscle spasms and bleeding blisters.*

As they travel across high, rocky terrain, they pass through deep saw grass and an area covered with prehistoric coral boulders as large as a house. These stones still clearly show permanent imprints of marine life and must have been deposited here a long time ago when the island first rose from the ocean's depths. The fossil imprints would make an excellent study for marine biology students; in fact, this entire island is one giant history book.

They cross a small creek and hear it babbling as fresh water cavorts over rocks and races to the river far below. As they go higher and higher, they come to a picturesque waterfall and pool. In this isolated setting, they talk about all the people back home they wish could see this view. Fog and clouds start rising from the jungle floor far below. Small cloud puffs swim by as they rest and dine on beef jerky and canned peaches.

The Doctor has a nagging concern about how they are going to get back across that raging river. He does not relish the idea of going through that adventure again.

As best as he can, Roger asks the guide about the river.

The native replies, "Bigfella reva himi gobinbi."

In this jungle paradise, natives always refer to anything big like a tree, ocean or river as masculine; so this basically means, "The big river will go away by and by."

The Doctor turns to Roger and says, "You know, I'd interpret that to mean: in case you two mud puppies are not aware of it, as soon as this rain ends, water runoff will continue for awhile. Then it will slow down its deposit into that small river below. The roaring torrent's force and the intensity will subside. And in only an hour or so it will return to its normal size and rate of volumetric flow."

The Doctor and Roger have a good laugh that relieves the stress of the raging river experience. Then the native gets to his feet as if to say, "Now, if you two boys are through with your picnic and laughter, maybe we can press on with your business. And, if you will hurry, maybe we can be through with this trek before long. And then we can go home."

[13-d] DAUNTLESS: Roger and the Doctor had to overcome yet another small obstacle at the Dauntless.

So, thus enlightened, the Doctor and Roger load up their gear and shoulder their packs. Unhurried, they prepare to move up to the crashed airplane site.

Looking back later on the situation, the Doctor wonders if Larry was really impressed at the two white men's patience. After all, they seem to be in no particular hurry to get to the plane. They demonstrated their calm, cool, self-control by stopping for an hour to rest and eat beside the waterfall.

Once the Doctor is fully loaded, he notices a perplexed look on Larry's face as he says, "Wego." This is, of course, intended to mean something like, "Well, now, Mr. Guide, you have seen our unbounded prowess and skill in jumping rivers and hopping over hills. You have been treated to a rest period and plenty of food to eat for your luncheon pleasure in this delightful and idyllic setting. And surely, by now, you must be well rested and ready for the remainder of this very important mission. So, come along now and let's get um' up and move um' out, so to speak."

The quiet little native seems to be able to read the Doctor's every thought as he calmly points to a spot about twenty feet behind Roger.

The two Americans turn to look and are speechless and stunned. There, covered by shadows and a carpet of moss, is a perfectly camouflaged Douglas SBD.

The two brothers walk all the way to the airplane before they take their packs off again.

"Yep!" the Doctor muses. "Larry must have really been impressed with our exhibition of self-control as we just took a break only a stone's throw from this plane. It would be terrible for our reputation if Larry thinks we didn't know the plane was there all along."

Research notes indicate this plane and crew were reported missing on a flight from the Solomons to Santo. It was presumed lost in the sea; but here it is, lying only twenty feet from where the searchers have calmly eaten their lunch.

An SBD is a single-engine dive-bomber that carries a single bomb in a rack under the fuselage. It has a two-man crew with a pilot up front and a gunner in the back seat. The gunner also serves as observer and radioman while on a busy mission. The plane is photographed and tail and side numbers recorded.

This is a rare wreck that did not explode or burn on impact. The terrain is a 45-degree incline and impact was heavy. The plane probably first entered the trees in a 20-degree nose-down descent. Perhaps he was very low on fuel after the flight from the Solomons. That would explain why this plane did not burn on impact.

A home computer could easily duplicate the accident using a digitizer for a slow motion study of the crash sequence. Perhaps, on that busy day long ago, the mountains and trees were shrouded in clouds and fog. Maybe it was even raining like today as the pilot descended to a lower altitude in search of Turtle Bay.

This crew's final few seconds began when the plane struck the first tree and the left outboard wing section sheared off. Then it began its final turn into a cartwheel. When it collided with this 45-degree slope, the right wing folded upward, but did not shear off the plane. The plane's nose slued left, then the propeller and engine cowling struck the slope.

The airspeed indicator froze in time and space and permanently recorded the speed of that last brutal impact at 200-mph. The fuselage broke in half, directly through the pilot's cockpit. Bolts holding his seat in place sheared, and the pilot, still strapped in his seat was hurled forward into the instrument panel. The impact's force was swift and the outcome mercifully sudden. The pilot was then thrown free of the wreckage and came to rest like an astronaut, still strapped to his seat. His parachute, raft, pistol and all his personal equipment remained undamaged as he began a long wait for someone to find him – hopefully, it would not be a mindless grave robber.

The crushed instrument panel is bent forward. It is complete, along with the two 30-caliber machine guns and boxes of ammunition. The cockpit and instrument panel remained upright and are still protected by the windshield and gun sight that peers forward toward an unseen enemy.

Rudder pedals, brakes, switches, and even the control stick seem ready for use. The control stick's red trigger switch still sends silent messages to both guns and radios. The engine and propeller are still wrapped in blue and gray cowling.

[13-e] TECHNOLOGY: This radio equipment from one crash site would all fit on a postage stamp-sized computer chip in today's technology. But in the 1940s, it was all handmade and each component was soldered by humans. Robotics, like space travel, was a subject for comic strips then. This radio looks like it could be cleaned up, dried off and many of the undamaged components would be fault free. The condition of the wrecks and equipment was of special concern because we were trying to anticipate what condition a pilot would be in after 50 years.

With two-thirds of the left wing gone and the right wing crushed and bent upward, the rear part of the plane was treated like a whiplash. Lightened by the loss of engine and pilot, it bounced straight up and landed upside down 30 feet away.

The tail did not touch the ground and still seems ready for flight. The intact tail section still has fabric drawn tightly over the rudder and elevators. A thick coating of moss has preserved the majority of the wreck, and wheels are still tucked neatly into their wheel wells and appear unscratched. The plane's upturned belly faces skyward and bright red dive brakes look like they were painted only yesterday.

Suddenly, a movement in the bushes under the rear cockpit startles the Doctor. The Aldis signal light, still attached by its electric cord, rattles bushes as it swings gently in a breeze. An eerie uneasiness prevails, as if the gunner is saying, "Here! I'm over here."

The rear gunner's compartment is like a visit to a historical museum. It has been lying upside down and has not been rained on, or covered with leaves and jungle trash. The controls, gun, seat and switches are all like new.

The Doctor ponders, "Did this crash really happen a half-century ago? It seems to have happened only moments ago."

The rear gunner has remained with his pilot and plane, and rests on his side still strapped to the seat. Both these young men are a silent tribute to all casualties of WW2 and will not be forgotten. They were, after a tour of combat, returning to Santo and Turtle Bay for rest and recuperation.

These two aviators were too young to suffer such an ignominious fate. But their sacrifice was made willingly, at a time when they knew that price would be paid by many. They are now in the permanent company of men whose memory resides at Turtle Bay.

This airplane was not a trainer, but a combat veteran of a shooting war. It still carries scars from field repairs to bullet holes inflicted by a spirited defense thrown up by a valiant foe. It was scheduled to receive some serious attention from the airfield maintenance heroes at MAG-11.

Roger and the Doctor have had a lesson in humility today as they realize that they sat and ate in the presence of heroes and never knew it. And now they know, and must leave this hallowed ground with a feeling of remorse that is almost overwhelming. The Accords must not be violated; they must take nothing, and they must leave nothing.

They fight an overwhelming urge to simply make the recovery and return this crew to Hawaii. But they cannot forget their agreement with the people who helped make this visit possible. To violate the code now is senseless and intolerable.

A deep feeling of regret overcomes both the Doctor and Roger as they realize they must leave, but these men must stay. They now fully realize that, "Take nothing and leave nothing" is an almost impossible requirement. It requires more discipline and understanding than they had planned for. In a sense, they both cheat, and violate the agreements because they bring with them, forever and indelibly imprinted on their brain, the memory of today's visit.

The Doctor is tempted to tune into another sureal visit, but choses not to impose.

This lonely mountaintop will not be forgotten. It is a place of remorse for two young lives lost for all time. Hopefully very soon, if Folly doesn't get to them first, they will be able to again grace the soil of their mother country – a country that will welcome them home with open arms.

[13-f] THE DOCTOR (left) AND ROGER: After three weeks on the trails, we were ready for a hot bath and hot meal. What we got was a cold river bath with soap. There were no razors so we just combed our beards. This was our last change of clean clothes, which we sleep in to ward off mosquitoes. Food for tonight was: prime fillet of beef jerky – well chewed, bis-kits – well gnawed, and coffee – well, I think it was coffee. For dessert we had a steaming cup of rice and baked fish, a la banana leaf.

The Doctor looks at Roger and notices he must be sweating around his eyes because he seems to be wiping them often; but, then, he may be catching a cold because he seems to be sniffling a little more often now.

However, it may be neither, and the Doctor looks away. The trail seems to be strangely blurred as the brothers reluctantly begin to leave this lonely mountaintop. The Doctor wipes his eyes and nose with the back of his muddy sleeve and they start the long walk back to the river.

The first three hours of the return trip is without conversation. Larry has been correct in his prediction about the river. As the three men reach the edge of the cliff, he points to what is now only a small stream.

Roger notes, "I'm sure glad we don't have to face a raging river again."

The Doctor nods and they start the long climb down to the river. After a short break for a snack, they climb out the other side of the gorge.

The journey back to Luganville is slow. Both men know they will never be able to put their full feelings on paper, and neither of them will be able to speak about this episode for a long time. Perhaps time will sufficiently dilute emotions enough to allow the Doctor to describe a visit to a lonely mountaintop some years later. Maybe that effort will put a different perspective on the emotional turmoil that future MIA searchers will encounter.

CILHI rightly demands that, when an MIA is found, the team must not disturb him or the site. A conscientious team will have the satisfaction of knowing by then that their search is over, and they have completed a very difficult task with each member of the team playing an important part. They will have done their job better than anyone has ever been able to do before them, and they must not make a mistake. If they do not control their impatience, they could destroy the last hope for a casualty's positive identification and final return to his home and loved ones.

DECEPTION UNVEILED

As Roger and the Doctor return to Hotel Santo, they are informed that the remainder of the team is on its way back into town. They are scheduled to arrive at road's end at about 2:00 tomorrow afternoon. Because this has been a long and tough day for Roger and the Doctor, they take a shower and welcome the opportunity for sleep.

In the morning, Roger and the Doctor locate a vehicle to use to rejoin the rest of the team in the final search area. Somewhere they find an entire case of soft drinks and a chest of ice to take with them. They know the team will be ready for something cold and refreshing after several days in the bush.

Hopefully, they will have good news and better results than the Doctor. It was rewarding to locate the Dauntless, but it was a disappointment to find it was not Bennett. However, it did eliminate another site from further consideration in future searches and provide another location and remains for CILHI to process.

The Doctor decides not to mention the Dauntless until he can get a satisfactory report on Ben's activities. He is afraid Ben will visit the SBD and become a part of the total desecration of a site. If Hardy is interested in filming an excellent subject, he can take the high road and produce an honorable documentary; otherwise, he will travel a low road – one which the Doctor is sure Ben and Hardy have already started to travel.

As Roger and the Doctor reach Brokestone, they meet a native they know from earlier trips into this area. He informs the Doctor that Laurel, Hardy, Folly, Ben, and Pam are all on the way out of the jungle and should arrive in about an hour.

The Doctor is dismayed to learn that the team is obviously not going to the final search area. He is almost certain they have not had time to search the assigned area and find Bennett. They have abandoned their search entirely for a reason the Doctor will soon learn. This turn of events was not fully expected.

When the team emerges from the jungle, they are surprised to see the Doctor and Roger standing in the clearing waiting for them. For some reason, Pam will not speak to anyone except Ben and Hardy. Ben is distant and will not discuss the results from the search area to which he was assigned. Ben and Pam stay together as if they are protecting each other from some threatening danger. The Doctor also notices that Laurel joined Hardy and Folly some time after he and Roger left.

At first the Doctor thinks they must just be exhausted from a long march and several days in the bush. But he soon realizes that they are somehow different and their silent mood is strained. They act like children who have done something they knew in advance was wrong.

The Doctor takes Roger aside and quietly tells him, "I am now certain of three things: (1) Ben did not complete the search as assigned; (2) he went with Hardy and Folly to film the Wimbo site; and, happily, (3) I am convinced they have not found Bennett. They did not have time to do what they have done and also go into the new area. Of course, thankfully, that means they have not looted Bennett's body and airplane."

The Doctor and Roger let out a huge sigh of relief because they know the Doctor's gamble paid off. Bennett is safe and undisturbed for now, and he is almost certainly in one of the two mysterious planes near Sara. They are the only two sites left in the primary search area that no one has reported or visited. Their exact location is unknown to anyone because of the old Chief's restrictions to outsiders.

The rest of the natives soon emerge from the jungle bringing, in addition to the normal camp gear, several large pieces of cargo. This extra gear and cargo has been wrapped in banana leaves and rags.

"What could they have brought out of the bush that is so important it needs to be wrapped?" the Doctor wonders.

The Doctor and Roger smile at each other because the entire picture is unfolding clearly; Ben's deception is becoming both apparent and public. It appears the entire group has joined together in desecration, and both Ben and Pam have now violated the CILHI Accords.

The last two natives who emerge from the bush have a long pole over their shoulders. Suspended beneath the pole is another banana-leaf-wrapped object that seems bulky and heavy. As they drop their load on the ground, a vine holding it in place snaps and leaves fall away. This reveals a fully assembled 50-caliber machine gun; and, from the appearance of other bundles, a total of six machine guns have been removed from the airplane they visited. Several ammunition belts are included in the natives' loads. The natives place everything in a pile, and their souvenirs include a Corsair's windshield, rear-view mirror, light control panel and radio components.

[13-g] UNTIMELY FATE: This one-inch thick, bullet-proof windshield was directly in front of the pilot of another Corsair. Even with the plane's destruction many windshields are undamaged and still clear when wiped off. This Corsair was a Dash one, with a bird-cage canopy.

[13-h] (right) JUNGLE PRESERVATION: This F4U Corsair is an interesting study in wreck preservation. It has had no protection and no attention since it crashed. Yet, this light panel is in good condition. The paint is still on the panel and all labels are readable. The switches click with the same new authority as they did on the last flight. The engines, though buried and constantly wet in the soft jungle floor, seem to be well preserved and loaded with reusable parts. While internal damage is common due to a crash's sudden stoppage, many engines are well preserved. We hope researchers and legitimate historians will study and record these aircraft.

The atmosphere immediately becomes very strained. It is similar to when a parent catches a child doing something he has been specifically directed not to do. Then the child is speechless when he gets caught. At best, a child will drop his head in shame for what he has done.

However, in this case, these grown men and women know what they have done is wrong, and they become protective of each other in an attempt to show strength and stick together.

The Doctor is reminded of the way Adam and Eve reacted when God confronted them in the Garden of Eden after the episode with forbidden fruit.

The Doctor tries to break down the barrier between Ben and Pam, but they try to become invisible. They must both now realize that their days on the search team have come to an inglorious end. They have completely looted an airplane and destroyed its historical significance.

Then the Doctor notices that all his gear, including research notes, is in the cargo, so he loads everything into the truck. When everyone is on board, they begin the long, silent ride back to town.

When they arrive at the hotel, Ben and Pam go with Laurel, Hardy and Folly and have a long, private meeting. It is obvious that whatever is adrift here is being led by Hardy, which is not really a surprise.

The Doctor quickly learns that the wreckage of both planes on top of Mt. Wimbo have been ravaged, and that Ben and Pam participated in filming of dog tags, bones, teeth and assorted remains for Hardy's disgusting documentary.

He immediately writes a detailed report for CILHI, and sends a faxed copy to Bowden. It is important to keep Bowden informed about what has happened. All he has learned is included in his report. The Accords require that Ben and Pam be identified, along with the part they played in this desecration. Of course, there is no choice but to fire both of them from the team for their part in the scandalous conduct.

Ben and Pam are not seen until three days later when Roger enters the restaurant to find them sitting alone. Roger joins them and discovers that Ben is belligerent and aggressive toward him for no reason. Pam is silent and will not speak to anyone. Whatever agreement they have entered into apparently includes an oath of silence.

Apparently, Ben still has all the team's supplies locked away in his room. This includes the team chart and research notes that were left in his care when the Doctor and Roger went searching for the Dauntless. Roger tries to talk to Ben and suggests that the time has come to get these differences straightened out and settled.

Ben makes an unfortunate error in judgment when he decides to show that he is "somebody" in front of his new girlfriend. From some unearthly depths, he dredges up a long diatribe of profanity against Roger and the Doctor. Roger tries to calm his attack and get a conversation started; but Ben, much to his misfortune, will not listen and continues his verbal attack against the heritage of both the Doctor and Roger.

Ben soon learns that his actions are not a very smart move because calm and gentle Roger finally loses patience with Ben's adolescent behavior. Roger reaches over, puts his hand on Ben's arm, and says, "Ben, I'm not the Doctor, and I'm not required to act like a gentleman and a scholar. I want all of those notes and charts, and Ben, I want them right now!"

Ben should have taken this warning at face value because he is somewhat overweight, out of shape and paunchy. He also has an irritating habit of constantly preening his hair as if he wants to make sure he looks picture-perfect if Hardy and his camera show up.

Roger, on the other hand, is a prison guard and no stranger to physical activity. He has learned to tell the difference between a blowhard and someone who poses a real threat.

Roger has read Ben all along, but Ben decides to try one more blast of profanity against the Doctor and Roger.

Finally, Roger's patience is over. With one stroke, he sends Ben flying out of his chair, skidding across the floor, scattering silverware and chairs, and becoming a crumpled heap in a corner against the wall. Ben does not enjoy the opportunity to fight back either, because Roger pounces on him like a cat. Ben is already bleeding from his mouth and nose, and Roger is about to do a little more attitude adjustment.

Finally realizing the error of his ways, Ben begins to cry and cower. He curls up in a fetal ball and sobs in despair as he pleads with Roger, "Please don't mess up my face."

Roger puts his face very near to Ben's own and growls, "I want those notes now, Ben."

Ben agrees to get the notes, so Roger releases him. Ben quickly scurries off to the safety of his room, calls the police, and tries to file a complaint against Roger.

When the Luganville police learn that Ben is illegally holding the search team's notes and charts, they refuse to accept his complaint. The native policemen encourage the Americans to settle their differences after they get back home.

Roger tells the policemen that he wants the papers from Ben immediately, and with no more delays. He informs them that, if the research notes and charts are not returned now, they will soon receive another call. Roger explains his intention to have the papers now or he will find Ben again before he can get off this island.

Ben and Pam retreat into their new inner circle with Folly, Laurel and Hardy. They all soon reappear with a woman who claims to be a lawyer that Laurel has hired. She attempts to practice her legalese on the Doctor who has joined Roger. He will have none of it.

The Doctor states his case clearly. "I do *not* need a lawyer. I want my charts and research notes intact and complete, and I want them right now. As for Ben, he's fired. Pam is also fired, along with Hardy. Laurel and Folly... well, they don't even work for me; but, just for they record, they're fired too."

He finally gets their complete attention when he addresses the lawyer directly, "After our property is returned, I'll give Ben and Pam enough money for their tickets home – on a plane separate from ours. But, lady, no notes, no money; and your clients can pay their way back home."

This seems to put the game on a level playing field with everyone using the same rules. In a few minutes, Hardy comes prissing back with the notes and charts, which he had transferred to his room for safekeeping.

It is obvious, from the notes' condition, that they have all been copied. Every single page has been put through a copy machine, and the Doctor suspects at least five copies have been made of everything. Of course, many of the notes are in the Doctor's own cryptic shorthand and they will never be deciphered.

With the original research notes and charts back in the Doctor's possession, he gives the lady lawyer just enough cash for Ben and Pam to buy return tickets home that day. He tells her, "I do not intend to pay any more of their expenses for hotel rooms or food as of right now."

Ben, Pam and their friends stay together and eat together as a group at the hotel for the next several days. But Hardy and his friends have to pick up the entire tab.

The Doctor and Roger learn that Folly's grisly collection of artifacts was brought into the bush along with the Doctor's letter from his wife. Hardy immediately assumed leadership, broke camp and suspended the search after the Doctor and Roger left to search for the plane in the south. They proceeded directly to Mt. Wimbo to recreate the finding of those two planes. They replaced dog tags, teeth, bones and personal effects Folly had stolen and covered them with leaves and twigs. They then set up cameras to portray the group stumbling across this wreck for the first time. They showed the identity of these remains on film and portrayed themselves as cowboy heroes.

The fact that Ben and Pam did not follow the Doctor's instructions was most fortunate for those who were truly searching for Bennett and not just out to create a role for themselves. If Ben and Pam had conscientiously performed as they were instructed, they would have found Bennett and his airplane, along with a small, added bonus. But, by their own choice, they were only able to film Ben and Pam in living color as they acted out roles in a diabolical deed of desecration. That is quite a legacy for Ben and Pam, but it was their choice.

Pam was probably swept along in the course of events and was nothing more than a victim of circumstances to the aftermath. That is unfortunate for her because she could have made contact with the Doctor at any time to resolve those differences, and she did not. It will be up to CILHI and the government to prosecute Ben and Pam for their crimes against American military personnel and property.

PETER'S MISSION

Time is almost over for this search year, but the Doctor wants to check out one more lead. Since Folly's plan has been put into action, he cannot send messages into villages. Folly and his pals are desperately trying to keep all information from the Doctor.

The Doctor contacts the local missionary who originally told Phyllis about Ben's treachery. He agrees to accompany the Doctor and Roger to the outlying village of Sara and help them attempt to contact Peter, a missionary the Doctor met several years earlier on the first trip.

Peter had then told the Doctor there were at least, "two planes about two hours away, well maybe twice that long for a white man."

Since that first meeting, the Doctor and Peter have always missed each other in their attempts to make contact. Peter has always been on a church trip into the bush when the Doctor passed through Sara. As they drive into the village this time, they find Peter at his church office in the village, much to their relief.

They talk with Peter for over an hour about his work there and his family. They tell him they are brothers. Peter thinks, "One must be a Chief because he is tall and silent." He is a large man with black hair and beard, and looks like a giant to Peter who is only five-feet tall and weighs 110 pounds. Peter remembers no one from the village of Sara who has ever been as big as this American.

This big white man speaks very little; he only looks at you with cold, piercing eyes. He is a wary and watchful man. Peter thinks, "This must be what a Centurion looked like in Bible days. He has the marks and scars of a warrior who has been in many battles." Peter decides this man can be a very good friend but could be a terrible foe. Somehow Peter senses that he is a kind and gentle giant of a man because he talks to children and gives them candy. Peter also notices that animals come to him when he calls them. He seems to be able to pet dogs and cats that Peter has never seen tamed before.

The other man is an older brother with tired eyes and hair that is beginning to gray. This man is a doctor and does all the talking to Peter about their mission.

Then they tell him about a young man who died in the Santo jungles long before Peter was born. They say they represent the family of the dead pilot, and it is the American custom to return the bones to the village from which he came.

The Doctor speaks of their friend, Reece Discombe, from Port Vila. Peter has heard about Discombe as a legend in stories and recalls that all the old chiefs speak well of the things he has done for the islands. He knows that Discombe was the first white man to receive citizenship in the Republic of Vanuatu. There are not many cars in the islands, but this man owns two. The license plate on the car he drives is simply a number "1"; his wife drives the other car and her license is number "2." This is a rank of distinction in the islands to which no one can compare.

The Doctor has been coming to the islands for several years now, and Peter has heard of the team he is leading on the searches. "They are good men on a hard mission," he realizes, "and it is obvious they will not give up this search until their friend is located."

Peter has heard many stories about the older brother. He thinks, "The stories of his walking strong in the jungle and searching at night with flashlights is incredible for a white man. Our natives avoid night travel and the island's white residents won't even venture into the jungle at night. This man seems to be without fear. His dedication to this search for his lost friend is like one would have for a brother or their own child. What type of friends are these who will travel so far and take such risks to search for a friend?"

Peter decides Discombe and Dr. Hutton in Vila are the best credentials anyone could ever need for an introduction. The two brothers are wearing distinctive raincoats with "MIA Search Team" printed on the back. Peter decides they are good men, and he will help them in their search for their friend, but he also knows they have some serious opposition from other whites in the islands. He has heard that the man called Folly is treacherous and has been telling the natives not to help these men. Folly has said all manner of things about them that Peter does not believe. Peter knows these men have become friends with several of the island's missionaries over the years; and, as a result, many packages of clothing and books have been sent from America. The crippled preacher in Santo is Peter's good friend and has helped these men. "Yes," he decides, "I will do everything I can to aid them in this search."

The Doctor asks several questions, but says they must leave the next day to return to America. He seems most concerned about the planes Peter told him about several years ago.

Peter tells them, "There is a plane with two engines just beyond the first mountain and another, smaller plane only a short distance from the first. They are in a very isolated part of the bush that, for years, was controlled by a very inhospitable tribe of natives. The Chief has only recently allowed me to enter and talk to his villagers.

"I learned about these planes about a year before I met you. I think that was about five years ago. Then I passed one of them about two years ago when I visited a remote village. I saw some boots and pistols but really wasn't interested in them."

The Doctor asks Peter, "Has any white man ever been to these airplanes?"

"No. Even natives from other villages do not enter into this Chief's area, so only a very few natives have seen them."

The Doctor is visibly relieved.

Peter does not want to pass on local gossip but he tells the Doctor, "I was recently contacted by a white man who lives in Port Vila. He is not a good man. He is exerting a very bad influence on the natives – trying to turn them against your team from America."

Of course the Doctor realizes that this man from Vila is Folly.

Peter continues, "This bad man is offering to hire natives to lead him to the site of any airplane in the jungle. He wants to collect the belongings of these dead men and pick up their bones. Some natives from Sara have worked for him in the past, but they say he is disrespectful to the dead and no 'Kastom rites' are observed.

"Our people, regardless of how remote their village, believe in some form of higher power. They also believe the dead go to a better place in their after-life. When it becomes necessary to disturb the dead, regardless of the reason, a formal 'Kastom rite' must be observed. Our natives know that this man is not being respectful to the dead Americans because he is moving their bones without a 'Kastom' ritual being performed in their honor."

The Doctor responds, "Yes, I understand. We have a reverence for the dead in our country also. That is why we are trying so hard to locate this airplane – because his family and friends want to return him to his homeland for a proper burial."

Peter explains, "This man from Vila has told stories about your American MIA search team, all of which I'm sure must be untrue."

The Doctor then asks, "Peter, have you told this man about the two planes?"

"No, nor do I intend to do so. He is a bad man as far as I know."

The Doctor is pleased with Peter's reply, but he is sure it will only be a matter of time before Folly hears a story about their location.

The Doctor must leave tomorrow to return to America, so he tells Peter more about their search for Bennett. Then he adds, "I will not be able to return to the islands until next summer, but Reece Discombe in Vila is helping us here in the islands."

Peter replies, "I have heard good stories from the village elders about Reece Discombe, but I have never met him."

The Doctor asks Peter, "Will you please contact Reece and speak with him in Vila if you learn any further information about the two planes? He may come to see you or send someone he trusts to see you if that is all right."

Peter agrees to this arrangement and promises to help in any way.

The Doctor has a good feeling about these planes, but he cannot delay his return home for the two additional days it would take to visit them this year. That part of the search will have to be scheduled into next year's search plan. Maybe, next year, there will be less distraction to the search and the team will be considerably smaller.

With mixed emotions, the Doctor and Roger bid farewell to Peter and promise to check in with him the following year. They have made a good friend, but it will be some time before they know how good a friend he really is.

SETTING A PLAN IN MOTION

The Doctor and Roger pick up Phyllis at Hotel Santo and take the afternoon commuter flight to Port Vila, where they go directly to Reece and Jean Discombe's home. Their hospitality is always like being at home with good friends. Jean is a superb cook and immediately starts trying to put a little weight back on the two weary travelers.

They tell Reece everything that has occurred and report the wreck sites they visited. The Doctor tells Reece what the Frenchman said, as well as what Peter said about Folly attempting to get the natives to withhold information from the search team.

When the discussion reaches the subject of meeting with Peter, Reece takes on a new degree of interest.

The Doctor says, "I'm certain the smaller plane near Sara is Bennett's, and I'm very concerned that Folly, Laurel and Hardy are making a concerted attempt to reach Bennett first. But I really cannot delay our return to America any longer. In fact, Roger must be back at work in three days. Unless you have an idea about how to make a quiet visit to Sara and the two planes, we will have to wait until next year.

"If Folly's plan goes into effect, it will open an entire Pandora's box for future search results. Folly has apparently already made some progress along those lines by hiring villagers who worked for him in the past," the Doctor adds.

Roger then describes in detail how this overall pattern could produce negative results for all future researchers and searchers. He says, "I'm afraid Folly might be able to lock out all search teams and sites, if he can get the local government officials to place all crash sites under his control by convincing them of his humanitarian interest. It would be disastrous if Folly and company are in charge of all crash sites and future search missions."

The Doctor adds, "Of course we know what they are up to. But will island government officials question their motivation for seeking such an appointment. They already have a track record of raiding and looting wrecks and bodies, and an equally important issue is what artifacts they sell in their museum."

Roger then asks, "If Laurel and Hardy, in the company of Folly, are successful in a bid to get government authorization, what will become of authorized searches for other MIA's?"

The Doctor replies, "If Folly becomes the exclusive government licensee and acquires permission to include searches in his concept of a tour service, no one will ever again be able to search in Vanuatu for anything unless they contract with him. It would restrict any legitimate future searchers and researchers alike, and it won't matter if the subject of their work is WW2 aircraft or other subjects of academic and historical interest. He will control all searches, sell team supplies and provide native labor.

"Folly's natives can then lead searchers aimlessly in the wrong direction for any search. When the dejected team returns to Vila, Folly can sell them the very artifacts they seek. He will be able to systematically strip each wreck site before a search begins. He can personally assure the failure of a search and then have a corner on the black market selling body parts and personal belongings. If anyone should accuse him of such pilfering, he will simply blame the natives who live in the nearby jungles."

The Doctor continues, "Folly has already told me natives are notorious for doing this, but I have never seen a native who collected artifacts and personal effects from the body of a dead American. Only Folly and company seem to be able to stoop this low, and they have done so with the help of two of our American searchers: Ben and Pam."

All three men are disturbed by this turn of events, but hopeful the government of Vanuatu will see through Folly's scheme. However, they are afraid to count on the government's wisdom coming in time to preserve Wayland Bennett from becoming another victim of their plan.

Roger comments, "I hear about a lot of 'best-laid-plans' of people who get caught trying to make such scams work, but this scam will be even more painful if Folly and company are able to pull it off. I'm just afraid the government of Vanuatu will never suspect the true intent of Folly and his friends because they will claim to do everything 'in the interest of tourism'."

Reece has been sitting quietly and listening to the Doctor and Roger discuss the problem. Finally he says, "I have lived in these islands most of my adult life. The natives here are not given to this type of conduct on their own. They are kind and gentle folk who spend their entire lives on these islands and have no interest in the outside world.

"However, as Roger has expressed, it is possible for white men to do these things. Natives and the government have a natural tendency to look up to a white man as their leader and superior. While natives will not do these things, white men can manipulate them. If those white people are multilingual and can speak the people's language, they can certainly make such a plan work in the jungle.

"I am unsure how the government could be deceived, but the three people you have named are all multilingual and capable of this scheme. They appear to have money to finance such a commercial venture and the expertise to set up the filming of their activities. They can sell this product to any of the world media."

All three men shake their heads and wonder what to do. Then Reece asks, "So, under the assumption that Folly is trying to control the search, how can we intentionally steer them away from the site of Wayland Bennett? At the same time we must assure his intact recovery when the right time comes. And I agree with you, Doctor, time is running out. There is considerable native interest in the reward you posted. Sooner or later, someone is going to report the site, and that information will certainly get back to Folly and friends. If they're trying to get to Bennett's plane before you, it will be completely stripped before you have an opportunity to see him come home."

For the next three hours, they devise a plan to circumvent any looting of the small plane in the jungle, and they do it for Wayland Bennett's sake. The next day, confident of the plan, the Doctor and Roger thank Reece and Jean for their hospitality and board their plane for return to the United States.

When the Doctor arrives in Texarkana, he learns that Ben and Pam have already been to visit Bowden.

Bowden tells the Doctor, "Ben was on the verge of tears and raving like a maniac. He was threatening to sue everyone in sight, including Wayland Bennett. He refuses to meet with you or Roger. He is such a coward, he even declines the offer to meet in any gymnasium of his choice."

The Doctor explains search events, and they agree to make an announcement that will remove some of the pressure from the Bennett search. It must be done skillfully and with a specific purpose in mind.

The next Monday, September 16, 1992, an article appears in the local newspaper, and reads: "The search for Wayland Bennett has become an emotional roller coaster for the family. In consideration of this Gold Star American family, it has been decided to call off all plans for the recovery of his remains. The search team and the family of Wayland Bennett wish to thank all of the supporters for their prayers and assistance in the searches."

Copies of this announcement and a thank you note are sent to Port Vila and appear in the local newspaper there as planned. As a result of this announcement, all local efforts in Vanuatu to search for Bennett cease.

In the absence of a race, Folly, Laurel and Hardy decide to take their time. Since there are now no other contenders in the race, they know they are in the best position to win. They become over-confident and slow down their efforts. The monsoon season begins soon, and the jungles are very quiet as almost all traffic to and from the bush ends.

Almost seven months later, in June 1993, two natives arrive in Santo completely unnoticed. In their single bag, they carry a simple camera and hitch a ride northward out of Luganville. Their final destination is the small village of Sara where they meet with a missionary.

Several days later, they return to Santo and leave immediately for Port Vila. When they arrive, they have a long meeting with Reece Discombe. Peter has also sent Reece a written report.

The two natives have visited a remote site and have pictures that will be very exciting for some people very far away from the shores of Espiritu Santo. Reece places their film in his bureau drawer for the night, planning to have it developed the next day. After it is developed, he will fax copies of the film to the Doctor in America.

The next morning is busy for Reece, performing tasks for Jean. He is certain, after last night's meeting with the two natives, that the Doctor will want to come to the islands very soon.

At 10:00 a.m., Reece is doing the final chore for Jean, when the ladder he is standing on slips. Reece suffers a severe injury and is airlifted to New Zealand for emergency treatment. He is unable to return to his home in Vila for several months, but he finally recovers and is back in Vila before the year is out.

Upon his return, he immediately takes the roll of film from his bureau drawer and has it processed. When he sees the pictures, there is no further guesswork about the result of the two natives' trip into the bush near Sara.

Reece contacts the Doctor in America, and his news makes the Doctor very happy indeed. The final chapter of *Search for the Lost Blacksheep* will soon begin.

CHAPTER 14

AN IMPORTANT DISCOVERY – 1994

THE DESECRATED PBY

Two native loggers, working in a jungle near Sara in January of 1994, report a twin-engine airplane wreck to local police, who notify government offices in Port Vila.

The wreckage is a PBY Catalina that crashed during WW2. It was loaded with two bombs for anti-submarine attack, in addition to the full crew compliment with machine guns. On impact, one wing tore off and the remainder of the plane burned. The two pilots were thrown from the plane with their intact bodies strapped into their seats. The other five crew members were scattered in and around the burned-out hulk, where they waited for over a half century to be recovered.

Just as expected, the team of Folly, Laurel and Hardy hears this news and springs into action shortly after the report is made to Port Vila. The trio immediately flies to Santo and goes straight to the local police station. Folly produces documents that proclaim him an expert in the identification of crashed American WW2 aircraft. With such documentation, Folly is passed into the crash location with no restriction on his activities.

Just as the Doctor anticipated in October 1992, Folly proceeds directly to the village of Sara, where he hires a native to take him to the crash site. Unknown to Folly, this native is the local missionary, Peter. Unfortunately, Folly will be the first white man to visit the wreck in almost a half century.

Upon arrival at the plane, Folly immediately strips the crewmen's bodies of all personal effects. He completely destroys the integrity of the remains and any opportunity to identify them from their personal effects. This is a senseless act by an incompetent "would-be and wanna-be," a grave robber and thief who wants credit for his discovery. His loot includes several pistols, watches, rings, bracelets, dog tags, rifles and a sack filled with wallets and money from victims' remains. He stuffs some of the most obvious bones into another bag, commingling them in a common sack without respect.

Folly's actions completely destroy the possibility of a professional recovery and identification process. The plane's data plates and identification numbers are also taken away from the site.

Peter carefully observes Folly's activity with extreme frustration.

Several days later the U.S. Army recovery and identification team from CILHI arrives at the site. They are appalled at the degree of disturbance and desecration. They methodically rope off the crash area to keep out curious natives while they try to make some order out of the mess that has been deliberately prepared for them.

That night, under the cover of darkness, Folly returns to the site and removes all remaining evidence of plane and crew identity.

Chaos reigns supreme the next morning, because even the natives know who raided the wreck site during the night. The natives seek a restraining order to prevent Folly from returning to the scene.

Folly immediately files a counter-appeal, asking that the American Army be prohibited from removing anything from the islands. He demands that no foreigner be allowed to remove anything without his approval, including crew remains and any personal effects.

The local government issues a court order to keep Folly and his pals in town, away from the site. The police confiscate items he pillaged from the plane and hold them at the station pending the case's final disposition. The court also denies Folly's request for a counter claim.

Folly even complains to the Ministers of Justice and Culture and History. They are, of course, honorable men in Vanuatu's government; but Folly and his two pals have hoodwinked these fine officers into supporting his demands for the time being. Soon, however, they will learn of his true intentions and withdraw their support of his plan.

Once Folly no longer has personal possession of the remains, he has someone in the Port Vila government offices file a complaint with the U.S. Ambassador in the Solomon Islands in an attempt to force the U.S. Army to leave everything in the islands. Folly claims he will contact the families of the deceased and arrange for return of remains and personal effects to those families. He demands the "mean old folks" at CILHI be forced to return the watches, rings, and personal effects that he secretly hopes to sell back to the families in America.

Fortunately the Embassy in the Solomons is a function of the mainland U.S. government, and these things just take time. In this case they take just enough time to allow the Army to complete the project as it has been outlined from CILHI in Hawaii. They know it won't be difficult to document Folly's immoral and unethical actions when the time comes. Yep, old Folly is full of audacity, among other things.

Peter continues to watch the activities closely to determine who is in charge of the operation to recover remains of the PBY Catalina crew. For several days the CILHI team is busy at work trying to identify the wreckage.

Peter smiles as he listens to a rumor that has started to circulate among the natives: "The Wayland Bennett search team will pay natives $40,000 in U.S. currency for the remains of Bennett."

Peter knows that a woman from Vila named Laurel, who speaks four of the languages spoken in the islands, is the rumor's originator.

Word has not yet filtered back to the site that police have the bones stolen by Folly. And already there is another rumor that the natives want $40,000 for each of the bodies recovered from the PBY.

Knowing this is also untrue, Peter watches and listens as the man who is spreading the rumor circulates among the natives with this lie. His name is Hardy. Peter thinks about what he knows about Hardy and ponders, "Hardy and Laurel are truly a matched pair. Their lifestyle is devious; their intent is to destroy hopes with their project; and, in the company of Folly, they become a tragic trio that turns legitimate dreams into a scheme of selling a hero's remains back to his own family. The hero's supreme sacrifice is replaced by a supreme insult to the tragedy endured by the hero's family."

Peter is most upset by the rumor that claims the natives have stolen the crewmen's bodies and are holding the bones for ransom, but he continues to listen as he thinks to himself. "It is time for our natives to go public in their own defense. Even though their lifestyle is considered primitive, those who live in Sara are indeed kind and gentle people. They don't know how to set in motion rumors such as these. Of course, the natives have no idea what 40,000 of anything is, and they have no concept of U.S. currency; yet, this elaborate scheme implies these natives are demanding money in return for the bodies. Most have lived in these jungles for generations and have always known where these planes are located. No one from this village has ever taken any of the artifacts or bones from the PBY, so why would they do it now? They have no interest in guns or artifacts, and a watch or bracelet has no meaning to them."

Peter observes the local Chief and natives as they ask the U.S. Army for the opportunity to pay their respects to these American dead by performing their ancient 'Kastom' ritual before any more remains are removed from this site or the islands.

He ponders, "Our natives have a basic understanding that is commonly taken for granted. These primitive natives believe all men have a spirit and will go to an afterlife existence. They know that remains of the dead are due a certain 'Kastom' ritual, no matter if it is a native or a white man who died long ago. If remains are to be moved, they must be afforded these final rituals as a matter of respect. These rites have been practiced in these jungles for centuries."

He is pleased to see the U.S. Army team agrees to allow them to pay tribute to these great American heroes. With simple respect and dignity amid the jungle's peace and quiet, these so-called uneducated natives perform ancient prayers and chants to their god on behalf of Americans who died in the PBY crash.

Their performance is completed with a sincerity that makes Peter proud of his fellow Vanuatu countrymen. He thinks, "What a shame

Folly, Laurel and Hardy don't have the common sense of these natives; they might have learned a little about human dignity and respect for their fellow man." From the shadows Peter watches and smiles.

As the recovery of the PBY bodies continues, it becomes apparent that a total of seven men were on board. Although Folly has demanded he be given all the rotten remnants of boots and gloves, belt buckles, coins and cigarette lighters from the bodies; all these items are necessary for an identification process to be complete. They will all go with the remains to CILHI in Hawaii.

Folly has shown where his heart lies as he has made every effort to disrupt the recovery of these remains. He has been allowed to display his true character just like the Doctor anticipated several months before.

Peter wonders, "What level of insensitivity must one person have for demanding personal equipment and belongings that has the name of the deceased on it?"

He finds it hard to believe Folly only wants these things for his museum. "I'm certain he is going to sell them back to the families he will contact about the dead Americans in planes he is able to loot. Folly probably thinks he can become rich on other people's grief."

Finally, as Peter watches the drama unfold, he senses that this team will be through with this site and its investigation in a few more days. It is almost time for Peter to make his next move. So far, his presence has been well disguised by a beehive of activity surrounding the PBY site. But this next move was planned months ago, and Peter begins to play out his role in the final events of a special recovery.

Peter mingles with the crowd and moves silently until he is standing quietly next to a female member of the U.S. Army team. Peter speaks to the Sergeant in a voice only slightly louder than a whisper, quietly explaining that he is a local missionary for his church and lives in Sara.

Peter then makes the notification that will forever exclude Folly, Laurel and Hardy from the one honor they will never participate in. "I want to inform CILHI of the location of yet another American airplane nearby." His notification to this Sergeant is confidential and urgent, then he silently returns to his position under a tree and watches the activity.

The Sergeant is surprised when the little native speaks to her at the PBY site, but she decides to do as he requests. "After all, what do I have to lose?" she ponders. She has been in the Army for 13 years and will soon transfer to another CIL unit like this, in another part of the world.

She gives a few orders and the Army team quietly divides into two separate groups. She announces, loud enough for anyone nearby to hear, that one group will continue final details at this site, while she and the other group return to town and complete paperwork at the local police station.

Before long, much of their equipment is loaded into bags and removed from the campsite. Five recovery team members bid farewell to the five who remain with the PBY. With their bags on their shoulders, anyone can see they are on the way back into Luganville.

The team walks down a trail and, as they get out of sight, Peter meets them. Without a word or fanfare, he motions for them to follow him into thick underbrush and away from the trail. They walk for an hour using a circuitous route through the bush, stopping frequently and listening to determine if anyone is following them. They move cross-country and leave no hacked foliage to mark their passing. During this walk they see no one and meet no one in the bush.

This walk with the recovery team is just as it has been planned, and no one knows they are here. Soon they enter a forest of densely packed underbrush and trees over 100-feet high. Only fluttering of wings disturb the peace and tranquillity as birds dart through trees searching for a place to rest for the day. A wild animal sound is occasionally heard; but most predominant is the sound of silence.

The team assigned to finish the recovery at the PBY continues to work, slowly. They have frequent meetings, slowly. And they have many quiet conferences, slowly. They take photographs and draw maps, slowly. They even write field reports and keep themselves busy, slowly. They are a methodical group of professionals. To a practiced observer they are accomplishing nothing, in reality they are killing time as a smoke screen for the rest of their team.

It's a little after midnight in America and the Doctor is alone in his dark living room, his mind thousands of miles away. All has been quiet regarding the Bennett search for several months, but he knows about the last few days' events on the island. He just got off the phone with Reece and knows the CILHI team is being led to the site of *"Susie-Q"*; so, he's like a child on Christmas Eve. He knows he won't sleep tonight and sighs, "One more night, old friend."

As he stretches out on the couch, he reflects on his meeting with the native missionary, Peter, and the assurances Peter made that have been followed to the last detail. The Doctor is appalled at the desecration visited on the crew of the PBY, but it could not have been prevented. He hopes CILHI will be able to sort out the mess. No matter which plane was reported first, the first one would have been looted. The Doctor deplores the actions of Folly and his gang, but his job has been to locate the intact wreck of *"Susie-Q."* He only wants to be certain the remains of 2nd Lt. Wayland E. Bennett are recovered undisturbed; that is where his responsibility ends. The fact that the PBY was the first one reported just made his job a little easier.

In Vila, Reece Discombe is still confined to bed after his injury. But, after his calls from Peter and to the Doctor in America, he has started to feel exceptionally well. He smiles at Jean as she serves lunch and adds her cheery, "Bon appetite, darling."

Reece looks at his watch and notes the date and time. It is almost time, he determines as he smiles and mumbles, "Wake up, old friend, it's time to begin your long journey home."

Jean turns and asks him, "Did you say something, Reece?"

He shakes his head and replies, "No Jean, nothing at all."

[14-a] NOTHING SPECIAL HERE – ONLY A DENSE JUNGLE: Can you see the F4U-1 Corsair? Can you see Lt. Bennett? May I introduce you to Buzz number 88, Navy 02608 and Lt. Bennett as he was found.

A LITTLE MAN NAMED PETER

In the jungles of Espiritu Santo, not far from the PBY and not far from the village of Sara, the small Army team reaches a location deep in the bush. Peter tells the Sergeant, "My instructions are to direct you to the site of this Corsair. According to the CILHI Accords, you are supposed to find this airplane and recover the remains for return to Hawaii."

All this baffles the Sergeant. "What plan is he talking about? What are the CILHI Accords? And how does he know what we are supposed to find and return?" None of her team has been given any information about this aircraft.

Peter watches closely as the CILHI team quickly sets down their packs and methodically starts unloading gear. They soon become very busy at this new site. Cameras are unpacked and the entire area photographed and marked off. They drive stakes into the soft earth and string is tied to them to mark off areas in which the soldiers will work. They are very careful to disturb nothing and are very efficient.

Peter helps two team members build a campsite. When the Sergeant offers to pay Peter, he refuses and says, "I have been paid by the American search team, and they will not need any other help."

Peter looks at his watch and remembers when the American MIA search team gave him the watch. That was when today's plan was laid out. These American still wanted the "Bones blong him," meaning: "the bones that belong to him." Peter remembers the meeting as if it happened only yesterday. Finally, he has been able to lead the right people to the right place at the right time.

Peter thinks about the day, not too long ago, when he came and photographed this same area with two natives from Vila who worked for Discombe. Peter realized then that the dead man beside the plane must be the friend the two brothers are searching for. He is pleased to see the plan has been successful, and no one has been able to violate these bones.

The Doctor knew the PBY would be violated by Folly if its location was reported first. Just as the two natives from Vila had predicted, the white man named Folly had come to the PBY and ransacked everything in sight. Peter knows the American Army team is not happy about that plane and those seven men who were disturbed. But Peter is proud to be part of the plan to insure that this little plane was not disturbed at all.

Peter spoke again with Discombe yesterday by telephone, and he told Peter the two American brothers will be notified. Silently, Peter begins to work on his sermon for Sunday; he has decided to preach on "Helping a Stranger in Need."

THE RECOVERY

These jungles were quiet and dark 51 years ago, and the ground was soft like it is today. The silence was suddenly disturbed by a hum that became a buzz, then a roar with a peculiar whistling scream. The plane slipped between giant trees to this final resting-place. The huge trees soon spread their giant branches over the newcomer to shield his rest from prying eyes. The undergrowth quickly sprang back into place to provide a blanket for this warrior from a place called America.

The rains came and washed away the pungent odors of gasoline, hydraulic fluids and hot oil. For several days the jungle's peace was broken by a deafening noise as other planes growled across the treetops in search of their lost friend, but they soon stopped coming. After a year or so, no one ever returned, and the peaceful serenity was undisturbed.

The Chief of this area believes in the old ways. For generations his territory has been off-limits to everyone, and no one has been allowed to bring in outside ideas or culture. He has held fast to this rule and even kept missionaries from coming to his village.

Now, stakes are placed in the ground and strings define the area to be studied by archaeologists and anthropologists. These forensic experts begin a detailed examination of the area around the wreck site. The brush and undergrowth are slowly cleared away, and parts of the wreckage become visible. This site will be much easier to define than the PBY because, for some strange reason, this airplane has never been disturbed. This wreck is in its original condition and, as the investigation proceeds, it becomes apparent that it has not been pilfered.

The team silently works in this quiet jungle with no distractions and Peter as the only spectator. The Sergeant is curious about the little native because he seems very secretive for some reason. He has only told them that he is a native preacher and did not want this plane to be looted like the PBY.

[14-b] Navy 02608: (left) An enormous force separated the complete center section, containing the retracted main landing gear, from the remainder of the airplane.

[14-c] Navy 02608: (right) This shattered hulk was broken apart by the impact. To the left is a section of the left wing flaps.

[14-d] Navy 02608: (left) Left wing and entire center section of wing was ripped out of the airplane.

[14-e] Navy 02608: (right) Left wing is upside down and shredded. The trailing edge and flap tracks are visible.

[14-f] NAVY 02608: (left) Landing gear is inside wheel wells. The violence of impact fractured the wheel.

    The wreckage is soon identified as an F4U-1 Corsair. It is a Navy plane, but the markings indicate it served U.S. Marines. The airplane is lying on its right side and the wings have been torn off at the wing root.

[14-g] NAVY 02608: (right) Left wing (without fabric) was shredded from impact with trees. Ammunition boxes were thrown out by the impact.

[14-h] Navy 02608: (above) Browning .50 caliber machine guns. Of almost 180 guns viewed, all seem restorable.

[14-i] Navy 02608: (right) A fresh box of 400 rounds of ammunition remains belted, folded and ready to fire from the left wing machine guns.

[14-j] NAVY 02608: Tail-cone of fuselage (left side) with tail wheel still retracted. No tail hook is installed.

    One wing flipped over and the wing's underside shows the landing gear folded into its bottom. The three wing guns are pointing south, while the remainder of the plane points north.

    The airplane came in to this place at a very high rate of speed. It impacted at a 60-degree angle with the left wing down approximately 20 degrees. Apparently the pilot made no attempt to pull-up when he crashed because elevator trim tabs are still in nose-down position.

Search for the Lost Blacksheep

[14-k] Navy 02608: (top left) The R2800-8, 18 cylinder, 2000-horse-power engine lies buried with propeller blade tips protruding from the earth.

[14-l] NAVY 02608: (top right) The engine and propeller were buried and the propeller is protruding from the mud and loam. Notice the cowl flaps.

[14-m] NAVY 02608: (bottom left) Engine (lower left) and cowling with cowl flaps closed for high speed in-flight cooling. Right side engine accessory service panel is open.

The engine lies buried in soft earth, almost hidden behind a clump of bushes. The propeller blade tips are curled and twisted, but remain attached to the engine's front. The instruments are ruined, but the airspeed indicator is stuck at 322 mph.

The impact was violent and the airplane is a jumbled mass of chunks and pieces. A fuel tank in the front part of the fuselage was ripped apart by impact and the hot engine ignited a small fire that burned for only a few minutes before all remaining fuel was consumed. The cockpit and pilot were untouched by fire.

One investigation and recovery team member is photographing fuselage wreckage. Near the tail on the left side is an American star and bars. Just in front of this are two numbers stenciled in white just under the cockpit. He clears away brush and moss from the plane's side and photographs the number "88."

[14-n] NAVY 02608: (right) Cooling duct and clamp attached to panel for access with clearly legible "Do Not Push Here."

[14-o] Navy 02608: (left) Perfectly preserved Star on left side of fuselage with remnants of moss and undergrowth clinging to paint.

[14-p] NAVY 02608: (Below) Fuselage lying with left side up. The Star is on top and "88" is just ahead of the Star and Bars.

The entire wing root and center section were ripped away during the crash. Sharp pointed debris is the landing gear door. A section of wing flap is to the right.

In front of this number on the fuselage is a faint white letter "Q." When he wipes the area to photograph it, he notices a dash mark in front of it. After he lifts away the moss and mud cover, he sees a partial word that means nothing to him. He records "S I E - Q" in his notes.

He speaks quietly to the woman in charge, "Sergeant, this number on the fuselage is '88'. Isn't someone looking for an airplane with this number on it?"

She remembers that an MIA search team from Texas has been combing this island in search of that plane and remains of a pilot from their hometown. "Yes, Bill, I heard something about their search two or three years ago. Look at the tail and see what the identification number is." But he has already looked for the tail, and it is not attached to the fuselage. He replies, "Sorry, the tail is not attached, but maybe we can identify it a little later in all this mess. Trees may have torn it off during the initial impact.

She stops what she is doing and thinks for a moment, then says, "Okay, Bill, check behind the seat on the forward surface of the armor plate. The data plate should be riveted to that steel plate."

Bill turns to look inside the cockpit and says, "Gotcha, Sergeant."

[14q] NAVY 02608: Native guide from the village of Sara looks inside the forward fuselage.

He carefully steps over a piece of wing and takes out a flashlight. What remains of the cockpit is a shambles. The pilot's seat attachments failed, and he was thrown forward into the instrument panel. The impact was so violent that the panel bent forward and instruments are broken.

Several pieces of white board are scattered inside the cockpit. Bill recognizes this as the pilot's navigation plotter on which he wrote his briefing information. The grease pencil used in 1943 is still attached to the plotter and some writing is still legible. "Lt. Benn... Lt.... ker, squadr... tics, Navy 026..., take off: 073... durati... 3+0... hr..., rendevo... gun... ry ...nge... 940, Maint... notes: lef... ing OK. Oil pres... nor...al, ...IL te...p n...mal."

This writing means nothing now; but, upon closer analysis, it will detail this flight. It was recorded a long time ago and shows this last flight as a normal day in a fighter pilot's life. It will later be deciphered to read: "Lt. Bennett, Lt. Crocker, squadron tactics, Navy 02608, Take off 0730, Duration of flight: 3+00 hours, rendezvous gunnery range 0940, Maintenance notes: left wing OK, Oil Pressure normal, Oil Temperature normal." In today's era of satellite navigation, this plotter is an antique; but, in WW2, it provided pilots with all the details they needed for their missions.

The throttle on the cockpit's left side is in full forward position and both landing gear and flap controls are retracted. Rudder pedals look almost new and the twisted cockpit's switches and levers still operate.

Bill thinks to himself, "Boy, this guy was moving!" He speaks to the Sergeant, "Didn't this airplane go about 400 miles an hour?"

*[14-r] HEART AND SOUL: This tattered and bent piece of metal hangs in a frame above the Doctor's desk. It is the "heart and soul" of an airplane. It was sent to the Doctor by someone who thought he might like to have a memento of the eight years he dedicated to the **Search for the Lost Blacksheep**. They also knew he had lived up to the "CILHI Accords," and had removed nothing from any crash sites he visited. As a token of his association with CILHI, he was presented with a commemorative coin that reads, "CILHI, Search Team." The commemorative coin is in the same frame and represents an end to **"The Promise."***

    She is lost in her own thoughts and does not look up from her work as she answers, "Yes."

    The data plate is still where it was originally mounted. It looks new and is undamaged. As Bill wipes away moss, he can read information from the metal strip. "Chance–Vought–Sikorski, Aircraft type: F4U-1, Customer Number 02608."

    He records this information on his work sheet and photographs the plate. He reads this to the Sergeant, who silently nods at his latest findings.

    She is clearing away brush in the area just outside the cockpit and has started to find scant remains of gloves and fabric. She finds remnants of a pilot's flying goggles and the radio headset earphones he was wearing. She brushes away some soft dirt around a piece of bright yellow rubberized fabric. It is the pilot's Mae-West.

*[14-s] Navy 02608: The man in the dark shirt is peering into the shattered cockpit. His hand is resting on the number "88." The spot where he is kneeling is where Wayland Bennett waited for us to fulfill – **The Promise.***

    While clearing away loose branches and sticks, she suddenly stops and whispers to herself, "These aren't sticks, they're bones."

    After she gingerly removes twigs and grass she can see that it is not only a bone, it is the pilot's complete skeleton! He is still wearing his flying gear and parachute. He is in the anatomical position of a young man taking a nap; lying on his left side with both arms in front of him.

She stands and steps out of the string-marked area that defines her work area. After notifying the team anthropologist that she has located the pilot, she starts to dig a hole in soft earth fifteen feet away. When the hole is two-feet wide and two-feet deep, she asks the archaeologist to make notes about that hole.

This hole is now a basic reference point for the surrounding area. It has been necessary for her to determine the depth of each layer of undisturbed soil so she will know what to expect when she begins to remove the remains. They measure the first layer of dark brown loam depth as ten inches. The second layer of light brown loam extends down to a depth of twenty inches. They photograph and describe the color and depth of each layer of this soil.

When the airplane crashed, it disturbed the natural layers of soil and, with a reference point from the test dig, she will know when she has reached the original stratification of layers and will not need to dig further for artifacts or remains.

She returns to her work around the skeleton and, with delicate care, makes each practiced move with planned respect. She is working with a hero; and, whoever he is, he died long before she was born. She knows he was a pilot and an officer, but he was also someone's son. Perhaps he was also a brother, a husband and even a father.

With a small paintbrush, she continues to brush away soft earth around the pilot. She thinks back to a briefing she attended about two years ago in Hawaii. She is a conditioned professional, but is not hardened against emotion. She vaguely remembers the topic of that meeting: something about a civilian research team from a MIA/BNR pilot's hometown that is attempting to locate his crash site. This is not a popular subject because recovering remains is CILHI's hallowed ground.

She wonders, "Why would anyone, especially a civilian team, attempt to locate an MIA? The cost must be enormous, and where do they get their money? Well, at least they are Americans; and, according to the briefing, they have met and periodically checked in with the Colonel." She then remembers, "The report said the civilian team leader told the Colonel all about what they learned in their research. They have also been making reports to the Colonel at the conclusion of each search season. For the Colonel to allow something like this is odd, but someone has mentioned that the Colonel has some sort of agreement with them."

She is somewhat puzzled because the mysteries do not end with that meeting two years ago. The way in which she was given the information about this airplane is also rather a mystery.

She finally realizes, "The native from the village was standing around watching us while we worked on the PBY. He was always in the background and seemed not to want to be noticed. He was even in Santo last week during all the commotion at the local police station. He was there when the natives asked for a court order barring Folly from the area. And he was there when the work had to stop while villagers performed some kind of tribal ritual over the PBY and the remains of its crew."

She frowns as she remembers the first time she saw the PBY. "It will take years to identify remains from that plane," she fumes. "The white man named Folly scrambled and mixed remains of all victims in one bag when he removed them from that site. It was a deliberate act and, for some reason, he is now trying to get Vanuatu's government to stop our removal of the bodies from the island."

As she continues to brush away dirt, she realizes that the skeleton has remained on top of the ground for all this time. "Why? How?" She records the maximum depth of her findings of bones and artifacts at ten centimeters. "That is less than five inches," she realizes. "At that rate this pilot could have waited on the jungle floor's surface for 100 years before he was covered by soil. It almost seems like this officer has been waiting for someone to come for him. Could he have known that someone would come?"

She remembers from her experience that the vast majority of these old WW2 wrecks exploded and burned on impact and wonders, "Why not this one?"

Many cases she has investigated included bodies on top of the ground, but scattered and eaten by wild animals. "Why not this one?"

Rarely does an airplane come to rest in one pile like this one; many have scattered their occupants all over a jungle where it takes weeks to recover them. She wonders, "Why has this wreck's pilot remained intact? He appears to have just laid down for a nap."

A coded message comes in over the communications set directly from the Colonel in Hawaii. "Transmit GPS coordinates and data plate information to CILHI."

She types in the GPS (Global Positioning Satellite) reference grid and data plate details into her small computer and transmits it to Hawaii. She also sends photos of the data plate and the number "88" on the plane's side.

She soon receives in a reply message, "F4U-1, Nr. 88, Navy 02608, Pilot BTB (believed to be) USMCR, Case Nr. reference 0060-94."

"Wow," she thinks, "this is a new twist. These remains already have a case number." She suddenly realizes, "This case is not going to be treated simply as an unknown; he will receive immediate attention upon return to the Lab."

This man is now known as "0060-94"; but his name, rank and service number will be determined by the scientific community at CILHI. Forensic pathologists, anthropologists, odontologists, radiologists and even archaeologists will examine him there.

Search for the Lost Blacksheep

While the remains are reassembled, the research office will reconstruct his entire military career. They will examine medical history and dental records for every minor detail. No holds will be barred as forensic specialties explore questions and details. One team will try to prove who he is, while another will try to prove he is not that person. The checks, balances and quality control proceedures the Colonel and scientists have worked out is incredibly accurate.

Once the research office is finished, it will send its results back to the lab where they will be compared with the assembled skeletal remains on a table. During this study of the remains, each bone will be checked to determine the victim's age, sex, weight and height.

She continues to brush soil away from the remains. She places the brushed dirt into a small pail that will be given to the anthropologists. Even this discarded dirt will be sifted through a screen and checked for any evidence that may be used in the identity process. This attention to the smallest details sometimes allows recovery and examination of dental fillings or shattered bones.

Early evidence indicates this pilot was killed on impact and simply rolled out of his plane when it stopped on its side. The crash occurred during an instant while Crocker was trying to shake cobwebs from his eyes following a hard pull-out from their last dive.

The Sergeant has seen no evidence to suggest this pilot survived the crash or suffered in any way. He may have been under the influence of a partial blackout and felt no pain when he crashed. Obviously, the small fire that burned quickly near his plane's engine did not burn him. This pilot was not paralyzed by injuries nor did he succumb to starvation or thirst. There was no time to experience panic and, since the canopy latches are still locked, he apparently made no attempt to get out of his plane.

"Perhaps it was a blackout," she briefly speculates, "but what proof remains?"

The Colonel allows no speculation about matters that are no longer important to a case. The only thing that is now relevant on Case 0060-94 is to recover all of the remains and artifacts that may be of some help in establishing his true identity.

Protocol will not allow anyone to refer to a set of remains based upon who they "think" he is. With the Colonel, it is an all-or-none procedure. The remains will pass the rigorous test for positive identification or they must remain an unknown. What is known to be factual in this case is a series of six numbers: "0060-94."

Working steadily with a small brush, she uncovers a small glint of gold and wonders, "Maybe it's a ring?" The wrist's carpal bones have been revealed and she finds remnants of a glove. Knowing she is in the vicinity of the pilot's hand she carefully exposes hand and finger bones. The finely engraved gold is fashioned into a ring that encircles one skeletal finger. She knows this was his right hand and she gently removes the gold ring and places it into an evidence bag.

The glove also contains shreds of gauze-like material and what appears to be strips of tape. "Apparently he had some kind of injury to that hand prior to his last flight," she surmises. She knows it may have no bearing on the case because minor injuries were frequently not reported to medics and would not be part of his records.

The gold ring is an uncommon design, without a central stone. It is in a style from pre-WW2, and her magnifying glass reveals lettering on the ring. "Texas High, 1941," she reads, then notices the initials "W" and "B." A deep scratch across the ring's face reminds her of something she learned in parochial school, "Upon his death, the ring of office a Catholic Pope wears is intentionally defaced." She finds it interesting that this ring is defaced, perhaps impact damage.

She continues her examination and notes that this pilot may not have been a Catholic because she finds no evidence of a Saint Christopher medal or bracelet. She finds no evidence of dog tags on the remains or near the body; then notes their absence on the field report.

Old stories, from WW2 men, indicate that pilots often did not wear their pistol on training flights in a non-combat zone, so she isn't surprised not to find one at this point. "If he had been on a combat flight," she realizes, "he would have worn all his identification gear, but not if it was a training flight."

She continues to work on the skeleton throughout the remainder of the day. Finally, when the recovery is complete, her field report log indicates she has recovered almost the entire skeleton.

Included in this recovery are artifacts other than the skeleton such as two rings, one gold and the other silver. She locates a total of sixteen teeth, some of which have fillings still in place. A silver cigarette lighter is recovered from his pocket along with several coins and remnants of his personal flying gear. Both boots are recovered and a belt buckle has been recorded and bagged.

[14-t] NAVY 02608: Associated small debris inspected by CILHI, not part of identification process – cooling fan, instruments switches, valves and panels.

For the next three days the team continues to examine this wreck for any further details or remains. The Sergeant expands the area of her excavation to insure she is leaving nothing behind that can be used in the final identification process. She separately packs each item recovered as she prepares the skeletal remains for transport. She notices that some of the bones are so fragile and eroded that they must be handled with extreme care in order to preserve them.

On the last evening, it rains hard most of the night. The next morning Bill notices rain has washed away almost all lettering under the cockpit. He ponders, "I wonder what 'SIE-Q' was supposed to mean, if anything?"

The team has removed this airplane soul (metal identification data plate) and its tail was ripped away in the crash. No numbers are now attached to the airplane. It has become a useless hulk, without numbers or a name to identify it. It can safely be abandoned to the jungle, which will soon cover its rough features with a smooth, dense camouflage of moss, vines and undergrowth. Maybe fifty years from now someone will stumble on this sight and wonder who died here; then the answer will be recorded in CILHI's vast computer network for retrieval whenever needed.

Now another critical work phase begins as CILHI tries to answer the question, "Who is this American hero?"

Working in the jungle like this requires extreme dedication and a high degree of self-discipline. For a moment, the Sergeant reflects on her military career. None of her hometown friends and relatives comprehend what she does in the Army. None of them will ever be able to appreciate the satisfaction she enjoys with a successful recovery like this one.

An intense feeling of pride develops at CILHI when they make a positive identification of recovered remains. This is the most gratifying part of the job she does for an MIA family: returning him to American soil for identification and return to his family.

A young WW2 pilot died here and waited a long time for someone like her to come for him. He was not mixed with wreckage and scattered across jungle floor, like so many others she has seen. Instead, he patiently waited for over fifty years on top of the ground; and, during that time, no wild pigs or dogs that roam the island in packs disturbed him.

She knows the forensics lab will have a field day with this case. A single-engine plane with one recoverable set of remains is a relatively simple case for CIL lab teams. The numbers and data plates have already identified the plane, and a missing pilot is listed on old loss reports. But she knows the Colonel will never accept old records as conclusive proof of his identity. The personal effects found with this pilot, such as the cigarette lighter and rings, will certainly provide a trail to his identity. The coins all have mint dates of 1943 or before, and will help establish the approximate year of the crash. The silver U.S. Marine Corps ring on his finger pretty much tells the story of his service – at least it will be a place to begin.

[14-u] Navy 02608: Native guide moving wreckage aside after CILHI recovery.

Early the next afternoon, this site is closed and the investigation comes to an end. With all their findings packed away, the team follows Peter back along the trail to the PBY site. No one knows where they have been for the last few days, and Folly will not have access to either site until they leave.

"Folly is such an insufferable boor, he really seems to be taken with himself. Well, everyone needs a fan club. Everyone knows one of the many problems with Folly is that he's a chronic, pathological liar," the Sergeant concludes.

As of now, she has the complete and untarnished remains of a Corsair pilot in her possession, plus all his belongings. Folly will not know of the discovery of this Corsair until after they leave the island, and he will not become aware of the pilot's true identity until September 1994.

Work at the PBY site is complete and the team ends all further work on that project as well. In Santo they gather bones and artifacts that were confiscated from Folly.

The Sergeant smiles, as she thinks of Folly, "The explorer and WW2 American airplane crash expert – what a joke he is. And what a bad joke the discovery of the Corsair is going to be, on him."

In her travels around the world to recover remains, she has met people like Folly before. There seems to be one on every island who is always "expert" at something. She smiles as she considers, "In Folly's case, his only known expertise is in shooting off his own mouth, something that also comes very easy for him."

FOLLY'S DRUNKEN REVELATIONS

Back in Santo, Folly is finishing a bottle of whiskey in a local tavern and telling his woes to an old buddy named Guthman, who is involved in similar black-market pursuits on another island. Folly is furious at not being recognized by the U.S. Army and has been raving about it to him.

Folly is unwilling to admit that he was really embarrassed by recovery events at Sara, which excluded him; but brags that he and his boys "have done a thorough job of pickin' over that PBY 'fore that bloody Yank

Army arrived." He remembers all the "goodies" he has at the police station in Luganville and gloats over the way they will turn a pretty penny on the black market from the tourists.

His tirade continues, "But then these bloody Yanks come to town an' act as if they want to take over the whole blimey island again. They din't e'en offer me a reward for bringin' all the bones an' stuff out. Bloody female Army Sergeant thinks she can tell me what to do," he fumes. "She restricted that whole area an' told the constable to guard it from all trespassers... as if I was trespassin' on sumthin' that din't belong to me! She sets up a bloody perimeter fence an' won't let anyone even talk to the members of her team while they work. Those blasted Yanks just give their females too much authority, if ya ask me."

Folly continues, "That female soldier also restricted any of the natives I sent up to that site from gettin' any further souvenirs from that PBY. Ya can be sure I'm gonna find a way to beat 'em. This bloody Yank airplane is gonna make me some real money," he exclaims, "not to mention the fact that I'll finally be afforded the respect of a real explorer. Now that I have that letter from the Civil Aviation Authorities, I'm already a properly recognized expert on the bloody Yank airplanes in the bush!" Folly gloats.

Guthman asks, "Hey mate, din't ya say that Yank Army has been at that crash site for several days now. Wonder what's takin' 'em so long?"

Folly replies, "My man there reported that part of the team left that wrecked PBY several days ago. S'pose to be comin' back to Luganville to pick up the bones I brought out. I tell ya' what, if they think they're gonna take all **MY** booty back to Hawaii, I've got a little surprise in store for 'em. I can't wait to see the look on that gal's face when she finds she can't take that jewelry an' money from the island." He pauses to take another drink of whiskey, then asks, "Where do ya think they are?"

"Maybe they got lost in the bush," Guthman chuckles.

"Yeh, maybe that native guide decided to see how much trampin' around they could stand! Ha! Wouldn' that be a joke on 'em."

They both laugh as Folly continues, "I contacted Laurel an' Hardy 'bout that PBY collection I brought out." He pauses, "You do remember Laurel, don't ya' mate?"

Guthman leers at his recollection, "Who can forget Laurel... me an' her... we had some fine times together. She knows how to make a man feel real good."

Folly snickers and says, "Yeh, nobody forgets that Laurel. She makes ya remember her. A toast to Laurel's talents."

"A toast!" Guthman echoes as they both down a glass of whiskey. By this time they are both getting a little noisy, but no one seems to care because that's the general climate of the establishment they're visiting in this evening.

After a few thoughtful moments, Folly resumes the conversation.

"Oh, yeh. We were talkin' 'bout that letter. You see, Hardy helped me write a letter to the Ministers of Health, Culture an' Justice. You know, those guv'ment officials were properly excited by Laurel an' Hardy. It looks like they'll stop those bloody Yanks from takin' the bones an' personal effects when they leave."

"You better hope it works or ya'r out a blimey fortune, mate."

"Yeh, but I've got the whole guv'ment of Vanuatu on my side. I've convinced those fools that I've only got this country's best interest in mind."

Both men laugh. They fill their glasses and Guthman toasts Folly, "To yar health 'n wealth, mate."

They empty their glasses and order another bottle before Folly continues, "You know, Hardy got the Director of Civil Aviation to identify me as an aviation expert. His letter is what gave me full access to the crash site an' let me get the collection of bones, guns an' artifacts out 'fore the bloody Yanks arrived.

"That letter makes it official," Folly boasts. "I'm s'pose to be treated as though I'm a representative of the guv'ment of Vanuatu. But that female sergeant wouldn' have none of it. She said she din't need any help other than her team. Then she ask' the constable to keep eva'one outta the area... no exceptions. At least I was able to get into that site one more time an' get the pistols an' some personal stuff I'd left 'hind."

Folly takes another drink and continues his boast, "I sure feel good 'bout the letter written by the Civil Aviation Authorities. I made a copy of it an' put a note on the bottom an' sent it to the American Embassy in the Solomons, 'long with a demand for the return of my property. Perhaps that Yank Ambassador there will stop that bloody Yank Army from takin' my collection off the island."

Folly takes another drink, then continues, "And, if they do take it to Hawaii, that Ambassador assured me that it'll all be returned to me after the identification is complete. Laurel an' Hardy have been talkin' to the Minister of Justice an' they've found an old memorandum of understanding that we can use agin' 'em. On the basis of that agreement, the Minister is demandin' the return of all artifacts to me. Accordin' to Hardy's meetin' with the Minister of Justice, the bloody Yanks will have to comply."

"What ya gonna do with all that stuff an' the money ya make off this deal?" Guthman asks.

"When my booty is returned, I'm gonna expand my shop to larger quarters. I'll be able to sell it all out in a matter of weeks after my new shop opens. As fast as I can clean up the stuff, they'll sell to the highest bidder. The jewelry an' money I got from the PBY crew will bring in at least a hundred grand."

"You'll be bloody rich in no time, mate," Guthman ventures, "I ain't neva' seen that kinda' green."

"Well, there's lots to be made in this business if'n ya can just get it goin' right, an' I'm sure in it to make eva'thin' I can. Then, one day, I'm gonna settle back an' have a bunch of these natives wait on my eva' wish! I sure could get yoosta that kinda life."

"To wealth," Guthman toasts.

"Here, here!" Folly cheers as he empties his glass, "When I returned to that PBY the other night, I took our pal Laurel as far as the village. She started a big rumor 'bout the Yanks makin' a reward of forty-thousand dollars. I sure woulda enjoyed stayin' around for the fireworks 'cause she has a way of gettin' the natives all stirred up. Then she got a couple more rumors started to keep the pot boilin'. You know, those rumors worked real well for a few days, but then they just seemed to die out. Someone up there must be interferin' with our efforts to discredit the Yank MIA search team.

"That bloody Yank doctor..." Folly lets loose a string of expletives directed at the Doctor's lineage, then continues, "him an' his bunch have been comin' over here for the past several years. Maybe after all the excitement 'bout the PBY is over, I can get back to searchin' for old Bennett they're lookin' for. I've decided that one of my major goals in life is gonna be to get to that airplane 'fore anyone else does."

Folly picks up the whiskey bottle and refills their glasses. As he sits staring into the brown liquid, he reflects back to when the American search team first came to these islands several years before. He remembers when one of his informants told him of their arrival.

Guthman, who is becoming quite inebriated, is presently lost in his glass of whiskey and doesn't really try to follow his friend's conversation as Folly begins where his mind has taken him. "This bloody Yank doctor's a strange type. He's got eyes that can look right through a person. Talkin' to him is like talkin' to an x-ray machine,... or a snake. Yeh, dat's what it's like – it's like lookin' in the eyes of one of dem cobras."

Folly takes another drink, satisfied he has finally figured out why the Doctor's eyes bother him. "That bunch sure wants that missin' pilot pretty bad 'cause they keep comin' to the island eva' year, tryin' to locate his crash site."

Folly pauses as he tries to recall details from their first meeting several years ago, he can still remember the pilot's name. "Now I 'memba, he was a bloody Marine by the name of Wayland Bennett. He was flyin' a Navy Corsair with a large number '88' on the side."

Folly grins as he thinks about what that plane and its pilot will be worth to him when he finds it. He's sure the natives will notify him just as soon as they locate it. "Den I'll claim all the remains an' booty, includin' the teeth, for my souvenir shop."

Folly takes a drink, then asks his friend, "ya know how persuasive Laurel can be?"

At the mention of Laurel's name, Guthman recovers from whatever personal journey his mind had wandered off on, and he wonders what he's missed. "Yeh mate, sure do," he replies.

Folly continues without realizing Guthman hasn't heard the last few minutes of conversation. "Well, even Laurel has tried to get to this Yank doctor; but, can ya believe, he turned her down flat."

Guthman shakes his head, skeptical that anyone could deny anything Laurel had to offer.

Folly continues, "Well, she was unfit to live with for a week after dat. Laurel usually gets her way, an' if she don't, the tantrums she throws are beyond belief."

Guthman ventures, "Yeh, I suffered one of her tantrums once. Thought she was gonna kill me."

Folly laughs, "If Hardy can get the Minister of History an' Culture to come on 'round to our way of thinkin', this pilot Bennett will go down in history... the history of my souvenir shop! Last year Hardy an' I figured the bloody Yank search team is spendin' thousands of dollars each year; in fact, they must be spendin' at least forty grand to come out here for a search. Hardy reckons as how those Yanks will pay at least that much for Bennett, or they won't get him at all. I've told my natives to tell the bloody Yanks nothin' 'bout crashed airplanes... an' I mean nothin'!"

Folly takes a drink of whiskey as he remembers Hardy's warning to never take this American Doctor for granted. He then tells Guthman, "Hardy says that doctor is wealthy an' a shrewd businessman and he has lots of real estate holdin's. Hardy's seen his office an' a clinic an' a train station he owns in that city where he lives. Can ya imagine bein' rich 'nough to own a train station. Wonder if he owns a train to go 'long with it? Well, Hardy says he also owns several airplanes an' has a fancy sports car an' a big speedboat. Wonder if dat's all true, but guess it is 'cause they say he spends his own money to come to the islands an' nobody is payin' him to do dis. I guess dat's why the doctor can afford to have morals an' principles... cause he's a blimey rich hoidy-toidy."

Folly thinks about the trouble the Doctor can cause to his plan, then continues, "When we find that Bennett plane, it'll be necessary to eliminate even the most remote possibility of the doctor knowin' anythin' 'bout it. Even Ben..."

Guthman wonders who Ben is, but doesn't bother to ask. He figures Folly will tell him soon enough.

Folly continues without interruption. "... told me that the minute the doctor gets wind of the plane bein' found, he'll be here the next mornin', all the way from America. I've a score to settle with him, an' I've got to make sure he's not involved in discoverin' that airplane in any way."

Folly has made sure every native he's been able to reach has been given the message to tell the Yanks nothing. Folly's mind wanders back to when the American team leader first hired him in 1988. Folly had taken some photographs of the first planes that he told the Doctor about. "One of the planes I took pictures of while I worked for that doctor was number '33' on top of Mt. Wimbo, an' there was 'nother plane nearby I took pictures of too. Well, I went back later an' took lotsa relics an' stuff outta one of the planes, includin' the teeth an' all the bones."

Remembering the profit he made on that venture he continues, "It's simply amazin' how much money a Jap tourist will pay for just one small bone of a dead Yank. I've heard they curse an' vilify that bone daily as dey say their prayers. I've already sold over twelve-thousand Yank dollars worth of souvenirs from that one plane alone. Dog tags an' the pistol will bring a fair dinkim profit indeed. Lots of bones an' teeth came from the Wimbo plane. Tourists who want to buy relics from a bloody Yank plane or pilot will give a grand for each dog tag. An they'll pay as much as fifteen-hundred each for rusty pistols taken from the pilot's body. Yeh, I think the bones from old Bennett an' the parts of his plane will bring in 'bout fifty grand 'fore I'm through."

Folly boasts, "We're also tryin' to get recognized as experts by the Vanuatu guv'ment. If eva'thin' goes well in the guv'ment offices, I'll acquire an international reputation as an explorer. Then those bloody Yanks can't call me a grave robber any more!"

"A toast to international explorer Fred Folly!" Guthman declares.

After finishing their glasses and pouring another, Folly resumes his diatribe, "'Cause Laurel can speak four languages, the guv'ment might put her in charge of all searches on this island. Hardy says we can charge the tourists over two-hundred grand per year, an' we'll split it all between us. Our sales to Yank tourists will be outdone only by the amount the Jap tourists will pay for Yank bones. And, with the friends Hardy is makin' in the guv'ment offices, he thinks I'll be appointed to the position of Curator of Native Resources an' Historical Artifacts."

Folly remembers the Doctor's reaction when he first showed him the collection and dog tags from Shafer's plane on Wimbo. "I offered to give the doctor one of the dog tags an' some of the bones, but the bloody Yank refused – what a self-righteous clod. He probably din't even know that dog tag is worth a grand. I can move merchandise like that on the black market any day of the week. But that stiff-necked Yank doctor is hard to get 'long with an' won't bend at all. Hardy says that he won't go 'long with anythin' or anyone he doesn't approve of."

Folly remembers meeting the Doctor at the hotel in Port Vila after he returned from the bush the first year. "That bloody Yank wouldn' even buy me a meal at the hotel. He just lectured me like a bloody school kid back in Melborne... actually preached at me, he did. Said my actions were a direct reflection on his precious search team. Said they would be viewed as 'the willful desecration of an American war hero's grave.' He also said dat, since I had been his employee, this unauthorized pilferin' of the wreckage was inappropriate behavior an' unethical conduct. Said I had broken those bloody CILHI Accords he keeps yammerin' about. You know mate, he even made me sign a paper pledgin' to abide by his rules 'fore I could go to work with him. What do I care 'bout what he had printed on a piece of paper. I'd sign away me own mither if'n it would get me what I want."

Guthman isn't surprised at Folly's statement. He's known for a long time that Folly's word is worthless. "He may call himself my friend, but I wouldn't trust him as far as I can throw him," Guthman thinks.

"The bloody Yanks had named that doctor the team leader an' he said he was responsible for the search team's conduct. Apparently he'd been designated by that pilot's family to conduct the search an' he said he felt obligated to represent 'em an' find their brother. He went on 'bout how he'd made agreements with CILHI, whoeva' that is. And then he said neither he nor any of his team would eva' be allowed to touch the remains of dose dead Yanks. Can ya believe dat, mate? Findin' somethin' an' not bein' able to even touch it?"

Folly is pretty worked up by this time an' rages on, "He then said he would have to *dis*-associate hisself an' his team from me; an' not have no future relationship with me in connection with searches. He bloomin' fired me, he did! Humph! Like that was my first time to be fired. An' he's treated me like a leper eva' since. But," Folly takes another drink and lets loose a string of expletives, "believe me, his day is a comin'; an' I think it's gonna be very soon by the looks of it. If I can just find that Corsair with Bennett still in it, I'll have it 'made in the shade,' as the bloody Yanks say."

Folly takes time to down another glass of whiskey, then continues, "Yeh, an' 'nother thing. Last time the Yanks came over here, Hardy had already been to America to meet with this doctor 'bout film the findin' of old Bennett. Betcha he plans to sell the film world wide. Well, Hardy found that doctor an' Bennett's family a little too hard to handle. Hardy had to cough up ten grand 'fore the doctor would even consider lettin' him go 'long on a search. Believe me, Hardy was sure burned up 'bout that.

"He said that doctor is the boss of eva'thin' even remotely associated with the searches. An' the bloody Yank has the entire support of Bennett's family an' friends. Hardy said it's impossible to reason with that doctor, an' he'll have to be disposed of from inside his own search team. Hardy tried to pay him to look the other way while the film was made, but that self-righteous bloke refused the money. Told Hardy money wasn't a factor for considerin', or even the object of this search. Can ya believe anyone turnin' down money like dat? He must be swarmin' in it!"

Guthman just shakes his head while Folly goes on, "So, Hardy 'ranged to meet 'nother Yank on that doctor's team, by the name of Ben."

"There's that name again," Guthman thinks. He says nothing but just continues to drink his whiskey and listen to Folly's ravings.

"Laurel had already gotten to know Ben the year 'fore an' she said he'd play 'long, for a price. Hardy paid Ben thirty-three hundred to go agin that doctor's authority an' cause a ruckus among the team members. That deal din't work out 'tall, at least Ben din't like the outcome. We're still hopin', howeva', that the doctor can be forced to resign or even be fired by that Yank pilot's family.

"Ben, Laurel an' Hardy spent a lot of time together in America; then made even more plans when the team got to the islands. The plan was for me to bring what I had left of the bones an' other things from the planes on top of Wimbo back to the mountain. When eva'thin' was in place, the revolt was gonna begin. But some of the events in Luganville went sour an' Hardy' plan began to unravel when the doctor got wind of what was hap'nin' there. Hardy knew if that doctor learned of the plan, he'd fire him an' anyone connected with him; but he tried it anyway. Too bad it din't work out, but I'd warned Hardy 'bout that bloody Yank doctor an' he wouldn' listen to me.

"Laurel an' Hardy, 'long with Ben, have a vendetta an' preoccupation 'bout the doctor. Hardy has spent lotsa money to get him out of the picture, 'bout forty grand so far, an' he's still not rid of him yet. Ben, the man inside the search team is my kinda guy. He's a likable sort of fellow who wants to see the doctor outta the way so he can take over the team.

"Hardy convinced Ben he'd be the star of the documentary, if he'd help get the doctor outta the way. Ben hated that doctor, 'cause he wouldn' let Ben be filmed by Hardy with the other planes they've found. Ben's eager to be a star, so Laurel an' Hardy have been able to stir him up into a frenzy. Well, as they say in America, 'there's a sucker born eva' minute' an' Ben is the prime example."

Folly grins as he remembers warning Hardy and Ben they would all be fired if the doctor found out about the bones. "Serves Hardy right for refusin' to listen to me. He said he had too much invested in this project already. Sure 'nough when that doctor found out what was goin' on with Ben an' Hardy, he fired 'em both. In fact he fired eva'one even remotely connected to Ben an' Hardy. That bloody fool thinks he can fire anyone who crosses him.

"Maybe, if Laurel had played her cards right, she could have done that job better. But the problem with Laurel is, she thinks she's still irresistible. She's always tryin' to run somethin', an' she's made a mess out of her opportunity this time. She approached the doctor in the restaurant in Vila one night an' tried to get him to come to her room so she could get him into a compromisin' situation. He told her in no uncertain terms that her proposition din't fit his life style. Acted like he was better'n her. After dat, he wouldn' even talk to her. In fact, he neva' even asked her advice on anythin' or let her do any translatin' for the team."

Guthman is so drunk by now, he's passed out in his corner; but Folly is oblivious to the snoring from across the table. He takes another drink and continues. "Laurel's conflict with that doctor caused her to lose face with some of the natives when she wasn't their interpreter. It'd be interestin' to know just what it would take to get to that bloody Yank doctor. I know Laurel an' Hardy have spent a lotta money tryin' to find out just what makes him tick. They've offered him money, booze an' sex; but, so far, he's never fallen for it. Oh well, they'll be back next summer to look for their pilot; an' we'll all have 'nother go at the good doctor then."

Folly falls into contemplation and remembers how their plan started to fall apart when the Frenchman got drunk and talked too much in Hotel Santo's restaurant. He starts talking again, "I told Frenchy to stay away from that preacher, but he likes to act crazy when he's 'round those do-gooders – thinks he's a better man than that pastor who was crippled in a motor car wreck in Australia some time ago. But, I tell ya, that preacher's still got more guts in his crutches than Frenchy's got in his entire body.

"But no, Frenchy had to tell the preacher he din't like preachers, missionaries, Yanks an' other foreigners. Told him he'd been to the plane out westa town, but refused to help the Yanks get to it. Well, that preacher thought Ben an' Hardy were with that doctor's team, so he told 'em all 'bout the plane Frenchy visited. Course, Ben neva' told the doctor 'bout that plane, 'cause he an' Hardy were savin' it for later.

"Then the doctor's wife had to find out. She met the preacher one day at Hotel Santo, and he asked her if the team was checkin' out the plane he'd told Ben 'bout. When she said Ben hadn't told them 'bout the plane, that blasted preacher told her the whole story. She began to put the pieces together an' then that cat was outta the bag."

Then Folly begins to berate himself, "Sure 'twas pretty slick how she tricked me into helpin' her. She knew I was goin' into the bush the next mornin' an' she said she'd heard nary a word from her man for several days. Said she wanted to send her husband a 'luv letter' to tell him she missed him an' all that mush. Even sent the blimey message into the bush by me, an' I was dumb 'nough to deliver it without openin' it. Yeah, she was pretty smooth with that story 'bout the luv letter.

"I handed his bloody majesty that letter, an' the Yank wouldn' even speak to me. That guy acts like some kinda Lord High Mayor, he does. But, no matter what else happened, Hardy an' Ben were determined to make their documentary in spite of that doctor. Laurel an' Hardy wanted to embarrass that doctor on that trip, an' Ben wanted to get even with him by gettin' him fired. Hardy wants to try to get the guv'ment to refuse to allow him to return on another search, but dat'll be tricky.

"Anyway, after the doctor read that letter I brought him, he called the team together for a meetin'. He told Ben to continue the search in the mountains, while he an' his brother returned to Luganville to check out a lead. We were all glad 'cause this would work out perfectly for Hardy' master plan an' now Ben was in a perfect position to cooperate, 'cause the doctor made him leader of the team that stayed in the mountains. As soon as the doctor was outta sight, Ben called off that mountain search the doctor had told him to do.

"Ben wanted Pam to join 'em in the plan an' be the female star in the documentary. She was reluctant at first, but Hardy convinced her the doctor had abandoned her an' wouldn' be back. Finally, Laurel was able to get Pam to go 'long with the plan, an' they went right off to the planes on Wimbo. When they got there, Hardy made it look like they were the first ones to find that plane number '33'. Course, by that time, I'd already put all the bones an' dog tags back in the plane. It did make a nice bit of film an' almost looked like an authentic discovery."

Folly snickers as he remembers, "that Pam was more fit at climbin' that mountain than Ben. She seems like a nice 'nough girl an' Ben was such a ham. She had trouble with Ben an' wanted to leave; but, finally, Laurel convinced her to stay with them rather than return to the doctor's team. Ben an' Hardy had planned eva'thin' out to the last detail, except they din't count on gettin' caught at the last minute."

Folly appears perplexed, "We stripped the planes on Wimbo again, but neva' dreamed that doctor would be awaitin' when we came outta the jungle. We probably looked kinda foolish comin' out, loaded down with 'nough machine guns to start a war. We all thought that doctor would go bonkers when he saw what we'd done to his precious 'time capsule of history.' But, even though he'd caught us all red-handed, he said absolutely nothin' when he saw what we had with us.

"The doctor sure is a strange fellow. You know, thinkin' back, it almost seemed as if he already knew what we'd done. How could that be? He just turned an' walked away like he was disappointed in eva'one for what they'd done. He knew Ben an' Pam had betrayed him. Ah, but revenge was sweet, the only trouble was it din't last long 'nough."

Folly frowns as he says, "Somehow, I keep gettin' a thought that he knows all 'bout what we're doin'. But Hardy says he's certain no one knows anythin' 'bout us sellin' bones back to the Yank families, an' whoever else we can.

"Hardy an' Ben wanted to keep all the charts an' notes that doctor had put together, an' that was the start of the last mistake. Hardy wanted to sell 'em back to that doctor for the money he'd had to pay to be on the search team; but Ben just wanted revenge an' planned to keep the notes an' neva' give 'em back. Well, neither one got their way.

"You know mate, I actually enjoyed seein' that bloody doctor's disappointment in his fellow Yanks. As the doctor an' his brother walked away, I mumbled, 'So solly, G. I.' just like the Japs would say it."

Folly pours the rest of the whiskey in his glass and guzzles it down. Then he turns and staggers off to see if Laurel will let him in for a visit

Search for the Lost Blacksheep

and a place to sleep it off. He's forgotten all about Guthman who's sound asleep in the corner. The police will find Guthman later when they haul all the drunks to the jail to sleep off the night. Neither Folly nor Guthman will remember much of their evening's conversation. But, some in the tavern weren't as drunk as they appeared, and they'll remember – you better believe they will.

[14-v] At some point, the Doctor's 10-year-old nephew, Justin, became enthralled by the story of Bennett's disappearance. This penciled drawing was his interpretation of the story.

Search for the Lost Blacksheep

CHAPTER 15

THE CILHI PROJECT – 1994
RETURNING TO BASE

With recoveries complete, the CILHI team is ready to return to Hawaii. On behalf of the entire recovery team, the Sergeant thanks the government, villages and people of Vanuatu, and especially the natives from Sara who assisted in the recoveries. She tells them that these recoveries could not have been made without their assistance.

On the long flight back to Hawaii, the Sergeant thinks about her upcoming transfer to the mainland. It has been almost eighteen months since her last leave and she is looking forward to seeing her family again. She plans to buy a car in California and drive it all the way to Delaware, driving for days and days in a long, straight line. The Hawaiian Islands are a beautiful place to be stationed and a fantastic duty assignment for an outdoors person like her; but she is ready for this transfer and her well-earned vacation.

"Maybe," she ponders, "the pilot we recovered from that Corsair will also get back home this year if nothing goes wrong in the identification process."

She remembers, "This mission has been different, almost from the very beginning. That PBY was heartbreaking; its recovery an absolute nightmare. It had already been looted, stripped and pilfered. It will take a long time to correct the damage, if it's even possible. The bones must be reassembled and positively identified according to rigid protocols; and the Colonel will be forced to ask for interment as an unknown for any of the crewmen whose identity cannot be confirmed.

"The damage done by that idiot who calls himself an expert is beyond explanation. Expert at what?" she ponders. "It's certainly not the recovery of MIA's."

She is upset at his interference. "Due to his 'expertise,' it will now take years to make a complete identification of those seven men in the Catalina. And it could have been so much easier on everyone if he had left it all alone.

"That crew had been left undisturbed in the jungle for over fifty years; then, just before we got there to make the recovery and easy identification, Folly executed the worst case of disturbance and desecration I've ever seen."

In her career with CIL units, she has investigated crashes and recovered remains from some of the worst places on the globe. She shakes her head as she thinks, "The worst part about Folly's 'expert' help was his senseless looting of the crew's personal effects. That was unforgivable because, until then, the wreck was pristine and undisturbed. He stole the personal effects and jewelry of each crewmember as methodically as if he had days to do the job properly. What a shame – the recovery and identification could have been so easy. The crew were all at or near their duty stations when the plane crashed and most were still strapped in their seats."

She remembers what she put in her report. "The pictures we took of the site when we arrived showed definite evidence of recent removal of watches, rings, bracelets, dog tags, and pistols from the bodies of that crew. The desecration and theft had all been completed no more than thirty-six hours before the arrival of the CILHI team at Santo."

As a matter of personal curiosity, she had checked passenger manifests for airline arrivals in Santo within that period. It seemed odd that Laurel, Hardy and Folly all arrived on Santo about 36 hours prior to the team and they all arrived on the same day, at the same time, and checked into the hotel at the same time. Hotel Santo's check-in log confirmed all this. The bar and restaurant charges after their arrival showed no charges during the day, only early morning and late evening.

She asks a question to which she already knows the answer, "Where were they all day, since none of them ate in the restaurant?"

She knows they all went to the police station together to present Folly's letter of credentials from the Civil Aviation Authority. These three non-government people then asked police to keep all foreigners out of the site until further notice from Folly.

"That really seems curious, particularly since the Vanuatu government had pre-approved our recovery of American remains."

She remembers it was reported that, "They all had large bags of bones when they returned to the police station in the evening. But there was no jewelry or personal effects in the bags they gave police."

"Why would all three of these non-officials feel such an overpowering urge to remove bones, when they knew our recovery team was en route?" she wonders.

Then she recalls, "On the other hand, the Corsair was a cakewalk as far as that recovery was concerned. It was a textbook recovery that had not been disturbed by any animals or humans. The remains were complete and should be comparatively simple to identify. This case will probably become a training film for new field recovery team members. This may be the only standard procedure I've ever seen in our CILHI lab. There are always complications in a case, but this one has no deviations from normal. The entire plane was in a very small crash area, and we were able to remove the entire skeletal remains and chart them.

"Still, it was strange to find two planes by accident on the same trip. Why was one so terribly ravaged by Folly and not the other? It's hard to imagine he didn't know about the Corsair that was so near to the PBY. Why would he focus all his attention on one plane and none on the other? The fighter plane site was small and contained, with no scattering of either wreckage or remains. A man with Folly's talents could have completely stripped it in one day, then moved to the PBY."

CILHI'S NEW LAB

As the sergeant begins to fall asleep, she thinks about the new CILHI lab in a remote corner at Hickham Air Force Base. It has state-of-the-art science and technology in a single building, and is undisturbed by traffic or normal duty routines of the sprawling installation.

After WW2, the Central Identification Laboratory of the Hawaiian Islands (CILHI) was formed. Prior to that time the group was known as the American Graves Registration Service (AGRS).

AGRS teams were composed of men who had no other assignment or were foul-ups from other units. Some were sent to AGRS as a punishment tour or an attitude adjustment program. Back in those dark ages after war in the Pacific, there were very few trained regulars left in the Army to supervise these new replacements.

The AGRS was not so technical then, and specialized training was non-existent. Even forensic lab offices and quarters were primitive. The old office in the piers and docks section of Honolulu harbor was an afterthought, placed there because AGRS recovery teams were bringing American dead back by the shipload into that harbor.

They chartered Navy ships, reclaimed all battlefield dead and emptied entire cemeteries into those ships. An entire ship loaded with dead bodies was an assignment of horror. The tropical heat took its toll on teams, and the smell aboard those ships was beyond belief.

Working every day in a primitive lab, with a shipload of bodies waiting for processing, put everyone in a state of tension. You had to try to process them as soon as possible. But, at least, they learned from those early years.

After CIL was formed, they were assigned to recovery, identification and return of remains to the next of kin for burial. A traditional military burial service is a formal affair, and provides a final salute to men who died in their country's service. That tribute includes official condolences from a grateful nation to the deceased's family.

But first the remains must be positively identified through a rigorous protocol. CILHI must review every known detail of a man's physical life, such as fractures and dental fillings. They must reconstruct his height, weight and even posture using state-of-the-art forensic science and medical technology. They also construct a documentation trail of orders and reports that placed the deceased in a certain plane on a specific date.

Computers store enormous amounts of information including remote details on action reports and war patrols. Information contained in CIL data banks today would fill half the warehouses in Washington if hard copies were all placed in one area. Computerized archives in Washington, Baltimore, Saint Louis, Arlington, Delaware and all other CIL's around the world are instantly available at a CIL lab's request. Almost every military record, report, document and personnel file is available by computer and ready to be called into use. With this level of science and technology, almost any question can be raised in a lab, and the answer is only a fingertip and a few minutes away.

The photo lab has undergone tremendous changes during the last quarter century and now includes the latest technology for detail, enhancement and computerized evaluation. They are able to photograph, x-ray and transmit all details to eminent forensic consultants halfway around the world.

As dental remains are being evaluated, questions can be faxed to special dental consultants at the University of New Mexico School of Dentistry. Or if a researcher has a question about the healing process of an eight-year-old fracture in a man who died fifty years ago, he can direct questions by computer, fax and phone to a professor at the Orthopedic Hospital in Denver.

On occasion, administrative details and disciplinary actions enhance a trail of assignments. The paper trail left by a victim's assignments can help pinpoint the date, time and place of his death. Within minutes details, which occurred long ago and are now a part of ancient personnel files stored in Baltimore, can provide answers in the quest for positive identification.

Sometimes, the only details available are rusty remains of a burned pistol. The lab will remove layers of rust and corrosion to locate a serial number. That serial number, on a shiny new pistol issued a long time ago, becomes of paramount importance. The computer can tap supply records that include all types of guns and weapons. Frequently, this is the last possible hope to tie a set of remains to something tangible, which can lead to his identity. Within minutes CILHI can assemble that data; then answers begin to accumulate.

For years there have been only questions about an MIA case, but in the CIL lab there will be no more questions, only answers. Old WW2 cases are often the hardest. In spite of technology, some old archives thousands of miles away have not been logged into computer files. Those files must then be manually searched, and enormous amounts of time are spent waiting. Someone may have to turn each page or open each box of dusty old files to find the required information.

A no-nonsense Colonel, who has worked at this profession for all of his adult life, heads the U.S. Army CILHI detachment. His entire military career has been in CIL units around the world and he will retire on September 1, 1994, after an exciting and interesting career. His assignments have included all American areas of conflict in this century. Although he has the reputation of being entirely without emotion, that is not exactly true. Today, he is reflecting on his career as he plans the work remaining before his upcoming retirement.

The Colonel is enjoying this new facility because it is evidence that one of his dreams has finally become a reality. He has lobbied higher command for years to get the latest technology into CIL labs. The Army has reached a pinnacle of technical and scientific skills with the opening of this new facility. The teams are no longer on temporary assignment to the unit, but have all been trained for this specialty because they requested this career field. This has also been a result of his effort over the years, and the CIL's are better now than when he came to them. He will proudly leave the Army with personal satisfaction of a job well done.

CILHI's staff of scientists and technicians has performed admirably in the past, and are now in the final stages of identification for several new cases. Like most other cases CILHI has recovered and identified, these will probably receive no thanks for well-done jobs either.

As each case is finished, it spells an end of hope for the deceased's family. They will no longer be able to delude themselves that his MIA status will someday be changed to a hero's welcome home. Without final evidence and remains to bury, there always remains a glimmer of hope in the deepest recesses of their minds that the designation of MIA/BNR is not final and will someday change. Hope is necessary; to be without hope is crippling to an MIA's family.

For each man who did not return home with his comrades, family and friends continue to hold onto that final straw of hope that he is alive somewhere, perhaps as a prisoner of war, and will eventually return. Or maybe he is alive in a foreign hospital, suffering from amnesia and unable to tell anyone who he is. No one wants to forfeit their greatest dream that a living miracle will some day come home to his loved ones.

Every case the Colonel has in his lab right now will end the same way – a family will face the inevitable. They will be forced to accept the unacceptable and forever give up all hope for an eventual safe return of their missing loved one. Each body in the Colonel's lab had designations of KIA, MIA, or BNR for many years. His lab staff will eventually cancel those designators and provide a positive identification. Their task is to prove, beyond a shadow of doubt and with scientific certainty, the case on a lab examining table is the remains of a family's final hope.

With CILHI's available science and technology, the Colonel can be absolutely certain about each case he recommends for identification. A burial with full military honors now requires a positive identification, with scientific confirmation, by experts on a CIL unit's permanent staff. Upon completion of identification protocol, a formal notification is made by CIL through the "Chain of Command."

This notification invites examination and inspection of all procedures used in the process by the deceased's military unit at the time of his death. The Army, Air Force, Navy or Marines appoint a board of Colonels who review final findings and conclusions of CIL experts. Their job is to question the conclusion and any part of the process that remains unclear to them.

CIL presents its findings when the remains in the lab match every question and detail concerning the man's life. These officers then review those details from the CIL science lab. If, after detailed evaluation and examination, they agree with CIL's findings, they authorize the final certification of a requested identity. But if even the smallest detail cannot be satisfactorily explained, all of the identification process is rejected and the entire identity protocol must start over.

If every question and detail are confirmed, the Board of Colonels will allow designated remains to be identified and assigned the name, rank and service number of the deceased as proposed by CIL. The burden of scientific proof is always on the deceased's remains. Those remains must measure up to those of a hero, and when they do measure up, "Johnny Comes Marching Home Again."

When processing a Marine identity, Marine Casualty Affairs and Navy Memorial Affairs work together to locate any next of kin. In most WW2 cases, parents are no longer living. A WW2 widow has probably remarried and has a new name. Many families have moved to other cities, and some to different states than at the time of his death. The entire family may have moved, leaving no forwarding address. It can become a very difficult task to locate the nearest relative of a serviceman who died in 1943; but Casualty and Memorial Affairs, along with the Decedent Affairs, leave no stone unturned in their search. Until this point, the family is unaware of what has transpired because no identity is assigned until lab science has been approved.

THE STORY BEHIND THE CASE

In April 1994, less than thirty days after the Corsair's field recovery, the highly skilled staff of experts is at work on several cases in the lab – including case number "0060-94."

The Colonel is deep in concentration when the Sergeant knocks on his door. He motions for her to come in. She is working on a case that she was assigned to recover in Vanuatu.

She explains her concern about an extraordinary amount of fax traffic coming in from the islands regarding the case designated as 0060-94. She is not accustomed to receiving demands from civilians, and people who live in the islands usually have no reason to communicate with the lab. However, three civilians who are not U.S. citizens are demanding access to information concerning remains she recovered from the Corsair.

Folly, Laurel and Hardy are threatening to write to Ambassadors and Embassies complaining about her lack of cooperation. Hardy claims to be with a worldwide news network, while Folly claims to be an aviation crash expert. They claim to be representatives of the Ministries of Health, Justice, and Culture in Vanuatu government offices.

In their latest fax, they demanded all details on the Corsair including the buzz number, tail number, pilot's name and last known address. They also want to know the name of the next of kin, his address and phone number. But, more importantly, they have demanded the return of all artifacts and personal belongings found and recovered with these remains including rings, lighter, coins, watch, pistol, Mae-West and boots.

She confesses a certain degree of concern about the demands, but is also curious about why this set of remains is so important. The people making these demands are not related to the deceased American pilot in any way and none of them are Americans.

The Colonel waves her into a chair to tell her the history of Case 0060-94, details she has not heard before. Taking time to reflect, he pours them each a cup of coffee, then begins to explain the events surrounding a search for an MIA/BNR who is now developing an identity and personality.

The Colonel tells the Sergeant about four friends who grew up together in a small Texas town and explains how they were all caught up in the events of December 1941. On the day Pearl Harbor was bombed, they had entered into an agreement and made a boyhood promise to each other. It was *A Promise* that the survivors of the war would insure return of any of their number who might not return.

"All four young men went to war, but one did not return from an island in the South Pacific theater. For decades, the three remaining friends waited patiently for the eventual return of their friend who has been declared KIA/BNR.

"These friends reached the age where they could no longer personally search for themselves and could not wait any longer for his return. They had to accept the fact that, if he did not come home soon, they would not be able to fulfill their *Promise.*

"In a final effort to gain his return, they found someone who would conduct the necessary research concerning his disappearance. When his research was over, they convinced him to conduct jungle searches for their friend. Of course there has never been a search conducted by civilians prior to this one; and, naturally, CILHI does not like to think of any search project that will be beyond their control or authority. The idea of a search by a group of amateurs was more than a little frightening to those of us in the lab as well as our offices in Washington.

"But the fellow they selected to conduct the research is pretty thorough, and has a track record of completing very difficult tasks. He knows how to do research, and is knowledgeable about both jungles and aviation. He is a professional pilot, was an Air Force instructor pilot, and is now a practicing physician. So he knows procedure as well as protocol. He is very tenacious and methodical in his work.

"Several years ago, as he first began the research, he put everything into a proper perspective when the family certified him as their legitimate DNOK and representative in this search.

"They gave him carte blanche authority to acquire information and conduct research. He spent months interviewing people, then they asked him to conduct the search itself. They gave him absolute authority to act as their sole representative and their spokesman. Although he is not related to this family, he speaks for them in all search matters. This fellow was able to find research information and acquire details that we frankly thought he would never gain access to.

"Civilians and townsfolk from this MIA's hometown seem to have been very supportive of the search through their prayers and assistance. The Doctor has put considerable time and effort into this project and appears to have invested a lot of his own money in it.

"The Doctor contacted CILHI back in 1988, before the searches started. He then visited us at the old Docks and Piers offices in 1989. He explained his intended mission and how he expected to conduct it. He told us he was an amateur in the MIA search and was not interested in searching for others.

"He asked me for an explanation of any rules and protocols in place, and wanted to know our recommendations for search team conduct while in the jungle. He even wanted to know what to do if they found remains in any airplanes they located.

"I was concerned that he might find remains we have not yet been able to recover and bring them to us in a duffel bag. I told him my concerns and that we could not participate in his search. However, he said he would agree to any procedures and protocols we felt were necessary. So I listed the basic rules: no photos, no contact, no recovery, no family notification, no media coverage, no announcements, no souvenir hunting and no attempts to recover or identify remains.

"The Doctor agreed to each condition I listed. Quite frankly, I was shocked when he agreed to abide by all the rules I gave him. He asked for nothing in return except to be able to call us on occasion to confirm new information he might discover.

"Every year for the past seven years, he called us just before he left Texas on one of his search missions or let us know if they weren't going that year. When he returned, he always filed a detailed report containing a list of all planes he visited and their identification numbers, location and the type of each plane he documented.

"To this day, he has never filed a report claiming to have found anything. He has never claimed credit for having been first to make a discovery of anyone's remains. When he goes to a wreck site, he plots its location on a team chart, just like we do. The Doctor always refers to his trip to an airplane as a 'visit,' never as a 'discovery.'

"So far, he has never violated his word to me, and, in fact, he refers to our agreement as the 'CILHI Accords.' He seems to have taken his agreement pretty seriously, and he has fired anyone on a team who violated one of the rules. Not being one of us, we have no choice but to consider him to be what he admits he is. He says he is an amateur and his only interest is the return of one man."

"So that's what the native meant by CILHI Accords," the Sergeant thinks as she sets spellbound.

The Colonel stands and starts pacing the floor. She knows from experience that something has happened that is bothering him and he gets right to it, "A couple of years ago, an independent photographer, whose name is Hardy, wanted to accompany the Doctor's team into the jungle. The photographer is a prissy little man who considers himself a giant in the documentary business. Well, the Doctor explained those simple rules to the photographer about what could be filmed and what could not. The photographer agreed to the 'CILHI Accords' in writing before the Doctor would allow him to follow them into the bush. The photographer even offered to pay some of the team's travel expense in advance, to show good faith before he could do any photography.

"But during that search, this photographer joined forces with another local named Folly and a woman named Laurel. Together, they decided to get some film of another plane that the Doctor had visited several years before. Folly had looted that plane of remains and artifacts. Hardy, Laurel and Folly filmed those remains and published the name of the dead pilot.

"Our intelligence on the island tells us the real business of Folly's group is to find airplanes before we do. They photograph the plane and pilot, then contact relatives in America. Folly has sold remains and personal effects to several American families and even some Japanese tourists.

"When the Doctor discovered what they were up to, he fired every one involved because they had violated the CILHI accords. Two of his volunteers, Ben and Pam, also participated in the filming of human remains; so he fired them and gave them only enough money to get back home the same day.

"The Doctor then filed a complete report with us about those people and their activities on the island. He gave us all the information he could obtain about names, dates, places and victims that had been violated. He even learned the names of some of the American families who had been contacted. The Doctor checked with those families and discovered how they were contacted. He also discovered, in each case, the charge for return of a loved one's remains and personal effects was over twenty-thousand dollars."

The Colonel tells her about the deception and intrigue caused by Ben and Pam, and the treachery they displayed which caused them to be fired. He recognizes Ben for what he really is. "Ben and Hardy came to my office after several calls from Texas. Ben personally tried to get me to deny the Doctor access to any information we might gain about Bennett. It's obvious Ben was personally making every possible effort to assure that the Doctor never found Bennett.

"Ben is a frustrated superstar, always wanting to run something but never knowing which way to run. He's a loser and way out of his league; and he acts like a small, pouting child when he doesn't get his way. I can think of a lot of terms to describe him like fake and phony; and there's also some vital qualities he lacks like class, character, honor and integrity. Ben is a man whose word means less than nothing, and he is available to the highest bidder. Ben was even foolish enough to allow himself to be filmed by Hardy while performing the worst type of grave robbing and desecration of an American war hero's remains."

The Colonel stops pacing and sits behind his desk. "All the Doctor's reports are in my private file in the records computer; perhaps it will not be in conflict with your project to review that file. The group that he fired did steal his team charts and research notes. They tried to blackmail the Doctor for their return, and at one point, I understand, it got pretty serious and physical. During a brawl at the hotel, one thief got a black eye and bloody nose. But, it's all in the Doctor's report. Don't let that file cloud your objectivity, Sergeant."

"Where is the report, Colonel?" she asks.

He hands her his computer access code, and says, "It is filed under the name of the MIA/BNR they are looking for. His name is 2nd Lt. Wayland E. Bennett, USMCR and was listed as missing in an F4U-1 Corsair. The Buzz number is "88," and the Navy identification number on the tail is 02608."

She looks at the Colonel and asks, "Have you read my field report from last month's recovery, Colonel?"

The Colonel smiles and tells her, "Yes, I have, Sergeant."

She stammers, "Those are the exact details I recorded during the recovery of 0060-94, so that must be who he is." The Sergeant instantly knows this is the wrong choice of words, but it's too late.

The Colonel is instantly on his feet, and coolly reminds her, "He must not be *anybody*. He should not be *anybody*. He is CILHI 0060-94. Your job, Sergeant, is to prove that he is *somebody*. And it must be proven beyond any reasonable doubt who he is."

The Colonel towers over her at a height of six feet and the look on his face tells her all she needs to know about his displeasure.

She groans to herself for the mis-statement. "What a stupid choice of words;" she acknowledges to herself, "everyone knows the Colonel is a stickler on assumption and presumption. He is only interested in scientific certainties that lead to a final conclusion. Even the new people assigned to this unit know better than to make this kind of a dumb mistake. No one ever uses words like *'must be'* or *'should be'* around the Colonel."

As she turns to leave, she composes herself and thanks the Colonel. She wants to apologize for her error, but knows better than to show signs of indecision and weakness around him. "Better just let it go for now," the Sergeant thinks.

As she leaves, the Colonel smiles to himself. She is a perfect example of the dedicated type of personnel assigned to the CILHI lab today. The Sergeant already knows more about field operations and recovery than he did when he became head of this lab years ago, and she knows more about current technology than he does now. She is a certified instructor in the photo lab and a master at recoveries. This Sergeant is more technically advanced in her training than any other person assigned to the lab. She is dedicated to her work and maintains the highest level of proficiency from her subordinates.

She has enjoyed her time in the islands, but has asked for a transfer to expand her level of experience, and he has reluctantly agreed to it. She will report to the CIL at Dover, Delaware, in another eight months. He knows she is deeply concerned about her slip of the tongue, but she is also the best investigator he has ever had assigned to his command.

A few minutes later in CILHI's computer lab, the Sergeant is reading the Colonel's private file on that MIA from Vanuatu. She surveys the Doctor's research data and field reports of searches he led. It is obvious this Doctor knows what he is looking for, and her recovery data points to that officer as being the one she recovered. But that data has not yet been proven; and, until that time, he must remain as CILHI 0060-94.

The Sergeant has never been allowed access to the Colonel's private computer files before. The information contained in these files is from private sources such as the Doctor. It has been personally investigated by the Colonel, but is unsubstantiated. Without a documented paper trail, the lab cannot use it; and she knows it can have no bearing on the science of identification in this lab. In a CIL there are no rumors; everything is limited to cold and unemotional data, details and facts. Always they search for answers, but never little personality features. Life stories, which can make a set of numbered remains on a cold lab table positively glow with a personality of long ago, are simply not allowed for consideration.

As the Sergeant scans the Colonel's computer record, she reads all the Doctor's research notes. She studies the dental records and recognizes them as copies of what she has in the lab notes. She reads where Bennett had fillings placed into his teeth at age twenty – only six months before his death. Medical records are also similar to what she has been working with in the lab. The Doctor's notes have all of the glowing personality of a man named Bennett. According to his research notes, the Doctor has had the opportunity to get to know Bennett quite well. Every document is in the proper sequence for a paper trail, and questions and answers follow them.

Some notes show a distinctive personality of a young man who died before she was born. Suddenly, she remembers the Colonel's warning not to let this affect her objectivity. She knows his admonition is correct, but she continues to read the Doctor's last report filed after his 1992 search. These notes are undocumented from a civilian doctor who has performed research and conducted jungle searches. Apparently this fellow is as thorough in his research as he is in his search notes and charts.

Because the Doctor is a non-military investigator, his notes will not be made a part of the original record. She acknowledges that he files excellent and thorough reports, and they're all included in the Colonel's file – one for each year and a full report on each airplane he visited and charted. He has worked on a systematic process of elimination in his search pattern. If he could be led to a site, fine; but if not, he searched the bush himself and without hurry.

This man intended to find Bennett, and he made assumptions in his notes and plans for his next year's search pattern. The Colonel is right; he does seem to be hard-nosed, but he is the boss according to Bennett's family. When he is in the bush, he has absolute authority and conducts the entire search like a military unit. In fact, she observes, he runs his team almost exactly the same way we do in the field.

She notices that he is a former pilot instructor in the U.S. Air Force and a practicing physician who does community service on the side. It seems like he has stood by his word to the Colonel on the CILHI accords, too. According to these reports, he fires anyone on his team who does not perform to the letter of that agreement with the Colonel. She chuckles as she reads about the last guy to cross swords with the Doctor. Seems as if the Doctor's brother, Roger, gave him a black eye and a broken nose; and it looks as though the guy deserved it, too.

She then reads the Doctor's letters to the Colonel that recommend earlier search team members for commendations. The Doctor pointed out that these team members were all volunteers who had to pay their own expenses on each trip. He urged the Colonel to consider recognition and an appropriate civilian decoration of the team. She sees Ben's name on the list and realizes that is the guy who later turned out to be a treacherous traitor to the Doctor and search team. She wonders if Ben knows the Doctor once recommended him for heroic performance as a volunteer. But that letter was written before the last search mission when they had all the trouble.

She closes the file and resets the security code. As she returns the code disk to the Colonel, she thanks him for allowing her special access.

When she turns to leave, the Colonel looks over his wire-rimmed glasses and asks her, "Who is on your lab table, Sergeant?"

But this time she is ready, and answers without a moment's hesitation, "CILHI 0060-94, Colonel."

A LONG, HARD DAY

The Sergeant decides to call the search team leader in Texas at 10:00 the next morning. There are some reports she needs to clarify and confirm. "I hope he's still in his office," she thinks. "I think it's probably about 5:00 p.m. there."

She is pleased when she is put directly through to the Doctor, and he seems like a friendly fellow who is easy to get along with. She senses no reservation in his answers as she asks questions she needs answers to confirm or refute in her field report. The Doctor is willing to answer any of her questions about his searches.

She heard rumors in the village of Sara and now she wants to know if they are true. "Doctor, we have a report that indicates you offered the natives a forty-thousand dollar reward for delivery of Bennett's remains to you and no one else. Is any of that true and would you care to comment on the rumor or it's source?"

She notices the Doctor is not the least agitated as he answers, "No, I have never offered any reward that can be misconstrued to mean anything like that. I posted Corsair pictures in jungle villages and Luganville that included the proper identification numbers for a pilot and his plane. The picture shows details such as machine gun wing locations, and the fuselage numbers and star. On this drawing, I noted that the search team will pay 500 dollars to the village Chief or anyone who reports this undisturbed plane and pilot's location to Mary Jane at Hotel Santo.

"The purpose of that small reward is to encourage natives to report the wreck site and to insure it will not be looted. The search team has never offered money for parts, bones, dog tags or any personal effects. All we want is information that can be given to CILHI, so you will be able to recover Wayland Bennett's undisturbed remains. If we are in the islands when the plane is reported, we will post our team as guards to insure its continued integrity until CILHI's arrival.

"As for a comment on who is involved, and why, that information has been filed with CILHI for some time and is on file with your Commanding Officer there."

She asks the Doctor her next question, "Doctor, do you have any interest in finding any other planes, such as a PBY?"

He responds quickly, "Well, of course, we do. We have an interest in any airplane we can visit in order to acquire its identity and location. This information is always passed on to CILHI officials, who then recover any crewmen at those sites. They are not the ones we're searching for; but, yes, we definitely will have an interest in any plane found in the jungle. As for our search mission, we are only interested in one airplane and one set of remains. We have no interest in trying to find a PBY, but if we find one we will report it to CILHI along with the tail number so it can be investigated and any remains recovered."

Now for the sensitive question, "Doctor, have you ever had an interest in dog tags, pistols or personal effects from these planes?"

Again the answer comes quickly, "No, we have no interest in collecting any artifacts from wrecks. We have been told that some natives collect such artifacts, but I have never seen a native wearing a dog tag. In fact, I don't even recall a native ever trying to sell any artifacts to our team. However, three people in the islands seem to have a new business enterprise in which they try to sell remains and personal effects to tourists. And I have reason to believe they are also trying to sell remains to the families of the deceased.

"I know that Folly picks up remains and personal effects. I also know that his friends, Laurel and Hardy, make home videos of their recoveries and take them to the deceased's family in America. They have asked for as much as $20,000 for return of a complete set of remains and effects that they have removed from a site. They do not report their dirty business to either the Vanuatu government or the U.S. government authorities because they are a black-market operation. In 1989, I was offered the opportunity to become a partner in this business and I declined. The people involved in this venture go by the names of Folly, Laurel and Hardy."

The Sergeant then asks one last question, "Doctor, do you have any knowledge of recent discoveries in Vanuatu?"

The Doctor does not hesitate in his answer, "Yes, I have some friends in the islands who daily fax me news and any information they receive. I am aware that a PBY has been found with seven men on board. I am also aware of CILHI's discovery and recovery of pilot remains from an F4U-1 Corsair. It is identified as Navy 02608, buzz number 88. The words *"Susie-Q,"* are painted just below the windshield. The remains of the pilot, who is believed to be Lt. Bennett, have been returned to Hawaii for identification processing. The tail of the plane was missing, but it was located 97 feet east of the point of impact. The aircraft has a birdcage canopy and no tail hook installed.

"A native waited until work on the PBY was almost complete before he told the recovery team about the Corsair. He is a missionary preacher by the name of Peter. And you, Sergeant, are the recovery team member he told about the Corsair. He asked you to keep everything quiet about the plane because he had been guarding it until your arrival."

She smiles as she hangs up the phone, "Nice work Doctor, that was smooth." She finally has a better understanding of all the odd things that occurred in connection with the report and recovery of the Corsair remains. She also knows why the native made the report to her, where he came from, and why the wreck was undisturbed and in such pristine condition.

She tries to remember, "What was it the native said when he spoke quietly to me at the PBY site. I think it was something like, 'According to the CILHI Accords, you are supposed to find and recover this plane.' Yes, that's what it was."

The Sergeant muses, "So, Doc, you knew where that plane was after all. You intentionally stayed away from it to keep Folly, Laurel and Hardy in the dark about its discovery. While you kept everyone else at bay, you arranged for us to get to it first. You also knew the first plane to be reported would be looted before we could get there. Knowing it was the largest and would probably be found first, you waited for the PBY to be reported. The PBY thus became the bait that forced Folly, Laurel and Hardy to show their hand and be exposed for what they really are.

"I wonder how long you've known about the Corsair? After eight years of research and searches, you knew where Bennett was. You kept your word to the Colonel and lived up to your agreement. You abided by the CILHI Accords to the very last so we could get to that airplane and Bennett before anyone else could strip it. My hat's off to you, Doc; that was well executed. And the Colonel, my Commanding Officer, knows every bit of this and has said nothing about it to anyone either. Because of your word to him, a code of silence exists in the case."

Still sitting at her desk and shaking her head in amazement, the Sergeant realizes, "The Doctor had the fame and fortune of this entire discovery in the palm of his hand, but he gave it all back to CILHI. All of the reports will show that we found the plane, we recovered the remains and we will get the credit for another identification process. But the REAL story behind this recovery is one about the Doctor and all the people who were involved in this search team's work."

The Sergeant looks through some paperwork on her desk, then takes an early lunch break, anticipating a long afternoon session in the lab. "I think I'll have a good lunch and go light on supper," she decides. "I've got to stay in shape for field work."

About 11:00 a.m. she goes into the stark and sterile lab, a huge room containing fifty stainless steel lab tables. On each table is a set of remains ranging from a few bones and personal effects to complete skeletons of the deceased. There is only a number to identify the case on each table under investigation. On some tables are pistols, dog tags, machine guns and all types of personal effects.

She walks over to one table which has a complete set of skeletal remains reassembled for examination. The bone x-rays are complete and the dental update has been finished. There are no previous dental x-rays and no recorded military x-rays of broken bones. With a tenderness not normally exhibited, she starts to work on the case again as she quietly says, "Well Marine, it's time for us to get your identification completed so you can go home."

As she looks at the collection on her table, she softly breathes a little prayer. "God, you've protected this young man's remains for a half-century so they can be returned to his family and friends. You've protected him from many things that could have scattered these remains from one end of the jungle to the other. You've provided a barrier against those who sought to desecrate his resting place and led us to him so we could bring him back here. Please guide me now so I can get everything in order for his official identification and final journey home."

She stands up and looks around the room after working for six exhausting hours. No one is in the lab; everyone has already left because their normal workday is finished. She gets a cup of coffee then goes back to the table. "No reason to leave yet. I can still work for awhile longer this evening," she tells herself.

Some people say the thought of working with all those dead bodies scares them. One man even asked her, "Don't you have nightmares about ghosts or skeletons getting up off those tables and walking around?"

She laughs as she remembers the look on his face. "Actually," she thinks, "I enjoy working in here alone sometimes. It's peaceful and I can concentrate without interruption. I think I even do some of my best work at those times. I also happen to believe if anyone did get up off one of those tables, he would be a friend and not an enemy."

She thinks about December 1941 and the four Texarkana lads who grew up together and went off to war. Then she pictures three elderly gentlemen who survived: Bowden, Carson and Sandlin the reports call them. She can tell from the Doctor's filed reports that these were good kids who became better men. "To remember for fifty-one years a promise made as boys is pretty impressive stuff in this day and age," she thinks. "However, to remember *The Promise*, then execute a search is quite a different matter indeed."

"And what of his hometown in rural America?" she wonders, "Only a handful of people there can even remember him; yet, they seem to have poured out their hearts and prayers as they also supported those search efforts. Have I ever made friends anywhere who would do such a thing for me?"

She looks at her watch and realizes it's the middle of the night in America. Bennett's friends are asleep in their beds while he's still lying here, waiting for some final details to be settled so he can be sent home.

"Yes, the Colonel's right; this case has started to take on a special personality. It's even causing me to put in extra time because I now have a special preoccupation with its conclusion. This is not simply about a young man named Bennett whose remains are lying on this table in front of me. This case represents all we do here, everything and everyone he died for, his friends and family, and the dedication they had to him. Yes, this case represents what we're all about here at CILHI."

So, for Bennett and his family, she continues to work. She wants to see the final outcome of his friends' dream. She thinks of the dedication displayed by the Doctor, his brother and the rest of the search team. And she wonders about other people she read about in the reports – the Discombes, Huttons and Forsyths – and the part they all played in this odyssey.

CILHI makes all recoveries and identifications; and, when the remains are sent home, our CILHI team never has any contact with either families or friends. However, in the case of Wayland Bennett, she has been afforded a rare insight to those waiting at home for the deceased. She has never become personally involved in a case like this before, and it has provided her a new perspective of her work. She realizes she's beginning to like it even more.

A couple of hours later she looks at the photograph of a smiling young pilot dressed in his flying gear – a photograph that was part of this man's 1943 obituary. She's been working at the table for eight hours now and is tired, but, since she has no plans for tonight, she keeps on working... and working... and working.

Finally, about 3:00 a.m., she stands up from the table; and, with a rare tear in her eyes, she whispers, "Okay, Lt. Bennett, you have some pretty nice friends and family waiting for you, and it's almost time for you to go home."

The basic recovery data is complete and re-assembly of remains has been finished. The administrative research has confirmed assignment of this aircraft to VFM-214 squadron on Santo for MAG-11 maintenance. All personal effects found on the pilot have been confirmed. There is a Texas High School in Texarkana, Texas, and Wayland Bennett graduated from that school in June 1941. He ordered a class ring that had no stone, but on the face were mounted initials "W" and "B."

The Mae-West has deteriorated somewhat and only about half remains; but it is still bright yellow and some of the printing is legible. The stenciled letters on the front that remain read, "..ETT, W. E...." While it is close enough to be a part of his last name, she knows the Colonel will never accept it as conclusive. While it is a valuable piece of corroborating evidence, the Board of Colonels will disallow it as proof.

No dog tags or identification card were found among the personal effects of these remains. However, study of bone structure for the man on this table has been subjected to a new computer program. Every bone recovered tells a story about the deceased. Some bones present a person's general health during his lifetime; others describe his posture. Parts of a skeleton even depict body weight. When the proper bones are recovered, like they were in this case, they are subjected to a computer analysis which provides total height in centimeters which is then converted to height in inches and feet. Bennett was five-feet, ten inches tall and CILHI 0060-94 is computed to be five-feet, ten-inches tall. The mathematical equation for such computations is extremely complex and wouldn't fit on a single-spaced typing page, but the results fit neatly into a small empty block on the form attached to Case 0060-94.

During the 1930s and 40s, dental records were primitive at best and were entered by hand. In 1942, induction centers were not equipped with dental x-ray equipment, so Bennett was given a dental examination using only visual inspection of his teeth, and military dentists provided Bennett with his first and only fillings in April 1943. Those old dental records generally match teeth she recovered at the crash site.

Odontology provided an even better confirmation in the developmental stage of his teeth, and forensic odontology went beyond those records in the lab. As a young man, Wayland Bennett's teeth were still developing and the apices were not yet in closure. As a young person grows older this small hole in the tip of a tooth's root will close. The teeth in the case 0060-94 have unclosed apices, which indicate the man was less than 23 years of age at his death.

There was only one problem that baffled her at first. As a 19-year-old young man, his wisdom teeth had not yet erupted through his gums. The findings of his induction dental exam reflected the absence of wisdom teeth numbered one, sixteen, seventeen and thirty-two. What the Sergeant recovered at the crash site complicated this. Still in place in the mandibular (jaw) bones of Case 0060-94 are four teeth which have been previously recorded as missing. Since this did not agree with the record, it becomes necessary to research procedures and protocol in place in 1942. After confirmation of those procedures, the lab must scientifically explain this phenomenon. How can previously recorded missing teeth reappear miraculously in skeletal remains 51 years after his death?

With the precise laboratory procedures of forensic odontology, this finding was subjected to a most severe dental examination and scientific scrutiny. The final analysis was that, in life, Bennett did have wisdom teeth just like everyone else; but they had not yet erupted through the gum tissue. Upon visual inspection, they really were not there and were recorded as missing at the time of his induction into the NAVCAD Flight training program.

When he received his final examination prior to going to Espiritu Santo, they still had not erupted. And, when he died in October, they still had not erupted. This was established by studying the teeth under microscopic examination. Those four teeth had never been used because there were no wear points and facets where they rubbed against other teeth.

While this may seem to be a simple explanation, it is far from simple. She ponders, "The Colonel will accept no presumptions on this case because he has taken a special interest in its final conclusion. He doesn't want any delay, and he has placed Case 0060-94 into the highest priority for some reason.

"In the years I've worked for the Colonel, I've never known him to take a personal interest in any case; however, in this instance, he's pressing all of the facility's scientific manpower onto this case. A case like this can normally be ready for positive identification in a little over a year, but he wants this case completed within the next ninety days! What is the hurry?" she wonders.

OFFICIAL CHANNELS

Meanwhile, in Washington, D.C., the offices of Naval Mortuary Affairs and the Marine Casualty Affairs Office are being kept aware of the status of #0060-94. They know that, for all practical purposes, the case is now complete. The Scientific conclusions have not yet passed final approval by the Board of Colonels, but a preliminary copy of the case has been faxed to the Affairs Officer in both of these offices. The Affairs officers know this means the case is near conclusion in the CILHI Commander's opinion.

The Colonel at CILHI rarely provides them with a head start on any case; but, when he does, it is for a good reason. If a case has the Colonel's endorsement, the identification is almost a certainty, and the Colonel's opinion is a 100 percent guarantee.

Inside the brown folder is a note that reads BTB (Believed to Be) Wayland E. Bennett. Included in the file is every photograph of the crash site and remains as they were discovered. Photographs and x-rays of all skeletal remains and field reports include determinations of forensic lab experts. Attached are opinions of some of the nation's foremost pathologists and dental experts. They fill pages with technical dialog; but they all come to the same conclusion on this case. The man in Hawaii is indeed Wayland Bennett.

At the bottom of the note is a cryptic message, "Twin sister dying of pancreatic cancer, please process accordingly."

There is no pressure applied on the Affairs staff and no request is officially made on behalf of the deceased that would be out of line. However, upon reading this note, the staff places other activities on hold while they devote their attention to searching for a Texas family. A member of this officer's family is a twin sister who may no longer exist by the time this case would normally be concluded. They recognize the urgency of this request since the prognosis of this illness indicates that Bennett's sister is terminal.

CILHI has already requested a Board of Colonels convene at the earliest possible date to examine the lab's findings. But very soon the Affairs Officers can see the possibility of a problem developing in their area of responsibility. Location of this family may be difficult, so the entire office starts an extensive search for remaining family members wherever they may be.

A computer scan of telephone listings turns up no member of this family in the city of record. Every listing is checked, but no one can remember the Bennett family. No one in the city of record with this name seems to be related to that branch of the family name.

Computerized death certificate records reveal the father's death in 1947, and the mother's in 1976. One of the brothers is also deceased, but even his family is no longer registered in the city.

The computer then provides contact with a Bowie County Tax Assessor's office located in the county seat. When she receives their letter *(Appendix R)*, she checks her records. They show the Bennett family owns no property and no taxes are being paid on any asset under that name. Another dead-end. Now where do they search?

The Bowie County Tax Assessor asks Julia, from the County Clerk's office, about the name Bennett from Texarkana since her computer records have drawn a blank. Julia then checks the County Clerk's computer records in search of the family. Another blank! The Bennett sisters have no marriage records and no birth records of any children in this county, so they must have relocated. Julia can find no records of current addresses on any of the surviving family in any of her computer files, so she returns to the Assessor's office. She has an idea who can help.

The Assessor listens while Julia tells her about a Texarkana doctor who has been leading a search for a man with this name. He has been searching in the jungles for this pilot and his plane for several years. The local newspaper has carried a story each year when the search team goes off to a jungle somewhere to search. The clerk even heard the Doctor speak once, and she thinks he may have current information on this Bennett family that Washington is looking for; maybe this is the same family. The clerk says she knows the Doctor and will call him to see if he can help.

Meanwhile, the Doctor is in an afternoon staff meeting with employees at his restaurant. It has been over a year since he was last in Vanuatu, but he knows Bennett's plane has been located. He also knows the remains were recovered before Folly and company looted them. He has copies of photos taken by two natives Reece Discombe sent to a crash site near Sara, but he shared this information with no one in Texarkana.

Because Ben and Pam live nearby, he has made certain they have no idea about this discovery. He is certain they would instantly notify their friends in Vanuatu if word got out that Bennett's plane has been located.

The Doctor knows he will probably soon receive a call from Washington advising him of the positive identification process's completion. Reece's photos clearly show remains recovered by CILHI, which should soon be confirmed as those of Wayland Bennett. He knows the procedures and protocols must proceed very slowly. He understands the requirement and wishes it could be speeded up, but this is no longer his case and he does not want to interfere with its progress by asking

CILHI unnecessary questions at this time.

His secretary hands him a note that reads, "Please call the Bowie County Tax Assessor's office as soon as possible on a personal matter."

"This is odd," he thinks as he reads the note. "I have all my taxes paid up. I wonder what this is all about?"

He excuses himself and walks into his office where he calls the Tax Collector's office. He tells the clerk who he is and asks to speak to Julia, who left a message requesting that he call her.

When Julia comes to the phone, she asks several questions he did not expect to hear from her. "Doctor, are you still searching for the pilot from Texarkana who disappeared during WW2?"

The Doctor's brow wrinkles. "Yes, I'm still looking for Lt. Wayland Bennett. Why do you ask?"

The clerk continues, "Well, I thought so. I've been following the newspaper reports on your searches for years, and I remember your name in that connection."

The Doctor replies quietly, "Thank you, you are very kind. How can I help you today, Julia?"

She continues, "Doctor, we just received a request from Washington that I cannot help them with, and I thought you might be able to."

He thinks to himself, "What an odd request from the clerk. Why would they want me to call Washington for them?"

He answers her with, "Well, I will if I can. What do they need? And, who are 'they'?"

The clerk explains that a request for information came from a Captain Black with the U.S. Marine Corps Casualty and Memorial Affairs office. "He wanted to know if we have any records on the next of kin for a Lt. Wayland Bennett in this area. He cannot find them, and he needs to give them an update on the status of Lt. Bennett.

"Our office doesn't have any information on this family. None of them have paid any property taxes in the county for over twenty years. But, I thought you might know how to reach them, since you have been involved with this case for so long. If you know the location of any family members, perhaps you could contact them."

The Doctor is somewhat relieved to finally learn the nature of her call. "Thank you for calling me, Julia, and I do have their names, addresses and phone numbers if you need them, or I will contact Captain Black with the information."

As the Doctor hangs up his telephone, he smiles because he knows now it will only be a short while before Lt. Bennett will be returned to his home in Texarkana.

The Doctor calls Capt. Black's office in Washington. He introduces himself as the family representative of the search and research project for Lt. Bennett. The Captain asks the Doctor to fax that information to him, and they will be able to discuss the matter in detail.

The Doctor faxes his letters of authority from the family to the Captain, then calls him again on the phone.

The Captain is a little more talkative now because he has a copy of the letter telling him he may discuss anything regarding the family with the Doctor. The Captain says, "Okay, I have it now. Do you know how I can reach any of the Bennett family who are related to Second Lieutenant Wayland Bennett?"

The Doctor replies, "Yes, I have all that information; but, may I ask, why you want to speak with them?"

The Captain seems evasive but simply says, "We may have developed new information on the location of their brother. There may have been some recent developments in the case."

The Doctor is confused at the failure of this Captain to understand the designation of the letter he has faxed. He reminds the Captain of his status in the matter and that any information is supposed to come to him.

The Captain will not budge and says, "I'm sorry sir, you have full designation to do research and to conduct searches until such time as Lt. Bennett is located. But after such an event occurs, you no longer have any status, and I must inform the family member who is the Designated Next Of Kin.

The Doctor is not upset by this turn of events, but he is also certain the family does not want to become emotionally involved in this matter until something definite is known. He tries one more time to get information, "Look, Captain, I am aware there is more than a little movement in this case. I know, for example, the wreck was reached in the early part of this year and the plane's wreckage has been identified as the Corsair Bennett was flying when he crashed. The remains of the pilot are currently at CILHI and the plane number is Navy 02608."

The Captain still will not budge, and the Doctor can see nothing to be gained by a conflict with anyone at this late stage of the game. He reads off the name, address and telephone number of the DNOK, which is Wayland Bennett's brother. The Captain is still very formal as he tells the Doctor the information he has just given will be very helpful.

The Doctor is not very impressed, but he knows the Captain is correct in his handling of this matter. The Doctor also realizes that an eight-year-old mistake has just surfaced. The family's letter of authority was to be in effect only until Wayland's discovery. It is not worded in such a way that allows the Doctor to remain in charge of the case from Capt. Black's point of view. The Doctor is out of the information loop for the moment and standard protocol rules are back in effect.

In Washington, the Captain is well aware of that detail and does not intend to transgress regulations in this case. This seems to be an important case and therefore must be handled "by the book."

The Doctor knows the Captain is right and nothing can be done about it now. Besides, this phone call with Capt. Black has proven that

Bennett will be home very soon. These Washington offices have not tried to contact the family in the last half century, so there must be a very good reason for them to want to do so now – probably to get shipping details of where Wayland is to be sent.

Officially, the Doctor has not been notified or informed of the status, but he knows how the system works. He picks up the phone and calls Wayland's older brother, Dr. Richmond O. Bennett, Jr. He is Chairman Emeritus of a major university school of business. During the war, he was a naval aviator and served as an instructor pilot, teaching young eagles to fly. After the war, he returned to college and received several degrees including a Ph.D. in business. Until his recent retirement, he taught principles of business to the leaders of tomorrow's America. Although retired, he remains an active man and is an avid hunter.

Long ago, Wayland completed a form for Miller that designated his father, Richmond Oliver Bennett, as his DNOK. Although his father is now deceased, Wayland's oldest brother bears their father's name and will be allowed to serve as DNOK because Wayland's forms are still on file. Richmond Jr. is a no-nonsense type of fellow, and covers up all the ground he stands on. He is, in effect, the boss of the search and administrator of the Bennett family's affairs. But he has given the Doctor unlimited authority to research and search for his brother. The letter he wrote made it perfectly clear that the Doctor does not have to ask for any further permission because Richmond and the Bennett family have given him absolute authority in the matter of the search.

When the Doctor calls, Richmond first thinks it is a routine status report. Then the Doctor explains the conversation with Capt. Black and advises Richmond of the need to consider plans for his brother's homecoming. There will be an enormous amount of detail in this event, and the Doctor tries to alert Richmond to that reality.

However, Richmond has other things on his mind of which the Doctor is unaware. The Doctor has not yet been told of the finality of Wanda's condition; in fact, he doesn't even know she is ill. Richmond assures the Doctor that, when Capt. Black calls, he will set into motion a pattern of understanding that the Captain will have no trouble accepting. He will inform Capt. Black that the Doctor is to be considered the family representative until the last note of "taps" is sounded at the funeral service.

Capt. Black does call Dr. Bennett, but does not inform him of Lt. Bennett's recovery. Instead he says he only wants to update his records and be sure he has the right family member. He explains that if something develops on the Bennett case in the future, he will contact Dr. Bennett.

The Captain makes no further attempt to provide a status report on remains because, at the moment, there is officially still no Wayland Bennett; there is only CILHI 0060-94 in Hawaii, but the Captain is not even authorized to release that information.

Soon, very soon, the Captain is back on the phone to the Doctor.

He informs the Doctor that his authority has been extended to representing the family in all funeral arrangements. When Bennett is identified and is ready to come home, the Doctor will be contacted for final instructions.

The Doctor is not fully aware of implications that come with this designation of funeral arrangements coordinator; but, if this is what the family wants, it will be done. The Captain informs him, "Dr. Bennett has directed the remains be held in Hawaii when they are found. You will come to a complete briefing by the CILHI team, and you are supposed to make the final arrangement for the funeral."

"Well," the Doctor says, "I started out as an amateur researcher and then became an amateur searcher. So, I guess it's not too much of a shock now to be an amateur funeral director."

The Doctor learned long ago that Wayland Bennett was a practical joker with his friends. Over these years the Doctor has grown to enjoy a special kinship with Bennett, and he chuckles as he realizes, "Well, Wayland you've done it to me again, old friend. Bowden warned me you would get to me when I least expected it; and, Wayland, you certainly caught me off guard this time."

Early in the search effort, the Doctor had drawn up the complete plan for a homecoming celebration for Wayland Bennett, which the family approved, rather than simply a traditional funeral service.

In December 1943, the family had held a memorial service at the Hardy Memorial Methodist Church. It took place less than ninety days after Reverend Mathison had prayed with Wayland for the safe return of all Americans. How ironic that his death had occurred so soon, and even more ironic were the reasons it would take so long to reach a final conclusion.

Several weeks pass after the last communication from Capt. Black. The Doctor is impatient and calls Washington for a status report on the identification process. He is told the administrative process of positive identification for remains is a very complex procedure. Confirmation takes time, but those who have endured the pain of waiting for so long must tolerate it.

The Doctor then calls the lab in Hawaii and is told that the forensics labs and all pathology have confirmed CILHI Case 0060-94, and scientific studies have been completed as well. All military records have been reconstructed and personnel files have been tested by the protocols.

The case is awaiting final approval of the identity by the Board of Colonels; then transportation orders will be issued. The Doctor is briefed on the usual procedures for transfer of remains. If a message of approval for the identity comes in today, the transportation order will be issued and Bennett can be on the next plane to California.

This waiting is beginning to take its toll on the Doctor. He hopes to see Wayland brought home before cold weather prevents public participation in the homecoming.

A LADY OF ELEGANCE AND GRACE

The phone rings in the Doctor's office, and it is Richmond calling to ask about progress on the case. The Doctor has heard nothing for several weeks and explains that it will surely be very soon. The Doctor is certain the case will be completed by late June and hopes the return of Wayland can be anticipated for the Fourth of July. Richmond then gives the Doctor news that Wayland's twin sister, Wanda, has a very serious health problem, which will limit the remainder of her life to a very few predictable weeks.

The Doctor previously learned that Wanda has mourned Wayland's loss every single day since his disappearance. Twins seem to share a special relationship with each other that other brothers and sisters do not.

As a young lady just out of high school, Wanda was already showing the characteristic beauty of a golden goddess. She had obviously inherited the natural smile and quick wit that was trademark to the always-smiling and ever-happy Bennett clan. Her laughter, like Wayland's, was naturally spontaneous and seemed to permanently enhance her personality.

The Doctor sits at his desk and remembers Wanda as being tall and dignified, with golden hair and a distinct tenderness in her eyes. But her graceful character hid a lifetime of private grief, and her charming personality endured decades of grieving. This aristocratic beauty suffered a lifetime of waiting, but her faith never failed her as day-after-day she endured the frustration of Wayland's continued absence. A special bond of love for her twin brother continued to exist in an undiminished state. He knows she has always been very religious and her daily prayer has been for Wayland's return as she maintained that basic human element called "hope."

Wanda is unaware of the events that have recently occurred in Espiritu Santo. She has not been informed about discovery of a Corsair named *"Susie-Q,"* or of a case in process known only as CILHI 0060-94. She is also unaware of the inquiries by Capt. Black and has no idea what the implication of the call means to the Doctor and Richmond. She cannot know that the entire force of the lab facility in Hawaii is exerting every effort in Wayland's behalf.

The Doctor's primary contact with the family is with Richmond. They both know the need for confidentiality, and this family has endured the emotional rollercoaster effect of intense hope each year that the search team goes to the islands. It has become such a drain each time they came back without Wayland, so the Doctor has only been communicating the latest developments with Richmond.

The Doctor has been rocked by the call from Richmond about Wanda's illness, and he immediately recognizes the finality of her condition. With the devastating diagnosis complete, the prognosis is terminal and the end will come in a very short time. He has practiced patient care for a long time and enjoyed the exhilaration of success as he treats some of his patients, but he has also seen the tragedies of incurable diseases that cannot be altered. The Doctor, like all health care practitioners, wages a constant battle against disease and infirmity in the human body; but he has never been able to accept this kind of news gracefully.

Wanda's condition is something that he knows he must accept as beyond his control, or the control of her attending physicians; but for this to happen now seems so unfair. It seems inconceivable that Wanda must go before Wayland comes home. Then he remembers a lesson he learned long ago and he realizes, "It is not my place to question a decision of the Higher Authority who has decided it's time for Wanda to come home. Perhaps a special reward is in store for her in that place; maybe she will view the ceremonies from a better seat."

The loss of a friend is always a blow, but for her to miss this homecoming, which she has waited for so long is beyond his ability to understand.

His office door opens and his secretary brings in coffee with her cheery smile and, "Good morning, Doctor."

But today his head is bowed, and he cannot look at her. Today he can only mumble a "thanks" and "hold my calls, please."

The hard-nosed Doctor is having a problem with his emotions, and he has to get it under control. As he struggles to come to grips with the news Richmond has given him, he remembers his days as an intern in college. He must shake off this emotion and get to work doing something constructive for someone else.

But he finds it's not always that simple. Today he is also wrestling with another personal dilemma, and he knows he is going to make the wrong decision. Long ago he was taught a basic rule that he found easy to live by and work with: "I will not lie. I will not cheat. I will not steal." But today he has reached an impossible decision that taxes that rule.

He made a promise, but now realizes he must break his promise to an old friend. Several years ago he had given his word to the Colonel at CILHI. He promised, he gave his word, and he agreed to abide by conditions of the CILHI Accords. Since that time he has never found it necessary to violate any of those tenants or conditions of that agreement. But this is different, and today he is going to do something he has not planned to do, ever.

As he reaches for the phone, he places a call to the Colonel in Hawaii. He plans to ask permission to tell Wanda of the latest status of the case.

The voice on the other end of the line drops another lead weight on the Doctor's shoulders when she says, "The Colonel is in Australia." The lady Sergeant with whom he spoke several weeks ago tells him, "He is in the final phase of recovering the long-missing crew of *'Beautiful Betsy,'* a B-24 bomber with a full crew on board."

The Doctor carefully explains the status of Wayland's twin sister to her and requests that she notify the Colonel as soon as possible. This was his last hope to maintain his promise, and it did not work. Perhaps, someday, he will have the opportunity to apologize to the Colonel.

As he picks up the phone again to call Wanda, he is having trouble seeing the numbers. His eyes seem to be blurring like that day on a mountaintop with Roger when they visited the SBD site. This decision is going against the grain; there's an ache inside that just won't go away. As he makes the call, he knows he will have to be held accountable for this act. He will have to publicly apologize for this, and it will have to be to the Colonel and his staff at CILHI. As he dials the number, he knows that the bond of friendship and respect he has with the Colonel will probably come to an end.

The Doctor swallows the lump in his throat as a soft, weak voice answers the phone. It is the voice of an old friend and, in his mind, the Doctor can see the photograph of the lovely twenty-year-old twin sister of another old pal.

He struggles with his emotions as he begins, and her reply to his questions is very feeble. "Hello, Wanda, how are you today, beautiful?... Richmond just called a few minutes ago and said you're not feeling quiet up to par... I suppose you're not going to be able to give me a golf lesson this weekend?... What a shame; maybe next week then... Are you comfortable?... I suppose everyone is spoiling you rotten, but that's okay, I'm sure you deserve it.... How are Cecil and the rest of your family?... I suppose Doris is getting ready to teach again this fall?"

The small talk aside, the Doctor finally gets to the point of the call, "Wanda, do you feel up to a talk? I want to tell you a story." The Doctor then breaks his agreement with the Colonel.

For the next two weeks, Wanda is at peace and relaxed. Her old smile returns and she speaks of Wayland often. For the first time in 51 years, she does not grieve for him. She is a very happy lady in spite of the devastating effects of her illness.

By now, it is late summer and Wanda is remembering happy childhood days at home with the family and Wayland. She is thankful for her husband, Cecil, and the family they have been blessed with. She chuckles as she remembers the way Wayland and three other neighborhood boys were always underfoot, looking for snacks from her mother. She smiles as she remembers her mother and how the family always teased her with that nickname they gave her. The smile grows as she remembers, "Wayland painted that nickname, *'Susie-Q,'* on the nose of his plane."

"Wayland will be home soon," she says to herself. "I'm so proud of him, and he looks so grand in his Marine officer's uniform. Those gold Navy pilot wings are his most prized possession and the pinnacle of his achievement."

Wanda decides to call Richmond and check on his cold. Her older brother is a paradox; as a professor and a Ph.D., he should learn to take better care of himself. But she knows, "When the ducks begin to fly, he will be right out there with them."

She calls Doris. "Big Sis" is now a retired school teacher, but she always seems to go back for "just one more year." She has always been such an influence on Wanda, almost like having a second mother and the confidant she has cherished and needed.

"Yes," Doris tells her, "I'm going to teach again this fall." But then Wanda hears the old familiar claim of "But, I think this will be my last." Wanda smiles. How many times has she heard that story from Doris?

Wanda visits with her beloved Cecil as they sit on the couch and hold hands like two teenagers. He has been her strength and her rock for all these years. She visits with her children who come by for a few minutes. They have made her so proud of them. All have graduated from college and have professional careers. They are all married and have given Wanda a noisy crowd of priceless grandchildren to love.

"How could anyone be more blessed by a merciful God than I feel at this moment?" she tells Cecil. She has had a very busy day today and is really tired, so she says, "I think I'll just lie down and rest for awhile."

Wanda, a lady of quiet dignity and infinite grace, is buried in quiet rolling hills of the Texas Hill Country she shared with Cecil.

After Wanda's services, Richmond and "Big Sis" Doris meet the Doctor at a restaurant. Richmond begins with, "Wanda, Doris and I talked last week just before she died. She wanted, and we want, you and Roger to go to Hawaii and see everything you feel you need to see and assure yourself of the status there. We want you to look at everything CILHI has collected that leads them to believe that Wayland is coming home soon.

"There are procedures that have to be observed by the authorities, and it will be best if you represent us in those details. We would like for you to make the final arrangements for the services and help with the schedule for his return. We would also like for you to look at the remains and be able to tell us you are satisfied with them. We do not want to have our memories of Wayland tarnished by having to do anything that would take away from our last time together.

"We would like for you to determine what personal effects would be appropriate for us to receive. Then we would also like for the CILHI labs to destroy everything else that has no meaning for us any longer. Make our thanks and appreciation known to the people there for their help with Wayland.

"We have a family plot in Texarkana which has a reserved space for Wayland's use. If possible, we would appreciate a military funeral service, and, possibly, a fly-over for his final tribute. It would be nice if the Blacksheep Squadron could do the fly-over, but we are sure that might be asking for too much. Will you and your brother do this for us?"

The Doctor just nods his agreement; it will be a moment or two before he is able to speak.

He knows how difficult this time is for the family, and how hard it is to cope with the loss of Wanda. In Richmond's case it is even more difficult because he has always been an active outdoorsman. He has been a naval officer, pilot, businessman and professor; but, right now, he is unable to share his grief for a little sister with anyone. And he does not feel he can do justice to managing the impending funeral arrangements and the hundreds of other details that must be fulfilled for Wayland.

Richmond also knows that the Doctor has drawn up a memorable final tribute for Wayland, and he is the one best prepared to put everything together. The funeral is to be a homecoming event, and it will be a time-consuming marathon for the one who must attend to all the details.

Doris and Richmond are right about the complexity and time-consuming nature of the homecoming event. They both feel Wanda tried so hard to hold on to life, so she could be here to welcome him home. It is heartbreaking to see her go, but even more so because it will be only a short time until Wayland comes home to stay. The loss of Wanda has been a crushing blow to them both, but the thought of her missing Wayland's return after waiting for so long weighs heavily on their hearts.

FORMAL NOTIFICATION

When the Doctor returns to his office after Wanda's funeral, he has a stack of messages on his desk. All of them will have to be answered, but one is of particular interest, and he returns that call first.

Capt. Black answers the phone and makes the usual formalities necessary in an official conversation. He then begins with, "Sir, I am aware that you are the designated and official representative of the family of 2nd Lt. Wayland E. Bennett. This officer was a casualty in the conflict of WW2 and has been missing since that time. Recently, the recovery of his remains was completed, and he was returned to Hawaii for the identification process.

"I am pleased to inform you of a decision by the Board of Colonels, which authorized a positive identification of Lt. Bennett. The remains have been subjected to the most strenuous testing of the CILHI laboratory. And the Board has agreed with the lab that all scientific studies of remains and records are complete. The forensic studies have been supported by the consultant's opinion and all concur in the final identification of these physical remains.

"The personnel records and administrative files leave no further question remaining about the identity of Lt. Bennett. The opinions all agree that, to a scientific certainty, the case that has been conducted as CILHI number 0060-94 is concluded. The disposition of those remains from this moment will be transferred to another command.

"The United States Naval Mortuary Center for Decedent Affairs and the United States Marine Corps Casualty and Memorial Affairs Center are at the disposal of the family of this officer. They await only a family decision regarding funeral arrangements and return of his remains for final honors. It is presumed the family will have certain instructions that we will be happy to assist them with.

"As you may not know, the offices of the CILHI labs have been aware of the terminal illness of Lt. Bennett's sister. We attempted to provide all assistance possible in the matter of speeding up this identification process in her behalf. This case would normally have taken over one year to complete. But, due to the special circumstances of his sister's illness, we have been able to conclude the identification processing in only four months.

"We have not notified the next of kin due to your unique position. If you choose to notify his family of this case's status, we await only their decisions. However, if you wish us to make the notification, we will gladly do so in our usual and customary formal notification procedure."

The Captain has been formal and official to the very last detail. The Doctor thinks he must be an incredibly efficient officer who does an unenviable job to such perfection.

The Doctor is elated to receive this official notification at last. But he is also filled with emotion at the loss of Wanda, especially since she was buried only yesterday. Perhaps God has a special treat in store for her that could wait no longer. It seems a shame she will miss the homecoming, but the Doctor vows to insure it will be done to perfection. It will be an event presented with dignity and respect for Wayland, and with style and class for Wanda.

He informs the Captain, "The family has expressed their wishes that my brother and I go to CILHI for a final meeting with the Colonel and his staff. Dr. Bennett has stated that we are to represent them in a private briefing on the full identification procedure and recovery records. Furthermore, it is their desire that personal effects be given to me or delivered with the remains. But, under no circumstances, are any of the effects to be returned to the islands of Vanuatu as certain individuals over there have requested."

The Captain agrees to the family's requests, but is surprised to hear no mention of the funeral arrangements and schedule. He asks, "When do you feel the family will want the funeral services to be conducted and by which funeral home? Also, when do you feel the family will want the remains to arrive in Texarkana?"

The Doctor responds, "Those arrangements are pending the outcome of meetings with CILHI."

As the Captain returns to his desk, he thinks about this strange twist of events at the closing of this case. A civilian who is not a member of the family is inserted into the loop of final arrangements. It seems most irregular for a civilian to be involved at this stage of the proceedings. He wonders, "Who is this man?"

The Captain calls CILHI and asks to speak directly with the Commanding Officer. He expects trouble from the Colonel after this set of requests. This Colonel is a stickler for procedure, protocol and propriety; and a request for a briefing from the Colonel and his staff concerning the outcome of any case is highly irregular. The Captain feels this situation may rapidly deteriorate when the Colonel is asked to call his team of experts together for the purpose of giving the Doctor a briefing. He is sure this request will not be taken lightly. When the Colonel comes to the phone, the Captain tells him of the family requests.

Again Capt. Black is surprised. The Colonel explains that he knows the Doctor and agrees to do everything that has been requested. Furthermore, he will do it personally.

The Captain is relieved; he concludes the call and sits back in his Washington Office to ponder these events, "Who is this Doctor, and how can he make such requests? Why has the Colonel himself agreed to personally conduct this meeting? They must know each other from somewhere before?"

CILHI BRIEFING

The Doctor and Roger arrive in Hawaii at 2:00 p.m. It has already been a long day, but they rent a car and proceed to Hickham Air Force Base. There is a new complex of low buildings in one corner of the sprawling air base. No large street signs announce one's arrival at this facility, only a small sign which says CILHI. As they enter the facility, the Army Sergeant who was on the Corsair recovery team meets them.

The Colonel is waiting for them in his office, relaxed and informal. He explains the staff meeting agenda and advises the Doctor regarding their formal briefing, which is scheduled for 0900 hours the next morning in the boardroom. "I will have the entire recovery team in the briefing, which will be a formal information session. You will both be allowed access to anything you wish to see, including photos and field reports that have been prepared for your study."

They briefly discuss the task that is assigned to CILHI and general procedures they follow on a case, but nothing is said about Bennett. The Colonel reviews recoveries of remains from different wreck sites around the world and shows them the charts they use in the field.

The Colonel remembers his first meeting with this Doctor seven years ago in CILHI's lab at the Piers and Docks area in Honolulu. He was then unsure about a civilian meddling around in the affairs of his command. Now, after having communicated with him each year by phone, fax and report letters; he feels as though he is talking to an old friend.

The Colonel knows the Doctor is a man of his word, and Roger is a loyal supporter of the team and his brother. When the Colonel first met the Doctor, he could sense a dedication to the single purpose of finding Wayland Bennett. He gave his word to the Colonel then, and he seems to have lived up to the letter of his agreement concerning the rules of protocol and confidentiality.

But, even then, the Colonel knew there was something about this Doctor which is not ordinary. He is courteous and respectful but, just beneath a facade of social graces, this man possesses a more commanding authority.

The Doctor has served in the military and, according to the computer, his life is *not* an open book. The Doctor has worked with some officers whom the Colonel has met before – shadowy types whose work is not normally discussed. In fact, some of the officers the Doctor worked with are legendary figures who the Colonel knows to operate "beyond command authority." The Colonel knows one of the legends of covert operations is a retired General, but he always seems to be around somewhere in uniform. No one seems to know who he works for and everyone knows not to ask, if he values his career. The General always handpicked his operatives, and the Colonel wonders if this Doctor may be a "sleeper."

He remembers trying to check on the Doctor several years ago because he was getting access to information that no one else could seem to find.

The Colonel talked to an old classmate in Washington who told him, "This Doctor was one of the General's top men and his right arm in the old days; a most active participant who always volunteered for the worst missions. He has no history that is accessible; and, for some reason, it all seems to be absent, missing or lost. He once had a reputation of walking a tightrope of the General's operation and was known by at least three different internal code names: The Snake in 1968, The Cobra in 1969, and The Hawk in 1970."

When the Colonel's friend started asking questions about those names, he received no further information from the computer. The next morning at 0800 hours, he was transferred to an obscure supply function in Saudi Arabia, with no warning of the reassignment and no knowledge about supply functions. After that incident, the Colonel decided it would be better not to ask any more questions.

The Colonel is conducting the briefing himself because, in the past seven years, this Doctor has shown neither temper nor excitement. He remembers, "The Doctor is always cool and methodical, but he does have one aggravating trait which I can't seem to get a fix on. This civilian subconsciously acts as though he's in command of something, even when he's talking to me. He seems only to tolerate my presence. I wonder who he is, and what he used to do. I think it would be a serious understatement to consider this Doctor and his brother to be just members of the team."

The Colonel knows they are much more. He also knows a little of what they have done and how. He knows about the help they received in the islands from Reece and Jean Discombe, Julian Forsyth, Dr. Ken Hutton and a native missionary who goes by the name of Peter. He is also aware of the regard in which the Doctor holds two Americans, Tom Chames and Harry Cornelieus, who were an important part of the team.

However, the Colonel also knows about Ben and Pam, volunteers who betrayed the Doctor's confidence in them, and the devious trio composed of Folly, Laurel and Hardy who did everything they could to prevent the successful outcome of this project. The Doctor recommended all search team members for recognition, except himself; but that was before their last trip to the islands. The Colonel has heard nothing else about the recognition or awards and has placed the recommendations in his private file marked "take no further action."

The Colonel knows the Doctor has lived up to his promises and to the CILHI Accords. But he knows even more and is about to test the Doctor's and Roger's patience to new limits. He ponders, "After what these two have been through, they may not take this next announcement gracefully."

Slowly, he asks the Doctor, "Are you aware of the most recent events in Vanuatu?

The Doctor has been receiving daily fax messages and news reports, so he has an idea what is coming up next from the Colonel.

The Colonel continues, "You know our government has a Memorandum of Understanding with the Republic of Vanuatu. The officials there in the Ministry of Justice and the Ministry of History have responded to demands from Laurel, Hardy and Folly, all of whom you fired during your last visit to the island. Joining them in these demands is your friend, Ben, whom you fired for collaborating with them in the acts of desecration. They are demanding the return of all artifacts recovered by CILHI during recovery of remains from the F4U-1 and PBY. In the case of Bennett, they are demanding an audit list and they expect all items to be returned."

The Doctor snaps, "Like what, for instance?"

The Colonel continues, "They want all personal effects returned as well as personal equipment. And they are demanding the order be inclusive of all items recovered. They want dog tags, watches, bracelets, rings, belts, boots, Mae-West, headset, coins, guns and cigarette lighter. They want both the class ring and the Marine Corps ring as well.

"Of course, those items were removed for the purpose of identification of the remains; and, since they're now a part of Lt. Bennett's identification package, they are exempt from the MOU. However, it seems Folly and his friends have convinced some people over there that these artifacts will greatly enhance the tourism industry. They have proposed increased travel to the islands as well as a major tourist attraction if the items are placed on display in his curio museum.

"Also, these people have convinced the Minister of Justice that an order should be issued for their return with Folly to enjoy full ownership. It seems that Folly has been receiving considerable telephone traffic and fax messages from Texarkana. Someone in your city is keeping them well informed, and they are very persistent in their demands."

The Doctor states, "Well, Colonel, I have the authority to decide what happens to Bennett's remains and personal effects... unless you're prepared to prove what part of the collection does not belong to Wayland Bennett."

The Colonel smiles and says, "The American Ambassador doesn't want this to become a big deal, so he's asked for your cooperation."

The Doctor very carefully measures his words, "Ab-so-lute-ly NOT! Folly and his gang get nothing. I am here to state that determination for the family. I want every single item placed on the table with Bennett. When I see them, I will decide what the family will receive under the heading of personal effects. Then, anything I don't take with me will be destroyed."

The Colonel insists, "I must respond to the American Ambassador before long with a decision."

The Doctor speaks through clenched teeth, "Do I have a standing in this part of the event?"

The Colonel nods and smiles, "Yes, you have the final say for the family; anything you wish to have will be labeled personal effects, and those items will be sent to the Marine Casualty Center in Washington."

The Doctor responds, "Anything I do not claim for the family, I want shredded and then burned. As the family representative, I will agree that what remains may be returned to the island curio shop for Fred Folly to use and sell as a souvenir."

The Doctor is smiling now, and the Colonel realizes he is on to his routine of business.

The Doctor asks, "Just how much fax traffic is being generated by that group of grave robbers?"

But the Colonel just waves the question off with a gesture which implies, "More than I've ever seen before."

The Colonel knows this Doctor probably has a copy of every message sent to and from Vanuatu, but he is not at all surprised. He thinks to himself, "Just as I thought, you do know what is going on over there on a daily basis."

The Doctor is relaxed, but the Colonel can see Roger is not. Roger is a quiet fellow who has said little but has listened and watched everything that has occurred. He is very observant, but the Colonel realizes this is not a man to push too far. The Colonel met Roger in 1992 when the two brothers brought in a report of the search events for that year. That report detailed how Ben and Pam were involved with Folly, Laurel and Hardy in the body snatching business. The Doctor's report explained in detail who was involved and how they made their documentary film. Of course, the Colonel thoroughly checked out the report and found it accurate. Folly's trio uses the documentary as a sales tool that they show American families who suffered the loss of a loved one.

The Colonel remembers that Folly's group also tried to steal the Doctor's research notes and team charts and copied them. This gave them an extraordinary amount of information, but nothing could be done about it then. The Doctor has accepted full responsibility and blame for the temporary loss of his confidential records. He regrets an error in judgment about Ben, who Folly, Laurel and Hardy used as a pawn.

The Colonel also knows that this big guy, Roger, is the one who went after Ben to get all the notes returned. The Colonel remembers what he carefully read in the Doctor's notes and speculates, "Poor old Ben only wanted to make a name for himself and show off in front of the girl. I bet that was a mistake Ben still has nightmares about."

An informant told the Colonel about that event, and he can easily imagine, "Roger reaching across the table and, with one swipe, rearranging Ben's attitude as well as his nose. Ben sliding across the restaurant floor, landing in a heap with broken dishes and scattered silverware. Then Roger on him like a cat, and Ben crying like a baby on the restaurant floor: 'Please don't mess up my face'."

He can imagine hearing Roger speak softly into Ben's ear, so no one else can hear, "You have two seconds and two choices, Ben, so what's it gonna be?" Then, after a pause, Roger whispering, "The notes and the charts, Ben. Right now! Or you can take your chances for recovery here in an island hospital, because I'm about to reschedule your travel plans."

In his mind, the Colonel can see Roger standing, one huge arm raising Ben up in front of his face and saying only two final words, "Now git!"

The Colonel sure wishes he could have seen Ben light out of there like his tail was on fire. That happened several years ago, but the story is as fresh in the Colonel's mind as if he heard it only this morning.

The Colonel returns to the present and says, "You understand. I have to tell you these developments; but we will also follow the family's wishes to the letter."

The Doctor knows his brother is upset, so he puts his hand on Roger's arm and addresses the Colonel. "The family and three remaining friends do not know of these developments in the islands. Nor are they aware of Folly's attempt to claim all of Wayland Bennett's belongings. I have never felt it necessary to bring up this subject with them, and now is not the time to add to their stress."

The Doctor had hoped this subject would just go away. However, with the demands and insistence to comply with the MOUs as interpreted by Folly and company, it is obvious that pressure will continue to be directed toward CILHI until a final disposition of those artifacts is settled.

"Perhaps it would be better to relieve the Colonel of this decision as soon as possible," the Doctor decides.

The Doctor clears the air with a question, "Who gets the first move, Colonel?"

The Colonel smiles, knowing what the Doctor is going to say. He answers, "Why, you do, Doctor. You represent the family of an American hero, and we're here to serve the family's last wishes in that regard."

The Doctor smiles, "Okay, I want the belt buckle, coins, rings, and lighter returned to the family. Out of respect for 2nd Lt. Wayland E. Bennett, a true American hero, I want each and every remaining piece of his personal belongings (specifically the headset, goggles, boots, Mae-West, and gloves) shredded. Then, Colonel, I want the shredded pieces burned. The ashes may be sent to Mr. Folly with my compliments. I want nothing of Wayland Bennett's to ever show up in Folly's curio shop museum of *'fine art.'* The data plate for the airplane wing does not denote Bennett's plane since it is only a sub-assembly parts plate and has no meaning for Folly; so, by all means, send it back in compliance with the MOU."

The Colonel is smiling because Roger is at ease again. With these details covered, they end the meeting at 5:00 p.m. and the Colonel invites the two visitors to dine with him at the base Officers' Club.

The Doctor declines as gracefully as he can because of another appointment. The Colonel is curious that they have another meeting so late in the day, and he can see Roger is also taken by surprise.

The Doctor continues, "General Robert Shaw asked us to pay a courtesy call on some old friends while we are here, and we want to take care of that obligation this afternoon."

The Colonel is surprised, but says, "Very well, perhaps I can tell you how to get to your next appointment. What is the name and I will look up the address for you."

The Doctor explains, "The names and addresses are all in the same place. We are delivering a message to them from the General at Punch Bowl National Cemetery."

Now the Colonel understands, "Very well, gentlemen, shall we reconvene tomorrow at 0900 hours?"

The Doctor nods and thanks the Colonel; then he and his brother leave. The Colonel stands at the window for a long time and watches as the two men drive away.

On the way back to Honolulu, Roger and the Doctor take a winding route to the site of Punch Bowl National Cemetery, set in the natural bowl of an extinct volcano. This awesome amphitheater was formed eons ago and commands an impressive view of a vast expanse of Pacific Ocean. There they fulfill a promise made to the General as they pay his respects to old friends from a time long passed. Here in honored glory are the names of heroes who will be forever etched into huge granite monuments and the hearts of all Americans. Some of them are unknown and other names are familiar: Bennett, Crocker, Nelson and Monger; but none can ever be forgotten in the hearts of free men and women in a place called America.

The next morning at 0850 hours, the two brothers drive into a CILHI staff parking lot. An escort is waiting for them and delivers them directly to the Board Room for a formal presentation. The room is tastefully appointed with all amenities necessary for getting right to the heart of important business. The long conference table has already been prepared with notebooks, pens and seating arrangements. This is to be a very formal meeting, indeed, and will be the last time that Wayland Bennett's case will be an open file at this facility. At the conclusion of the meeting, Bennett will receive travel orders for transfer to his final destination.

The Colonel enters the room at precisely 0900, followed by his staff, which fills the conference room. They have brought all their corroborating notes and records to present in the identification of Lt. Bennett. The staff includes laboratory professionals, identification team, recovery team, historical research team, forensics, pathology, radiology, odontology, medicine, anthropology, archaeology, photography, and records research and coordination.

Introductions are made all around and lights immediately dim. As a hush falls over the darkening conference room, a movie screen slowly descends from the ceiling and the briefing begins. The expert presentation includes a CILHI definition and the task with which they are charged. It provides a short history and presentation of some recoveries and difficulties that have been previously encountered. This smooth slide presentation blends into an area that is becoming familiar to the Doctor and Roger. It is more specific to a recent case history.

With an idea of what they do and how their mission is accomplished, the film gently eases into Case 0060-94 and how it became a mission for a recovery team. This case is odd because it has no origination report. This case, it seems, came to a recovery team while they were working another recovery case not related to 0060-94.

A field report was delivered to a female Sergeant, along with a suggestion for the team to divide itself and prepare for a return to base camp in town. As they travel back along a trail, they are led cross-country to this new site, which has not been disturbed since the day it crashed. The area has always been under the rule of a Chief who shunned outsiders until only recently. This explains why no one else on the island knew of its location.

The slide presentation shows an undisturbed crash site and an overgrown airplane before recovery began. It shows an archaeology dig and explains the reason for this field reference tool. It presents the undisturbed remains of the pilot and the location of those remains in the wreck site. The recovery demonstrates how a team performs field tests and protocols to insure that nothing is left behind.

The photographic records of both discovery and recovery have all been assembled. The remains have been subjected to the highest technology and painstakingly reassembled. The height and weight have been computed in the lab work sheets, and the field reports include proximity to the aircraft from which this pilot was removed. The aircraft's history and assignment have also been collected, and its maintenance details at MAG-11 are complete.

After two hours of concentrated presentation, the meeting becomes a walking tour of an ultra-modern facility known as CILHI. Few questions are necessary, but staff presentations leave out no answers. These professionals are proud of their work and eager to assure a family or its representative that no question remains unanswered.

As the Doctor and Roger are led into a laboratory, they both know they are in the inner sanctum of the acronyms: CILHI, KIA, MIA and BNR. This is the end of a war for this lab's customers. Here is where grief starts to end. This is where all further hope stops for an MIA's family, which has refused to accept the finality of death. Because, when he leaves this place, he will no longer be an MIA or any other acronym; he will be on the way home to his family, who have waited so long for his return. As he leaves these doors, he will again have a name and not just a case number. This is the place where healing is allowed to begin for a family.

This is not a place of the past; it is a starting place of the future for loved ones who can now experience "closure." Customers of CILHI have no rank when they enter and are all subjected to the most rigorous scientific tests known to mankind. When they leave here, they proceed without delay to Travis Air Force Base in California where they will be dressed out in their finest uniform with gleaming brass, spit-shined shoes and medals in place. They will be ready for their final, formal inspection.

CILHI has served a long and impressive list of highly respected guests, and performance of their staff and teams here is nothing short of miraculous to a layman. Here miracles of the identification process are accomplished on a daily basis. It seems that the only miracle CILHI does not do is raise the dead. But then, you see, that is not their mission assignment; and, besides, they leave that part of the job to Someone who is better qualified to perform such tasks.

As they walk among stainless steel tables, they see the extent to which this lab must endeavor on a daily basis. Finally, they stop at a table covered with a gleaming white linen drape.

The Colonel asks the Doctor, "Will you be able to positively identify

Wayland Bennett, based on our research and these remains?"

The Doctor says he can, if specific components are available.

As a drape is withdrawn, the Doctor leans forward for a better look at the skeletal remains on the table. It takes only two seconds to find what he is looking for. He quickly examines the dental collection, then he rises and states to the Colonel, "This is Wayland Bennett."

Based on CILHI's presentation of their verification proceedures and the physical evidence, there is absolutely no doubt in the Doctor's mind that the man he has searched for during the past eight years is here in this lab. The Doctor is totally certain about this identity, and there can be no doubt in his mind concerning this officer.

The dignity and final respect displayed by the CILHI staff to these American casualties is impressive and leaves a lasting impression. The people of CILHI are in good company because they work in the presence of heroes. All CILHI's clients died while in service to their country, and, whether during combat or training, that makes them all heroes.

Back in his office, the Colonel stands before the civilian searchers, reaches into his desk and removes two medallions. The Doctor and Roger both receive a special commemorative medallion from CILHI. The inscription of "CILHI Search Team" is indeed an honor for them both.

The Colonel speaks, "I had a request for some of these to be given to some folks once, but, something happened and I wound up with these two extras. I can't imagine anyone who deserves them more."

As the Colonel shakes their hands, he admonishes them, "The next time I meet you two, if you don't have this on your person, you will have to buy dinner. It has been a pleasure and an honor to work with you for the past several years."

The Doctor knows the time has come, and the staff is all assembled in the conference room for farewells. He cannot delay his announcement any longer. The Doctor begins his speech with, "I am glad your staff is here, because on behalf of the Bennett family and friends, I want to express their most sincere appreciation for your assistance in the research and search for Wayland Bennett.

"No one seems to know very much about what you do here at CILHI, but perhaps that can be remedied when a book is written about this search and homecoming. The courtesies you have all extended to our search team were many, and we could have accomplished very little without your assistance. Our city, the family and friends of 2nd Lt. Wayland E. Bennett want to take this opportunity to express our deepest appreciation for your assistance.

"Unfortunately, I have a confession that I must make to the Colonel and his staff. I regret to inform you that I did violate the CILHI Accords and my agreement with you personally. When I knew you had the unconfirmed remains from the Corsair, I was certain they were those of

Bennett. I waited, and I waited for the day of confirmation of his identity. I waited until I knew that Wanda, Lt. Bennett's twin sister, would be unable to live until his return. I even attempted to reach the Colonel, but he was in Australia on a recovery.

"And, on that day, I called her and spoke with her at length about her brother. I told her the whole story, as I believed it to be at that time. All of what I told her was true, and you have since proven all statements made to her then to have been correct. I told her that his airplane had been found and positively identified. I also told her that the full set of remains and personal effects had been recovered and were all in this lab in Hawaii. I told her that he was back on American soil in the hands of Americans. I told her, in good faith, that he would be home in Texarkana in only a few days.

"That was two weeks before she died. But I could not, in good conscience, let her go without being told of his coming home and of the hero's welcome we have planned for him. I received official notification from Capt. Black the day after her funeral. But, in telling her, I broke my word to CILHI, to you the staff, and to the Colonel. I want to acknowledge my actions and to tell you the reasons for them. But, for whatever those reasons, I now publicly apologize to all of you."

After a moment of silence, there are a few sniffles and the blowing of a nose or two. Then there are a few smiles as the Colonel rises to speak. He says, "Your honor is intact Doctor, and your ethics have never been in doubt. To tell you the truth, if I had been in your shoes, I would have done exactly the same thing you did. You see, I too know the code of honor, and in my view you did not lie, or cheat or steal. And besides, I already knew you had told her. I called her myself two weeks after you did, but she had already died."

CHAPTER 16

HOMECOMING FOR LT. BENNETT
SEPTEMBER 1994

After the CILHI meeting, 2nd Lt. Wayland Edward Bennett receives his final set of orders. The day he has waited for so long has finally arrived. He will soon be home, laid to final rest beside his dear parents. Many have worked and prayed toward this day and it has finally arrived.

Bennett is flown from Hawaii to Travis Air Force Base in California. There his remains are arranged in the proper anatomical position in a shiny steel coffin, and he is outfitted with the finest dress uniform. A pure white linen cloth covers the remains. Then a new, perfectly pressed, blue dress uniform is placed over the remains of the officer inside the casket. His medals adorn the breast of his tunic. Above these medals are the Naval Aviator's Gold Wings of which he was so proud. A Second Lieutenant's gold bars are pinned on each shoulder. All the brass is polished to perfection and the white hat cover is spotless. The dress white web belt and brass buckle are without blemish.

Lt. Bennett is now ready for his final inspection. He is ready to meet his escort and guard of honor who will insure that he reaches home on time and in the style befitting a war hero.

As is U.S. Marine Corps custom, Lt. Bennett will be afforded an escort that will accompany him from the time he departs California until he receives his final salute at the graveside services. The escort and guard of honor must, by tradition, be an officer of equal or higher rank. Since Lt. Bennett is a pilot, the escort must also be a Naval Aviator.

Captain Corey Thomas, an active duty pilot, is selected as Wayland Bennett's final escort. Capt. Thomas is revered by his men because he is a "Mustang," an officer who came up through the ranks. He enlisted in the Marine Corps and served for several years as an enlisted man. He then went to night school and self-improvement classes as he attained the rank of Sergeant. When he applied for Officer Candidate School, he was accepted and sent to Pilot Training, which he completed with ease. He is an outstanding example of today's young officers who serve their country's needs as enlisted troops, officers and pilots. His decorations of parachute wings as well as six full rows of medals on his chest are proof that this is not a "Gee Dunk" hero. This man is one of the proud, and one of the few; he is a Marine.

Capt. Thomas is introduced to Lt. Bennett in California and they travel together by commercial airliner to Shreveport, Louisiana. There news media and a Texarkana Funeral Home hearse meet them. The news media have all covered the research as well as the searches; and they are now ready and waiting to record Lt. Bennett's homecoming and report it to everyone in America. The escort and Lt. Bennett are chauffeured home in style and arrive in Texarkana at five in the afternoon. Capt. Thomas hovers around Lt. Bennett as he undergoes his last minute inspection. In a few minutes, he will begin to receive guests who have come to welcome him home and pay homage to his service and sacrifice to his country. Lt. Bennett lies in state for three days.

[16-a] HOMECOMING: When Wayland Bennett finally came home, he lay in state for three days and was visited by hundreds of friends, family and classmates. On September 16, 1994, a welcome home service was held in the same church where the memorial service was held in 1944, with the same photographs on a table in front of the casket. And on this day in 1994, Wayland Bennett was there. Thousands at a special service on the federal courthouse steps welcomed him home, and millions learned of the day from newspapers and TV all across the U.S.

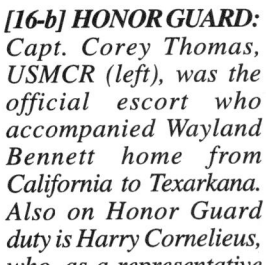

The "Lost Blacksheep" has finally been found.

[16-b] HONOR GUARD: Capt. Corey Thomas, USMCR (left), was the official escort who accompanied Wayland Bennett home from California to Texarkana. Also on Honor Guard duty is Harry Cornelieus, who, as a representative of all the local Veterans organizations, stood guard over Wayland Bennett as he lay in state. He was one of the first to volunteer and became a member of the team that searched the jungles.

Wayland Bennett is once again in the same room with his old boyhood friends and chums. When the Bowden, Carson and Sandlin families come to call, there is an air of happiness and relief – not of grief and sorrow. The Bennett family gathers from far and wide to attend the auspicious occasion of this American hero's return to Texarkana.

[16-c] BENNETT FAMILY: The Bennett family gathered for the long-awaited return of the Lost Blacksheep.

Robert and Frances Sandlin were the very last people from Texarkana to see Wayland, when he left the United States en route to Espiritu Santo. These friends are also the first to welcome him home as he returns. They are waiting for him as they have been doing for the past half-century, and they have not waited in vain.

Search team members report for the three day vigil, as well as doctors, ministers, lawyers and judges, along with hundreds of other ordinary American citizens. The Vietnam Veterans of America are on hand, and Harry Cornelieus stands watchful guard over the sleeping man for whom he helped search. Veterans of Foreign Wars and American Legion members have also waited for his return, and they, too, visit and pay their final respects.

Bennett is visited by his old girlfriends and dancing partners. His classmates and skating partners are also there. All surviving members of the Texas High School graduating class of 1941 are there, just as though the teacher is about to call roll again.

Reece and Jean Discombe travel from halfway around the world to pay tribute to an American who died before they were married, one they helped bring home.

ORCHESTRATING A HOMECOMING

Capt. Tatum Young, who graduated from the Virginia Military Institute, joins Capt. Thomas in his vigil in Texarkana. Capt. Young has been in the U.S. Marine Corps all his adult life and serves as Inspector and Instructor at the Marine Corps Reserves Texarkana Bulk Transportation Unit. He is an officer and a gentleman and one of the "ground guys." He is not a pilot, but a meticulous and methodical officer who wants all the "I's dotted and all the T's crossed."

Capt. Young, a stickler for protocol, is assigned as Casualty Affairs Coordination Officer (CACO) and is responsible for this funeral from a military's point of view. He has done this for many casualties in the past; however, he has found this funeral to be quite different from any he has ever been involved in before. When he learned that a civilian is somehow in this loop, directing things, making schedules and planning events, he told himself, "I'm gonna try to get along with this guy, but I'm not gonna like him at all."

While standing guard beside the casket, Capt. Young thinks back to when Robert Bowden introduced him to the Doctor several months ago. At the time, Capt. Young found the Doctor "too direct, too informal, too formal and besides," he thought, "he knows things about this funeral he won't even tell me." Now, he thinks about what has taken place and mentally starts telling Wayland Bennett all about it:

"You know Lieutenant, the Doctor told me during our first meeting, 'Today, 2nd Lt. Wayland Bennett is being recovered half way around the world in the jungles of Vanuatu and his remains will be taken to CILHI labs in Hawaii for identification.

" Of course, I wondered, how can he know this information? This guy's a local Doctor, and he's telling me what an Army unit is doing in the middle of a jungle 7500 miles from here! Now, how can a civilian know all of those details?

"Then I got really nervous when the Doctor informed me, '2nd Lt. Bennett is to be given a full Military Honors Funeral in Texarkana. And we want the local Marine Reserve Unit to take full charge of the funeral and honors.' And, on top of everything else, the Doctor informed me they were requesting that I be designated to tend to all the little details that accompany a normal military funeral.

"I remember thinking, 'Yep! I'm sure I'm not gonna like this guy. At all! I don't know who this guy is, and I don't care who he thinks he is; I don't do funerals and honors on demand from a civilian off the street.'

"Well, you know what, Lieutenant, I was stunned when I received orders to serve as the Officer in Charge and take over details of the 'Full Military Funeral and Honors for Second Lieutenant Wayland Bennett.' That was exactly what the Doctor had predicted.

"I called the Doctor that morning, and he invited me to come over for lunch at his restaurant. It was a marvelous steak dinner that I didn't get to eat because the Doctor was giving a play-by-play scenario on how this funeral is going to unfold. I just couldn't seem to get the grasp of all this because the Doctor still had answers to questions I hadn't even asked.

"I don't know who the Doctor is, but he's fast on giving instructions and very slow to accept the word, 'No.' But the Doctor does know how to give orders. He seems to start every sentence (or is it an order?) with the same opening: 'The family of Lt. Bennett would like..., wants..., requests..., suggests..., would appreciate....'

"But I soon acquired a new appreciation of the Doctor. I guess you know, the Doctor has spent the last eight years researching and searching for you. He has a private practice and was an Air Force Instructor Pilot; but, most of all, he was once in this Texarkana Marine Reserve unit.

"I soon learned that he is always working about three problems and two telephone calls at the same time, and seems to be able to handle anything that comes his way.

"It wasn't long until I started getting an idea that the Doctor has gone quite mad – about the time he told me the overall plan for your homecoming. He told me, "The funeral will have a full-blown cortege going from the front of Union Station right up the Texas-Arkansas state line to the Federal Courthouse and Post Office.'

"I started to tell him, 'We only do things like this for Generals,' but he didn't seem to understand.

"Without skipping a beat, the Doctor said, 'Right,' and continued to give instructions on the way he wanted the cortege to proceed. 'The coffin will be placed on an antique baggage cart from Union Station and covered by a U.S. flag. It will be taken six blocks in this fashion and will be propelled by ten veterans from various wars.'

"I was really beginning to worry when I realized all these veterans were not in the Marine Corps, and many of them were in wars that were over before I was even born. And he was telling me that he wanted me to place my Color Guard exactly on the state line and lead this gaggle of old soldiers.

"But he just kept going, 'They will be followed by the Honorary pallbearers: Bowden, Carson's representative, Judge Sandlin, Roger, Harry Cornelieus and myself.'

"You know Lieutenant, most of this crowd hasn't marched in my lifetime – three of the pallbearers even served in the war with you and many are senior citizens. I suddenly realized there would be no semblance of a uniform.

"According to the Doctor, the cortege is going to include all of your family – on foot – and many of your old classmates and childhood pals. You know what, Lieutenant, some of these people have never marched and most have never seen any type of military duty?

"Furthermore, the Doctor explained that many area high schools will turn out classes and provide a drum corps and at least 100 students will be marching in the cortege.

"By this time I started checking my notes and scratching my head. All I could think of was, 'Why me, Lord? What did I do to deserve this? Is this Doctor going to ruin my career? Please don't let me mess this up!' I had already taken two pages of notes, and the Doctor was showing no signs of slowing down yet. My steak was cold long ago.

"You know, Lieutenant, I may be known as a nit picker when it comes to the proprieties of protocol, but the Doctor really made my day when he announced that a large number of dignitaries will be present on the steps of the Post Office and Federal Courthouse.

"Then he said, 'Just a few VIPs.' He then began to list the proposed attendees which include Senators, Congressmen, State Representatives, at least a Two-Star Air Force General, seven full Colonels, five Lt. Colonels, two state governors and the mayors and city council members of both Texarkana, Texas, and Texarkana, Arkansas. Then he added, 'There will be a few proclamations on the steps of the Post Office; and, in addition to the local newspaper, at least four television stations will be live for the entire ceremony.'

"Did you know, Lieutenant, that even local church bells will toll for you on that day. This idea of a cortege with old veterans involved still scares me. Something this formal is a large task, but to do it with untried troops who can no longer perform commands is something to think about. This affair is one of the largest I've ever seen, and it's gonna be covered by nationwide media.

"You know, the thing that really worries me most is that some of these old veterans might just die in the street. Then, of course, someone must make sure the flag doesn't blow off your casket and into the street. If I had my own men, I could guarantee it wouldn't happen. But...

"And now I have more to worry about... the weather. Any good Marine will always have an alternative plan for weather contingencies, but the Doctor is making plans for this event as though it will be a bright and shiny day. And every weatherman in the four-states area says it will rain, and then rain some more, and then come up a terrible storm.

"Whenever I ask about this little problem, the Doctor looks at me with eyes like a cobra and informs me, 'It wouldn't dare.'

"You know, Lieutenant, the Doctor sure is slick in some of his maneuvers. I'm amazed how things seem to just fall into place. Some events have occurred as though they were designed to fit into this master plan and no other way will work.

"But one thing really did get to me. Last week the Doctor informed me that he wanted the Marine Blacksheep Squadron (VMA-214) to do a flyover at the cemetery. Now I know, Lieutenant, in your day the Blacksheep flew Corsairs out of Espiritu Santo, but now they fly AV-8b Harrier jump jets out of a home base at Yuma, Arizona.

"Well, I made it clear this would never happen; but he just can't seem to understand the word, 'No!' I've explained that the only Marine to receive a flyover at his funeral in the memory of most Marines was when Colonel Gregory "Pappy" Boyington died in 1986. Colonel Boyington was buried with full military honors at Arlington National Cemetery just outside Washington, D.C. Even though you're only a Second Lieutenant, the Doctor thinks I can just snap my fingers and get a four plane jet flyover all the way from Yuma, Arizona. I told him, 'It's just not going to happen.'

"Well, the Doctor then wrote a letter and personally hand-delivered it to me. Part of the letter introduced him and said he'd been searching for you for the past eight years. Said he understood the inability of the Marine Corps to furnish the flyover and to not worry too much about it.

That, even though many dignitaries would be in attendance (and he listed each one of the VIPs he expects), you were just a hometown Marine so he understood.

"He said he had been able to secure the services of U.S. Air Force pilots on training missions, who had already agreed to fly the graveside "Missing Man" formation. They would also be able to fly the same over-flight formation above the welcome home ceremonies on the Federal Courthouse steps where you will be presented back to the community.

"When he gave me the letter, he told me to just send it through normal channels and see what happens. I forwarded the letter through channels to my superiors marked 'Information Only.'

"Well, an odd thing happened three days later. I received a message, and it said that four of the VMA-214 pilots will be practicing bombing and navigation exercises on September 16, 1994, and will not be at the base for dispatch to a funeral flyover. Of course, funeral flyovers could not be authorized even if they were on the base. The letter ended with the usual technical jargon about 500 feet high and 400 mph, the coordinates, and that squadron records indicate the planned attack will turn onto the target at precisely 4:15 in the afternoon.

"You know, when I handed the message to the Doctor and apologized for not being able to produce the Blacksheep Squadron, he read it, smiled and said, "Yeah, well you know how Marines are." Then he turned and walked away. Just like that, with no further comment.

"You know, he must be getting tired; that's the first time I've seen him give up so easily. Well, this has been interesting. Maybe I could get to like this guy a little... eventually."

Suddenly Capt. Young realizes that, for the past several minutes, he has been talking to someone who can't even hear him. He shakes his head and mumbles, "You know, the Doctor must really be getting to me, here I am talking to a dead Marine."

HOMECOMING

The civilian MIA research and search team for Wayland Bennett was a first and only event of its type to be attempted; and the twin cities of Texarkana, Texas-Arkansas, are the first and only cities to bring home one of its own MIAs by intent.

It is September 16, 1994, and Second Lieutenant Wayland E. Bennett has come home to a hero's welcome. The historic event is attended by thousands of people who march right up State Line Avenue, the main street that runs right down the state line in the downtown business district.

Hundreds of thousands view it on television, and local newspapers devote entire sections to Wayland Bennett for several days. The national wire service picks up the event and passes in on to every city in America for newspaper and television coverage.

The cortege begins at the old Union Station train depot, which sits on the state line as an historic landmark in Texarkana. Wayland is placed on a baggage cart that is almost 100 years old, and a Marine color guard leads the way and sets the pace. Texarkana's Texas and Arkansas High Schools supply their marching drums to beat a step set by the Marine color guard.

During the six-block walk, all business comes to a stop as local police stop traffic and re-route vehicles during the ceremony on the Federal Courthouse steps. As the cart carrying Wayland Bennett rolls through the streets, television crews run to keep up with the procession and film its progress from every conceivable angle.

TEXARKANA'S OLD SOLDIERS [16-d] These men served in WW2, Korea and Vietnam. They placed Wayland Bennett on a railway cart and escorted him up State Line Ave. No old soldiers dropped dead in the street and it didn't rain – it wouldn't have dared.

[16-e] (left) ...AND THEY CAME TO WELCOME HIM HOME: Thousands attended and millions read of the day and the way Lt. Bennett came home.

[16-f] HOMETOWN FRIENDS: (below) To Wayland Bennett's right are Judge Sandlin, Robert Bowden, D.A. Carson's representative, Roger, the Doctor, and Wayland's family, along with thousands of hometown friends.

Search for the Lost Blacksheep

[16-g] WELCOME HOME: Senators and congressmen, mayors and governors proclaimed Lt. Wayland E. Bennett Day, and the Master of Ceremonies welcomed home one of "America's few, the proud, the Marine." Many military officials paid homage to Wayland exactly 51 years after his last call home to his parents. This day had a special meaning for all who celebrate POW/MIA observance day – we brought an MIA back to our community.

When the procession arrives at the courthouse steps, Wayland Bennett is presented back to the community from which he came. As the Master of Ceremonies welcomes Wayland home, he invites the dignitaries to make their presentations in the very moving ceremony. All the dignitaries have proclamations for recognition of September 16, 1994, as 2nd Lt. Wayland E. Bennett Day. Texas and Arkansas Governors both make their recognition statewide in his honor.

[16-h] BACK HOME: The search team leader addresses the community as Lt. Bennett is officially presented back to his home town – Texarkana, U.S.A.

The Doctor makes a statement on behalf of the search teams and reminds everyone that this day holds other significant meanings. First, it is the National Day of Recognition of POWs and MIAs everywhere. Second, it is the anniversary of the last time Bennett spoke to his family in 1943. Third, it is the birthday of the lady Sergeant who was in charge of the recovery of Bennett in the jungles of Vanuatu. He also thanks everyone who supplied the means by which this team was able to continue the search year after year.

When the Master of Ceremonies resumes the schedule, he asks the old veterans to return 2nd Lt. Wayland Bennett to the Honor Guard commanded by Captain Young. Bennett is then transferred to Hardy Memorial Church for the final service.

The memorial service at the Church is a poignant event that corresponds with the service held in Bennett's absence 51 years earlier. Now, in a packed sanctuary, Bennett is the guest of honor as his own minister recalls the days when Bennett grew up in this church. He asks everyone to remember one of Bennett's last acts in this city was in this church where he came to talk and pray with his pastor. The minister then asks the filled church to pray with him for the blessings of a merciful God to be bestowed on Bennett and his family this day.

[16-i] HONOR GUARD: Captain Young's U.S. Marine Corps Honor Guard receives Lt. Bennett.

[16-j] (right) SALUTE TO A FALLEN COMRADE: Capt. Tatum Young, Inspector-Instructor of Texarkana's U.S. Marine Corps Reserve executes his salute to a fallen comrade, Wayland Bennett, who died before the Capt. was born. Capt. Young and his troops performed flawlessly during what was, perhaps, the most stirring funeral service ever seen in Texarkana.

Bennett and his honor guard are then transferred to Hillcrest Cemetery and the family plot, where a site has long been reserved for him. The headstone is complete with the inscription, "God is now my co-pilot."

Capt. Young commands an Honors Service that is absolute perfection. The rifle squad is placed in perfect formation with their weapons at the ready. Upon command the seven squad members fire as one. As they repeat this function of the service, it is clear that Capt. Young and this squad have been practicing for some time. Their performance is flawless as rifles crack out the farewell of a 21 gun salute.

[16-k] 21 GUN SALUTE: The 21 gun rifle salute performed by Texarkana's U.S. Marine Corps Reserve unit was perfectly coordinated and picture perfect. These young men brought tears of pride to many who attended this final salute to Lt. Bennett. This unit is named after an Iwo Jima Navy Cross winner for heroism and valor – Pfc. D.A. Carson, a fellow Marine and one of Wayland Bennett's best friends while growing up.

The bugler must be on loan from the New York Philharmonic Orchestra because he never misses a note. The haunting refrain leaves a lump in everyone's throat. As Captain Young and his First Sergeant address the flag, it is folded to perfection in the world famous fashion and form. The Doctor wonders how many times they must have practiced this folding to make the three stars come out on the last fold of the flag. As Capt. Young makes his final salute to Lt. Bennett, he turns and presents the folded flag to Dr. Richmond O. Bennett, Jr., Wayland's brother and DNOK (Designated Next Of Kin) for just such an event as this.

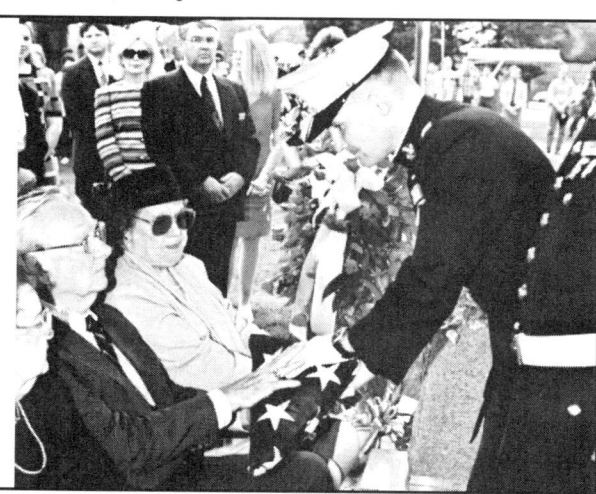

[16-l] PRESENTATION OF THE FLAG: Dr. R.O. Bennett, Jr., as the DNOK receives the folded flag of our nation from Capt. Tatum Young, and the thanks from a grateful nation for his brother's sacrifice.

As the flag is placed into the hands of the brother, Capt. Young turns to face the First Sergeant and salutes. The time is exactly 4:15 in the afternoon. As he does so, the earth shakes as four jet fighters streak past their designated target at a prescribed 500-foot altitude and 400 mph. They certainly hit their target with a high degree of accuracy this afternoon. At this precise moment one of the fighters pulls up and out of the formation; then flies off into the sun, climbing out of sight as he wings his way toward heaven.

In the cemetery, there is absolute silence because no one can speak. There is not a dry eye or a still heartbeat on this day for Wayland Bennett is now at home.

[16-m] FULL MILITARY HONORS: This photo now hangs in the "Blacksheep Squadron" Ready Room in Yuma, Arizona. While they were making a long range, precision navigation and bombing strike on some obscure target, they must have "accidentally" stumbled into a final photograph at the conclusion of someone's funeral in which the deceased received "Full Military Honors." Just in front of the Sergeant's salute are four AV-8b Harrier jump jets practicing some sort of formation flying... I guess. I couldn't see them well enough to identify them.

*[16-n] NOT A DRY EYE: At 1615 hours, 16 September 1994, the Blacksheep (VMF-214) struck their target with a high degree of accuracy. Not an eye was dry and not a heart was still as a final fulfillment was achieved of **THE PROMISE**.*

[16-o] MILITARY ENTOURAGE: Capt. Tatum Young (left) & Capt. Corey Thomas (right), and four "transient" pilots of VMA-214, who are known only by their call signs: "Reifer," "Norton," "Troll" & "Droopy."

Search for the Lost Blacksheep

[16-p] MUTUAL INTERESTS: Dr. R.O. Bennett, Jr., the older brother of Wayland Bennett, talks with a member of the Black-sheep. Dr. Bennett was a Naval Aviator in WW2, assigned to teach young pilots to fly.

The Doctor looks across the casket at Capt. Young, who is not exactly certain what has just happened. As their eyes meet, the Doctor winks at the Captain.

The Captain nods his understanding and thinks, "This is a perfectly shabby way to do business." Then, as the service concludes, he remembers that day when the Doctor seemed to give up. That was the day the Captain told the Doctor the "Blacksheep" would not be able to do a flyover because they were doing training missions.

As the Doctor moves alongside Capt. Young, he whispers, "You seem surprised, Captain? Something startle you?"

Capt. Young tries to sound angry as he growls, "How did you know?"

The Doctor explains, "I thought I recognized those target coordinates on your message."

"Where are the coordinates for?"

The Doctor smiles and says, "Guess."

Capt. Young finally realizes he was wrong as he thinks, "I guess I finally did get to like the Doctor."

[16-q] FRIENDSHIPS: (Left to right) Robert Bowden, Reece Discombe and The Doctor relive the friendships made by the team while searching for Wayland E. Bennett.

*[16-r] THE END OF A LONG SEARCH: Reece and Jean Discombe traveled half way around the world to pay their last respects to someone they never knew – for whom they were totally committed to their part in the drama of **The Promise**. They were valuable friends to the search team and remain dear friends today.*

And so, on this day, Bowden, Carson and Sandlin are finally able to fulfill their **Promise** given so long ago. No old veterans die in the street, the wind does not blow the flag from the casket, and it does not rain. It wouldn't have dared!

[16-s] "GOD IS NOW MY CO-PILOT": A good ending for an MIA story and a proper final tribute for Lt. Wayland Bennett, "The Lost Blacksheep."

POSTSCRIPT

Excerpt from a speech given by the Doctor on September 16, 1988, after the first trip to Vanuatu in search of Wayland E. Bennett

Today, some things have changed in our world – some for the better. In 1943, it took 20 days to reach Espiritu Santo island; today it takes only one. During WW2, the islands were primitive and remote; now, they are modern and accessible. And while many may have forgotten the memory of this fallen warrior, his friends and family continued to dream of the day when Bennett would "come marching home."

With declarations of "war is over and peace at last," the world tried to return to what it was and what it should be. Some still hope for the world to become what it can be. Since the war ended, lives have been lived and careers have flourished. But, in the hearts, minds and dreams of three boyhood pals, **The Promise** continued to smolder. According to the calendar, our bodies begin to require more attention as we age. Finally, at an age when their own bodies would no longer allow them to hack down jungles and search in sweltering heat, they made another proclamation of their own – a simple statement, "The time has come."

I was enlisted by Robert Bowden, a boyhood pal of Wayland Bennett, last year. When Bowden told me Bennett's story, he asked me if a search could be mounted; then if I could lead the search. When he asked me to consider conducting such a trip, it caused me to also consider the odds for such a search. I had been planning a vacation to Australia and some South Pacific islands, but this was an unexpected challenge. In this consideration I was forced to admit, the time has come for Bennett to get a few "yes" answers for a change.

These search missions will make a few of those "yes" answers available, and they will lead to a call for change. I reminded Bowden that the jungle is not something to be toyed with. It is dark, wet, disease-infested and full of wild animals. Jungles do change with time, but only to get worse. This case was already 45 years old, and any chances for a full recovery during the Bennett family's lifetime are rapidly diminishing.

If you are planning to join me in this search for our MIA, you must first realize that this will not be just a camping trip. It is to a foreign nation that is a real live jungle. A searcher will only sacrifice sweat, money and time, while Bennett and his friends gave their lives.

Who among us can be too busy? Who among us will be able to deny this need? And who cannot afford to be among the noble part of any community who will attempt to do this impossible thing?

There is an old saying, "Whether I win or lose the endeavor, let me do my best." This effort is for a man, a family, but more importantly, it is for a community. This may be the most enriching event of this decade because it represents our honor and an obligation. It is also a commitment to the memory of unity, when a nation joined together for a common cause. I thank God for the guidance to be among the first to volunteer for this effort, and I hope that you will be likewise inclined.

I do not know one member of the Bennett family at this time, but I have met the principals through basic research, and they seem like folks who live next door. I never met the parents and I have not yet met the brothers and the sisters – but Wayland Bennett made his gift of freedom to me while I was still in diapers. And so, if this shall be a test of my commitment to repay a long-overdue debt to a long lost American son, then let it be so. Let it be now that you and I try. Our success will not be measured by what we bring home. Nor will our failure be measured by what we do not find. Our success is to rise to this opportunity and occasion to try. Our failure will be in not having tried at all.

Excerpt from Keynote Speech given by the Doctor at the U.S. Marine Corps Birthday Party on November 6, 1994

As a Marine our first impressions were of duty, honor and tradition. As tough as our training was, it created a bond of faith in one another. The friends made then became comrades in arms. The trust that developed transcended blood, sweat, tears and time. It became an invincible attitude. The memories of hardships faded into dedication to excellence. And then the belief, the word, the pact, the contract – *Semper Fidelis* – always faithful to the nation, to the Corps, and to each other.

Fifty-three years ago a *Promise* was made among friends; fifty-one years ago that pact was forged in blood. A boot, a recruit, a cadet was trained as a pilot. He chose to become a Marine. Within six months, he would pay for our freedom by his supreme sacrifice. And so, as a life was given, a contract began. Eight years ago, I was told the story of this young Marine and of his loss in South Pacific jungles. One of my earliest reasons for accepting this challenge was in the pledge, *Semper Fi*.

One of my earliest thoughts of the successful conclusion of that project was of this night, and of this opportunity to return him to you at this U.S. Marine Corps Birthday Celebration. The honor of forever being a Marine was his. The honor of helping to return him home was mine. The honor of retelling this story will be yours. It is not a story of the searchers. It is not a story of the sponsors. It is a story of Marines.

An Interview with the Doctor following the Homecoming Ceremonies

Reporter: *The Homecoming ceremonies were a beautiful, stirring experience for Texarkana residents as they got to see a hometown boy brought home. Can it happen in other cities as well?*

The Doctor: The city of Texarkana is no different from any other city with an MIA/KIA/BNR. The difference is that Texarkana demonstrated its commitment and dedication to one man's return as a lasting example to every other city in America. We can just imagine the pride that is felt citywide because Lt. Wayland E. Bennett is home. Any American city can research and search for an MIA/KIA/BNR. It is time consuming and costly, but it can be done. Lt. Bennett now rests at peace in his rightful place – in his family's plot in American soil, right next to a lady he once knew as *"Susie-Q."*

Reporter: *The Homecoming was a tremendous outpouring of patriotism and display of military pomp. How important is all that?*

The Doctor: The ceremony was a stirring example of grassroots American patriotism that is alive and well. Our country is free and at peace today because of our military's efforts to keep us that way. Men and women have fought and died all over the world for those freedoms and we appreciate their sacrifices. All Americans should pray that we may continue to enjoy the blessings of a merciful God.

Reporter: *You speak frequently in churches and never hesitate to credit God for his help in your work. Why is that?*

The Doctor: I believe in giving credit where credit is due, and I know God walked with me every step of the way in those deep jungles on the other side of the world. Lt. Bennett and many other Americans made their sacrifices to insure our freedoms and rights, including freedom of expression and individual opinion as well as free speech. I enjoy telling a good story about what God has done for me. If anyone resents those stories and comments associated with religious freedom, then perhaps he will be equally interested in my next comment: TOUGH!

Reporter: *You recently referred to other planes and pilots who were "sleeping in Vanuatu's jungles." How many did you actually find during your search?*

The Doctor: I won't give you an exact figure because, in all honesty, I cannot state that our search team was the first to visit some of those crash sites. Neither will I make any claim for recovery of remains that were rescued after the Bennett searches. We were, however, able to update charts and reports that have had no activity for generations. As a result, more may be known today about the crash sites in Vanuatu because of our cooperative efforts with CILHI.

Reporter: *You referred to CILHI's work and introduced several people who were important in the search effort. How important are friends to a search such as this?*

The Doctor: It was never a one-man show, and no one can ever complete a project of this nature without the assistance of others such as CILHI. Many people also helped us here at home and their help can never be repaid, but they were able to see the fruits of their labor in his return home. It was a particular point of pride to see people like Dr. Gene Joyce, who helped us early in the research project, standing on the courthouse steps as Lt. Bennett was presented back to his home town.

In our efforts to find Lt. Bennett, we also made good friends who will last a lifetime including the Discombes, Huttons and Forsyths from Vanuatu. They were invaluable help to us in the islands and we might never have found Lt. Bennett's plane without them. Any search team must make friends in their search area if they expect to carry on from one trip to another. We also lost some friends along the way who were not dedicated to the final outcome of the mission.

Reporter: *It sounds like CILHI played a very important role in bringing Lt. Bennett home.*

The Doctor: The professionals at CILHI possess the ability and training to completely re-assemble the mortal history of a stranger who died in the defense of his country, decades before these investigators were even born. Their dedication is matched only by the science and technology they use on a daily basis. Their standards can identify a victim fifty years after an air crash. To assure such accuracy, they attempt to verify who forensic science says he is and not just who they "think he should be."

Reporter: *Sounds like they have a difficult task.*

Doctor: CIL teams methodically retrieve and research even the most obscure and seemingly unimportant details from warehouses of records and archives of historical data in order to make a positive identification. To fully comprehend the magnitude of this task, one must realize that:

(1) There are no fingerprints, scars, tattoos, features or dogtags.
(2) Only partial skeletal and dental fragments still exist.
(3) Very few, if any, of the victim's family or friends are still alive.
(4) There are usually no living witnesses to the event.
(5) Remains have often been subjected to scattering, mixing, erosion and destruction.
(6) Sightseers, curiosity seekers, souvenir hunters and scavengers may have disturbed remains.
(7) Remains have undergone years of exposure to nature's elements after the initial impact, explosion and fire.

Perhaps the single most difficult factor in an MIA recovery is that he is usually missing far from civilization. Airplanes have a nasty habit of crashing about 300 feet from a mountaintop in the most remote and inaccessible part of a jungle mountain range, rarely near the bottom, near villages or accessible roads. The crash site is often several days from any hint of civilization. Crashes often occur on large islands where natives, and occasionally cannibals, are the only residents – and they seldom speak your language. Temperature, heat, weather, mosquitoes, snakes, spiders, wild animals, and poor food and water supplies are daily fare for a CIL team assigned to bring an MIA/BNR home. After all, if it were easy to find, it would have been discovered long ago.

Reporter: *Why does it take so long to locate these crash sites?*

The Doctor: A plane may have exploded and burned after it crashed. The jungle then reclaimed the area with fresh undergrowth and overgrowth. Over a fifty-year period, trees may even sprout right in the middle of the wreck site and hide even the largest WW2 four-engine bombers from air discovery. Local natives may visit these wrecks but they have no interest in them and don't report them because they are unaware of their significance to Americans.

An MIA/BNR family may find this all incomprehensible, but this is how things happen and it is not our government's fault. After all, the crash site must be found and reported before CIL teams can start the tasks of recovery, research, identification and return to their homes and loved ones. From the bottomless pit of despair, the family of an MIA can only see a very limited view of the enormous task assigned to CIL teams, and to Casualty and Decedent Affairs. But these people do care, and are dedicated and committed to the task they undertake on a daily basis.

Reporter: *Why have some criticized your project?*

The Doctor: Our mission took eight years and there were those who wanted quick glory for their efforts. Any team will encounter "would-bes and the wanna-bes," but that is to be expected. Some people may even resort to treachery and blackmail if they do not receive the credit they think they are due. A search team must plan for this and conduct its search accordingly. Any leader and his team will be criticized and ridiculed by some for undertaking such a task. At times I even doubted my own sanity; but, by persevering, a leader may even find within himself a new person – someone who can take time to help solve a national dilemma by exposing it to America's "private sector." He may even help do, on a vacation, that which is so difficult to do on the diplomatic stage.

Reporter: *What was the biggest problem you encountered during your search efforts?*

The Doctor: The most glaring problem that surfaced was not in what we did as a team, but in discovering despicable acts of body snatchers and grave robbers who tarnish the name of Vanuatu's government in an arena of international relations and foreign affairs. Each of their "expert" efforts destroy the possibility of returning an MIA home to a hero's welcome. It is a sad state of affairs that allows these individuals to continue their miserable activity. Hopefully, they will soon be deported from the islands for their negative contributions to the good name of the kind and decent people of Vanuatu. Their acts and deeds erode the very fabric of common decency and humanity.

Reporter: *Who were these people and where were they from?*

The Doctor: They live in Vanuatu and I will not give you their real names but will simply refer to them as Folly, Hardy and Laurel. Hardy, a photographer, is a vile and despicable person who will go to any lengths to "get even" with any adversary. Laurel is what women like her have always been. Morality is not a burden to her, and she belongs to anyone with a low moral character to match her own. She will always be easy to find because her permanent address is on the bottom of the pile. Folly is an opportunist who owns a "souvenir" shop on the islands and fancies himself an explorer. He is really just out to make a reputation and fortune for himself and has made every effort to gain acceptance into a prestigious international explorer's club. One hopes people of his class and style will never make it.

Reporter: *Sounds like you have no use for those three?*

The Doctor: In Texas it is no longer acceptable for gentlemen to have a showdown in the street at high noon. How unfortunate that is because this cowboy ain't no gentleman, and I'm standin' in the street against bums like these, anytime, podnuh.

Reporter: *But what about problems you actually had as a team?*

The Doctor: I must admit that I made some mistakes during our searches. Some were due to inexperience while others were simply due to wrong assumptions. Some were threatening and dangerous, while others were amazingly funny and embarrassing. Although often funny or amusing, these instances highlight the necessity for careful consideration of all search management. A team leader has many opportunities for mistakes because he must plan for so many details in an area of vast cultural differences. Language and interpretation is a very real problem to overcome and often magnifies even the smallest omission. But mistakes can, in retrospect, provide a good laugh as mine did for me on several occasions.

Reporter: *I know you had to raise all the funds for the search from private benefactors. Was there anything left from the rescue operation and, if so, what will happen to it?*

The Doctor: We did raise funds each year to conduct the search, and there was a substantial amount left after all expenses were met. Lt. Bennett's family and friends donated most of these surplus funds to the Disabled American Veterans for purchasing a van to transport veterans to the V.A. Hospital. The remaining funds were donated to the Vietnam Veterans who participated in the homecoming services. By the way, if I ever write about this experience a portion of the profits will be donated to veterans' organizations. The Bennett family has declined any monetary gain whatsoever from this or any ensuing projects.

Reporter: *If given the opportunity to conduct another search, would you do it?*

The Doctor: It took us eight years of research and five searches to reach the point where we could experience this day; but, if I had to do it all over again, my answer would be a resounding "yes!" And the conditions would remain the same. The success of our team will not be measured by what we brought home, but our failure would have been measured if we had not tried. I think anyone who had the honor to be a part of the Bennett search team will say the same thing.

Reporter: *What would you do differently next time?*

The Doctor: A lot! On another search I would probably choose more team members who know how to pray for one thing. Perhaps the sheer numbers of their prayers would be more effective than those of the leader alone. But next time, most of all, people would be selected who will not wait so long to begin praying.

Reporter: *Do you really feel that the team's religious belief has a bearing on the search?*

The Doctor: Yes, God was the most important member of our team. If fact, if I participate in another search such as this, I will probably be sure not to take any atheists along. They are simply too brave for mere mortals, such as me, to work with on such an adventure. It's hard to imagine a searcher who would even contemplate doing what the Bennett team did without God's help. It is even more difficult to imagine being with a team member who has no one to turn to when he gets into a jam. I'm not claiming to have all the answers but, on searches for MIAs, I will be even more selective of volunteers in the future.

Reporter: *How important is the composition of the team?*

The Doctor: Well, I sometimes felt as though I was just working from one impossible situation to another. It was never my skill alone that brought about Bennett's successful return. It was always a team effort. Team members must work together and humble themselves to the point of asking for help. It is always very tough trying to lead a search team in the jungle, even for a short time; but it would be tougher still if hemmed up in the jungle with companions who are not smart enough to know when or who to ask for help.

Reporter: *What would you tell another team leader who wants to do what you did?*

The Doctor: Be prepared for the humbling effect of such a search. At times, searchers may be in deep trouble and plagued with problems. They may become sick, tired and exhausted; and their leader will have to carry the private burden of efforts that could end in failure. A leader will obviously care about what he's doing or he won't be there in the first place, but he will need Someone to turn to in his hour of despair. If he doesn't already know how, he will soon learn to pray. Since no one wants to follow a leader who doesn't know where to look for answers, his first prayer each day should be for God's care and guidance.

Any team leader must also keep a healthy sense of humor, not only for himself, but also for the rest of the team. No one on the team must ever adopt the attitude that everyone is laughing at him or his mistakes. An effective leader can both lead the team in the search and lead them in a search for laughter and amusement. In the bush, you will find very tough going at times, and a little smile goes a long way toward making someone's day out there. When the laughter is over, you can always get back to the serious part of the search mission.

Reporter: *You have spoken in area churches and club meetings about this search and many want to know if you plan to write a book about it. If so, what will you write?*

The Doctor: Well, let me answer your question with a possible scenario. Suppose you just run out and research and search for your own MIA. You may even be able to find him and see him recovered. If you are lucky, he will be identified and returned to a hero's welcome in his hometown. You can then observe as your fellow Americans pay homage to him, opening and closing their efforts with a prayer. Watch as his neighbors welcome him home as a hero; then, as an amateur, just sit right down and write a book. You may even include epithets, cursing and all manner of filthy language and tell your story in a fashion that would embarrass a gutter rat. That is your right because your MIA paid the price to make your rights a reality. But watch to see if your book is accepted or rejected by churches and schools across America.

You can be certain any book I write about this search won't be like that. Anything I write will be in a fashion that will make Wayland Bennett smile a little, and maybe even laugh a little. He might even enjoy it enough that he'll occasionally shed a tear. I'll also write it in a manner that will keep Wayland a little excited, perhaps even keep him spellbound on a dark rainy night. But, you can be sure, anything I write will be presented in a way that a lady of elegance and grace would have approved. She will never read the words I have to say about these past several years, but she knows they will be from my heart.

Reporter: *Are you referring to Wayland's twin sister who died recently?*

The Doctor: Yes, she was a source of inspiration for us all and they are now together forever. In your mind's eye, can't you see her and Wayland walking hand in hand down streets of gold. I can almost hear them laughing as Wayland tells her how much he enjoyed my mistakes and the trouble I went through. And, maybe one day, they'll even enjoy my amateurish efforts in writing a book about the ***Search for Wayland Bennett – The Lost Blacksheep.***

APPENDIX

A	Crossing the Equator	317
B	Turtle Bay Data	318
C	Casualty Report	319
D	From the Commanding Officer	320
E	From the Squadron Leader	321
F	Official Notification	322
G	The Family Responds	324
H	Broken Hearts	325
I	"Pappy" Wrote Mrs. Bennett	326
J	A Sister's Plea	326
K	Natives Observed A Crash (Robertson's Letter)	327
L	Detailed Search Report	328
M	Cover Letter	334
N	The Search Continues	335
O	Forty Years Later	336
P	Always A Helping Hand	337
Q	White Men Don't Do That!	338
R	The Beginning of the End	339
S	Please Bring Him Home	340
T	Parables of the Flight Line	341
U	The U.S.A.	343

In the Royal High Court of the Realm of Neptune in and for the District of Equatorius
The People of the Realm of the Deep
vs.
2nd Lt. Wayland E. Bennett USMC of the U.S.S. Mount Vernon
Subpoena
Filed 27th September 1943 A.D.

I HEREBY CERTIFY, That I have served the within subpoena on the herein named person on board the U.S.S. MOUNT VERNON in sufficient time previous to the crossing of the equator by said vessel, to permit the defendant to prepare an ample defense to such charges as appear therein.
Hon. Peg Leg, Deputy
Davy Jones, Clerk

Subpoena and Summons Extraordinary
The Royal High Court of the Raging Main

REGION OF THE SOUTH SEAS
DOMAIN OF NEPTUNUS REX §§

To Whom May Come These Presents
Greetings and Beware

WHEREAS, The good ship MOUNT VERNON, bound south of the Equator and
WHEREAS, the aforesaid ship carries a large and loathsome cargo of landlubbers, beachcombers, guardo-rats, sea-lawyers, lounge-lizards, parlor-dunigans, plow-devotees, park-bench warmers, chicken-chasers, hay-tossers, four-flushers, draft-dodgers, feather-merchants, Boston sheiks, Scollay cowboys, asphalt arabs, bridge sharks and other foul creatures of the land, falsely masquerading as seamen, of which low scum you are a member, having never appeared before us; and
WHEREAS, THE ROYALE COURT OF THE RAGING MAIN will convene on board the good ship U.S.S. Mount Vernon, on the 27th day of September and WHEREAS, an inspection of our Royal Muster shows that it is high time yours sad and wandering nautical soul appears before OUR AUGUST PRESENCE;
BE IT KNOWN, That we hereby summon and command you Wayland E. Bennett, Now a POLLYWOG to appear before the Royal High Court and Our August Presence on the aforesaid date at such time as may best suit OUR pleasure, under penalty of eternal pickling.
You will accept most heartily and with good grace the pains and penalties of our Trusty Shellbacks and answer to the following charges:
CHARGE I. In that you have hitherto willfully and maliciously failed to show reverence and allegiance to our Royal Person, and are therein and thereby a vile landlubber and pollywog.
CHARGE II. That you are a Hot Pilot;
CHARGE III. That you sometimes pile it too high.

Disobey this Summons Under Pain of Our Swift and Terrible Displeasure.
Our Vigilance is Ever Wakeful, Our Vengeance is Just and Sure.
Given Under Our Hand and Seal.

NEPTUNUS REX
Ruler of the Raging Main

ATTEST:
Davey Jones
His Majesty's Scribe

[A] CROSSING THE EQUATOR: Lt. Bennett's mother wrote in a letter that Lt. Bennett called her from San Diego, California, on the 16th of September, 1943. That letter and this document help pinpoint the time Lt. Bennett was there.

AIR FIELD DATA
TURTLE BAY AIRFIELD, ESPIRITU SANTO, NEW HEBRIDES

LOCATION - Turtle Bay Field (Fighter No. 1) is on the east coast of Espiritu Santo Island just north of Peterson Pt. on Peterson plantation.

LAT. - 15 degrees, 22 minutes, 45 seconds South

LONG. - 167 degrees 11 minutes East.

ALTITUDE - Sea level.

MAGNETIC VARIATION - 10-1/4 degrees East.

LANDMARKS - It is the most northerly of the four fields. Turtle Bay lies to the east.

DIMENSIONS - Runway NW-SE (293 degrees) - 4800' x 150'. Graded to 330 feet wide. Taxiways are on both sides through dispersal area.

SURFACE - Surface is 12" coral with good natural drainage. A watering system has been installed for wetting the runway.

LIGHTING - Semi-permanent boundary lights are available; one set of stationary. Truck-mounted floodlights.

OBSTRUCTIONS - Obstructions above 40-1 glide ratio within five miles.
- N - Hills to elevation of 363', trees near runway.
- NE - Unknown other than trees near runway.
- E - Mafia Island with hill and trees – elevation unknown.
- SE, S, & SW - Trees near runway.
- SW - Hills - elevation unknown.
- W - Mt. Turi to elevation of 1791'.
- NW - Hills to elevation of approximately 984'.

INSTALLATIONS - Bunkers, Revetments and Dispersal Areas - There are 50 hides on both sides of the runway and hard-stands for 160 planes - VF, VSB and VTB. Repair and Maintenance - The field has limited facilities of its own but can draw on those cited under this heading under Bomber #1. It has AvGas bulk storage. Miscellaneous - The field has a control tower, ready rooms, a compass rose, aerological tower, and photographic laboratory.

This document was previously top secret but has been declassified

[B] TURTLE BAY DATA: *These details would have been invaluable to the Japanese but were closely guarded secrets until after WW2 came to a close.*

U. S. NAVAL AND MARINE AIRCRAFT
EXPENDED OUTSIDE THE CONTINENTAL LIMITS
OF THE UNITED STATES
TO ALL CAUSES
7 DECEMBER 1941 to 15 AUGUST 1945

Evaluation Section (Op 23-V-3)
Air Branch
Office of Naval Intelligence

DATE	TYPE PLANE	BUREAU NUMBER	SHIP OR SQUADRON	BASE OR PLACE	AREA	NAME OF PILOT
OCTOBER 1943						
18	F4U	17424	VMF-214	NEW HEBREDES	SoPac	Lt. Oliver K. McMahan
20	F4U	02315	VMF-214	NEW HEBREDES	SoPac	Lt. Herbert Holden, Jr.
22	F4U	02608	VMF-214	NEW HEBREDES	SoPac	Lt. Wayland E. Bennett
JANUARY 1944						
3	F4U	17915	VMF-214	VELLA LAVELLA RABAUL	SoPac	Maj. G. Boyington
3	F4U	02723	VMF-214	VELLA LAVELLA RABAUL	SoPac	Capt. G.H. Ashmun
APRIL 1944						
7	F4U	56263	VMF-217	ESPIRITU	SoPac	1st. Lt. H. M. Shafer
7	F4U	56334 (of VMF-225)	VMF-217	ESPIRITU	SoPac	2nd. Lt. L. W. DeCamp

THIS DOCUMENT WAS PREVIOUSLY TOP SECRET BUT HAS BEEN DECLASSIFIED

[C] SOUTH PACIFIC MIAs: *These are a few selected excerpts from a much more detailed aircraft losses report. When we acquired this list during our research, it promptly identified the squadron to which the plane and pilot were assigned. VMF-214 was the "Blacksheep Squadron." Note the October 22, 1943, entry.*

**HEADQUARTERS, MARINE AIRCRAFT GROUP ELEVEN,
FIRST MARINE AIRCRAFT WING, NAVY NO. 140
(ONE FOUR ZERO),
C/O FLEET POST OFFICE, SAN FRANCISCO, CALIFORNIA.**

15 December, 1943.

Mrs. R. O. Bennett
Texarkana, Texas

My dear Mrs. Bennett;

I am writing you in regard to the death of your son on October 22, 1943. At this time it is possible to release the few details that we have.

Your son was on an authorized training flight in a fighter type airplane. He was practicing maneuvers in preparation for transfer into a combat zone. During this flight, your son failed to pull his plane out of a high speed dive and was seen to crash into the jungle. It has been impossible to recover his body as the jungle in the interior here is impenetrable.

Your son gave his life for his country and you should be proud of him. He was a distinct loss to us in the group, and to the Marine Corps as a whole.

Please accept my deepest sympathy.

/s/ J. A. SMOAK,
Lt. Col., USMC.

[D] **FROM THE COMMANDING OFFICER:** *In the adapted for TV series, "Blacksheep Squadron," an actor brilliantly portrayed the part of a "Colonel Lard," with some interesting similarities to the relationship Boyington experienced with his superior, Lt. Col. J. A. Smoak, on Espiritu Santo.*

**MARINE FIGHTING SQUADRON 214
NAVY NO. 140, c/o FLEET POST OFFICE
SAN FRANCISCO, CALIFORNIA.**

21 December, 1943.

From: Major Henry Stuckert Miller USMCR.

To: The Commandant.

Subject: Second Lieutenant Oliver Kriel McMahon USMCR, reported missing 18 October 1943, and Second Lieutenant Wayland Edward Bennett, USMCR, reported missing 22 October 1943.

Enclosures: (A) An unsealed envelope addressed to Mr. Oliver Roberts McMahon, *(address omitted to protect privacy)*, containing a letter from Father Thomas F. Gorman, a letter from me, and Lieutenant McMahon's accident form.

(B) A copy of my letter to Mr. Oliver Roberts McMahon, contained in (A), for Headquarters files, if needed.

(C) An unsealed envelope addressed to Mr. R. O. Bennett, Texarkana, Texas, containing a letter from me, and Lieutenant Bennett's accident form.

(D) A copy of my letter to Mr. R. O. Bennett, contained in (C), for Headquarters files, if needed.

1. I was a captain and officer in charge of a unit of fighter pilots attached to Headquarters Squadron, Marine Aircraft Group 11, which unit included Lieutenant McMahon, when he was reported missing 22 October 1943.

2. Please forward (A) and (C) upon approval.

/s/ HENRY STUCKERT MILLER

Originals forwarded to NOK...1/24/44

[E] FROM THE SQUADRON LEADER: *The unhappy task of notifying the families began with the squadron leader who would forward it up the chain of command. While it presents good living room TV enjoyment about the sadness of losing one's pals in war, it hardly compares to the real emotions necessary to write these letters for a real experience. One must therefore marvel at the emotion imparted to the family during these times by such men as the squadron leaders of the combat units.*

MARINE FIGHTING SQUADRON 214
NAVY NO. 140, c/o FLEET POST OFFICE
SAN FRANCISCO, CALIFORNIA

21 December 1943

FROM: Major Henry Stuckert Miller USMCR
TO: R. O. Bennett.
SUBJECT: Second Lieutenant Wayland Edward Bennett USMCR.
ENCLOSURE: Accident form.

    1. The Marine Corps Manual specifies that upon the death or honorable disappearance of a member of a unit overseas, that his commanding officer shall write to his next of kin stating the circumstances of such death or disappearance. On 22 October 1943 I was officer in charge of a training unit of fighter pilots to which your son Wayland was attached. I assure you that in fulfilling the duty specified, I am putting into somewhat official form statements and sympathy which are none the less genuine because put forth officially, and which I would have wanted to send you regardless of the requirement referred to.

    2. On Friday morning, October 22nd, we were doing routine training (the unit to which I refer was not this squadron). The weather was excellent. All that I can say about your son's accident is that another of our pilots saw your son's plane crash into the jungle some fifteen to twenty miles away from our base. The nearest habitation was about ten miles away. The jungle in that area grows to a height of at least one hundred feet, and is of a density which can not be appreciated until one has attempted to go through it. The other pilot fixed the location of the crash by reference to a bluff and certain local terrain features, and immediately flew back to our base with a report. For the next few days he, other pilots in our unit, and I searched the location of the crash, flying at a slow speed just over the treetops, hoping to find some sign of life or at least to see the airplane. Then for two weeks the Operations Officer at our base continued our aerial search. Two different parties made efforts on foot to reach the location of the crash and were turned back by the jungle after several days on the way. The only conclusion which could be reached was that the jungle had swallowed the airplane and its pilot as if it had been a crash at sea.

    3. November 4th another pilot and I inventoried your son's belongings and turned them in to the Post Quartermaster. This was also in accordance with provisions of the Marine Corps Manual.

    4. November 26th at five o'clock in the afternoon a service in your son's memory was held by our Protestant chaplain. Your son had come out to this area with a group of lieutenants with whom he had flown for about a year. Only they, a captain then attached to our unit, and I were present, and the service was brief, but nothing could have made it's impression go deeper. What the chaplain said was that one with whom we had lived and flown had left us, and that we would not see him again, but that we would not forget him. We are not training now, and we have not forgotten him.

5. At the time of the crash I had known your son about two weeks. To me he seemed one of our most capable and level-headed pilots. I knew that in his cadet course he had an outstanding gunnery record and on the very morning of the accident had asked him to take charge of that most important and difficult part of our training. Your loss is irreparable — and so is that of the Marine Corps.

6. At least in aviation units, each person is required to complete an accident form, in duplicate, upon attachment to any unit. A copy of your son's is enclosed.

7. I might add that a federal statute known I believe as the Naval Aviation Cadet Act of 1942, provides, or did provide, that upon the death of a former cadet, $500 should be paid for each year of his active service to such beneficiaries as he should have designated. Each cadet is supposed to complete applications for the benefits of this statute while he is still in training. However, to make sure, each member of our unit was required to fill out such forms again, and I still hold a carbon copy of the transmittal letter to the Bureau of Personnel of the Navy Department, which letter enclosed the completed forms and listed the names of those for whom they were enclosed.

/s/ HENRY STUCKERT MILLER

Original forwarded to NOK — 1-24-44

[F] **OFFICIAL NOTIFICATION:** *The letter on these two pages from Major Miller officially notified the family of Bennett's crash.*

Texarkana, Texas
March 20, 1944

Maj. Henry Stuckert Miller, U.S.M.C.R.
c/o Fleet Post Office. San Francisco, Calif.
Dear Maj. Miller:

    Your letter about the death of our son 2nd Lieutenant Wayland E. Bennett has been very gratefully received by his family (his parents, two brothers and two sisters). We can't begin to tell you how much we appreciate the letter from you. It spoke your sincerity from first to last. We are very glad his friends had the memorial service for him. On the 11th of November we had a service at our church, of which he was a member. It brought some degree of comfort to us. It was a very beautiful service, with his picture in his flying outfit, on a flag draped table banked with flowers. The remaining members of the family were here: the oldest, R. O. Bennett who is an Ensign in the Navy and an instructor at the Naval Air Station at Dallas, H. Wayne Bennett Y1C, U. S. N. R. and was then in N. O. P. in San Francisco; Doris, the older sister, a hostess for Braniff Airlines and Wanda, Wayland's twin sister, who is a senior in college and is a pre-med student.

    We are crushed. We can't begin, even yet, to think straight. It was so soon, we knew he was a natural flier, he was so happy in all his training, and we knew he was capable of handling his plane. It could not have been a human fault and must have been a fault of his plane. He was so sure his plane would stand by him. I'm sure he was happy even to the last minute.

    Please understand how we thank you for saying the beautiful things to us about Wayland. You judged him rightly. He was always cool and level headed. He was so proud of his gunnery record, but would only say, "I guess I was just lucky."

    We are so grateful for your efforts in trying to locate his plane. Do you suppose there was a chance that he parachuted out and may be in the jungle alive? If searchers can't get in, could he not also be unable to get out if he did parachute to safety? Do you suppose the natives could be hired to search until they find the plane and hunt for his body?

    We will give any reasonable reward to them if they will only bring his body to the base. One thousand dollars or whatever it will take. Can you give me the name of the pilot who saw Wayland's plane crash? We know Lieut. Harry Johnson of Birmingham, Ala. went over with him. Major Miller, can you tell us why we never had a letter from Wayland after he left the states? He called me on the telephone on the night of Sept. 16. That was the last. We don't know, even, what day he sailed. He was always so good to write. No one had letters from him.

    We are so proud of you Marines. You are wonderful. I'm so glad my son made the grade and could have his commission in the Marines. I listen breathlessly to the radio until I get all the news I can of the Marines. My prayers are for you all. May God hasten the day when it is all over. Please let us hear from you again. Tell us if there is a possibility of rewarding the natives to keep up the search until they find the plane and my son's body.

    All the family join me in sending you our best wishes.

                                    Very sincerely,
                                    /s/ Mrs. R. O. Bennett
                                  Texarkana, Texas, U.S.A.

[G] THE FAMILY RESPONDS: *Mrs. Bennett's response to the official notifications mirrors the response of many mothers following the loss of their sons during WW2.*

Texarkana, Texas
August 10, 1947

Marine Commandant Vandygriff
Washington, D.C.   (Received Aug 20 1947)
Dear Sir:
    I am writing you asking you to please renew your efforts to locate the wreckage and remains of my son, Lieut. Wayland Edward Bennett.
    020609-1
    DGU-296-hn.
    His plane crashed with him on Oct. 22, 1943, on Espiritu Santo, New Hebrides. By referring to his file you can get the exact spot where he went down.
    Others whom we know that crashed on this island were Lt. McMahon. Oct.18, found 10 days or two weeks later — (My son with Maj. Stuckert Miller searched for Lt. McMahon) Lt. W. L. Crocker Jr. not found. On Oct 22, my son and Lt. Wm. Leroy Crocker Jr. Worcester, Mass. went out together, Bill Crocker came back and reported the crash of my son's plane which was a Corsair No. 02608 with a large "88" on the side. Bill reported the right wing of my son's plane buckled at about 5000 ft. My son was assigned to Major Gregory Boyington's Blacksheep Squadron, VMF-214. His first combat would have been over Rabaul, where Maj. Boyington went down, but was liberated after Japan's surrender.
    Lt. Bill Crocker went on the Rabaul trip and returned to Espiritu Santo in about seven weeks. He was lost over Espiritu, I'm confident he was searching in the vicinity of my son's crash for some sign of him.
    Another person, a Major I believe, was with Lt. Crocker.
    About a year later Robert Bowden, another Texarkana boy, and who grew up with my son, was sent to this same island. He came to visit me when he got back home. He says he thinks the jungle can be penetrated and a thorough search made for the many boys we know are there. He talked with Americans who were in the "Malaria Control" and they are of the opinion that the jungle can be gotten into. Many roads have been made for their work.
    Our hearts are broken. Our boys wanted to come home and the least our government can possibly do is to bring home everyone that can be brought. My son knew he was selecting the most dangerous branch of the service when he chose to be a fighter pilot in the Marine Air Corps. Yet he never faltered. He lacked one month being 21 years old when he crashed. We knew he was a natural flier. (His sister and a brother also are pilots) But he was the best.
    America to us mother's means our boys. I'm afraid it doesn't mean much to us without them. Again I'm asking you to please send some means of search there and find as many as possible of the many who are still there.
    I shall be especially glad to get a letter from you telling me about what can be done. Have the islands above mentioned been turned back to the British and French?
    Thanking you for your patience in reading my letter.
                    I am
                    Very truly yours,
                    /s/ Mrs. R. O. Bennett

[H] BROKEN HEARTS: *Mrs. Bennett's urgent plea for the military to find her son and bring him home.*

Documents file, Wayland Bennett

Some time after the end of WW2, my mother Mrs. R. O. Bennett, received a letter from Major Boyington expressing his sorrow and offering his condolences for the death of her son, Wayland E. Bennett, 2Lt. USMCR. Lt. Bennett had been assigned to Squadron 214, commanded by Major Boyington, shortly before his death in October 1943 when his F4U-1 airplane crashed.

After reading the above mentioned letter I handed it back to her, my mother. I am the older brother of Lt. Bennett.

I have not seen the letter since that time and do not know what has happened to it.

Sincerely,
/s/ R. O. Bennett

Seal and stamp of
Notary Public

[I] "PAPPY" WROTE MRS. BENNETT: *This letter, from Wayland Bennett's brother, confirmed his mother's receipt of a letter from "Pappy" Boyington concerning her son's death.*

To Whom It May Concern:

I have cancer of the pancreas. My life expectancy is very limited. Anything you do to expedite the return of my brother's remains will be appreciated.

My name is Wanda Bennett Knox, the twin sister of Lt. Wayland E. Bennett, U.S.M.A.C. deceased. My brother served under Col. Boyington, squadron 214, later known as the Black Sheep Squadron. I read the letter Col. Boyington wrote my mother, after the war telling us that her son flew next to his plane in formation flying. I recall Col. Boyington's hand writing indicated a tremor or unsteadiness. My brother completed his Marine Corps flight training in California and was later assigned a new Corsair which he named "Susie-Q" after our mother. As he was one of the first to fly a Corsair, he helped with the indoctrination of new arrivals in the Corsair at the base on Espiritu Santo.

My brother was 20 years old when his plane crashed and killed him. He was very proud to be a Marine officer, a pilot, and to serve his country under Col. Boyington. The letter written by Col. Boyington indicated that he too was proud of Wayland's accomplishments and happy to serve with him.

Sincerely yours
/s/ Wanda Bennett Knox

[J] A SISTER'S PLEA: *This letter was written by Lt. Bennett's sister in early 1994, before she became aware of his exact crash location. He had not been positively identified. The letter was written to provide her statement of having seen the letter from Boyington to her mother. She was not made aware of his recovery and the identification of his plane and personal effects until later when it was certain that she would not survive until his homecoming.*

May 1944

Major Palmer
"Somewhere in Espiritu Santo"

    Bushmen from the village of MATILITILI have just come in with a Very Light pistol, two revolvers and a burnt invoice book from a plane that crashed at Panarabi. This place is about one days march from here for the natives, I would say a day and a half for your people.

    From the information that I have gotten from them it seems as if this crash occurred about three weeks ago as the natives say, "close up time month he dead" which means it was about the end of the last quarter, of the last moon, from what I gather.

    The plane burst into flames in the air. On asking what time of day this took place they said after Kai-Kai at night so I would say around 8 p.m. They say it was a twin engine plane or as they say "him he got two propeller," though one fellow was positive it had "four propeller." Any way two engines and propellers are there to be seen so they say. When they went next morning there was no sign of any of the crew, One bad thing is that they say there were knives lying around with the handles burnt off which makes it look like there were no survivors.

    Perhaps this might be the twin engine bomber you mentioned was missing when you were here. If you sent a party to investigate they want to be fit and well shod as I know this trail well and it is hard going in parts. I should think two would be enough as I will supply the guide and carriers.

    Now Major, I must thank you on behalf of the boys and myself for all the gifts delivered by Lieutenant Beinor. It was far too much for the little we were able to do and if at any time we are able to assist the Marines' Air arm we are here to command.

                                  With sincere regards,
                                    Yours sincerely
                                    /s/ W. T. ROBERTSON

[K] **NATIVES OBSERVED A CRASH:** *Mr. Robertson was a plantation owner who lived near the north shore of the island of Espiritu Santo during the war. He was very helpful in the searches and recovery of many of the casualties that occurred there during the period of intensive air activity in which many American planes crashed. He understood the natives and was able to pass on information to the military that would help facilitate searches when they saw planes crash. This letter led to the search described in Appendix L.*

JPP/fd
**HEADQUARTERS SQUADRON, MARINE AIRCRAFT GROUP ELEVEN
MARINE AIRCRAFT, SOUTH PACIFIC, c/o FLEET POST OFFICE
SAN FRANCISCO, CALIFORNIA**

4 June 1944

From: Major John PALMER, U.S. Marine Corps Reserve.
To: The Commanding Officer, Marine Aircraft Group Eleven.
Subject: Crash of PBJ 35087, trip to the site of.
Enclosures: (A) Letter from W. T. Robertson. *(see Appendix K)*
  (B) List of personnel missing from operational flight of PBJ 35087.

1. On Saturday 18 May, 1944, the following teletype message was received at Marine Aircraft Group 11:

"To Major Palmer from Lt. Pierce. Twin engine plane located one and one half days Coast Watch Station 5 near Jordan River, Information no survivors. Equipment found as follows: 2 Smith and Wesson 38s serial 412534 and 396551. One "Very" pistol E-050343. Information from Mr. Robertson."

Amplification of that message, which was sent from Coast Watch Station 5 at the time it was being decommissioned, was found in a letter from Mr. Robertson (copies attached) which he had no means of sending "out" to any American unit without dispatching natives on a trip of four or more days to the southwest coast of Espiritu Santo and back. (Mr. W. T. Robertson is the only white resident of the central and northern sections of Espiritu Santo, He is notorious for his generous and interested cooperation on problems of the American forces).

2. The pistol numbers were communicated to Marine Bombing Squadron 423, and it was thereby established that the plane was PBJ 35087, Squadron number K 104, Engine numbers 33374 and 33331, which had been missing since about 2132 hours on 22 April 1944. (A list of personnel aboard the plane at the time is attached to this report). The report which follows includes not only factual information, but has been drafted also to give background as to conditions encountered by the jungle search and rescue parties in this area.

3. On Sunday, 14 May, the next day, after having conferred with Major Hyatt of IV Island Command and with Air Center Operations, a party from Marine Aircraft Group Eleven proceeded by amphibian plane to Mr. Robertson's residence at the southwest corner of St. Phillip's and St. James's Bay. The composition of the party was:

Major John Palmer, USMCR, Marine Aircraft Group 11.
2d Lieutenant R.R. Wilson, USMCR, Marine Aircraft Group 11.
2d Lieutenant E.J. Caroselli, USMCR, Marine Bombing Squadron 423.

At Mr. Robertson's the party was increased by the addition of:

Willie's Son, Shadrach, Shoum-Shoum, Harry, Markwell, and Ghee-Ghee.

4. The equipment of the party was extremely light in accordance with the belief that the mission over the most difficult terrain on the island could best be accomplished by white men unaccustomed thereto by pushing in to the objective and on out again at a rapid rate of march. The party's gear included the following:

1 so-called jungle hammock each
1 khaki slacks and 1 long sleeved shirt each
1 khaki shorts and 1 short sleeve shirt each
1 pair field shoes each
2 canteens each
1 .45 cal. pistol for all of the party
1 machete (short-bladed) each

1 sheath knife each
1 sun helmet each
2 small flashlights
"K" rations, compasses, first aid gear, haversacks, small presents for natives, etc.

5. At Mr. Robertson's, preparations were carried out for the start of the journey to be made at dawn. Packs were made up on the basis of the amount of food per officer and per native it was computed would be required for the trip in and out plus a small margin to allow for possible delays which might result from sudden rising of the rivers, incapacitation of personnel, etc. The route which would be followed was discussed with the native who was to be our guide, but with a lack of very enlightening results. The party later learned why it did not get more definite ideas as to where its objective lay, the comparative advantages of following one river system or another one, where it was most practicable to cross the watershed, etc.

6. The party left Mr. Robertson's plantation shortly after sunrise on Monday, 15 May. The first part of the route was through a number of pasture-like openings in the jungle where the going was excellent. After about a 2 1/2 hour's walk the Apouna river was reached; it was then left again and paralleled at a distance of about a mile for another 2 hours. (Here it may be said that this country, and that further upstream, would be made literally impassable, even more so than the terrain around the Jordan and it's tributaries, by the constant rise of the river after heavy rains lasting for more than one day. Fortunately the party only encountered one sustained several day rainy period, it lasted only eight hours). The first crossing of the Apouna was made at a fairly good site, and the party stripped, bathed and got cooled off and refreshed before starting on. It is estimated that by the time the coast was reached again on the return trip a total of 55 river crossings had been made. Practically all of these of course involved wading with shoes and socks on, and subsequent marches frequently over the fairly large boulders in the river bed with the same shoes and socks in a constantly immersed condition. The travel over the rocks in the river bed was, for each member of the group, far more arduous than the anticipated rugged going of dense jungle travel. Everyone had good field shoes, however, and soon learned to keep going from one likely-looking boulder to another with considerable speed, the thought being to get to the end of that tedious terrain as soon as could be. Some hours after "lunch" had been eaten, the party's pretty well sustained pace still had not brought it to the anticipated point where a turn to the left would be made away from the river. By that time ankles were quite sore from wrenches, feet were considerably barked up, and the leg muscles strained and a little shaky. There was a great unwillingness to move on again soon after each rest, and a growing feeling of disrespect for one of the principal thoroughfares of Central Espiritu Santo. About 1500, when the direct rays of the sun and the reflected and retained heat of the rocky valley were at their worst, Mt. Tabwemasana ("two breasts") was sighted. The hills soon came closer to the river, and the river narrowed and was more rapid. The native leader also speeded up, which disheartened the members of the group until they were told that the cause was the probable proximity of a "native" village.

7. A halt was called at 1600 and despite a general desire to lie down for a "short" rest, camp was made and gear stowed against the coming of darkness and possible bad weather. It was learned from the natives that the "village" was on the opposite side of the river and (to them) "no distance at all" away. There was no desire to visit the primitive metropolis to inspect it's inhabitants or to collect its curios. Dinner was quickly eaten, and denying itself the solid pleasure of around-the-campfire philosophies, the party, to a man, entered their jungle hammocks.

8. Tuesday 16, May, 1944, camp was broken and the site-known to the natives

as MATILITILI — left for a further march upstream. A moderate drizzle of rain commenced but was interrupted every half hour or so by short spells of sunshine. The character of the country changed violently and the way led through river gorges and via many distance-wasting detours into the jungle to get past impassable canyons. At the end of four hours walking the expedition came into country somewhat resembling that of the lower Apouna. Boulder jumping was again in order, and some of the well known leg muscles, which had been used extensively the previous day, were again brought into play. The way then became quite noticeably steeper, and once more foliage closed in on the riverbed, which wound continually between increasingly higher mountain peaks.

9. A particularly pointed discussion broke out between the coast natives and a pygmy chief who materialized on the dawn start of the trip at MATILITILI. The denouement was that agreement had not been achieved when a choice of river crossing points had come to the top of the agenda. From this the party's sole, but not able, "beche-la-mur" linguist subsequently, with liberal use of a rare virtue, learned that his guide from the coast was — should the pygmy be right — about 1 watershed, 3 mountains, and 7 hours off course if he insisted on continuing as he planned. The chart (Army Air Force #29 was the best available but of course gave very little detail) had been practically memorized by that time and it was decided — but with disturbing misgivings because of the known reliability of the coast native — to back the pygmy's contention. The party made the crossing, backtracked down river a short distance and, with a last glimpse of Mt. Tabwemasana — then looking quite impressive went under the jungle canopy and started up the bed of a very small and swift brook. Here it was discovered that most of the "K" rations were completely spoiled. Chocolate bars were mildewed in the center, biscuits and cookies were pulverized, and other items — with the exception of meat and cheese in cans — were contaminated.

10. 1000 hours — Elevation about 800 feet — Weather: Oppressive, threatening. Equipment: reduced to knives and rations for one meal. The brook was left in about 20 minutes' time, and the course changed to go straight up the face of a jungle covered peak of then unknown elevation. The pygmy hill-dweller, tiny and putting but little weight on the slushy banks and the small roots and vines by which he hauled himself up, waited frequently for the plodding progress of the more highly developed humans trying their very best to follow him. The gradient was so steep that it was not possible to put one's foot forward when climbing-a disconcerting factor as the first half hour wore on. Rest, resume, conjecture, as to when the route would start circling up the peak, instead of tackling it so directly. Heart pounding, shortness of breath, Rest, On again. Tired, too soon again this time. It's getting late though — better keep going just a little longer before stopping. Murmuring from party in a tone to be distinguished from the jocular one of the river bed travel. No answer; on a little further. Rest, Resume, but with some protest. This work calls for everything one has. Wonder if there won't be a little bit of light in the bushes and overhead trees in just a minute which will mean that the summit is in sight. Falling and sliding backwards more often now. One member of the party stops where he has fallen, closes his eyes, no comment from anyone. Slightly longer rest. Resume. All natives except pygmy also tiring visibly now. Feel like resting about 12 steps after starting. Whole procedure depends on pulling oneself up by the arms. Think that this is the most unsatisfactory footing possible, except loose shale or slick ice. Don't want to over do this , not too much strain on heart. Rest. Feeling that the longer the rest, the harder to start up again. Upon order to resume, first open complaint about hardship, too severe climb. Terrain exactly the same as two hours before; no sign of summit. Rest requested soon after resumption of march. Rest. Complain, upon resumption, about leg (right) giving out.

Climb maintained. Rest. Two members of party lie quite still. Eyes closed. Resume once more. Discouragement, at seeming lack of progress; practical hopelessness of really getting anywhere. Inquiry as to one's own capacity for endurance. Second member of party has acute pain (stomach). Rest, all three members of party collapse at spot where they stop. Now know literal meaning of word exhaustion. Haven't been like this for many years. Certainly the finest thing in the world now would be just one half hour's sleep. Other two seem to have passed out completely. Late as the devil — can't stay here tonight — malaria. Pygmy said the natives would never climb up here with our heavy gear in which the mosquito nets were left. Left it at the bottom. Got to get back there tonight or at least two of the three of us sure to contract malaria. Others obviously done for. Any use trying to go on alone when distance yet to be covered is unknown? (Pygmy says "Plane him far too much"). Bitterly disappointing to go back now. Failure of a mission. But Robertson said I am held in higher respect by natives than any white man who had attempted jungle here. Maybe it's only a just accomplishable few minutes further on. Might as well do the utmost. The pygmy seems to be trying to get me to understand as he says, "One boy he stop along two — fellow masters. Boy altogether him go along me, go along plane." Must be saying to leave these two and he and I will go to the plane. Feeling inclined to run the rest of the way, to get it over with. Probably exhilaration. Same tough going as before, though. Exhilaration tapering off. Unencumbered now, why stop? Curious to see just how far this freak peak really can go straight up like this. Wish the anatomy would take it better. Why can't heart and lungs shift into very low gear for this sort of work? Why that old completely "done in," feeling again, when dragging along so very slowly? Rest, I suppose. Climb — slip — fall — miss vines — get lower vines — but they carry away — scuff leg — land — bruise backbone — don't care — don't swear. Try getting up that one again — toughest yet — don't make it, but get angry now. Make it climb some more. This has got to be near the top. Have been going vertically now in terrific heat for exactly four hours. Eight half hours, And each half hour divided into climbs that seem to last an eternity and rests that are over as soon as they start. Probably fool hardy and other fellows were smart. Why should this have an indefinitely stretchable limit? Mustn't stay holding on to trees with eyes closed. Should either get going or sit down and rest. Rest. Going again. Not going to try to puzzle things out anymore. Can't make so much difference in any case. Unimportant. Nothing's important. Kind of gray and fuzzy. Shake head violently. Pygmy turns to right. Follow him. He's going down- can't be. Route has only leveled off, completely. Unaccustomed to anything but up, I guess! Soon get so can do a jog trot on level route. Child's play now. Must be between 3000 and 4000 feet high. Lost track of even rough computations, way back. But believed before that crash would be just over summit. Surely not too far down other side. Here we go down. Pygmy finally says it's very near now. Discover presence of nerves while letting down near vertical banks. Burned branches of trees in sight. This is it.

    11. The highest area burned by the impact of the plane was about 350 feet below the summit of the mountain. Which is about 2 1/2 miles (air-line between peaks) to the north east of Mt. Tabwemasana. The elevation was about 3100 feet. The impact area extended vertically another 350 feet and was no more that 75 feet wide. It consisted of a narrow but high rock wall with a ravine at the bottom. The plane, freakishly enough, appears to have struck the exact center of this rock wall. It must have been on a westerly course, and just failed to clear the top of the mountain. It obviously exploded on impact, killing all personnel, and then burned. The largest piece of the plane which was left was one wing section which was torn off by impact with trees apparently and thrown to one side unburned. There was nothing left of the

fuselage as such. The article of paramount interest which was found was a remote compass dial, the hand-set pointer on which was set at 255 degrees, a compass heading which it is entirely possible that the pilot would have been steering at the time of the crash. There was no evidence that the crash occurred from any failure of material. The story of the natives who heard the crash impact was to the effect that is occurred roughly about 2000.

12. The personnel of the plane were discovered under a carpeting of green and black blow flies. Near the top of the impact area the first remains were found, later further down and to the northward more were come across. Still more in two more places in the center and further down. It was impossible definitely to establish the number of persons who died there but there could well have been seven. No tags, teeth, or other means of identification were forth-coming despite the fact that the so-called remains were probed and examined with a hunting knife. The largest section of human anatomy found was a spine with a few attached ribs. Everything had been badly burned and showed the effects of having been in the weather and at the mercy of flies for a period corresponding to that which had elapsed since the time of the reported crash — namely about 24 days. Planes of Marine Aircraft Group Eleven during periods of many days provided a most thorough search coverage, and it is believed that the plane in question crashed without any of it's personnel making parachute landings in the jungle. The natives of this region confirm this. Burial was given to the remains, and a cross was erected. Before leaving the site all secret and confidential gear, which has not already been destroyed or sufficiently obliterated by the crash and fire, was destroyed.

13. On the way back the other two members of the party were met. They had a refreshing sleep, during which time passed more quickly than they realized. Upon awakening they had moved further along the route toward the crash. The trip down was trying, despite the assistance of gravity and the fact that one could do considerable sliding. The unremitting peril of falls resulting in incapacitating injury kept everyone tense, and made the trip seem to last an eternity. Before reaching the bottom there was considerable debate as to whether an attempt should be made to MATILITILI that night or whether camp should be made along the river where the gear was cached. It was decided to carry on.

14. The little party, as it went into its second hour of travel along the river, consisted of three intensely fatigued individuals, all dragging pretty badly. A heavy rain started and continued — heavily — for the next eight hours. Darkness was therefore premature. That did not facilitate crawling along certain ledges overlooking the river which had been none too readily passable when the party had come up-stream under favorable conditions. The rock was like soapstone, it was wet and the visibility close to zero. Camp was nowhere near as close as the party heartily hoped it were. Rain. Completely immersed. Panicky start of a slip down from un-seeable poor footing on a huge rock. Diving off into the jungle after the natives — losing them in the now pitch black darkness — yelling against the rain — going on-growing like automatons — insensitive — feeling that a limit of suffering had been passed and that it didn't make any difference now. Incredible, eventual, arrival at the camp site. Unbelievable down pour of rain — still. Decision to go to the shelter of a native house "just across the river." No one falls down in the river; just as well, because no one would have cared. On the other side a hold up in the line. Soon see why. We are trying to go straight up again. These people live above the river, come to it often, and yet have nothing resembling in the least a "decent" trail. Incredible going. Terrain as bad as the mountain but made worse by lack of visibility and downpour which doesn't take even a short recess. Everyone wants to quit, to lie down in the mud, in the rain,

in the underbrush, and get two things: sleep and forgetfulness of all recent and present misery.

The intoxication of exhaustion — fine technical label! Time just disappears as an entity with which one is concerned. We practically collide with one grass shack. Destination. Shelter. Fire. Rest. Party is required to eat hot dinner despite unanimous desire to pass out instantly. Literally unreal, looking around fire which is inside hut. Cooking dinner — for whom, why, away out here, with most primitive of all aborigines looking on. Certainly are some funny ways of helping with a war. Time between eating last of dinner and sleep: approximately 1/100th second.

15. At sunrise the next morning the party's leader put, out his decision of the previous day to remain in the region and try to find a missing pilot (Lt. A. Pappas, USMCR). This plan had been come to because of the constant presence of large numbers of planes over a point a few miles to the southward of MATILITILI. It as felt that if someone were in that jungle area, perhaps injured, the party should not leave for the coast but should endeavor to get information from the natives and from the plane as to what bearing should be taken to go further in and get the pilot. This was put to the other members of the party and each expressed a desire to return to the coast as soon as possible. Permission was given for both of them to go.

16. The next two days were spent with the pygmy family (consisting of two men and four women), and were, though of course uncommonly interesting, without occurrences with which this report will be lengthened. A rumor, however, appears to have gained some currency, to the effect that when the party penetrated the almost completely virgin pygmy country, one of it's members was obliged to kill a pygmy "who was attacking him with a blowgun," The party had no differences of a serious nature, with any of the natives.

17. On 19 May a message was dropped from a plane ordering the party's representative to leave for the coast as there was no reason to presume that the pilot who was missing was down anywhere in the surrounding region. The trip to the coast was started early the next morning and completed in 6 hours, a reduction of 2 hours from the time made on the trip in. Because of weather no planes called at the plantation until the next day, when the expedition leader returned to his base, made verbal reports on the result of the trip to the Commanding Officer of Marine Aircraft Group 11, to Major Hyatt of IV Island Command, and to Air Center Operations.

/s/ John Palmer

[L] DETAILED SEARCH REPORT: *The exquisite eloquence and accuracy of this search report (on the previous 6 pages) is astoundingly appropriate to our searches a half century later. If this time frame is of any use to research it should be noted that there has been no change in the conditions of a search or to the life-style of the resident natives of the interior of the island. Major Palmer's apparent "dry wit and piercing sense of humor" is indeed enjoyable to a reader who has had similar experiences and interests. The author chooses to omit actual names out of respect to the memory of those members of the crew and their families. Of particular interest is the necessity to take nothing as a souvenir. Even the serial numbers of the pistols can become an all-important piece of evidence necessary to identify the remains of the occupants of a crashed airplane. Thus the all-important rule for a search team to adhere to of "take nothing and leave nothing," becomes important to not contaminate the site.*

KV11/A16-3/(jrw)
(2160)

HEADQUARTERS, MARINE AIRCRAFT GROUP ELEVEN,
MARINE AIRCRAFT, SOUTH PACIFIC,
c/o FLEET POST OFFICE
SAN FRANCISCO, CALIFORNIA.

11 June, 1944.

From: The Commanding Officer.
To: The Commanding General, Marine Aircraft, South Pacific.
Subject: Report on Jungle expedition to locate crash of PBJ 35087.
Enclosure: (A) Copy of subject report.

1. The enclosure is forwarded for information.

2. This report is not to be considered as an administrative report, but is a narrative report indicating the difficulties encountered on this, and other expeditions into the jungle in search of lost aircraft.

3. Administrative control of the Marine Bombing Squadron Four Twenty-Three was not vested in Marine Aircraft Group Eleven at the time of the crash, hence Marine Aircraft Group Eleven did not order a board of investigation to inquire into this accident.

/s/ J. S. HOLMBERG,

Copy to: IV Island Command;
         Com air center, EBON;
         CO, VMB-423;
F I L E   Return to

HISTORICAL DIVISION
HQ., USMC, Room 3235
ARLINGTON ANNEX

[M] COVER LETTER: *This letter accompanied the search report (Appendix L).*

**HEADQUARTERS
604TH QM GRAVES REGISTRATION COMPANY
(LESS SECOND & THIRD PLATOONS)
PACIFIC ZONE APO 954**

7 Sept 1947

SUBJECT: Investigation of AGRS Case 1322, Espiritu Santo Island, New Hebrides

To: Commanding Officer, 604th QM Graves Registration Co.

    1. Team No. 5 left the LST 711 at 0515 and arrived at the beach at 0545 hours. Mr. Robinson had arranged for our guides the previous day and they were prepared to take us to the scene of the crash.

    2. We immediately started out and encountered many difficulties, especially heavy swamp and jungle. There were two high streams to cross and we had to remove our shoes and wade across up to our waist lines. We arrived at the scene of the crash at 1030 hours, position 166 degrees, 52 minutes East, 15 degrees, 17 minutes South.

    3. A thorough search was made through the debris, but no signs of any remains were found. It is my firm belief that the occupant of this plane was incinerated. The plane was broken into a number of sections, and the cockpit was fused with the engine, caused by the terrific fire when the plane crashed.

    4. For identification one metal tag was taken from part of the cockpit with the following inscription: Eastern Aircraft Division, General Motors Corporation, Linden, N.J., U.S.A., Serial No. 1325, Navy Model FM2, Class VF, Serial No. 15126, U. S. Motor No. R1830-56. Part of the plane had the following painted in red, a pair of dice with number seven showing. Underneath the dice, in square printed letters, in black paint, "Come Eleven."

    5. Parts of the plane were brought back as evidence. Photographs were taken. We then had lunch and immediately proceeded back to the LST arriving at 1630 hours.

COPY   /s/t/WILLIAM J. O'NEILL,
                                         1ST LT. QMC
                                         Team Commander

[N] THE SEARCH CONTINUES: *A plane was found, but it was not Lt. Bennett's "Susie Q."*

August 22, 1988

Santo Hotel
Higgenson Blvd. 178
Luganville, Espiritu Santo, Vanuatu.

Dear Mary Jane:

This will advise you that at least 5 people will arrive at your establishment on approximately 15 Sept. 1988 for about a 10 day stay. Arrival and departure dates will depend on connecting flights.

The purpose of our trip is to locate an F4U-1, Corsair, single engine fighter, which crashed on 22 Oct 1943. We wish to locate the remains of the pilot, for return to his home and family. Our search will be an humanitarian endeavor. We request the assistance of the local people in this search and we are willing to pay for those services. We will need supplies, transportation, and guides. We solicit the assistance of local chiefs and elders who can lead us to any known site. Our principal goal is to locate the undisturbed site of the wreck and the remains of the pilot. We will offer a $500.00, U.S.D. reward for the undisturbed site of these remains. Local authorities will coordinate the recovery, by U.S. authorities, of the remains.

We also request the names of English speaking clergy who may be helpful in our search and the use of interpreters and guides. Please feel free to contact this office in the event of any information or question that you may have in this regard.

Sincerely
/s/ (The Doctor)

[O] FORTY YEARS LATER: *This letter of intent to the hotel owner also alerted the Chiefs and clergy of the islands. It notified them of the first possible date for our plans to search and our goal of undisturbed remains. Local authorities were aware from the beginning that we would pay the reward and that it was to be a project that would go through proper channels for recovery.*

Tuesday, August 23, 1988

Dear Mr. Bowden,

Thank you for your telephone call yesterday. As I told you, we are about to leave on vacation. I have many matters on my mind (and my secretary and her equipment have even more) so that I can reply only by this long-handed note.

Enclosed are copies of the following.
1. Map of Espiritu Santo.
2. Roster, as of 4 Nov. 1943, of the training unit to which Wayland belonged.
3. My 21 December 1943, to R. O. Bennett.
4. 20 March 1944, reply from Mrs. R. O. Bennett.

I trust the enclosed are of some assistance. I am most interested in the plan you have described and hope you will let me know what develops.

Yours respectfully,
/s/ Henry S. Miller
Colonel, USMCR

P.S. I recorded Wayland's aircraft as 88-02608, probably meaning the BuAer number was 02608, and the number on the fuselage (both sides) was 88.

[P] **ALWAYS A HELPING HAND:** *Henry S. Miller, although busy in a professional schedule, was always helpful to our research. This letter was his response to a telephone call requesting information. He still maintains a ready access to all the notes he took during the war and is an absolute wealth of information to a researcher. Boy, wouldn't it be great to spend a day with him in a fishing boat in the middle of a lake. I'm sure he is a treasure of stories about the priceless experiences he had.*

Matevulu College
B.P. 149
Santo

25th October, 1988

Dear Doctor

Thanks for your recent phone call and the offer of the reward. It is indeed a formidable task to cover 100 square kilometers of Santo dark bush. It is at least a 25 km walk to the area of the proposed search. The search could possibly be conducted by talking with many of the people who live in the area.

Harry, Aki, Okes, and Garae have all been building fences since you left the island. They described you as "the long fella man merika," and said that "you were a strong walker," and, "that you were the first white man they knew of who walked in the bush at night with a torch light." They say that, "you are unafraid of anything in the bush." For these natives to say things like that about you is the beginning of a legend. They look forward to your return and to walking with you again. They seem to be quite taken with the idea that you are not afraid to go into the "dark bush" alone. White men do not normally go into primitive villages unless they are a good-sized group.

/s/ Benny Cherick (principal)

[Q] **WHITE MEN DON'T DO THAT!** *This letter conveys the impression that the Doctor made on the natives during the first search.*

DEPARTMENT OF THE NAVY
24 Apr 94

County Clerk
P.O. Box 248
New Boston, TX 75570

Dear Sir:

    I am writing this letter to request your assistance in locating the descendants of a former member of your community.

    In October 1943, a young Marine Officer was killed while piloting an aircraft on an authorized mission off the coast of Australia. We have information that would be of great interest to members of his family and are most anxious to locate them.

    However, the only relative listed in our records at the time of death was his father and we assume he is now deceased. Therefore, we wish to contact any other members of his family that may be living in your community, or elsewhere, if their whereabouts are known.

    Our hope is that through tax, property, voter, death or whatever records are available, that you may be able to assist us in locating a family member. The Marine pilot was named Wayland Edward Bennett. He was born in Texarkana on November 21, 1922. Our information indicates that in October 1943, his father, R. O. Bennett, resided at *(address omitted to assure privacy)* in Texarkana.

    Unfortunately, this is all the background we are able to provide. We would greatly appreciate any assistance you may be able to give us and wish to thank you for your time and effort in this matter. If you wish additional information, please contact me at the enclosed phone number. A prepaid, self-addressed envelope is enclosed for your convenience.

                      Sincerely,
                        /s/ Casualty Section
                        Personal Affairs Branch
                        Human Resources Division
                        By direction of the
                        Commandant of the Marine Corps

[R] THE BEGINNING OF THE END: *When the Doctor received notification of this letter, it became apparent that the search was about to become public knowledge. Also, it began the announcement that Wayland Bennett was finally about to receive his final orders, transferring him home to Texarkana, U.S.A. However this letter also began to tell another story — Wayland Bennett's twin sister, Wanda, would not be able to be here for his "homecoming."*

To Whom It May Concern;

      This is to certify that we, the nearest surviving kin of Lt. Wayland E. Bennett, being own siblings of Lt. Bennett, authorize the Doctor to escort Lt. Bennett's remains from Hawaii to Texarkana, Texas for burial in the family cemetery plot in Texarkana.

      Further, we request that the Doctor be allowed access to all information regarding recovery of Lt. Bennett's remains; that the Doctor be allowed to inspect all items found with the remains at the crash site and be furnished an official list of such items; that the Doctor be allowed to inspect contents of the casket; and that the Doctor receive Lt. Bennett's personal effects and other items recovered with remains in order to deliver these items to Lt. Bennett's family.

                                      Respectfully,
                                        /s/ Dr. R. O. Bennett, Jr.
                                        /s/ Doris Bennett Williams
                                        /s/ Wanda Bennett Knox

*Signed and sealed
by Notary Publics*

[S] PLEASE BRING HIM HOME: *This letter, from Lt. Bennett's family, authorized the Doctor to inspect and accompany Lt. Bennett's body back to Texarkana.*

PARABLES OF THE FLIGHT LINE

And so it was, in the 13th hour of the sun, in the *land* of the burning concrete;
    that the heavy laden lay down their wrenches, and lifted up their voices in prayer
    toward the center cubicle from which all things begin.
And as the benders of the wrenches assembled in prayer,
    there ariseth great clamor, weeping, and lamentations,
    for they are heavy of eye, sore of feet, and weary of limb.
Their toils have been indeed great. Surely now the master will give them rest.
Then there is a great hush, for the hallowed portals of the center cubicle opens,
    and the master and his disciples come forth from their sanctuary
    and don their dark glasses and sun helmets,
For Lo! the sun is painful even unto them.
And a disciple steps forth and speaketh unto them,
    — of **the** maximum effort on the morrow
    and calleth on the benders of the wrenches to give freely and
    cheerfully of their labor, for the maximum effort surpasseth all earthly things.
And another disciple cometh forth and speaketh in riddles of reports
    and of analysis, and of manhours, and of the glory of the system.
Then there is a great hush, for the master himself cometh forth to speak,
    and he sayeth of them,
"Return ye to you labors, and if the maximum effort be a great success,
    surely on the second Sunday of next week ye shall have an hour of respite."
And one of the braver of the benders of wrenches ariseth and maketh great harangue,
    and speaketh to the master, saying,
"Surely thou hast not so soon forgotten thy promise,
    that on this night thou wouldest give us rest.
And the master was exceedingly wroth and speaketh in a thunderous voice,
    and the benders of the wrenches weep and murmur,
"Yea, verily, we *are* of the accused."
And the master speaketh yet again,
"Hear ye my judgement, for ye are of the unfortunate.
Ye shall henceforth maintain twice as many aircraft,
    but we shall give unto you no meter leads,
    and ye shall forage throughout the land for new pans.
And I shall send my inspectors to work mischief among thy people,
    and to harass, and spy upon thee.
And great will be the plague that shall be visited upon thee.
Yea, verily, thou shall come to know the torments of the time cards."
And the benders of the wrenches rend their clothing and sit in ashes,
    and plead for mercy, but the master is ever unforgiving.
Then the master and his disciples turn away from their places
    and go thence unto the places from whence they came,
    under which rivers of beer flow, and abideth therein during the darker hours.
And the benders of the wenches return to their tasks
    and revile the flapped wing monsters and one sayeth,
"Yea verily, Hell is our heritage and we must abide therein."
                  Ye end.

[T] Parables of the Flight Line *(previous page):* *The Doctor acquired this document some time between 1957 and 1960, while he was stationed at Naval Air Station, Agana, Guam. The Doctor was assigned to the United States Navy, Airborne Early Warning, Patrol Squadron VW-3 and flew over 2000 hours of radar patrol missions in the Lockheed Super constellation (WV-2 radar picket reconnaissance plane). This airplane carried a crew of 32 men and patrols were in excess of 20 hours. It had bathrooms, galleys, bunks, and maintenance support equipment on board. It even had a combination safe for the documents. This was before the days of spy satellites, but this was the most advanced intelligence gathering airplane in the Navy fleet and the most comfortable by far. It was pressurized and air conditioned, and the crew chief was required to be the best cook in the world, and he was.*

The maintenance troops who kept these behemoths flying were truly the unsung hero's of the Navy. They represented an Espirit de Corps much the same as the mechanics of MAG-11. The assignment to Espiritu Santo must have been a brutal assignment with no relief and no time off. Demands of non-stop work for the non-stop war were a burden only the mechanics can appreciate.

While the Doctor did not write "Parables of the Flight Line," someone captured amazingly accurate description of the hardships of the "ground guys" and their work day. It was written about the mechanics who kept planes in the air long enough to win the war. No amount of credit will ever be enough to salute these men. It is hoped that the parable will bring back some of the fonder memories of the days when they had to sweat and toil in the hot tropic sun. They deserve to be acknowledged for their efforts and the Doctor is proud to endorse it, and forward it to higher command for approval.

The U.S.A.

The United States is an unusually large island, bisected in the center by the Mississippi River. Everything east of the river is a suburb of the capital of this section of the country. It is called Brooklyn. Everything west of this river is called Texas. Some sections have local names, such as Maine, Iowa or California.

Do not be cajoled into sleeping in one of the big soft innerspring beds that are common in the States. Many cases of curvature of the spine have resulted from this practice. To be sure that you have a good night's rest, sleep on the floor.

Almost all theaters have roofs, so carrying a raincoat, cushion, and poncho will attract attention to you and make people think you are peculiar. Many of the movies you see will be new and entertaining; if this bothers you, you may get up and leave. Because you will be under a roof, remember that you will not be able to look up and see the stars; by the same token, you will not get rained on.

Radio is more complicated in the States. One must learn to tune the station dial as well as the volume control to select one of the numerous stations. Listen carefully, for the programs are seldom repeated. Avoid television for the first few months, as it is entirely too involved.

Food is generally plentiful, but in some localities, powdered eggs are almost unobtainable. You will be forced to eat the shell covered kind, but even these will not be of the cold storage variety, so you may have to age them yourself if you are unable to become accustomed to the fresh taste. On restaurant menus you will find an item called, "Steak and Mushrooms." This is a native dish, but some people will learn to like it almost as much as stew. There is a type of milk which comes in bottles. This is not as rich as canned milk, but is a fair substitute for the reconstituted and powdered varieties you have been enjoying.

The country is composed of two general types of people — Democrats and Republicans. In the eastern part you will find subdivisions known as Yankees and Rebels.

The Quonsets are piled on top of each other, sometimes as high as 60 in one pile. You win not usually be able to enjoy the invigorating sound of the rain on a tin roof, every hour on the hour – and sometimes in between.

You will find out there is no place in the States where it is hot and humid all year round, so no one will accept that as your reason for drinking. Neither will you be able to use the excuse that liquor is so cheap you can't afford not to drink. You will have to think of another excuse, such as home-sickness for the islands. (Applications for overseas duty will be received in the main lounge at 0900 hours in the morning.)

[U] The U.S.A.: *After living in the tropics for years, the philosophers of wit came forth with more pearls of wisdom. The men of the island hopping campaigns were able to combine their wishes and apply it to yet another of the many things they missed most. The following is a collection of the things they looked forward to when they arrived back in the States. It is also one of the things they will remember about the islands during the days of their service in the Gardens of Eden. The author is unknown.*

GLOSSARY

AVENGER (Grumman – TBM or TBF): All-metal, single-engine plane with folding wings and a tail hook for carrier use. Carried one torpedo for attack on enemy ships. President George Bush flew this one-pilot, two-crew plane in WW2.

BUNKER: A storage site for men and equipment during an attack. Normally a fully-enclosed earthwork such as a bomb shelter. Varied from one-man size to large enough to house many men or entire airplanes.

CARGO MASTER (Douglas – DC-4 or C-54): A four-engine, all-metal civilian airliner that was the largest support plane used extensively during WW2 as an instantly available cargo and troop transport. It normally had two pilots and two additional crewmen. Bennett co-piloted a C-54 while in San Diego.

CARRIER (Aircraft Carrier – Flat Top): Naval combat ship that usually carried complete squadrons of fighters, dive bombers, torpedo bombers, equipment, supplies and ground crewmembers in addition to normal ship's crew. The top deck was a flat surface on which planes took off and landed. Cables stretched across the rear flight deck landing zone with aircraft loaded with fuel and bombs in front of this area, so there was no margin for error. To stop in extremely short distances, pilots lowered the plane's tail hook to catch the cable as they landed. Whereas most pilots landed on a non-moving shore base with a 200-foot wide by 5000-foot long runway, Naval Aviators landed on a specific 75-foot wide by 500-foot long area of a carrier that was usually moving at about 30 mph. Takeoffs and landings often occurred on totally dark nights in rain-swept seas and carriers sometimes hid from the enemy up to 100 miles away while its planes were attacking. When a Naval Aviator completed his mission, he had to find his carrier without lights and radio signals to lead him home, then land on it, regardless of combat damage or injuries, because he didn't have enough fuel left to go anywhere else.

CATALINA (Consolidated – PBY): A twin-engine amphibian airplane designed to land at sea or on land by using retractable wheels and floats. It had an all-metal fuselage and fabric covered wings and tail. It was manned by two pilots and five other crewmen. PBYs were used as Patrol Bombers and in Search and Rescue of downed airmen at sea. Many were stationed at Espiritu Santo and several remain in shallow diving waters of lagoons and channels there. One famous WW2 unit was the Black Cat Squadron. PBYs were also dressed up with bombs, torpedoes, machine guns, depth charges and other types of "local manufacture ordinance" that they delivered with astounding accuracy. A crashed Catalina with seven crewmen aboard was retrieved by CILHI at the same time as Bennett's recovery, but it was not a clean recovery because bounty hunters had plundered it.

CILHI: Central Identification Laboratory Hawaiian Islands

CILKO: Central Identification Laboratory Korea

CILTI: Central Identification Laboratory Thailand

COAST WATCHER (Coast Watch Station): Before the days of radar, Allied forces positioned these individuals at strategic points where they could scan the seas with binoculars. If a Coast Watcher spotted a plane or a ship, he radioed specific information to headquarters including the ship's type, number in the fleet, and speed and direction of travel. Their names and call signs were secret. They helped orchestrate many attacks on Japanese shipping and also reported for rescue the position of airplanes that crashed at sea. They were partially responsible for the rescue of John Kennedy as well as a Blacksheep pilot at Espiritu Santo.

CORSAIR (Vought-Sikorski – F4U): A single-engine, first-line fighter plane with one pilot and no other crew. It carried six .50 caliber Browning machine guns and had an all-metal fuselage and fabric cover over a metal-structured tail and wings. Carrier based Navy and Marine fighters had a tail hook or arrester hook to stop the plane in extremely short distances and folding wings to take up less space on carriers, allowing more to be assigned to a single carrier.

DALLAS HUT: A disposable, prefabricated plywood square structure providing living quarters for up to ten men. It had screenwire-covered windows to keep out mosquitoes and closeable wooden window flaps to keep out rain; but, with window covers down, they were like a tropical sauna with no breeze to cool the inside. None still exist at Turtle Bay.

DAUNTLESS (Douglas – SBD2C): A single-engine dive bomber and scout plane with one pilot and one crewmember. It was all metal with folding wings and a tail hook for carrier operations. Dive bombers could penetrate the enemy defense perimeter; then, when directly over an enemy ship, push over into a steep dive similar to that of a "kamikaze" attack. This fast dive, occasionally straight down at the enemy ship, let them get as close as possible to the target before releasing their single bomb. When this drama was over, the pilot had to pull out of the dive before he hit the ship or crashed into the nearby sea – assuming he was not shot down by the enemy ship's guns or a "hornet's nest" of defending fighter pilots. These very angry Japanese had everything to gain and nothing to lose by putting up a rather spirited defense and hot reception to unwanted visitors when an attack was directed at their aircraft carrier. Dive bombers were unable to carry either enough or large enough bombs to always actually sink a large enemy ship; however, it would be enough if they could damage the ship in any way that would lower its ability to fight, defend itself, maneuver evasively or maintain speed. A crippled war ship could then become a primary target for Torpedo Bombers, PT boats, PBYs and fighters. Fighter attacks on large battleships or aircraft carriers served as a distraction and caused enemy gunners to focus on the attacking fighter, often allowing dive bombers or TBMs to slip a torpedo into the ship's side and cause even more damage, possibly sinking the ship. This teamwork was a ballet of death for participants on both sides. Their sacrifices were high and necessary. Each battle or engagement was needed to seriously reduce the enemy's ability to mount either a defense or an attack.

GOONEYBIRD / DAKOTA (Douglas – C-47 or DC-3): An all-metal, twin-engine plane with two pilots and one mechanic crew. They could carry 20 parachute troopers or mail, cargo and crews between bases in the Solomons and New Hebrides. They also acted as mother ships to escort and lead fighters from rear to forward areas. They were classified as non-combat but were an easy, unarmed target for any marauding enemy equipped with a gun. The C-47 gained fame as a major support plane when flying the "Hump" in China during WW2. The Doctor's friend, Capt. Oliver R. Smith, Sr., was a C-47 pilot who flew various supply routes in the Pacific and frequently had to "duck into clouds to hide from Japanese fighter planes." Even ducking into clouds was not without risks because the clouds also hid another enemy to all pilots – mountains. At the same time Bennett was being recovered in 1994, a C-47 was discovered in China that had been flying the "hump" and ducked into a cloud. Its crew has been returned home to America. The C-47 also found fame through extensive use in the "Berlin Airlift." She then just seemed to get tired of being pushed around and took on a more aggressive role as "Puff the Magic Dragon." Decked out with machine guns and gattling-gun-style cannons, she was able to sweep and saturate entire areas of jungle with devastating effects during the Vietnam conflict.

HELLCAT (Grumman – F6F): A single-engine, first-line fighter plane with one pilot and no other crew. It had six .50 caliber Browning machine guns and was all metal with folding wings and tail hook for carrier operations.

HIDE: A ground area where aircraft are parked under trees with other camouflage. Elaborate devices including paint colors and schemes were often necessary to hide aircraft from the eyes of enemy pilots and intruders.

KAYDET (Boeing – PT-17): A single-engine, wood and steel-tube construction plane with fabric covering. It was a primary training plane with one pilot and one student. They were modified to spray for mosquito control in many areas of the South Pacific during WW2.

LCVP (Landing Craft Vehicles and Personnel): Although smaller than the LST, the LCVP served a similar purpose by delivering smaller loads into a beach where it was unloaded in a similar fashion. Personnel were sheltered behind the steel front door as the craft approached the beach. It then lowered and became a ramp for disembarkation. This often happened while looking right down the gun barrels of the property defense system (dedicated enemy soldiers), which was waiting and ready to saturate the boat's exposed interior and occupants the instant the door opened. The occupants were often very brave American Marines.

LIBERATOR (Consolidated – B-24): An all-metal, four-engine, long-range bomber with two pilots and eight other crewmembers. Francis Sandlin, a "Rosie the Riveter" who built some of these, worked on one named "Beautiful Betsy" that disappeared during WW2. It was recovered and her crew returned home in 1994.

LST (Landing Ship Tank): A ship that transported huge amounts of cargo and supplies including tanks, troops and trucks. They were driven onto beachheads and intentionally grounded; then huge doors swung open in the ship's front and cargo was unloaded directly onto the beach. It was considerably lighter after the cargo was removed so it would re-float, then be backed away from the beach into the sea and returned to a larger freighter for another cargo load. LST-711 was used by the American Graves Registration Service after the war to deliver search parties to areas where men had been killed and buried as battlefield casualties. Graves were opened and the remains returned to Hawaii for identification and return home.

MAE-WEST: A bright yellow, rubberized floatation gear that slipped over an airman's head and around his neck like a horse collar. It was inflatable by two CO_2 cartridges or by blowing it up with a rubber hose, and kept the airman afloat until he could get his raft inflated and climb aboard. Bennett's Mae-West still had part of his stenciled name legible when recovered.

MITCHELL (North American – B-25 or PBJ): An all-metal, twin-engine, medium bomber with two pilots and five other crewmen. They also acted as mother ships to lead fighters from Espiritu Santo to Solomons and combat bases. Several Army B-25s were secretly loaded onto the Navy Aircraft Carrier "Hornet" in 1942 and the ship quietly slipped out of its American port. It traveled across the Pacific Ocean and, when it arrived within a few hundred miles of Japan, they took off and bombed Tokyo and several other target cities in the "Empire of the Rising Sun."

MRE (Meal Ready to Eat): A complete meal in a sealed package used by troops on field maneuvers. They are also available in sporting goods and surplus equipment stores, and were the answer to the search team's needs for field rations.

NAVCAD (Naval Aviation Cadet): A recruit navy candidate for pilot training, commissioned after successful completion of all training requirements as an Officer and Naval Aviator. They are given the opportunity to choose Marine or Navy service, but all are Naval Aviators and are required to be proficient in takeoff and landing aboard carriers.

NAVIGATION PLOTTER: A 24-inch-square, navigation marker board used by Naval Aviators to record information they will need to complete their mission. During a secret briefing prior to take-off they are told the proposed speed and direction of movement of their carrier during their mission; and, if no enemy contact is made during that time, where the carrier will be when they return... MAYBE! Bennett's plotter was still readable after its long sojourn in the jungle.

PILLBOX: A small concrete bunker or dome-shaped cover for a ground defensive position that protects a rifleman or machine gun nest.

PSP (Perforated Steel Plating): Two-foot wide by ten-foot long strips of steel plate with tabs along one edge and slots on the other. When two pieces are laid alongside each other, slipping the tab of one into the slot of another joins them. A dirt, mud and crushed coral landing strip can be covered with PSP and made useable in two or three days.

PT BOAT: Patrol boat with nine-man crew, designed to operate against aggressor fleets attacking shore-based installations. Constructed of wood with three engines that gave them attack speeds in excess of 50 mph. They were about 60-feet long and carried four torpedoes and several dual-mount .50 caliber Browning machine guns. The book and movie "PT-109" chronicled President John Kennedy's adventures while commanding one during WW2.

QUAD-MOUNT MACHINE GUN EMPLACEMENT: A defensive position, usually located at the end of a landing strip, where as many as four machine guns or cannons are bolted together for intense concentrated firepower. They can be used against any intruder from the air, land or sea.

QUONSET HUT: A prefabricated metal-corrugated building used for storage, shops, warehouses and offices. Of the hundreds built during 1942 and 1943 on Espiritu Santo, many are still in good condition and have been in continuous use. Some are now used as churches, convents, health care clinics and libraries.

RADAR (Radio Detection and Ranging): The use of radio beams to detect the presence of one or more targets and establish their distance, direction of travel and speed. It is a valuable tool in combat areas and replaced some Coast Watchers.

REVETMENT: An aircraft parking area, usually composed of earth walls or mounds surrounding an individual plane on three sides to protect it from enemy machine gun fire and the effect of exploding bombs during an attack.

SEABEE: The world famous U.S. Navy Mobile Construction Battalions, composed of several hundred men who are skilled in construction professions. They arrive during the fight and must fight along with a Marine Landing Force. They do not stop when the battle is over, but quickly build an airfield for airplanes to land on, repair shops, warehouses for the supplies and parts, and offices from which to manage a major construction effort. They must then build complete kitchens and hospitals to support the thousands of men assigned to the newly acquired property, which was recently wrested from a reluctantly-evicted tenant. SeaBees also built docks, piers, streets and roads. They built Turtle Bay Fighter Strip Number One in approximately 30 days on land that was a coconut plantation!

SENTRY (Guard): An armed soldier, sailor, or Marine who is standing guard on a post with authority to use his weapon whenever necessary.

SNB (Beechcraft – Army/Airforce C-45 or Navy/Marine SNB): All-metal, twin-engine light cargo plane. Because this non-combat plane had two pilots and could carry five passengers, it was used for inter-island transport as an air taxi. Many were used in New Hebrides and one is well preserved on the southern beach.

SWORDFISH (OS2U): A single-engine, all-metal airplane with one pilot and one other crewman. It was used with normal wheels for carrier or shore-based landings. Installation of floats for landing and take-off from water made it valuable as a scout or observation plane. They were also mounted on catapults and launched from battleships or cruisers requiring intelligence data of the surrounding sea. Upon return from the mission, they would land beside the ship on the ocean and be hauled back aboard by a crane.

TEXAN (North American – Army/Airforce AT-6 or Navy/Marines SNJ): An all-metal, single-engine, advanced trainer with one pilot and one student. It was not outfitted with guns or bombs because it was designed for non-combat use. They were used extensively at Turtle Bay to familiarize new pilots with the Corsair.

WILDCAT (Grumman – F4F): A single-engine, second-line fighter plane with one pilot and no other crew. It had four .50 caliber Browning machine guns, folding wings and a tail hook for carrier operations. It had inadequate power, guns and speed when matched against a Japanese "Zero" fighter plane. These obsolete planes were flown extensively during the early stages of WW2 until replaced by Corsairs and Hellcats.

ACKNOWLEDGMENTS

Prior to the search for Lt. Wayland E. Bennett and his Homecoming, I was perfectly content to read what other people wrote and leave the writing to someone else. I never even dreamed of writing a book, nor did I consider myself an investigative reporter or historian. I was also quick to admit that research was not my favorite pastime. However, as I embarked on this search, I knew research was of unquestionable importance, and I was compelled to assemble all available facts and keep detailed records.

Even before the last note of taps sounded on Wayland Bennett's Homecoming Day, I knew I had to put this experience into a permanent record so others could know what a difference a few caring individuals, who refused to forget a Promise, could make in the world today. But I also knew it could not be just the story of three boyhood friends who didn't forget their Promise to a hero who could not come home. Likewise, it is not just the story of a family who waited years before they could have a closure to their grief. It is definitely not just the story of the Doctor or team members who sacrificed and labored diligently for eight long years. Nor is it the story of so many people in this young man's hometown who were willing to support the effort with their prayers and finances.

It is all of these things and so much more. It is the story of a hero who was willing to serve and die for his country. It is the story of great American patriotism and the untiring efforts of those who keep the home fires burning brightly. It is a story which must be told... a story that can bring about healing in our land and a renewed hope for families who still wait for their son, brother, father or grandfather to come home.

While writing this story, I found it necessary to create narrative and dialogue as I imagined it; and, in some instances, I might not have gotten all the details just exactly as they happened. I have also supplied fictitious names for some individuals who wished anonymity and for those who would be adversely affected if their true identities were known.

I offer my thanks to those who helped us in our project, and I offer my sincerest apology for any errors that might have found their way into this story, be they errors of omission or errors of commission. I assure you, I have tried to remain true to the situation. If any reader has problems with the journalistic liberties I have taken, he can simply relegate this story to the vast storehouse of fiction; however, I hope he will remember that it is based on very real individuals in very real situations doing very real things. And, if my apology is not enough, I hope you will simply allow this book to serve as a guide to others who are searching for their own MIAs in the hope they will be successful in their effort.

This has never been a one-man project, and I want to recognize the many who assisted in the research project and the searches for ***The Lost Blacksheep.*** It would be impossible to individually acknowledge the contributions of the many people and organizations that played an important role, and those who contributed money, supplies, information and their prayers. Therefore, I simply say "thank you" to those unnamed American patriots who felt the need to participate, as they could, in the fulfillment of *The Promise.* God knows the role they played, and He will be the one to ultimately reward them accordingly.

I gleaned valuable information in the course of this project from several sources. I wish to express my gratitude to all those who assisted me in retrieving information lost amid almost fifty years of forgetfulness. The official as well as unofficial assistance from people in all walks of life is greatly appreciated. There were also several authors who wrote about the time and area in which Lt. Bennett served, and I wish to thank them for the assistance their works were to our research.

About the same time Wayland Bennett was in Espiritu Santo, another young Naval Officer was assigned there. James Mitchner's recollections were later immortalized in stage productions, a best selling novel and a classic movie by the name of *Tales of the South Pacific.*

Major "Pappy" Boyington and his unique Squadron are well-known to Americans today as a result of his best-seller, *Baa Baa Blacksheep,* which became a television series through adaptation into *The Blacksheep Squadron.* It should be noted, however, that the actual Blacksheep Squadron was not composed of rogues and misfits portrayed in this television series, but brave and competent men who were proud to serve their country in time of war.

Frank Walton's historical chronicles of the action and lives of men assigned to these islands became a very important research reference about WW2. His book, *Once They Were Eagles,* is a must-read for any devotee of history and research and an excellent primer for anyone who would consider writing a book about that era.

I want to thank everyone who suggested I write this book and encouraged my efforts. I appreciate those who read my manuscript in its various stages, and those who helped with the final proofreading including Dr. Mark Oglesby. And a special thanks to my Editor and Optimum Publishing for making it possible for you to read these words.

I am also grateful for the untiring efforts by the unknown, unrecognized, and unsung heroes of any military family's grief – the teams of the Central Identification Laboratories and the Casualty and Decedent Affairs teams who are right out in front trying to help these families. One must see their expertise and professionalism to fully appreciate it. This book is not written for or about CILHI; but it could not have been written without them. When an MIA/BNR comes home, it is in large part due to the people of CILHI and their commitment to the excellence of their performance which is their part of ...*The Promise.*

The search for Wayland Bennett was long and hard. It took eight years of on-going research and several searches. But this is not a story about hardship, it a story of perseverance and commitment to a purpose. While this is a story with a certain amount of sadness, it is also full of happiness. Although it is the story of a family's grief for a loved one, it also contains the celebration of this same family when they were able to welcome him home. Such an experience could never be written as a comedy, although some of our antics did become quite comical. Likewise, it could never be presented as a serious study in the tragedy of mankind, because we often had such need for laughter. And, as I acknowledge the dedication and commitment of those who served as volunteers, I am reminded of how we laughed and cried together as we shared the disappointments and failures. But, I will also always appreciate the good memories of our search for Wayland Bennett – *The Lost Blacksheep.*

Finally, I want to especially salute all those who searched, and all who will search in the future.

The Doctor

MEET THE AUTHOR

Dr. Danford A. Bookout is a pilot, chiropractor and author, who is highly respected by all who know him. He is actively involved in many civic affairs in Texarkana, USA, and is on the Board of Directors of several organizations including the Boy Scouts of America.

The task of returning 2nd Lt. Wayland E. Bennett to his hometown, family and friends was the type of challenge Dr. Bookout enjoys.

He is a veteran of both the U.S. Naval Air Force and the U.S. Marine Corps. He has over 18000 hours flight time and his accomplishments include 180 international aviation records that he set when he flew around the world in the ***Texarkana Baby***, his single-engine Piper Lance, in 1986.

He has flown both single and multi-engine airplanes for government, commercial and private use over both land and sea. He is a certified flight instructor and was the outstanding instructor pilot for the U.S. Air Force while instructing in Oklahoma. He was a pilot for the U.S. Postal Dept., the U.S. Atomic Energy Commission, and a commercial airline.

Dr. Bookout has lived in Texarkana most of his life and is the only Texarkana resident to receive the "Keys to the City of Texarkana." One of his hobbies has been the purchase and restoration of Texarkana's Union Station, a railroad station built on the Arkansas-Texas state line in 1929.

He was presented membership in the Blue Max Society by the Governor of Texas, and was presented some of his aviation awards by President Bill Clinton and "Pappy" Boyington of the Blacksheep Squadron.

Dr. Bookout is also the author of two more adventure novels to be released in the near future: ***Blue-Chip Three-Zero*** and ***Voyages of the Guardian Angel***. He is committed to writing books that contain no profanity, sex, drugs or alcohol; with the kind of heroes that young people today can look up to and pattern their lives after.

A portion of the proceeds from the sale of ***Search for the Lost Blacksheep*** will be contributed to veteran's organizations.